SAP PRESS e-books

Print or e-book, Kindle or iPad, workplace or airplane: Choose where and how to read your SAP PRESS books! You can now get all our titles as e-books, too:

- ▶ By download and online access
- ▶ For all popular devices
- ▶ And, of course, DRM-free

Convinced? Then go to **www.sap-press.com** and get your e-book today.

Getting Started with SAP HANA® Cloud Platform

 PRESS

Miroslav Antolovic
Getting Started with SAPUI5
2014, 462 pages, hardcover
ISBN 978-1-59229-969-0

Bönnen et al.
OData and SAP NetWeaver Gateway
2014, 666 pages, hardcover
ISBN 978-1-59229-907-2

Paul Hardy
ABAP to the Future
2015, 727 pages, hardcover
ISBN 978-1-4932-1161-6

James Wood
Object-Oriented Programming with ABAP Objects (2nd edition)
2016, approx. 450 pp., hardcover
ISBN 978-1-59229-993-5

James Wood

Getting Started with SAP HANA® Cloud Platform

Bonn • Boston

Editor Kelly Grace Weaver
Copyeditor Melinda Rankin
Cover Design Graham Geary
Photo Credit Shutterstock.com/80853385/© Ventura
Layout Design Vera Brauner
Production Kelly O'Callaghan
Typesetting SatzPro, Krefeld (Germany)
Printed and bound in the United States of America, on paper from sustainable sources

ISBN 978-1-4932-1021-3
© 2015 by Rheinwerk Publishing, Inc., Boston (MA)
1st edition 2015

Library of Congress Cataloging-in-Publication Data
Wood, James, 1978-
Getting started with SAP HANA cloud platform / James Wood and Robin van het Hof. -- 1st edition.
pages cm
Includes index.
ISBN 978-1-4932-1021-3 (print : alk. paper) -- ISBN 1-4932-1021-1 (print : alk. paper) -- ISBN 978-1-4932-1023-7 (print
and ebook : alk. paper) -- ISBN 978-1-4932-1022-0 (ebook) 1. Cloud computing. 2. Database management. 3. SAP HANA
(Electronic resource) I. Hof, Robin van het. II. Title.
QA76.585.W66 2014
004.67'82--dc23
2014039990

Contents at a Glance

Dear Reader,

If you've ever bought a programming book from SAP PRESS before, my guess is that you're already familiar with the work of James Wood. Well, it's my pleasure to welcome you to his latest endeavor: *Getting Started with SAP HANA Cloud Platform*. It's rare to find an author who is thoroughly talented, always professional, and never misses a deadline—but James is all of these things. (He also, for the record, makes a mean bowl of Texas chili.) I consider myself very lucky to be his editor.

Of course, with apologies to John Donne, no book is an island. And this one wouldn't have happened without the help of several collaborators, especially Matthias Steiner, champion of SAP HANA Cloud Platform and, well, champion in general. My thanks and gratitude are due to all involved.

But enough with the thanking, right? It's time for you to dive in. And when you're done, let us know what you thought about *Getting Started with SAP HANA Cloud Platform*. After all, your comments and suggestions are the most useful tools to help us make our books the best they can be! We encourage you to visit our website at *www.sap-press.com* and share your feedback.

Thank you for purchasing a book from SAP PRESS!

Kelly Grace Weaver
Editor, SAP PRESS

Rheinwerk Publishing
Boston, MA

kellyw@rheinwerk-publishing.com
www.sap-press.com

Contents

PART II   Core Development Concepts

7   Developing HTML5 Applications 289

8   Securing Cloud Applications 325

PART III   Advanced Concepts

11   Extension Scenarios with SAP HANA Cloud Platform 461

Foreword by Matthias Steiner

We live in a time of accelerated change, in a world in which companies fight over market share on a global scale. In this competitive environment, it's more important than ever for enterprises to focus on their core business, to differentiate themselves from their competitors, and to provide products and services that deliver immediate value to their customers. Software has become a key enabler to help companies adapt to changing market trends by both streamlining and reinventing their internal processes as well as empowering them to develop innovative solutions. As such, it's up to us developers to lead this digital evolution and shape a world that is driven by software.

Having made a living as a software architect for more than a decade, I understand that developing enterprise software solutions is far from being a trivial task. Complex system landscapes, ever changing business requirements, and pressing timelines are not an exception, but the norm. Consequently, developers need first class tooling that supports them in their daily tasks and enables them to focus on their job: converting business requirements into viable software solutions.

This is the problem space that SAP HANA Cloud Platform addresses: It's a design and runtime environment designed from the ground up to empower developers to build, extend, and run next generation business applications in the cloud. Based on SAP HANA, SAP's in-memory technology platform, this Platform-as-a-Service (PaaS) offering provides customers and partners with the comprehensive set of services and capabilities needed to efficiently develop business solutions for an increasingly connected world.

Nowadays, where everything from people (social media), to companies (business networks), up to individual devices (Internet of Things) are connected to each other, the cloud has became the catalyst for a global digital business transformation. It's the backbone of the mobile movement and the enabler for big data scenarios requiring lots of computing power. With SAP HANA Cloud Platform, SAP offers a cloud platform that enables developers to support their companies—and ultimately their customers—to leverage the opportunities accompanying this transformation.

In this book, James, Krassi, John, and Riley provide a comprehensive overview of SAP HANA Cloud Platform and its related technologies and how they support companies to extend their business into the cloud. Based on their vast experiences gained as development consultants over the last decade, James and John are able to holistically address these aspects and cover both the business and the technical perspective. Their expertise is ideally complemented by the inside view provided by my colleagues Krassi and Riley, who both have been driving their respective topics internally at SAP. Together, their domain knowledge is second to none.

The book focuses on concrete development scenarios and as such primarily targets solution architects and developers interested in understanding how to develop software solutions that excel in hybrid IT landscapes comprising both on-premise systems and cloud solutions. Starting with a general overview of cloud computing and SAP HANA Cloud Platform, the authors move on to address everything from getting started, to key technologies, up to advanced topics such as developing extensions for on-premise solutions and cloud applications alike.

After reading this book, you will understand the full potential of SAP's PaaS offering and how to leverage it for your own needs. Moreover, you'll be equipped with a great set of examples to kick-start your own development projects based on SAP HANA Cloud Platform. As such, I hope you enjoy reading through this book—and I ultimately look forward to welcoming you to the fast-growing community of cloud developers.

Happy coding!

Matthias Steiner
Cloud Platform Evangelist and SAP Mentor
SAP HANA Cloud Platform

Preface

Since its initial release in late 2012, SAP HANA Cloud Platform (SAP HCP) has flown under the radar for many within the SAP community. However, with the release of the new SAP S/4HANA business suite and a continued push to integrate recent cloud software acquisitions, such as SuccessFactors, Ariba, and Concur, SAP HCP has begun to emerge as one of the key components in SAP's overall cloud strategy. In essence, you can think of SAP HCP as the hub of the modern SAP technology landscape.

With that being said, if you picked up this book because you want to learn what SAP HCP is all about, your timing couldn't be better. In the months and years ahead, SAP HCP skills are sure to be in great demand. Whether you're a seasoned SAP developer looking to transition your skills or a non-SAP developer looking to jump onboard the SAP cloud bandwagon, we think you've come to the right place.

Target Group and Prerequisites

This book is intended for developers who are interested in learning how to develop applications on SAP HCP. Notice that we don't say *Java developers* or *ABAP developers*. Because SAP HCP is an open platform that offers a *bring your own language* (BYOL) approach to development, developers from all walks of life are welcome here.

Having said that, there are a few important prerequisites for being able to navigate through the material we cover here. Because this is a book about cloud application development, there is a natural expectation that the reader is reasonably familiar with core concepts, such as web application development, Internet technologies, and so forth. Although we do attempt to provide gentle introductions to new technologies wherever possible, this book cannot possibly cover these topics at the depth required to successfully develop cloud applications.

Structure of the Book

In many ways, we found that our biggest challenge in writing this book was in putting some structure around it. From the point we embarked on this journey until the time we finalized the manuscript many months later, SAP HCP experienced incredible growth. In the end, we had to narrow our focus to the core concepts and technologies that represent the essence of SAP HCP.

Part I: Foundations

In this section, we introduce SAP HCP and show you how to get up and running with the platform. This brief introduction sets the stage for the hands-on portion of the book.

- ► **Chapter 1: Introduction to SAP HANA Cloud Platform**
  In this chapter, we introduce you to the cloud computing phenomenon and SAP's cloud strategy. Here, we attempt to establish the positioning of SAP HCP with the cloud and SAP landscapes.

- ► **Chapter 2: Getting Up and Running**
  This chapter introduces the various SAP HCP account types and shows you how to set up a free developer account that we'll use to develop sample applications. We'll also show you how to install and configure the relevant SAP HCP development tools.

Part II: Core Development Concepts

In this section, we roll up our sleeves and demonstrate how to create custom web applications on SAP HCP. Along the way, we cover key logistics concepts and also consider key enablement services that can be used to round out the design of production-quality applications.

- ► **Chapter 3: Developing Java Applications**
  In this chapter, we'll show you how to create Java-based web applications using the core Java EE APIs: Servlets, JavaServer Pages (JSPs), and Enterprise JavaBeans (EJBs). Along the way, we'll become acquainted with the Eclipse IDE and SAP HCP SDK and demonstrate how these tools are used to test and debug Java applications.

▶ **Chapter 4: Managing and Deploying Java Applications**
This chapter explores some important logistical issues to consider when developing Java applications. Specific topics of interest include source code management, automated builds, deployment, and continuous integration. Also included in this chapter is an introduction to source code management with Git—a concept that we'll revisit in Chapter 7 when we consider HTML5 application development.

▶ **Chapter 5: Developing Native SAP HANA Applications**
In this chapter, we show you how to create custom applications based on the native SAP HANA programming model. We begin by showing you how to set up SAP HANA instances within an SAP HCP account and then move into the specifics of creating new SAP HANA XS applications and developing SAP HANA-specific development objects. By the end of the chapter, we'll have completed development on a fully functional mobile application that can be used to browse through the titles in a fictitious online bookstore.

▶ **Chapter 6: Consuming Cloud Services**
In this chapter, we teach you how to consume some of the key enablement services included with SAP HCP: the Persistence Service, Connectivity Service, and Document Service. To better demonstrate how these services are used, we develop a custom Java application that integrates features of all these services to create an approximation of a production-quality application.

▶ **Chapter 7: Developing HTML5 Applications**
This chapter explores the creation of lightweight HTML5 applications based on the relatively new HTML5 programming model within SAP HCP. Here, we provide a step-by-step demonstration that shows you how to create a new HTML5 application, synchronize its Git repository, and develop custom HTML5 application content. Along the way, we'll introduce you to the new SAP Web IDE and also show you how to incorporate SAPUI5 technology into HTML5 applications.

▶ **Chapter 8: Securing Cloud Applications**
This chapter rounds out the core development section of the book by showing you how to secure SAP HCP applications. Here, we take a holistic approach and survey the various security-related libraries and services provided with the supported SAP HCP programming models. In the latter half of the chapter, we also explore key components of the Identity Service as we consider how to implement authentication with SAML and authorization using OAuth.

Part III: Advanced Concepts

In this final section of the book, we explore some of the more advanced features and services of SAP HCP. Here, we show you how to apply basic concepts learned in Part II towards large-scale integration and/or extension scenarios, mobile access, and more.

▸ **Chapter 9: Working with SAP HANA Cloud Portal**
In this chapter, we introduce you to SAP HANA Cloud Portal, a lightweight portal service bundled with SAP HCP. Here, we'll show you how to create custom portal/mashup sites and integrate disparate content types using the OpenSocial API.

▸ **Chapter 10: Introduction to SAP HANA Cloud Integration**
This chapter provides an overview of the SAP HANA Cloud Integration (HCI) service built into SAP HCP. Here, we provide a base-level introduction to SAP HCI and see how it can be used in integration scenarios.

▸ **Chapter 11: Extension Scenarios with SAP HANA Cloud Platform**
In the final chapter of the printed book, we demonstrate how SAP HCP can be used to build extension applications for SAP's existing cloud products (for example, SuccessFactors). We outline the integration points that are currently in place, and then explain how the majority of the different features covered throughout the book can be used in tandem to create complex extension scenarios.

▸ **Chapter 12: Introduction to SAP HANA Cloud Platform Mobile Services (online only)**
This online chapter introduces SAP HCP Mobile Services, an SAP HCP service that can be used to develop custom mobile applications. Specific topics of interest include service consumption, an overview of the SMP SDK, and the bundling of SAPUI5 applications as hybrid applications. This chapter is available for download from *www.sap-press.com/3638*.

Conventions

This book contains many code examples demonstrating syntax, functionality, and so on. To distinguish these sections, we are using a font similar to the one used in many integrated development environments to improve code readability (see Listing 1). As new syntax concepts are introduced, we will highlight these statements using a bold listing font (see Listing 1).

```
public class MyClass {
  public void someMethod() {
    try {
            InitialContext ctx = new InitialContext();
            ...
        }
    catch (NamingException ne) {}
  }
}
```

Listing 1 Code Syntax Formatting Example

Using Code Examples

Throughout the course of this book, we'll be developing many sample applications that demonstrate key concepts in context. In order to make it simple to download working copies of these applications, we created a public repository for the book's code bundle on GitHub. The repository URL is *https://github.com/ bowdark/hcpbook*. This same information can also be downloaded from *www.sappress.com/3638*.

Where appropriate, we've included readme files with the various examples to show you how to configure them for deployment with your own SAP HCP trial account. Otherwise, you can generally find instructions for installing and deploying these applications within the chapters that cover them.

If you run into any problems with the examples, you can email the author directly at *jwood@bowdark.com*.

Acknowledgments

Putting together a book like this is a lot harder than it might seem, and would not have been possible without the assistance of a number of key individuals. These people generously offered both their time and expertise to make this book the best it could be, and for that we're very grateful.

Special Contributors

At the top of this list is Matthias Steiner, who, in addition to providing the foreword for this book, also provided lots of useful feedback regarding the long-term direction of the product and so on. Matthias was also very instrumental in helping assemble the complete author team.

Along those same lines, we'd like to thank Rui Nogueira and Thomas Grassl for helping us connect with the SAP HCP development team, as well as Sujit Hemachandran and Vivek Mangaonkar for their support in answering SAP HCI queries.

Finally, a shout out to the SAP HCP development community on SAP SCN for providing useful feedback as we prototyped example applications and tried out new features. Any time we ran into an issue, someone on these forums would respond in record time. It's a true testament to how far the SCN community has come.

Friends and Family

It's hard to take on a project like this without having the support and backing of family and loved ones. With that being said, the authors would like to extend the following thanks:

- James Wood would like to thank his wife Andrea, his sons Andersen, Parker, and Xander, and his daughter Paige for accommodating many long nights burning the midnight oil. James would also like to thank his dog Kirby for her incessant snoring, which became the book's main soundtrack.

- John Mutumba Bilay would like to thank his wife Hermien and his boys Ralph, Luc, and Ruben for their encouragement and unconditional love. John would also like to thank his colleagues at Rojo Consultancy for their support and feedback.

- Krasimir Semerdzhiev would like to thank the complete SAP HCP development team spread around in Germany, Bulgaria, and Israel, who made SAP HCP happen. He would also like to thank his SuccessFactors and SAP Jam product management and engineering colleagues for being such reliable counterparts. Last but not least, he would like to mention his partners in crime—Filip Misovski, Stanimir Ivanov, and Segev Lev—for forging the SAP HCP extension story going forward.

Final Thanks

And last, but certainly not least, we'd all like to say thanks to our editor, Kelly Grace Weaver. Kelly's simply the world's greatest editor and an even better person. Her saintliness was certainly put to the test on this project, and we could not and would not have been successful without her. This also goes for the rest of the crew at SAP PRESS who worked tirelessly behind the scenes to make this book a reality.

PART I
Foundations

In this chapter, we introduce you to the SAP HANA Cloud Platform and describe its positioning in the evolving SAP technology landscape.

1 Introduction to SAP HANA Cloud Platform

Since the initial release of SAP R/3 in 1992, SAP landscapes have primarily existed in isolation, being nestled safely within the nurturing confines of the corporate firewall. However, with the explosion of cloud computing and mobility in recent years, this has begun to change. Now, customers are looking to expand the limits of their SAP landscapes to support integration with cloud applications (provided by SAP or otherwise), mobile access, and the Internet of Things (IoT).

To address this ever-widening gap, SAP introduced SAP HANA Cloud Platform (SAP HCP). In this chapter, we'll get to know SAP HCP and learn how it will play a central role within the SAP technology landscape in the years to come.

Further Resources

The main product page for SAP HCP is *hcp.sap.com*, and serves as a valuable resource for SAP HCP material: trial systems, documentation, and more.

1.1 Introducing SAP HANA Cloud Platform

According to the SAP help documentation, SAP HCP is "an open, standards-based, and modular platform as a service for rapid development of on-demand applications." This definition is a bit of a mouthful, so let's take this point-by-point:

► First, we find that SAP HCP is a *Platform-as-a-Service* (PaaS) offering from SAP. Although we'll have an opportunity to explore this distinction in further detail in Section 1.2, for now, it's enough to simply note that SAP HCP is a platform that can be used to (rapidly) develop and deploy web applications in the cloud.

▸ SAP HCP is an open environment that offers developers lots of choice as it relates to the selection of programming languages and models, development tools, and so forth.

▸ In addition to being open, SAP HCP is also heavily standards-based, being developed from the ground up to support standards from leading standards organizations such as the W3C.

▸ Finally, we learn that SAP HCP is a modular platform that can be customized to meet the needs of all customer types and use cases.

In simplified terms, you can think of SAP HCP as a platform that customers can rent access to from SAP to develop and deploy applications in the cloud. From a technical perspective, this platform is not so different from application systems that are installed on-premise, such as the SAP Composition Environment. The primary difference is that SAP assumes responsibility for purchasing and maintaining the hardware, software, and other infrastructure-related concerns so that customers can focus on application development concerns.

A Brief History

Even though SAP HCP more formally came into prominence in the latter part of 2014, it's actually been around for quite some time. In late 2011, we were introduced to the first incarnation of the product, which at that time went by one of several different names: SAP NetWeaver Cloud, SAP NetWeaver NEO, and, in many circles, just NEO. At that time, the product offering was fairly modest, consisting mostly of a Java application server and a series of basic cloud enablement services. This changed considerably over the course of the next 18 to 24 months, as new features and services seemed to be popping up on an almost weekly basis.

> **NEO vs. AS Java: Are They the Same Thing?**
>
> One of the prevailing myths around NEO (and, by extension, SAP HCP) is that its Java application server is basically just a port of SAP's on-premise AS Java application server into the cloud. In reality, though, the two application servers have two entirely different code bases. For a variety of reasons, it made sense for SAP to start from scratch with NEO so that it could run optimally in the cloud.

By mid-2013, NEO had reached a sufficient level of maturity that SAP began to quietly position it as part of their long-term cloud strategy. Around this same time, SAP decided to drop the NetWeaver/NEO naming in favor of the name we recognize today: SAP HANA Cloud Platform. From here, the product really began to pick up momentum as we saw the scope of the platform expand to include support for native SAP HANA development, HTML5 applications, and much more.

By the time the annual SAP TechEd/d-code conferences rolled around in late 2014, SAP HCP finally hit center stage as a key component in SAP's cloud strategy and vision. In many respects, this milestone marked the end of SAP HCP's infancy. Now, we look ahead to the emergence of SAP HCP as a production-ready platform for deploying cloud applications. With significant commitment and backing from SAP, the future of SAP HCP looks to be very bright indeed.

1.2   The Cloud Computing Revolution

Even though it's been a buzzword for quite some time, many people still have a hard time wrapping their heads around what the cloud is exactly. For some, it's a magical place where their music files live. For others, the cloud is a wild frontier that's much too insecure to trust with precious IT resources. Somewhere in the midst of all this chatter is an idea that's so simple and yet so powerful that you almost wonder why we haven't arrived at it before. With that in mind, in this section we'll take a look at the cloud computing revolution.

1.2.1   What Is Cloud Computing?

To a large extent, cloud computing is one of those stream of consciousness ideas whose origin is difficult to trace to any one particular individual or organization (see boxed note ahead). Like many economic trends, it's a concept that evolved organically as a result of the convergence of several key market conditions:

▸ A proliferation of inexpensive hardware components (e.g., multicore CPUs, main memory, and disk storage)

▸ Expanded availability of high-speed network access

▸ Continued advances and innovations in the fields of hardware virtualization

> **Note**
>
> To a certain extent, Antonio Regalado settled the origin of cloud computing in a 2011 article entitled "Who Coined 'Cloud Computing'?" (*MIT Technology Review*, 2011). Here, he traced the origin of the term back to an internal business strategy document published by Compaq Computer Corporation in November 1996.

As these technologies and market conditions converged with one another, it became apparent to many technology companies that it would be possible to bundle access to computer resources and sell this access to customers using an on-demand, pay-as-you-go subscription model.

This idea, in and of itself, is not a novel concept. Indeed, hosting and co-location of server resources have been successful business models in the IT world for quite some time. The difference with cloud computing is that provider companies aren't just standing up a handful of servers here and there to meet the demands of a particular customer. Instead, providers are building up huge server farms that, due to their overall size and computing power, can scale to meet the needs of hundreds or even thousands of customers at a time. This kind of economies of scale allows providers to provide access to computer resources at a fraction of the cost it would normally take to provision the same resources on premise.

To summarize, we can simply say that "cloud computing" is a term used to describe the packaging and distribution of computing resources as a *commodity*. Of course, as is the case with most commercial offerings, the way that these resources are bundled can vary greatly. Therefore, in the next section, we'll consider some of the more prominent service models that have emerged in the cloud computing space.

1.2.2   Understanding the Cloud Computing Service Models

As the idea of cloud computing really started to take form in the mid-2000s, it quickly became apparent that there was not a "one-size-fits-all" service model that could possibly satisfy the needs and demands of customers looking to jump onboard the cloud computing bandwagon. Therefore, before too long, lots of specialty shops popped up offering a la carte services, such as online data storage and backup, application hosting, and more. When the dust settled on all this, three broad categories of service models had emerged:

▸ **Infrastructure-as-a-Service (IaaS)**

IaaS is a service model in which providers offer access to base-level computing resources: servers, disk storage, and so on. Although the resources themselves are normally virtualized, the end product looks and behaves for consumers in almost identical fashion to infrastructure resources configured on-premise. Some of the more prominent IaaS providers in the market as of the time of writing include Amazon, Microsoft, and Google.

▸ **Platform-as-a-Service (PaaS)**

As the name suggests, the PaaS service model offers customers a full-fledged computing platform. Here, in addition to virtualized hardware resources (as part of an IaaS offering), PaaS also includes an installed operating system (OS), one or more programming environments, and general-purpose services, such as database access. Collectively, these platform resources offer developers everything they need to develop applications within the cloud. Some of the more prominent PaaS solutions in the market as of the time of writing include Amazon Web Services (Amazon AWS), Force.com, Google App Engine, and Microsoft's Windows Azure.

▸ **Software-as-a-Service (SaaS)**

SaaS is just that: software that's provided to customers as a service. Here, as opposed to commercial off-the-shelf (COTS) packages customers have historically installed on-premise, the installation and maintenance of SaaS solutions is managed exclusively by the software provider. This frees customers from the headaches of maintenance, but also restricts their ability to customize the software. Although most SaaS solutions are somewhat configurable, the scope of what can be enhanced is fairly limited by comparison.

The positioning of these three service models within the cloud computing paradigm is shown in Figure 1.1. This service stack provides customers with the flexibility they need to choose the model that works best for them. Starting from the bottom up, it's important to note that the higher you go within the service stack, the more abstracted the offering becomes. For example, when customers purchase licenses for a SaaS solution, they're not only buying access to the software itself; included in this offering are the underlying platform and infrastructure resources upon which the software's deployed. In addition to simplifying the buyer experience, this also makes it possible for customers to be up and running with a particular software package in mere minutes as opposed to the days, weeks, or months that are normally required to stand up a new server and install software packages on-premise.

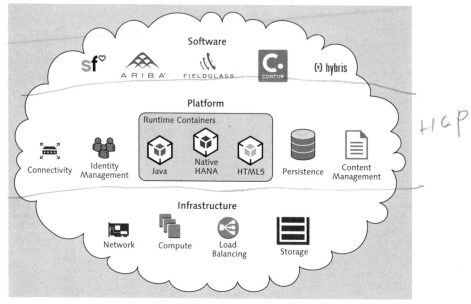

Figure 1.1 Understanding the Cloud Computing Service Model

Because this is a book about SAP software, you're probably wondering how SAP's various cloud-based offerings fit into the service model diagram shown in Figure 1.1. These relationships are highlighted in Figure 1.2.

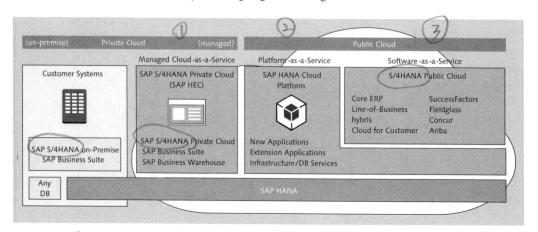

Figure 1.2 Overview of the SAP Cloud Strategy

Considering the overview diagram contained in Figure 1.2, let's focus in on some of the various components that make up SAP's cloud strategy:

- **IaaS** (for SAP is managed cloud)

  As opposed to traditional IaaS offerings, which provide generalized access to hardware resources, SAP's IaaS offerings consist mostly of hosting services. This starts with the *SAP HANA Enterprise Cloud* (SAP HEC), which is a hosting service that allows customers to run their SAP Business Suite and/or SAP Business Warehouse (SAP BW) systems on a private cloud that's managed by SAP.

  In addition to SAP HEC, SAP also provides SAP HANA-related infrastructure services as part of SAP HCP. For customers who have previously purchased an SAP HANA license, SAP provides *SAP HANA Infrastructure Services.* Net new customers have the option of subscribing to *SAP HANA DB Services*, which bundles infrastructure and license subscriptions together. In either case, SAP provides the hardware infrastructure to stand up an SAP HANA instance in the public cloud.

- **PaaS**

  As noted earlier, SAP HCP is SAP's PaaS offering. As you can see in Figure 1.2, SAP HCP runs in the public cloud and undergirds SAP's SaaS solutions by providing a rich set of application services that can be used to develop extension applications and the like.

- **SaaS**

  Over the course of the past several years, SAP has built up a fairly large cloud application portfolio that blends core ERP functions with applications that were attained via acquisitions (e.g. SuccessFactors, Concur, Ariba, and so forth). In early 2015, this portfolio of applications was given a common name: *SAP S/4HANA*. SAP S/4HANA is the next generation of SAP Business Suite, and will ultimately unite these applications into a full-scale cloud application suite. As you can see in Figure 1.2, SAP S/4HANA customers will have the option of deploying SAP S/4HANA on-premise, on the public cloud, or privately as part of a managed cloud solution. This flexibility allows customers to slowly move to the cloud and choose how much control they wish to delegate to SAP in terms of maintenance.

  Though SAP S/4HANA represents the future of SAP's SaaS offering, we should also make mention of another SaaS offering that exists at the time of this writing for small/mid-size businesses: *SAP Business ByDesign*. SAP Business

ByDesign is an integrated, turn-key offering that allows small businesses to stand up a lightweight SAP Business Suite in the public cloud.

Throughout the course of this book, our focus will be on SAP HCP and, more specifically, the *SAP HANA App Services* portion of the overall SAP HCP services offering. This distinction is highlighted in Figure 1.3 and Figure 1.4. As you can see, SAP HANA App Services builds on top of the infrastructure services provided as part of the aforementioned SAP HANA Infrastructure Services and SAP HANA DB Services to include all of the services you would expect to find in a PaaS offering: application containers, enablement services, and so forth.

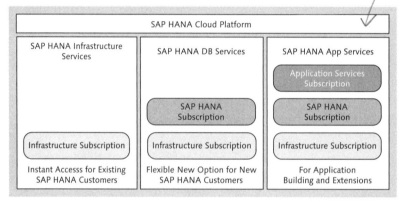

Figure 1.3 Overview of the SAP HCP Services Model (© 2015 by SAP SE. All rights reserved.)

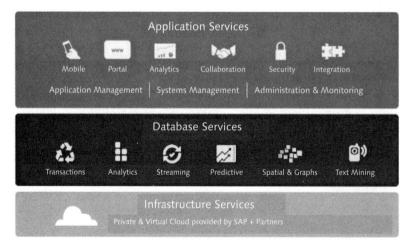

Figure 1.4 SAP HCP Services Model in Detail (© Copyright 2015. SAP SE. All rights reserved.)

1.2.3 Some Historical Perspective

In his book *The Big Switch: Rewiring the World from Edison to Google* (W.W. Norton & Co., 2013), Nicholas Carr tells the story of Samuel Insull, a brilliant business-man who was among the first to see the practical benefits in packaging and selling electrical energy as a commodity. Such a notion might seem obvious in these modern times, but the concept was met with a considerable amount of opposi-tion at the turn of the twentieth century. Indeed, among these opponents was Thomas Edison, Insull's former boss and long-time mentor. Believing that direct current (DC) was the only way to reliably transmit electricity, Edison felt that it was impractical to attempt large-scale distribution, because DC couldn't be trans-mitted very far.

Insull saw things very differently. With ever-improving electrical dynamos and the advent of Nikola Tesla's alternating current (AC), he felt that all of the foun-dational pieces were in place to establish large-scale power plants that could reli-ably transmit electricity for miles. Insull followed through with his vision and established the Commonwealth Edison Company, a prototype for modern electri-cal utility companies in the United States and eventually around the world.

After building up his infrastructure, Insull initially found that driving customer adoption was difficult. At the time, power supply systems were mostly built and managed internally by customers. Because even the smallest of power outages was viewed as a huge risk to production operations, customers were naturally very concerned about stability and generally felt that it was best to manage this risk in-house. Through a bit of shrewd marketing and negotiating, Insull was eventually able to convince a few strategic customers to give his services a try. Once the word of success spread, it didn't take long for other customers to see the viability of the model and jump on board.

Over the course of the next 30 years or so, this trend would continue to the point that hardly any companies in the United States operated their own power supply systems. Through centralization and economies of scale, electrical utilities were able to produce electrical power much more efficiently and reliably at a fraction of the cost. In time, companies simply could no longer afford to go it on their own.

Fast-forwarding about 100 years, we find that cloud computing is experiencing some of the same growing pains that the electric utility industry faced in the early twentieth century. As a relatively new and somewhat abstract concept, many customers are frightened and skeptical of the promises made by cloud software and infrastructure providers. After years of installing and maintaining large and complex IT systems, the notion of relinquishing control of that infrastructure to a third-party vendor seems unfathomable.

Despite all of these (valid) concerns, there's simply no denying the economics of cloud computing. Much like electricity, IT infrastructure is something that's destined to become a commodity. The question is no longer *if*, but *when*. For companies bold enough to take the plunge, cloud computing offers a wide range of potential benefits:

- **Reduced operating costs**
  Operating an IT infrastructure is a very costly enterprise — one that's difficult to fully quantify when you consider the costs of racking and stacking servers, real estate, power consumption, sustaining a competent support staff, and so on. Cloud computing doesn't eliminate those costs, but it certainly goes a long way towards consolidating and reducing them. Plus, it's important to remember that we're not talking about short-term gains. In the long run, cloud computing providers will become more efficient and therefore more economical.

- **Reliability**
  Because cloud providers are focused squarely on providing a handful of services, there's a considerable amount of research and effort that goes into building up a reliable infrastructure. Indeed, when you read the articles that describe the lengths that providers such as Amazon and Google go through to provide near 100% uptime, there's really no comparison with what most IT organizations can manage internally in terms of disaster recovery, failover, and so on.

- **A lowering of the entry barrier**
  For small startup companies, cloud computing lowers the entry barrier, because it eliminates the capital expenses normally associated with building data centers, procuring hardware, installing and configuring software, and so on. With the offer of elasticity, most cloud providers offer subscription models that can grow with a business over time.

- **Faster turnaround times**
  Normally, the time it takes to procure a server, mount it, configure its software, and get it up and running is measured in weeks and sometimes months. Cloud providers, on the other hand, can often spin up fully functional instances in a

matter of minutes. For customers that are looking to innovate right away, there's simply no comparison.

▸ **Universal access**
With data centers scattered around the world, most cloud providers make it possible for a customer's user base to access IT resources from anywhere in the world. In general, the only thing a user needs is a public Internet connection.

If history is any indicator, these benefits will eventually outweigh the negatives to the point that customers feel they can no longer afford to stick with the status quo. Right now, most companies are as much in the business of IT as they are in manufacturing and/or selling goods and services. This is an unsustainable model that will inevitably change. In the meantime, we'll likely see lots of hybrid models that allow customers to take their time in migrating towards the cloud.

1.3   A Strategic "Glue" Component for SAP

Because SAP has such a wide customer base, it's not practical to close up shop with its on-premise offerings and transition into a cloud-based solution provider overnight. For a variety of reasons, many of SAP's customers will be slow to move towards a public cloud offering, and some may never get there. Recognizing this, SAP has formulated a cloud adoption strategy that supports hybrid landscapes that mix and match cloud-based offerings with on-premise solutions.

At the center of this strategy lies SAP HCP, which is effectively the glue that holds everything together. In this section, we'll briefly consider how SAP HCP satisfies this important role in SAP's cloud strategy.

1.3.1   Challenges of the Hybrid Landscape

Although the hybrid landscape offers customers the flexibility to move towards cloud solutions at their own pace, it also presents plenty of challenges. To put this into perspective, let's consider a customer that has historically run its human resources (HR) department using SAP ERP Human Capital Management (HCM) module on premise. Now, let's imagine that the customer decides it wants to improve its talent acquisition capabilities with SAP's SuccessFactors SaaS solution. At this point, the customer's HR solution is distributed between SuccessFactors running in the public cloud and SAP ERP HCM running on premise.

In order to be successful, these two solutions will need to collaborate with one another in different ways. It probably goes without saying that they'll need to exchange data with one another, but integration really goes beyond a handful of interfaces. True process integration requires streamlined process flows that automate task flow between groups of users that may work in different modules at different times.

From a functional and productivity perspective, users within the HR department need to have a unified experience. If you've ever (redundantly) maintained data in two or more systems at a time, then you probably have a sense for what we're talking about here. To the end user, it doesn't matter if the software's coming from SuccessFactors in the cloud or SAP ERP HCM on-premise; the user just wants a simplified set of tools to do his or her job.

1.3.2 Where SAP HANA Cloud Platform Fits In

If you think about the challenges considered in the previous section, it's plain to see that customers require certain extensions to cloud and/or on-premise applications in order to be successful. Because the nature of these application extensions can vary significantly depending on the customer's business requirements, a general-purpose development platform is needed.

As you progress through this book, we think you'll find that SAP HCP fills this role quite nicely. To put this into perspective, here are some highlights of what SAP HCP can be used for:

- Using the various runtime containers, you can build and deploy custom or extension applications using the Java, native SAP HANA, and HTML5 programming models.
- Using the SAP Cloud Connector component, you can connect with on-premise and third-party services in a secure and reliable manner.
- You can design mashup portal sites that aggregate content from SaaS applications, extension apps, and third-party applications.
- You can build interfaces to exchange data between cloud and on-premise systems.
- You can create custom mobile applications that leverage data from cloud and on-premise systems in a secure manner.

As you consider these possibilities, we should point out that the scope of solutions deployed on SAP HCP is not limited to custom applications developed by customers. Because SAP HCP is an open platform, the SAP partner ecosystem (and even SAP itself, for that matter) can also target SAP HCP as a means for developing and distributing extension applications.

Because of its flexibility, it's quite likely that many industry-specific innovations within the SAP landscape will make their way over to SAP HCP. As more and more SaaS offerings become closed off for custom development, SAP HCP will become the one place where customers and partners can come to develop application extensions. For developers who enjoy working with SAP HCP, this is an exciting and intriguing possibility.

1.4 Summary

In this chapter, you were able to gain a better understanding of what SAP HCP is and its role in the next-generation SAP technology landscape. Specifically, you learned how SAP HCP is positioned as a PaaS offering in SAP's cloud strategy. As you progress throughout the remainder of this book, we'll be expanding on the high-level concepts reviewed in this chapter in order to see how they're applied in real-world implementation scenarios.

Before we delve into specifics, though, we first need to take care of a few administrative items. Therefore, in the next chapter, we'll show you how to obtain access to an SAP HCP account, set up your development tools, and get up and running with SAP HCP.

In this chapter, we'll take a look at what it takes to get up and running with SAP HCP application development. By the end of this chapter, you'll have everything you need to begin developing live applications on the platform.

2 Getting Up and Running

Now that you have a feel for what SAP HCP is from a conceptual perspective, you're probably itching to take it for a test drive and see what it can do. We'll have a chance to do just that in Chapter 3. However, in the meantime, there are several administrative items that we need to sort out.

First of all, in order to do any real work on SAP HCP, we need to get our hands on an SAP HCP developer account. This account will be used to log onto the platform, allocate and assign resources, deploy applications, and more. We'll explore the account provisioning process in Section 2.1. In Section 2.2, we'll take a quick inventory of what's included with an SAP HCP account. Finally, in Section 2.3, we'll show you how to set up SAP HCP development tools on your local machine. With these tools in place, you'll be ready to hit the ground running in Chapter 3 when we start getting our hands dirty with application development.

2.1 Obtaining an SAP HCP Account

In order to access SAP HCP, we must apply for an account with SAP. In this section, we'll take a look at the various account types offered by SAP and see how they differ from one another. We'll also show you how to set up a free developer account that you can use to take SAP HCP for a test drive.

2.1.1 Understanding the SAP HCP Account Concept

In many ways, SAP HCP accounts are not unlike the accounts you set up with utility companies, such as your local electricity or Internet service provider. If you have ever had the pleasure of setting up one of these accounts, then you're no doubt familiar with the basic procedure:

1. First, you choose among the various account types and/or service plans offered by the service provider.

2. Then, you enter into some form of contract agreement whereby you as the customer agree to pay a certain fee, and the provider agrees to provide the requested services according to the service level agreements (SLAs) set forth in the contract.

In the context of SAP HCP, accounts are used to determine the scope of resources/services a customer wishes to procure from SAP. Once a customer registers for an account, the account becomes the key to accessing the platform, deploying applications, and much more.

At the time of this writing, SAP offers three different account types: developer, customer, and partner. These account types differ in terms of pricing model, the amount of cloud-based resources allocated, and usage conditions. Let's take a look at each of the available account types in detail.

Developer Accounts

The first account type that we'll take a look at is the free developer account. This account type is provided for developers who wish to explore SAP HCP and see what it has to offer. Unlike other SAP trial accounts that you may have worked with in the past, the SAP HCP developer account never expires, so you can continue to use it as a trial or sandbox account indefinitely.

For the most part, developer accounts provide access to the majority of features and services provided by SAP HCP. However, because this is a free account, SAP does limit the amount of resources you can consume using this account. In particular, as of the time of writing, developer accounts come with the following limitations:

- You can only run a limited number of applications at a time.
- Only 1 GB of database storage and 1 GB of document storage is provided.
- Only one user can exist per account.

Customer Accounts

As the name suggests, customer accounts are accounts that customers purchase from SAP in order to host productive applications in the cloud. Unlike the more limited developer accounts, customer accounts offer full access to SAP HCP productive services as well as 24-7 support from SAP.

In order to support a wide range of customer types, SAP offers a multitude of configuration options, which allow customers to choose the configuration that best meets their needs. You can obtain a pricing sheet and browse through the various configuration options by logging onto the SAP HANA Marketplace at *http:// marketplace.saphana.com/New/SAP-HANA-App-Services/p/1808*. In most cases, you can choose the target configuration and purchase the customer account right from within the SAP HANA Marketplace. After the initial purchase, customers have the option over time to purchase more resources from SAP as the need arises.

> **Tip**
>
> To ensure fast response times for productive applications, customer accounts are hosted in regional data centers that are in close proximity to the target user base. At the time of this writing, SAP has three data centers, covering the Americas, Europe, and Asia-Pacific regions.

Partner Accounts

This account type is provided for SAP partners who are interested in building cloud-based applications and selling them to customers. Access wise, partner accounts are similar to customer accounts in that they have access to the full set of SAP HCP productive services. However, because these types of accounts are normally used for development and prototyping, the amount of allocated resources tends to be less than for your average customer account. That being said, SAP will allow partners to purchase more resources as needed.

For more information about this account type and the SAP PartnerEdge program, log on to *https://www.sapappsdevelopmentpartnercenter.com*.

2.1.2   Registering for a Free Developer Account

If this book is your first foray into the world of SAP HCP, then it probably makes sense to start your journey by registering for a free developer account. The steps required to sign up for a developer account are as follows:

1. Log onto the SAP HCP trial account landing page at *https://account.hanatrial. ondemand.com*, as shown in Figure 2.1.

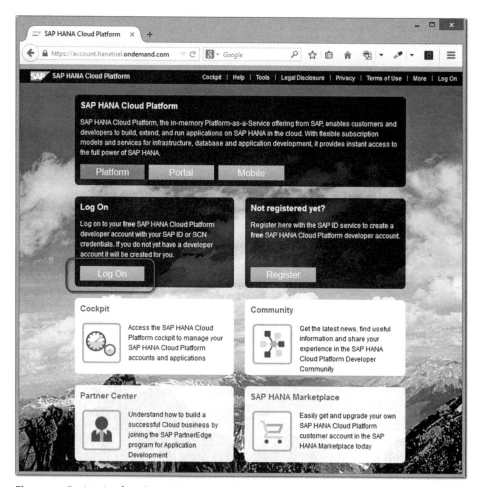

Figure 2.1 Registering for a Free SAP HCP Developer Account: Part 1

2. From the landing page, click on the LOG ON button. This will bring up the LOG ON page shown in Figure 2.2. From here, you have one of two options. If you already have an SAP ID or SAP SCN account, then you can plug in your account credentials into the LOG ON form and click on the LOG ON button to link this account with your SAP HCP developer account. A quick acceptance of the license agreement, and you're up and running.

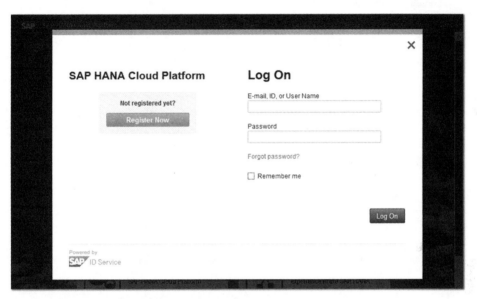

Figure 2.2 Registering for a Free SAP HCP Developer Account: Part 2

3. If you don't yet have an SAP ID and/or an SAP SCN account, then you'll need to create one by clicking on the REGISTER NOW button shown on the left-hand side of the screen in Figure 2.2. This will open up the REGISTRATION window shown in Figure 2.3. Here, you must specify a minimal amount of contact information and agree to the terms and conditions in order to register. After you submit the form, you'll receive a confirmation email, via which you can confirm the registration and activate your account.

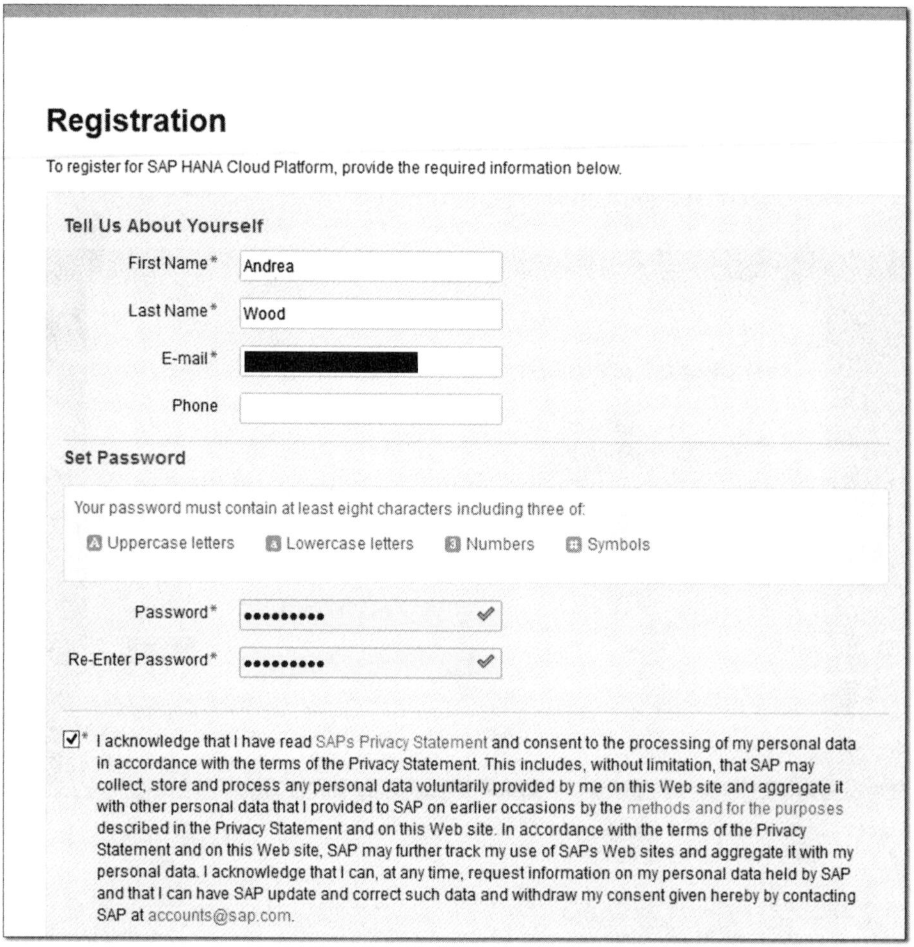

Registration

To register for SAP HANA Cloud Platform, provide the required information below.

Tell Us About Yourself

First Name* | Andrea

Last Name* | Wood

E-mail* | ████████████

Phone |

Set Password

Your password must contain at least eight characters including three of:

Ⓐ Uppercase letters   Ⓑ Lowercase letters   ③ Numbers   ⊞ Symbols

Password* | ●●●●●●●●● ✓

Re-Enter Password* | ●●●●●●●●● ✓

☑* I acknowledge that I have read SAPs Privacy Statement and consent to the processing of my personal data in accordance with the terms of the Privacy Statement. This includes, without limitation, that SAP may collect, store and process any personal data voluntarily provided by me on this Web site and aggregate it with other personal data that I provided to SAP on earlier occasions by the methods and for the purposes described in the Privacy Statement and on this Web site. In accordance with the terms of the Privacy Statement and on this Web site, SAP may further track my use of SAPs Web sites and aggregate it with my personal data. I acknowledge that I can, at any time, request information on my personal data held by SAP and that I can have SAP update and correct such data and withdraw my consent given hereby by contacting SAP at accounts@sap.com.

Figure 2.3 Registering for a Free SAP HCP Developer Account: Part 3

Regardless of the approach you take, the account creation process ends with you logged onto the SAP HCP Cockpit application shown in Figure 2.4. As you can imagine, we'll be spending a considerable amount of time in this cockpit as we develop and deploy applications, provision resources, and so on. Therefore, it's a good idea to bookmark the cockpit's page for future use: *https://account.hana-trial.ondemand.com/cockpit*. Also, if this is the first time you've ever accessed SAP HCP, we'd encourage you to take a look around the cockpit and become acquainted with the various tab pages, which will give you a sense of what's included with your SAP HCP account.

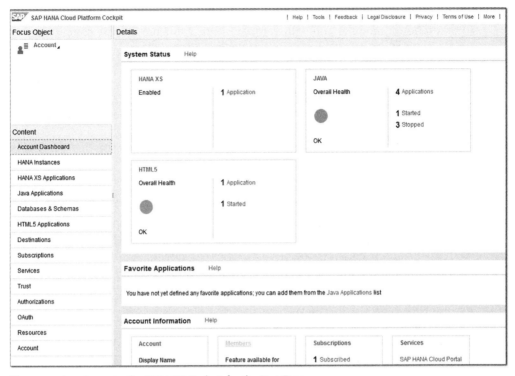

Figure 2.4 Logging onto the SAP HCP Cockpit for the First Time

2.2   What's in the Box?

Now that you've gotten your hands on a shiny new SAP HCP account, let's take a moment to unwrap the packaging and see what's included out of the box with SAP HCP. In addition to helping you understand more about what SAP HCP provides on a technical level, this brief analysis will also help you recognize the types of tools you'll need to install and configure in order to start developing SAP HCP applications.

2.2.1   Application Runtime Containers

As we noted in Chapter 1, SAP HCP was designed from the ground up to support a wide variety of programming models. This BYOL (bring your own language) approach lowers the entry barrier to SAP HCP by allowing development teams to leverage preexisting skillsets when migrating to the platform.

Java
HANA
HTML5
see Fig 1.1

In order to support multiple programming languages, SAP HCP employs the use of a series of modular and lightweight runtime containers. These containers provide a secure and scalable runtime environment for running applications based on a particular programming model (e.g., Java).

Next, we'll take a closer look at the types of runtime containers included with SAP HCP. We'll also look ahead a bit and see what other container types SAP has on the roadmap in the near term.

Runtime for Java

Going back to the days when it went by the codename "NEO," SAP HCP has always had excellent support for Java-based application development. From a technical perspective, the Java applications that we develop are deployed in a specialized runtime container called *Runtime for Java*. Figure 2.5 illustrates the basic architecture of Runtime for Java. As you can see, the basis for this runtime environment is the Compute Unit. As consumers of SAP HCP, we can think of Compute Units as virtualized host machines complete with their own CPU(s), main memory, disk space, and an installed operating system.

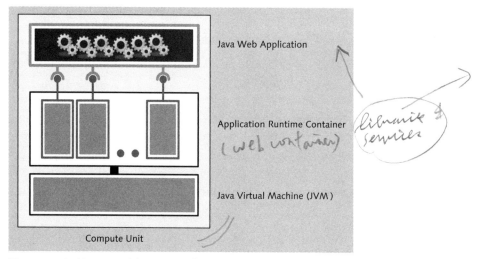

Java Web Application

Application Runtime Container
(web container)

*libraries &
services*

Java Virtual Machine (JVM)

Compute Unit

Figure 2.5 Architecture of the Runtime for Java

From a Java development perspective, the basis of a Compute Unit is the *Java Virtual Machine* (JVM). Here, SAP utilizes a proprietary JVM derived from Oracle's

HotSpot JVM called the *SAP JVM*. Compared to the default JVM provided by Oracle, SAP JVM offers a number of useful features related to debugging, memory profiling, and instrumentation.

On top of the SAP JVM, we have the *Application Runtime Container*, shown in the middle of the architecture diagram contained in Figure 2.5. If you're familiar with Enterprise Java development, then you can think of the Application Runtime Container as being analogous to web containers you may have worked with, such as Apache Tomcat or any of the number of leading Java EE application containers on the market. In essence, the Application Runtime Container furnishes our Java-based web applications with all of the libraries and services they need to get the job done.

As of the time of writing, SAP allows us to configure the Application Runtime Container according to three different profiles:

▸ **Java EE 6 Web**
This profile provides the full complement of APIs offered by the *Java EE 6 Web* profile. Here, in addition to Servlets and JavaServer Pages (JSPs), we also have access to Enterprise JavaBeans (EJBs), the Java Transaction API (JTA), the Java Persistence API (JPA), and more. These APIs simplify the enterprise application development process by assuming ownership of lower-level technical concerns, such as transaction management, object-relational persistence, and so on. For more about the Java EE 6 Web profile, see the boxed note ahead.

▸ **Java Web**
According to the online help documentation, the Java Web profile offers "a subset of Java EE standard APIs typical for a standalone Java Web Container." An example of a typical web container is the popular Apache Tomcat container. Such containers provide support for developing Java web applications using Servlets, JSPs, and so on. They do not, on the other hand, support the entire Java EE API. This means that you cannot utilize other Java EE-based technologies (such as EJBs) on the Java Web container. Of course, you still have access to the full Java SE library, as well as all of the custom SAP HCP service APIs.

▸ **Java Web Tomcat 7**
This profile (which is in beta release as of the time of writing) offers similar functionality to the Java Web profile. The primary difference is that the web container for this profile leverages the Apache Tomcat 7 web server without

49

modifications. This implies that certain cloud-based services will not be available at runtime.

What Is the Java EE 6 Web Profile?

The Java EE 6 Web profile was introduced in conjunction with the Java EE 6 specification. Conceptually, you can think of the Java EE 6 Web profile as a stripped-down version of the Java EE stack. Here, a subset of the common APIs used to develop Java-based web applications were grouped into a separate profile that application server vendors could use to build lighter-weight application containers. Naturally, such profiles make a lot of sense for cloud-based software providers such as SAP.

As developers, it's only natural to assume that "stripped down" implies "less awesome." In this case, however, we think you'll find that the APIs that were taken out have little to do with cloud-based application development. For example, it's probably unlikely that you would need access to RMI/CORBA-based remoting when developing web applications in the cloud. In other cases, you will find that there are cloud-based services that offer features that are similar (and arguably better) than the missing Java EE APIs. We'll find examples of this as we progress throughout the book.

One final distinction we should make here is with regards to EJB support in the Java EE 6 Web profile. Although the profile does include support for EJB development, it utilizes a specialized specification called *EJB Lite*. EJB Lite is a subset of the EJB 3.1 specification that provides support for session beans (stateful and stateless), singleton beans, and the associated container-based management features. Notably absent here are message-driven beans, JAX-WS endpoints, remoting, and backwards compatibility to EJB 2. Because these features aren't really used for web application development, this omission doesn't really impact the way we approach application design, but it's important to understand the differences all the same.

We'll have an opportunity to delve into Java-based application development beginning in Chapter 3.

Further Resources

You can access the Java web help documentation online at *http://help.hana.onde-mand.com*. Within the SAP HANA CLOUD PLATFORM section, navigate to JAVA DEVELOPMENT • RUNTIME FOR JAVA to learn more about the latest innovations in this space.

SAP HANA Runtime

One of the distinguishing features of SAP HCP is its built-in support for in-memory computing with SAP HANA. This support exists on two levels:

▸ **Basic database access**

In this scenario, applications are developed using a general-purpose programming language (such as Java), and the SAP HANA database is used as the underlying database. Here, the SAP HANA database is used just like any other relational database management system (RDBMS), providing access using standard SQL.

▸ **Full-scale native SAP HANA development**

In this scenario, applications are built from the ground up using native SAP HANA-based development artifacts (e.g., SQLScript-based stored procedures, server-side JavaScript, and custom view types). This approach is ideal for the development of analytical applications, which deal with lots of data.

In the latter usage scenario, the native SAP HANA development objects are deployed on the *SAP HANA Runtime*, which is essentially a cloud-based *SAP HANA Extended Application Services* (SAP HANA XS) instance.

What Is SAP HANA XS?

If you're not familiar with SAP HANA XS, then a brief introduction is in order. In essence, SAP HANA XS introduces a full-featured application server that sits directly on top of the SAP HANA database. This application server can be used to develop web applications based on technologies such as SAPUI5, server-side JavaScript, and native SAP HANA development objects (e.g., SQLScript procedures and analytical views).

Because SAP HANA XS sits on top of (and is tightly integrated with) the SAP HANA database, native applications deployed on this application server enjoy the benefits of having localized access to data. By eliminating the overhead of transferring data from the database tier to the application tier, native applications can churn through large amounts of data very quickly. For this reason, SAP HANA XS is well suited for building analytical applications and the like.

Within SAP HCP, the SAP HANA XS application server plays a similar role as Runtime for Java: It provides an application server that we can use to create web applications. Here, we can go about constructing SAP HANA native applications in much the same way that we would develop such applications on-premise.

To put all this into perspective, consider the basic architecture of an SAP HANA native application deployed on SAP HCP. As you can see in Figure 2.6, the client tier of this application is based on SAPUI5 technology. The SAPUI5 content is served up to clients by the SAP HANA XS engine, which includes a built-in web server. Because of the ubiquitous nature of HTML5, such content can be consumed by PCs, tablets, or smartphones without requiring the installation of any client software (e.g., the SAP GUI client).

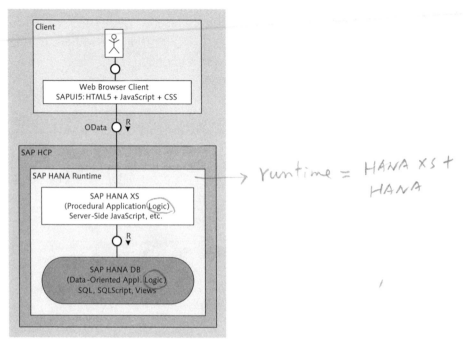

runtime = HANA XS + HANA

Figure 2.6 Basic Architecture of an SAP HANA Native Application

On the server side of things, we can see how the application logic is distributed between the SAP HANA XS engine and underlying SAP HANA database. Which layer(s) we choose to implement our logic depends largely on the requirements. For example, if all we're doing is performing simple CRUD (create, remove, update, and display) operations, then basic SQL/SQLScript should generally suffice. On the other hand, if the requirements call for lots of procedural logic, then we'll need access to more general-purpose language, such as server-side Java-Script. In this case, it makes sense to exploit the capabilities of the SAP HANA XS engine in tandem with pure SQL/SQLScript.

The communication channels between the client tier and the SAP HANA XS back-end are primarily defined using the OData protocol. This REST-based protocol is used to create lightweight web services that can easily be consumed via JavaScript and SAPUI5 widgets. We'll have an opportunity to see how all this comes together in Chapter 5.

HTML5 Application Container

For UI-centric application scenarios, SAP HCP also provides support for the deployment of HTML5 applications. These lightweight applications are deployed to a Git repository, from which their static resources (e.g., HTML, JavaScript, and CSS) are served up via a shared dispatcher service embedded within SAP HCP itself. We'll learn more about how all this works in Chapter 7.

More Runtime Containers on the Horizon

As of the time of writing, SAP has made it made it known that there are plans for dramatically increasing the scope of SAP HCP language support based on strategic partnerships with Cloud Foundry and Docker. Once this integration is in place, SAP HCP will truly support BYOL through a series of new runtime containers that are more generic in nature. For now, support for most of the popular cloud development languages must be deployed via the Runtime for Java via third-party implementations, such as JRuby, Jython, and so forth.

2.2.2 SAP HCP Enablement Services

As a true PaaS solution, SAP HCP provides much more than just a series of standalone runtime containers. It includes a series of enablement services that provide an abstraction around the access and consumption of cloud-based resources. Table 2.1 contains a list of the more prominent services provided by SAP HCP as of the time of writing. As you're reading this, keep in mind that the service offering continues to expand, so it's definitely a good idea to periodically check in with the SAP HANA Cloud Documentation to see what's new.

Service	Description
Persistence Service	This service provides an abstraction on top of relational database instances deployed in the cloud. This abstraction provides developers with a common interface for accessing database instances while at the same time shielding them from the underlying complexities of scaling databases in the cloud.
Connectivity Service	This service provides developers with a means of transparently communicating with remote services that could be hosted either on-premise or elsewhere on the Internet.

Table 2.1 Enablement Services of SAP HCP

Service	Description
Document Service	This service provides access to a content repository for storing unstructured content. It can also be used to implement a sort of virtualized file system as needed.
Identity Service	The term "Identity Service" is the name given to a series of security-related services or features integrated into SAP HCP. Some highlights in this offering include support for single sign-on (SSO) scenarios, identity federation with the Security Assertion Markup Language (SAML), and authorization based on the OAuth protocol.
Feedback Service	This service provides a framework for implementing user feedback scenarios in cloud applications.

Table 2.1 Enablement Services of SAP HCP (Cont.)

2.2.3 Higher-Level Services

In addition to the core services described in Section 2.2.2, the SAP HCP PaaS offering is rounded out by a series of higher-level application services that provide specialized capabilities needed in certain cloud-based application scenarios. Next, we'll highlight a few of the more prominent services included in this offering.

SAP HANA Cloud Portal

SAP HANA Cloud Portal is a cloud-based portal solution that makes it easy to create lightweight portal sites that combine cloud applications, cloud application extensions, and on-premise content to create a seamless UI experience. By using open standards like HTML5 and OpenSocial, SAP HANA Cloud Portal makes it easy to integrate content from disparate sources without having to reinvent the wheel. We'll see how this works firsthand in Chapter 9.

SAP HANA Cloud Integration

In many respects, you can think of *SAP HANA Cloud Integration* (SAP HCI) as a cloud-based version of SAP's on-premise SOA middleware tool, *SAP Process Integration* (PI). This is to say that SAP HCI is a cloud-based middleware service that allows you to develop integration scenarios in the cloud. These scenarios might be needed for one-time uploads of on-premise data or ongoing real-time lookups to on-premise systems. We'll discuss SAP HCI in more detail in Chapter 10.

SAP HCP Mobile Services

This service is used to help developers roll out mobile applications. Some of the more prominent features provided with SAP HCP Mobile Services include the following:

▶ Support for user onboarding

▶ Security and authorization services

▶ Support for implementing native push notifications

▶ Support for implementing offline support for mobile applications

▶ Administration and monitoring of mobile applications

We'll take a closer look at SAP HCP Mobile Services in Chapter 12, which is available for download at *www.sap-press.com/3638*.

2.3   Installing SAP HCP Development Tools

In the previous section, we learned how SAP is really focused on positioning SAP HCP as an open and inviting platform for developers. Although this openness is unquestionably a good thing, it does make the task of setting up our development environments a little bit more complex, because there are so many types of development objects that we have to account for.

In this section, we'll take a look at what a *typical* tools setup looks like so that you'll have the necessary tools in place to work through the examples described in this book. We emphasize the term "typical" here because tool configurations will tend to differ in subtle ways between developers. Fortunately, because SAP HCP is standardized around the extensible Eclipse integrated development environment (IDE), these differences usually amount to the installation of a few plug-ins here and there.

2.3.1   Setting Up the Eclipse IDE

SAP elected to standardize the SAP HCP toolset around the open-source Eclipse IDE. This approach allows SAP to leverage the built-in development functions of the core Eclipse IDE and merely supplement with SAP HCP-specific features as needed. Plus, because Eclipse is arguably the most popular IDE in the world, it offers the added benefit of requiring little to no introduction for the average developer.

In this section, we'll take a look at how to set up a new instance of Eclipse and install the relevant plug-ins from the SAP HCP Tools library.

Installing the Java SDK

Before you can install Eclipse, you first need to make sure that you have the appropriate version of Java installed on your local machine. Although modern versions of Eclipse only require the installation of the more lightweight Java Runtime Environment (JRE), we recommend that you go ahead and install the full Java SE software development kit (SDK), which is available online at *www.oracle.com/technetwork/java/javase/downloads/index.html*. This will ensure that you have the full complement of compiler tools needed to carry out various development tasks.

When installing the Java SDK, you'll want to download the version that best fits with the target Application Runtime Container profile you plan to work with in Runtime for Java (refer back to Section 2.2.1). For example, as of the time of writing, the available container profiles are based on Java EE versions 6 and 7. Therefore, if you're working with the Java Web Tomcat 7 profile, then you'd want to download and configure version 7 of Java SE.

Downloading and Installing Eclipse

In order to maximize flexibility, SAP developed SAP HCP Tools to work with most recent versions of the Eclipse IDE. Therefore, if you already have a recent version of Eclipse lying around, it should be possible to install SAP HCP Tools on top of that instance if you so choose. However, given the large number of plug-ins associated with an SAP HCP Tools instance, we recommend that you download and configure a separate instance of Eclipse for SAP HCP development.

To download Eclipse, go to *www.eclipse.org/downloads* in your web browser. From the main DOWNLOADS page, download the latest version of ECLIPSE IDE FOR JAVA DEVELOPERS for your target operating system, as shown in Figure 2.7.

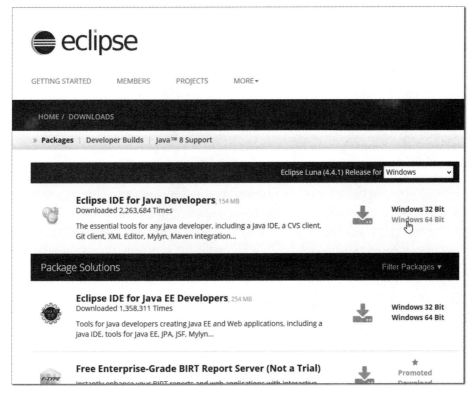

Figure 2.7 Downloading Eclipse IDE for Java Developers

The installation bundle that you download will be a zipped archive that you can unpack to a directory of your choosing. Once you unpack the bundle, you can launch Eclipse for the first time by opening up the ECLIPSE folder and running the executable eclipse file (e.g., eclipse.exe).

As Eclipse loads for the first time, you'll likely be presented with the WORKSPACE LAUNCHER dialog box shown in Figure 2.8. Within this dialog box, you must select a directory on your local machine that Eclipse can use to store project artifacts and the like. Normally, it's a good idea to select the USE THIS AS THE DEFAULT AND DO NOT ASK AGAIN checkbox so that Eclipse will use the selected directory as its default location. That way, Eclipse won't pester you about choosing a location

every time you launch it, and you'll know where to look to find development artifacts created from within the IDE.

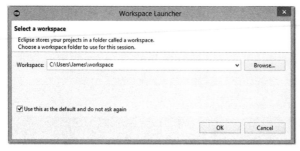

Figure 2.8 Selecting the Default Workspace Location in Eclipse

If all goes well, Eclipse will eventually load in a window similar to the one shown
in Figure 2.9. If you're new to Eclipse, then we recommend that you browse
through a tutorial or two to become acquainted with the IDE layout, Eclipse-spe-
cific terminology and features, and so on. For the most part, we think that you'll
find that Eclipse is fairly intuitive, but like most IDEs, it does have a few idiosyn-
crasies.

Figure 2.9 Launching Eclipse for the First Time

Before we move on, we should probably make mention of one minor housekeeping task you should be aware of if you're working behind a proxy or firewall. Because Eclipse receives its updates over HTTP connections, you must configure your proxy settings in order to extend Eclipse for use with SAP HCP. To configure a proxy server connection, perform the following steps:

1. From within Eclipse, select the WINDOW • PREFERENCES menu option within the top-level menu bar, and then drill into GENERAL • NETWORK CONNECTIONS.

2. From the NETWORK CONNECTIONS panel shown in Figure 2.10, select the appropriate schema (e.g., HTTP and/or HTTPS) in the PROXY entries table, and click on the EDIT... button.

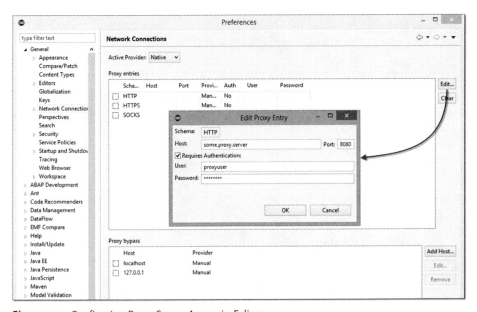

Figure 2.10 Configuring Proxy Server Access in Eclipse

3. Then, in the EDIT PROXY ENTRY subdialog box, enter the proxy host name and port, as well as authentication details as necessary. Click on the OK button to confirm your selections.

4. Finally, as necessary, you can use the PROXY BYPASS table to configure a list of hosts that you want to access without using the proxy server.

Installing the SAP Development Tools

At this point, you should have a vanilla version of Eclipse installed on your local machine. Although this Eclipse instance is fully functional, it doesn't come equipped with any SAP or SAP HCP-specific features. To add these features, we must download and install the necessary plug-ins from SAP. This can be achieved by performing the following steps:

1. To begin, we need to log on to the SAP Development Tools for Eclipse installation site, available online at *https://tools.hana.ondemand.com/#cloud*. As you can see in Figure 2.11, this site provides installation sites for several recent Eclipse distributions (e.g., Eclipse Luna 4.4 and Eclipse Kepler 4.3 as of the time of writing). Copy the URL for your version of Eclipse onto your clipboard.

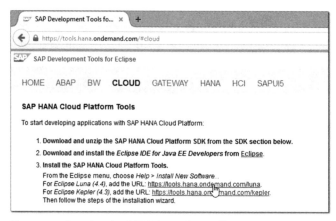

Figure 2.11 Locating the SAP HCP Tools Installation Site

2. Next, open up the Eclipse IDE, and select HELP • INSTALL NEW SOFTWARE... from the top-level menu bar.

3. This will open up the INSTALL dialog box shown in Figure 2.12. From this screen, paste the installation site URL copied in step 1 into the WORK WITH input field, and click on the ADD... button. In the ADD REPOSITORY dialog box, give the repository a name, and click on the OK button. By naming the repository, we can use the same repository later on to check for updates and update the software as needed.

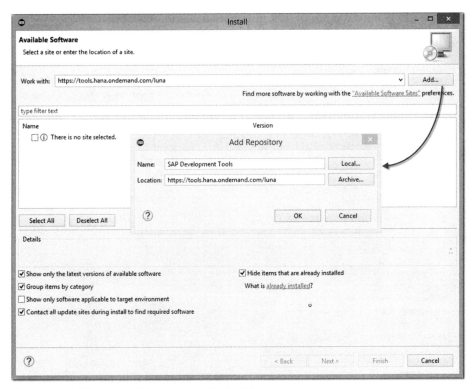

Figure 2.12 Adding an Available Software Site in Eclipse

4. After the repository is defined, click on the NEXT > button to move to the next step in the installation wizard. At this point, Eclipse will connect to the installation URL and search for available plug-ins to install.

5. At the AVAILABLE SOFTWARE step shown in Figure 2.13, you'll be provided with a list of available software items to install. For the purposes of this book, the main items of interest will be the SAP HANA CLOUD PLATFORM TOOLS, SAP HANA TOOLS, and UI DEVELOPMENT TOOLKIT FOR HTML5. These items will ensure that we have the necessary components in place to develop SAP HCP-based Java applications, native SAP HANA applications, and HTML5 applications based on SAPUI5 technology. Of course, you can also choose other items of interest as desired.

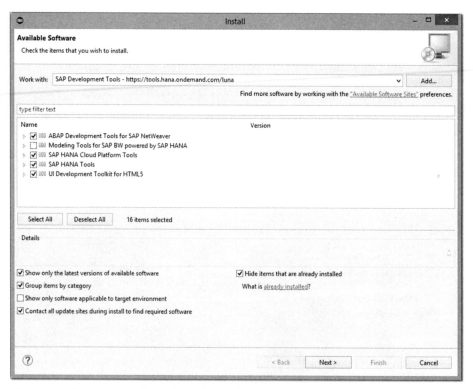

Figure 2.13 Choosing the Software Items to Install

6. Finally, once you choose the relevant items you wish to install, you can continue through the installation wizard by accepting all of the defaults. At this point, Eclipse will download and install the relevant plug-ins.

As you're running through the installation process, keep in mind that this step can take quite a while if you have a lot of items selected and/or a slow network connection. If all goes well, Eclipse will finish installing the plug-ins and let you know that it must restart in order for the changes to take effect. After the restart is complete, you should be greeted with a revised welcome page, similar to the one shown in Figure 2.14. Here, you'll notice a few new SAP and SAP HCP-related items that have been added to the welcome page.

Figure 2.14 Revised Welcome Page after SAP HCP Tools Installation

2.3.2 Downloading the SAP HCP SDK

In addition to the SAP HCP-related plug-ins integrated into Eclipse, SAP also provides a standalone SDK that includes a series of useful tools and examples to kick start the development process. Among other things, this SDK includes the following:

▸ Platform API Java Archive (JAR) files

▸ API documentation

▸ A local SAP HCP runtime instance that can be used for offline testing

▸ A command line tool that can be used to administer SAP HCP instances

▸ Loads of full-scale example projects with annotated source code and documentation

The SAP HCP SDK can be downloaded from the same site we used to locate the Eclipse installation site for SAP HCP Tools: *https://tools.hana.ondemand.com/# cloud*. As you can see in Figure 2.15, SAP provides separate SDKs to support the different Application Runtime Container profiles available in Runtime for Java. For a variety of reasons, we strongly recommend that you select the SDK version that coincides with your selected profile. For the purposes of this book, we'll be downloading the SDK for the Java EE 6 Web profile, because it contains the comprehensive set of features needed for our demonstrations.

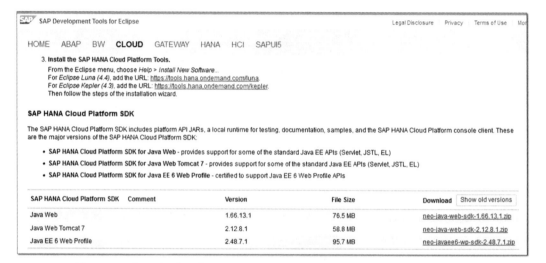

Figure 2.15 Downloading the SAP HCP SDK

Once you download the SDK version that's right for you, you'll want to unpack the ZIP archive to an easily accessible directory on your local machine. After the ZIP file is unpacked, we highly recommend that you browse through the SDK folder structure and take a look at all of the goodies SAP provides.

> **Tip**
>
> For a variety of reasons, we would recommend that you refrain from nesting the SDK folder too deep within your local file system. Doing so can cause issues with the local runtime due to extraordinarily long file names.

Setting Up the Local Runtime Environment

As we noted earlier, the SAP HCP SDK includes a local runtime environment that allows you to test SAP HCP applications on your local machine. Although you can administer this local runtime environment from the command line, it's much more convenient to install the local runtime environment as an available server runtime in Eclipse. This integration can be achieved by performing the following steps: Fig 2.16, 2.17, 2.18

1. Start Eclipse, select the WINDOW • PREFERENCES menu option, and expand the SERVERsubmenu.

2. Inside the SERVER submenu, select the SAP HANA CLOUD PLATFORM node. This will open the SAP HANA CLOUD PLATFORM panel shown in Figure 2.16. Within this panel, you'll want to configure the relevant attributes as follows:

   ▶ LANDSCAPE HOST
   This attribute needs to point to the host of your target SAP HCP instance. If you're using the free developer account, then the landscape host will be `han-atrial.ondemand.com`. Otherwise, it will be `hana.ondemand.com`.

   ▶ SDK LOCATION
   In this field, you'll want to specify the directory that you unpacked the SAP HCP SDK to.

   ▶ ACCOUNT NAME
   This attribute is used to keep track of your SAP HCP account name so that SAP HCP Tools can automatically propose this value whenever you perform actions that require you to specify your SAP HCP account.

   ▶ USER NAME
   This attribute is used to keep track of your user name so that SAP HCP Tools can automatically propose this value whenever you perform actions that prompt you to authenticate with the server-side SAP HCP instance.

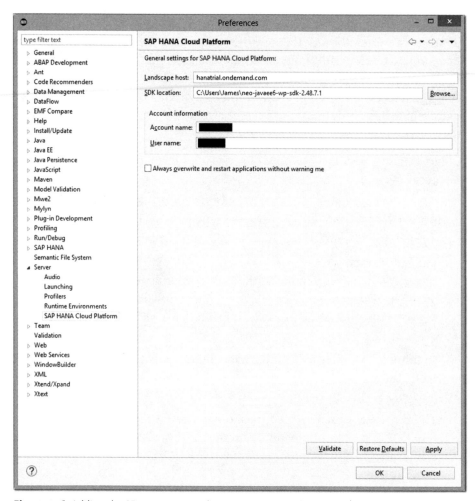

Figure 2.16 Adding the SDK Location to the SAP HCP General Settings

3. Once you've configured the directory location for the SAP HCP SDK, you'll want to switch over to the Server • Runtime Environments node. From here, you can configure the SAP HCP local runtime environment by clicking on the Add... button. This will open up the New Server Runtime Environment wizard shown in Figure 2.17.

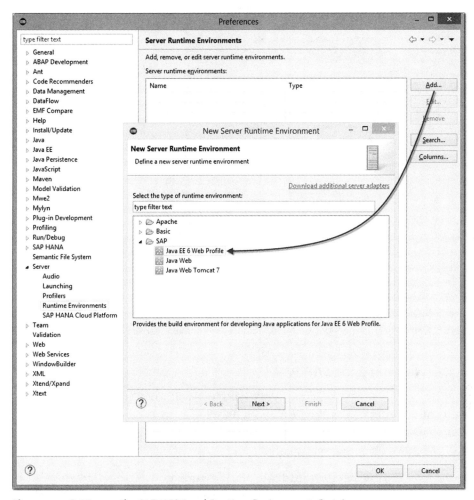

Figure 2.17 Setting up the SAP HCP Local Runtime Environment: Part 1

4. From the initial wizard page, expand the SAP folder, and choose the appropriate local runtime environment based on your selected Java profile (see Figure 2.17). Click on the Next > button to continue.

5. At the next screen (shown in Figure 2.18), you have an opportunity to choose the location of the local runtime environment from your local machine. Because you configured the SDK location previously, this directory will be proposed automatically, so simply confirm the selection by clicking on the Finish button.

Figure 2.18 Setting up the SAP HCP Local Runtime Environment: Part 2

2.3.3 Installing the SAP JVM

One last item that we would encourage you to install when setting up your development environment is the SAP JVM. As we'll learn in Chapters 3 and 4, this optional step allows us to tap into some of the powerful profiling capabilities of the SAP JVM when tuning Java applications.

The SAP JVM can be downloaded from the same downloads page we used to download the SAP HCP SDK: *https://tools.hana.ondemand.com/#cloud*. In the SAP JVM section of the page, simply download the appropriate bundle for your OS configuration. You can find installation instructions for your particular OS in the SAP HANA Cloud Documentation available online at *https://help.hana.ondemand.com/help/frameset.htm*. Here, browse to JAVA DEVELOPMENT • GETTING STARTED • INSTALLING JAVA TOOLS FOR ECLIPSE AND SDK • INSTALLING SAP JVM.

After the SAP JVM is installed, you can associate it with the set of installed JREs in Eclipse by performing the following steps:

1. Open up Eclipse, and from the main menu select WINDOW • PREFERENCES.

2. Expand the JAVA • INSTALLED JREs folders, and click on the ADD... button.

3. This will open up the ADD JRE installation wizard shown in Figure 2.19. Accept the default STANDARD VM option, and click on the NEXT > button to continue.

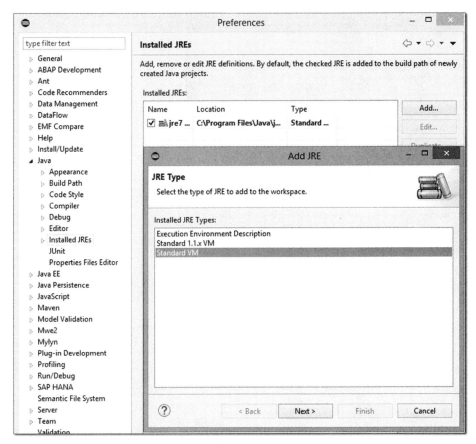

Figure 2.19 Adding the SAP JVM as an Installed JRE in Eclipse: Part 1

4. On the next screen, you must browse to the directory location in which you installed the SAP JVM. Once you select the directory, the JRE name and system libraries will be configured automatically. To confirm the configuration, click on the FINISH button.

5. Finally, after the SAP JVM is configured as a JRE, you'll want to select it as the default JRE by clicking on the checkbox adjacent to the NAME column (see Figure 2.21). With this setting in place, all new Java-based projects will be automatically configured to utilize the SAP JVM as the target JRE.

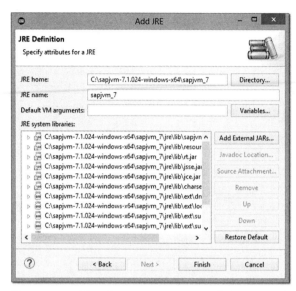

Figure 2.20 Adding the SAP JVM as an Installed JRE in Eclipse: Part 2

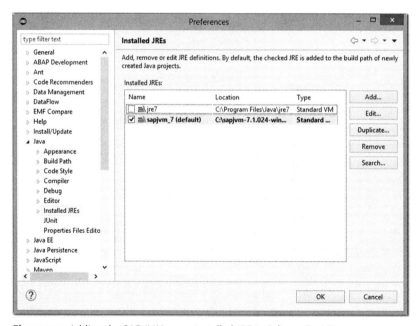

Figure 2.21 Adding the SAP JVM as an Installed JRE in Eclipse: Part 3

2.4 Summary

In this chapter, we were able to work through all of the prerequisites for developing cloud-based applications on SAP HCP. With these administrative tasks out of the way, we're ready to proceed with some hands-on development exercises. We'll get things started in Chapter 3 by learning how to develop Java-based web applications.

PART II

Core Development Concepts

In this chapter, we'll show you how to develop Java-based applications for SAP HCP. This gentle introduction will serve as the foundation for more advanced topics covered in later chapters of the book.

3   Developing Java Applications

Despite boasting an open, bring-your-own-language (BYOL) approach to cloud-based application development, SAP HCP definitely has some strong ties with Java. In terms of core language support, Java's been around the longest (going back to the days when SAP HCP went under the code name "NEO"). As a result, it's not surprising to learn that Java is the most mature language offering within SAP HCP.

This history, in and of itself, doesn't make Java a better language choice than other languages supported by SAP HCP. However, it does mean that there are many more Java-based application examples and resources available online to browse through when kick starting your own development projects. Therefore, even if you don't have plans to utilize Java in your daily work, it's not a bad idea to understand how Java is used on SAP HCP so that you can at least follow along and understand how to adapt these examples for the language of your choice.

In this chapter, we'll demonstrate how to develop Java-based web applications for SAP HCP. Although our intent with this chapter is to provide a gentle introduction, we should point out that this chapter should not be seen as an introduction to the Java programming language. If you're a fairly experienced programmer, then you should probably be able to follow along with the examples provided in this chapter, but we would strongly recommend that you read through some of the reference materials described in Section 3.5 if you plan on performing serious Java development on SAP HCP.

3.1 Overview

In Chapter 2, we spent some time analyzing the Application Runtime Container for Java applications deployed on SAP HCP, *Runtime for Java*. We noted that Runtime for Java can be configured according to several profiles based on a customer's needs or preferences. From a developer's perspective, the impacts of the profile choice come down to just how much of the Java EE API they have to work with. In all cases, the foundation is set with the core Java SE and Java Servlets/JSP APIs. However, only in the case of the Java EE 6 Web profile configuration do developers have access to EJBs, for instance.

On top of the Java SE/EE APIs, SAP HCP provides a series of services (such as the Persistence Service and Connectivity Service) that can be used to fill in the gaps exposed from the Java EE libraries that are not available within SAP HCP. As we'll learn in Chapter 6, these services are in many ways easier to work with in a cloud context than the core Java EE libraries/services.

The third (and arguably most important) piece to the Java development puzzle is the vast community of open-source projects and libraries that can easily be integrated into Java web applications deployed on SAP HCP. This means that preexisting Java-based web applications built on frameworks such as Spring MVC, Struts, and so forth can be deployed pretty much as-is on SAP HCP.

When we put all these pieces together, we end up with a blank canvas that can be filled in a lot of different ways. For example, UI-centric applications can be built using a mixture of HTML5 with Servlets/JSPs, SAPUI5, or any number of the available open-source UI frameworks out there in the Java space. Similarly, APIs can be built using EJBs or plain old Java objects (POJOs).

Because we could scarcely enumerate the various library and framework permutations, much less demonstrate them, our approach in this chapter will be to stick to the essentials by showing you how to build basic web applications using the Java Servlets/JSP APIs. In the chapters that follow, we'll then build on this foundation and show you how to incorporate third-party libraries and frameworks, cloud services, and more.

3.2 Creating Java Web Applications

At the end of the day, any Java-based SAP HCP application that we develop must be deployed as a Java Web Archive (or WAR) file. Inside this WAR file, we can include a wide variety of resources, including Java class files, Servlets/JSPs, and static HTML artifacts. Although we'll be looking at many of these different resource types as we go along, we thought it appropriate to start things off with a very simple Java web application based on Servlets and JSPs.

To guide our demonstration, we'll be developing a simple application via which users can maintain a reading list. Here, we'll create a simple JSP form to display the reading list and add additional titles. On the backend, we'll develop a faceless, Servlet-based controller class to collect and keep track of the reading list entries. This application, though trivial, will provide us with an opportunity to learn how to work with the Eclipse IDE and observe how Java web applications are packaged. Plus, it will give us a chance to play around a bit with the local runtime environment packaged with the SAP HCP SDK. Without further ado, let's get started.

3.2.1 Creating a Dynamic Web Project in Eclipse

To get things started, we need to open up the Eclipse IDE and create a new Dynamic Web project. This project type is the default project type for building Java-based web applications and is included as part of the Eclipse Java EE development tools. To create a new Dynamic Web project, we must perform the following steps:

1. Open Eclipse, and switch to the JAVA EE perspective. If you've never accessed this perspective before, you can do so by choosing WINDOW • OPEN PERSPECTIVE • OTHER... in the top-level menu bar and selecting the JAVA EE list option.

2. Once the JAVA EE perspective is opened, create a new Dynamic Web project by selecting the FILE • NEW • DYNAMIC WEB PROJECT menu option, as shown in Figure 3.1.

Figure 3.1 Creating a Dynamic Web Project in Eclipse: Part 1

3. This will open the NEW DYNAMIC WEB PROJECT wizard, as shown in Figure 3.2. In the first step, specify the basic coordinates for the project, including the following:

▸ The project name (e.g., EXAMPLE03_01).

▸ The location where you want to store the project artifacts within the local file system. Normally, it makes sense to keep the USE DEFAULT LOCATION checkbox selected, as this will ensure that the project artifacts get stored in the default Eclipse workspace.

▸ The target runtime environment (i.e., the local runtime environment you set up whenever you downloaded the SAP HCP SDK).

▸ The version of the Dynamic Web module you wish to create. Here, the numbers in the DYNAMIC WEB MODULE VERSION list correspond with versions of the Java Servlet API. Unless you have a compelling reason to configure it otherwise, we strongly recommend that you choose version 3.0, as illustrated in Figure 3.2.

Figure 3.2 Creating a Dynamic Web Project in Eclipse: Part 2

4. After the basic project coordinates are set, proceed forward through the project creation wizard by clicking on the NEXT > button. For the most part, you can accept the proposed defaults at the intermediate steps. However, at the WEB MODULE step, we recommend that you select the GENERATE WEB.XML DEPLOYMENT DESCRIPTOR checkbox, as this will automatically create the web project's web.xml file and ensure that it's linked up with the Eclipse Java EE toolset.

5. Finally, once all of the settings are configured, click on FINISH to confirm your selections and create the project. At this point, Eclipse will create the project folder structure and generate relevant project files, such as the aforementioned web.xml file.

Figure 3.3 shows what the project looks like in the ECLIPSE PROJECT EXPLORER view once it's been created. Here, we can see that the project creation wizard has furnished us with everything we need to get started with development, including the following:

❶ Underneath the JAVA RESOURCES node, you can see that a folder called SRC has been created to store our Java source code files.

❷ The project also contains references to all of the libraries needed to build Java-based web applications. This includes the basic Java SE libraries, Java EE libraries, and SAP HCP-specific libraries.

❸ A WEBCONTENT folder mirrors the structure of the WAR file that will be used to deploy our web application. As you can see, this includes the aforementioned prebuilt WEB.XML deployment descriptor.

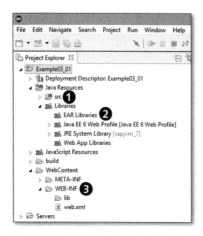

Figure 3.3 Basic Structure of a Dynamic Web Project in Eclipse

The last step in the project setup process involves the creation of a Java package to store our Java source files. To create a new package, simply right-click on the SRC folder and select the NEW • PACKAGE menu option, as shown in Figure 3.4. Then, in the NEW JAVA PACKAGE dialog box, specify the package name using the familiar Java package naming convention based on reverse Internet domain names (see Figure 3.5).

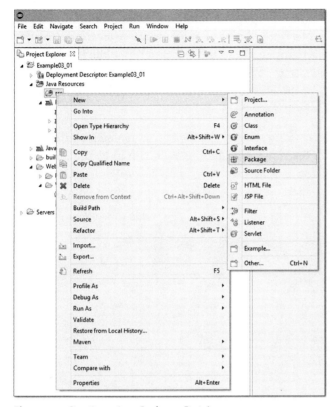

Figure 3.4 Creating a Java Package: Part 1

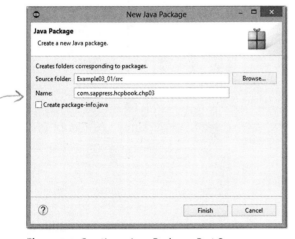

Figure 3.5 Creating a Java Package: Part 2

3.2.2 Building the Servlet-Based Controller

With our Dynamic Web project now in place, we're ready to begin developing the actual application artifacts. In keeping with the traditional model-view-controller (MVC) paradigm, we'll start our development from the bottom up with the creation of a hybrid model/controller layer. As mentioned earlier, we'll implement this layer using a faceless Java Servlet class.

To create the Servlet, right-click on the development package created in Section 3.2.1 and choose the NEW • SERVLET menu option, as shown in Figure 3.6. Then, in the CREATE SERVLET dialog box (Figure 3.7), specify the Servlet class name (ReadingListServlet), and click on the FINISH button to confirm your selection and create the new Servlet class.

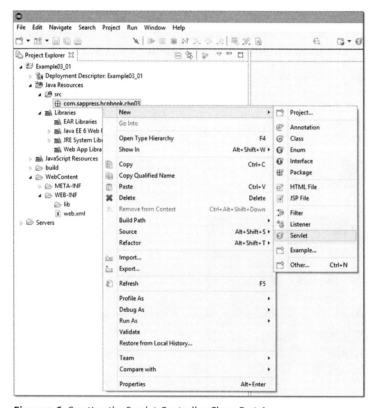

Figure 3.6 Creating the Servlet Controller Class: Part 1

Figure 3.7 Creating the Servlet Controller Class: Part 2

After the Servlet class is created, we'll want to plug in our custom application logic inside the doPost() method, as shown in Listing 3.1. Here, the logic is pretty straightforward:

1. First, create a variable of type java.util.List called readingList. This variable will be used to store the book entries in the user's reading list. Because our trivial application is not backed by a database, we'll simply store this transient collection inside the user's session context. Note that once this list instance is created, we'll simply fetch it from the session context in subsequent calls to simulate access to a persistence store.

2. Next, retrieve the name of the book the user wants to add to the list by using the getParameter() method of the HttpServletRequest variable passed via the Servlet container. Here, we're retrieving the book's name via an HTTP request parameter called book.

3. Then, add the book to the reading list by calling the add() method of the readingList list object. While we're at it, we also update the session context with another attribute called itemCount that allows us to keep track of the number of books in the reading list.

4. Finally, use the javax.servlet.RequestDispatcher class to (re)direct the user back to the JSP form so that he or she can browse and/or make further updates to the reading list.

```
public class ReadingListServlet extends HttpServlet
{
  ...
  protected void doPost(HttpServletRequest request,
                        HttpServletResponse response)
     throws ServletException, IOException
  {
    // Retrieve the current list from the user's session:
    List<String> readingList = null;
    HttpSession session = request.getSession();
    Object o = session.getAttribute("readingList");
    if (o == null)
    {
      readingList = new ArrayList<String>();
      session.setAttribute("readingList", readingList);
    }
    else
    {
      readingList = (List<String>) o;
    }

    // Add the selected item to the list:
    String book = request.getParameter("book");
    if (book != null)
      readingList.add(book);

    // Also keep track of the number of items in the list:
    session.setAttribute("itemCount", readingList.size());

    // Reroute the user back to the main reading list form:
    RequestDispatcher rd =
      request.getRequestDispatcher("index.jsp");
    rd.forward(request, response);
  }
}
```

Listing 3.1 Implementing the Servlet Controller Logic

3.2.3 Creating the View Layer Using JSPs

As we noted earlier, the view layer for our application is implemented using JSPs. To create the JSP form, perform the following steps:

1. Right-click on the WebContent folder and choose the NEW • JSP FILE menu option, as shown in Figure 3.8.

2. In the NEW JSP FILE dialog box (Figure 3.9), enter the JSP file name (e.g., index.jsp), and click on FINISH.

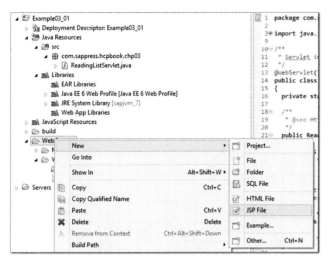

Figure 3.8 Creating the JSP-Based View: Part 1

Figure 3.9 Creating the JSP-Based View: Part 2

As you can see in Listing 3.2, the form UI is implemented using some basic HTML5-compliant markup and a few well-placed JSTL scriptlet tags. These tags are used to simplify handling of the dynamic reading list data. Underneath the reading list, we've included an HTML form that allows users to add additional books to the list. As you might expect, this form is linked back to our ReadingListServlet to update the reading list.

```
<%@ page language="java" contentType="text/html; charset=UTF-8"
    pageEncoding="UTF-8"%>
<%@ taglib prefix="c" uri="http://java.sun.com/jsp/jstl/core" %>
<jsp:useBean id="readingList" scope="session"
             class="java.util.ArrayList" />

<!DOCTYPE html>
<html>
<head>
  <meta http-equiv="Content-Type"
          content="text/html; charset=UTF-8">
  <title>HCP Book :: Chapter 3 :: My HCP Reading List</title>
  <link href="css/style.css" rel="stylesheet">
</head>
<body>
  <h1>My HCP Reading List</h1>
  <table class="readingList">
    <tr>
      <th>Book Title</th>
    </tr>
    <c:forEach var="book" items="${readingList}">
      <tr><td><c:out value="${book}" /></td></tr>
    </c:forEach>
  </table>
  <section>
    <form method="post" action="ReadingListServlet"><div>
      <label for="inpBook">
        Book: <input id="inpBook" name="book" />
      </label> 
      <button type="submit">Add</button>
    </div></form>
  </section>
</body>
</html>
```

Listing 3.2 Implementing the JSP-Based View Layer

3.2.4   Testing the Application Locally

With all of the code now in place, we're ready to test our application. Because we're dealing with a pure Java-based web application, we could technically test this application on most any Java web server. However, because the target run-time is ultimately SAP HCP, it makes sense to run our test using the SAP HCP local runtime that's bundled with the SAP HCP SDK. The steps required to test our application on this local runtime are as follows:

1. Create a new run configuration within Eclipse by right-clicking on the project folder and choosing the RUN AS • RUN ON SERVER menu option, as shown in Figure 3.10.

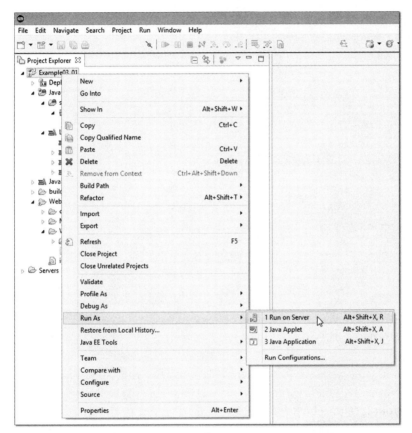

Figure 3.10 Testing the Reading List Application: Part 1

2. This will open up the RUN ON SERVER dialog box (Figure 3.11). Here, select the server instance that you want to run your application on. Because this is the first time you're running an application on the SAP HCP local runtime, choose the MANUALLY DEFINE A NEW SERVER radio button option so that you can configure the SAP HCP local runtime as a server within Eclipse. This configuration amounts to the selection of the appropriate runtime environment from within

the SAP server type selection list (Figure 3.11). Click on the NEXT > button to continue.

Figure 3.11 Testing the Reading List Application: Part 2

3. On the next screen, select the target HTTP port for your new local server instance. Normally, you'll want to choose an available 8000 series port (e.g., 8080) on your local machine for this, so it's usually best to simply go with the default port selection proposed by Eclipse.

4. Finally, trigger the deployment/test by clicking on the FINISH button. At this point, Eclipse will attempt to deploy your application onto the target SAP HCP local runtime instance. The SAP HCP local runtime environment will be started if it's not started already. Assuming the deployment is a success, the default index.jsp file will be loaded into an embedded browser window, as shown in Figure 3.13.

Figure 3.12 Testing the Reading List Application: Part 3

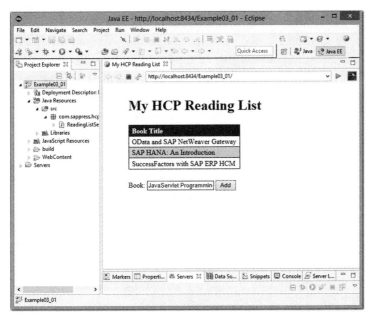

Figure 3.13 Testing the Reading List Application: Part 4

Once the application's deployed, you can play around with the reading list and test the application flow to see how the Servlet and JSP components interact with one another. We should also point out that you have the option of copying the URL from the embedded browser window in Eclipse during the course of your testing and pasting it into the address bar of your favorite browser (e.g., Google Chrome, Mozilla Firefox, etc.) so that you can better approximate the end user experience.

3.3   Working with EJBs

As we noted in Chapter 2, the Java EE 6 Web profile provides support for EJB development using session beans. This allows us to factor our business logic out of the presentation layer (i.e., Servlets and JSPs) and into a series of session beans. Although we could conceivably achieve the same designs using POJOs, there are several benefits to be gained by using EJBs, including built-in transaction management, security, pooling, and more. With that in mind, this section will demonstrate how to integrate EJBs into our Java-based web applications.

3.3.1   Refactoring for EJBs

To illustrate how to work with EJBs, we'll refactor the reading list application that we developed in Section 3.2 by moving all of the business logic from the Java Servlet tier into a session EJB. Because we don't have a persistence layer yet, we'll approximate this by defining our EJB as a stateful session EJB. That way, our EJB can keep track of the individual reading lists, and our Servlet/JSP layer can focus on rendering the UI content and controlling page flow.

To kick off the refactoring effort, we elected to create a brand new Dynamic Web project and then copy over all the resources from the original reading list application. With this new project in place, we're ready to proceed with the development of our new EJB component. The steps for creating the EJB are as follows:

1. Right-click on the main project node and select the NEW • OTHER... menu path, as shown in Figure 3.14.

2. In the wizard selection dialog box (Figure 3.15), expand the EJB folder and select the SESSION BEAN (EJB 3.x) entry. Click on the NEXT > button to proceed.

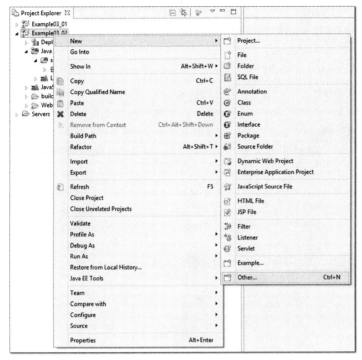

Figure 3.14 Creating an EJB in a Dynamic Web Project: Part 1

Figure 3.15 Creating an EJB in a Dynamic Web Project: Part 2

3. This will open the CREATE EJB 3.x SESSION BEAN dialog box (Figure 3.16). Within this screen, there are several important properties that you need to configure for your EJB:

   ▸ The target JAVA PACKAGE and CLASS NAME.

   ▸ Within the STATE TYPE list, you need to choose whether the session EJB will be STATEFUL or STATELESS. For the purposes of our example, we've chosen the STATEFUL option, because we want our EJB to keep track of application state. Most of the time, though, we prefer to go with the default STATELESS option, because it's more efficient.

   ▸ Because you want to incorporate EJB method calls into the Servlet/JSP tier, you need to configure a local business interface for the EJB. This is achieved by selecting the LOCAL checkbox in the CREATE BUSINESS INTERFACE section.

Figure 3.16 Creating an EJB in a Dynamic Web Project: Part 3

4. Once you've confirmed your selections, click on the FINISH button to go ahead and create the session bean.

After the wizard is completed, we can see that there are two new source files added to our project: one for the session bean itself and the other for the local business interface. In the next section, we'll learn how to add our business logic to these source files.

3.3.2 Implementing Business Logic in an EJB

To begin developing the business logic, we start with the local business interface. This interface will define the business methods exposed to the Servlet/JSP tier. For the purposes of our reading list application, we created the four methods shown in Listing 3.3. These methods will allow users to add and remove titles from the reading list, obtain a live copy of the reading list, and determine the total number of entries in the list.

```
@Local
public interface ReadingListManagerBeanLocal
{
  public void addTitle(String title);
  public boolean removeTitle(String title);
  public int getCount();
  public List<String> getReadingList();
}
```
Listing 3.3 Defining the EJB's Local Business Interface

As you can see in Listing 3.3, the local business interface looks pretty much like any other Java interface. The only EJB-centric element is the @Local annotation, which allows the EJB container to identify the interface as a local business interface.

After you save your business interface, you'll notice that the session bean class has been flagged with a little red ERROR icon within Eclipse. Because our session bean implements the local business interface, the error is indicating that our session bean contains unimplemented methods. To fix this problem, simply click on the ERROR icon in the margin to the left of the class definition statement and choose the ADD UNIMPLEMENTED METHODS option, as shown in Figure 3.17. This will add empty versions of each of the business methods to our session bean.

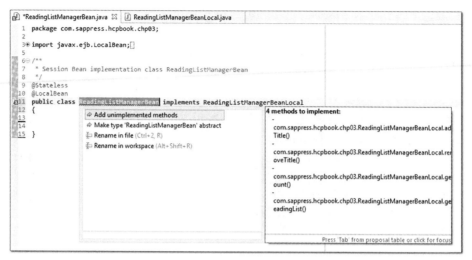

Figure 3.17 Adding Business Methods to the Session Bean

For the purposes of our rather trivial application, the implementation logic for the session bean itself is pretty straightforward. As you can see in Listing 3.4, the business methods basically leverage the capabilities of the `java.util.List` collection to maintain the reading list. With the minimalistic design of the EJB 3.x specification, the only real EJB-centric content here is the `@Stateful` and `@LocalBean` annotations. These annotations provide the EJB container with the metadata it needs to determine how to deploy the bean (e.g., as a stateful bean).

```
@Stateful
@LocalBean
public class ReadingListManagerBean
   implements ReadingListManagerBeanLocal
{
   private List<String> readingList = new ArrayList<String>();

   @Override
   public void addTitle(String title)
   {
      readingList.add(title);
   }

   @Override
   public boolean removeTitle(String title)
   {
      return readingList.remove(title);
   }
```

```
@Override
public int getCount()
{
  return readingList.size();
}

@Override
public List<String> getReadingList()
{
  return readingList;
}
}
```

Listing 3.4 Implementing Business Logic in the Session Bean

3.3.3 Incorporating EJBs into Servlets and JSPs

Now that we've created our EJB, let's see how we can incorporate it into the Servlet/JSP application layer. To begin, we'll refactor the ReadingListServlet introduced in Section 3.2.2 to utilize our stateful session bean.

Under normal circumstances, we'd utilize dependency injections to inject the EJB into our Servlet, as illustrated in Listing 3.5. However, this approach doesn't work for our particular use case. This is because we need a separate stateful session EJB instance per user. This means that we need to create and store the stateful session EJB instance in the user's session scope.

```
import javax.ejb.EJB;
public class ReadingListServlet extends HttpServlet
{
    @EJB
    ReadingListManagerBeanLocal readingListManager;

  protected void doGet(HttpServletRequest request...
  ...
}
```

Listing 3.5 Utilizing Dependency Injections to Access EJB Resources

To handle our unique EJB access requirements, we introduced a helper method called getListManager(), as shown in Listing 3.6. This method performs the following steps:

1. First, it checks to see if an instance of the stateful session bean exists within the user's session.

2. If it doesn't, it requests a new instance to be created via a JNDI lookup and stores that in the user's session context. We'll see where the lookup string is configured momentarily.

3. Finally, the derived session EJB handle is passed back so that it can be used to perform business operations.

```java
private ReadingListManagerBeanLocal getListManager(
  HttpSession session)
{
  // Access/create the reading list manager EJB from the
  // session context:
  ReadingListManagerBeanLocal readingListManager = null;
  readingListManager = (ReadingListManagerBeanLocal)
    session.getAttribute("readingListManager");
  if (readingListManager == null)
  {
    try
    {
      // If the EJB hasn't been created yet, go ahead
      // and create it:
      InitialContext ctx = new InitialContext();
      readingListManager = (ReadingListManagerBeanLocal)
        ctx.lookup("java:comp/env/ejb/ReadingListManager");

      session.setAttribute("readingListManager",
                           readingListManager);
    }
    catch (NamingException ne)
    {
      ne.printStackTrace();
    }
  }

  return readingListManager;
}
```

Listing 3.6 Accessing and Storing the Session EJB Handle in the User's Session

In order to perform the JNDI lookup, we need to modify the web.xml deployment descriptor file to include an `<ejb-local-ref>` tag, as illustrated in Listing 3.7. Here, we specify the lookup string by using the `<ejb-ref-name>` subelement.

```xml
<?xml version="1.0" encoding="UTF-8"?>
<web-app...>
  ...
  <ejb-local-ref>
    <ejb-ref-name>ejb/ReadingListManager</ejb-ref-name>
```

```
    <ejb-ref-type>Session</ejb-ref-type>
    <local>
      com.sappress.hcpbook.chp03.ReadingListManagerBeanLocal
    </local>
  </ejb-local-ref>
</web-app>
```

Listing 3.7 Adding the EJB Reference to the web.xml Deployment Descriptor

With the session-based bean instance lookup in place, the implementation of the
doPost() form handler method within the Servlet becomes quite straightforward.
As you can see in Listing 3.8, we're simply using our getListManager() method
to obtain a reference to the session bean and then calling its addTitle() business
method to add a new title to the reading list.

```
protected void doPost(HttpServletRequest request, HttpServletResponse
response)
  throws ServletException, IOException
{
  // Fetch the EJB list manager:
  ReadingListManagerBeanLocal readingListManager =
    getListManager(request.getSession());

  // Add the selected title to the list:
  String title = request.getParameter("title");
  if ((title != null) && (! title.equals("")))
    readingListManager.addTitle(title);

  // Reroute the user back to the main reading list form:
  ...
}
```

Listing 3.8 Calling EJB Business Methods in the Reading List Servlet

If we need to access the EJB from within the JSP layer, we can simply retrieve it
from the user's session, as shown in the scriptlet code excerpt contained in Listing 3.9. Normally, this sort of access would be brokered by an intermediate Servlet controller class that fetches the relevant data from the EJB layer and stores it in
the request context so that it can be read within the JSP. However, there are those
rare occasions in which direct access to an EJB is warranted, so it's nice to know
it's there if you need it.

```
<%@ page language="java" contentType="text/html; charset=UTF-8"
    pageEncoding="UTF-8"%>
...
<%
```

```
try
{
  ReadingListManagerBeanLocal readingListManager =
  (ReadingListManagerBeanLocal)
    request.getSession().getAttribute("readingListManager");

  java.util.List<String> readingList = null;
  if (readingListManager != null)
    readingList = readingListManager.getReadingList();
  else
    readingList = new java.util.ArrayList<String>();

  request.setAttribute("readingList", readingList);
}
catch(Exception ex)
{
  out.println("EJB Exception: " + ex.getMessage());
}
%>
...
```

Listing 3.9 Accessing the EJB from within the JSP Layer

You can find a completed version of this application in the book's source code bundle, available for download at *www.sap-press.com/3638*. There, you'll find that we implemented other functions, such as remove, to make the application a bit more interactive. Obviously, this still barely scratches the surface of what's possible with the core Java EE APIs supported by SAP HCP, but at least it shows you what you need to get started. In the next section, we'll take a look at how to debug and tune your Java web applications.

3.4 Debugging and Tuning Java Applications

For simple demonstration apps like the ones we've created throughout the course of this chapter, there's usually not too much that can go wrong. However, as you begin to develop larger, production-quality applications, you will no doubt encounter situations in which it's difficult to pinpoint locations in the code that are causing application errors, poor performance, or both. With that in mind, in this section we'll cover a couple of tools that you can use to perform some root-cause analysis of your code.

3.4.1 Debugging a Java Web Application

Because most application errors are a result of an inadvertent mistake, it can be difficult to pin down the statement or statements that are causing the problem. In these situations, it can be helpful to run through the application with a debugger so that you can step through the code line-by-line to see where things go awry. Although it can be a challenge to debug Java web applications in some environments, SAP HCP makes it easy to launch debugging sessions on demand.

Regardless of whether you're debugging web applications deployed on your local SAP HCP instance or a cloud-based SAP HCP instance, the steps for launching a Java web application in a debugger session are as follows:

1. Before you start the debugger, you first need to set breakpoints in areas of the code where you suspect things may be going wrong. This can be achieved within the normal source code editor window in Eclipse by simply double-clicking on the gray panel adjacent to the line of code that you want to stop at (see Figure 3.18).

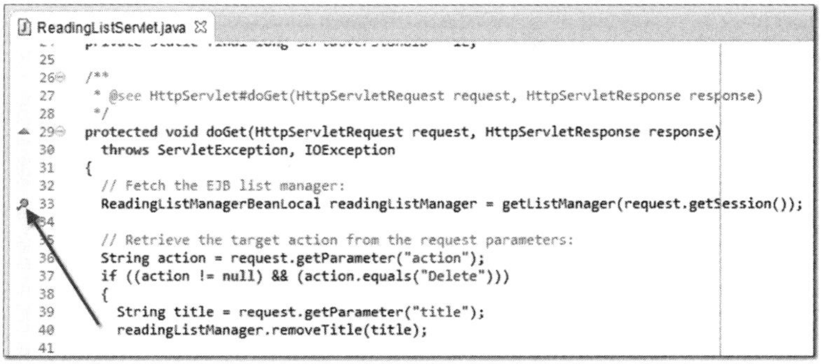

Figure 3.18 Setting a Breakpoint in the Java Source Code Editor

2. Once your breakpoints are set, launch the debugger by right-clicking on the project node and selecting the DEBUG AS • DEBUG ON SERVER menu option, as shown in Figure 3.19. This is analogous to the RUN AS menu option you've used to deploy/launch your applications in normal mode.

3. This will launch the DEBUG ON SERVER wizard screen (Figure 3.20). From here, simply choose your preexisting server (or create a new one as needed), and click on the FINISH button.

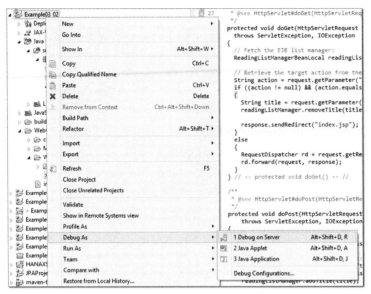

Figure 3.19 Debugging a Java Web Application: Part 1

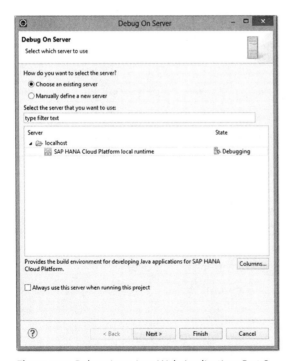

Figure 3.20 Debugging a Java Web Application: Part 2

4. If the target server is not running in debug mode (which should be the case here), you'll likely encounter the dialog box shown in Figure 3.21. This prompt is basically advising you of the fact that the server will be restarted in debug mode. Obviously, this is no big deal for local SAP HCP instances, but it could be a bigger deal for shared cloud-based instances in which other users are testing, so proceed with caution. For the purposes of this demonstration, accept the mode switch by clicking on the OK button.

Figure 3.21 Debugging a Java Web Application: Part 3

5. After the server is (re)started in debug mode, Eclipse will launch your web application in a local browser window as per usual. However, depending on where you set your breakpoints, the application will eventually be preempted by the debugger session, which assumes control of the processing. At this point, you will likely be prompted to switch to the Eclipse Debug perspective, shown in Figure 3.22. From here, you can debug through the application and try to track down the problem areas in the code.

As you can see in Figure 3.22, the Debug perspective is broken up into several content areas. Depending on your configuration, you should have the following views displayed on the screen:

▶ Debug
In this view, you can see the current stack trace for the running application thread.

▶ Variables
This view can be used to browse the contents of variables that are currently visible in the section of code that you're debugging.

▶ Breakpoints
This view is used to manage the breakpoints that are currently set in the source code. You can also use this view to create new ad hoc breakpoints as needed.

▶ CODE VIEW

This modified view of the source code allows you to trace through the code line-by-line as necessary.

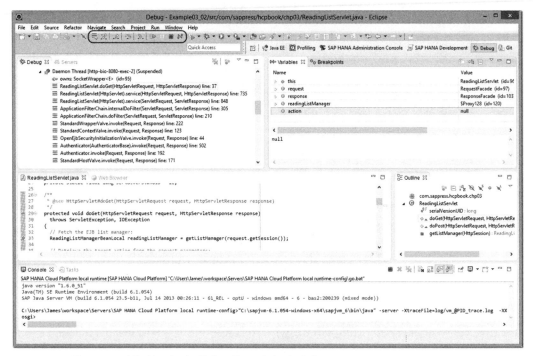

Figure 3.22 Working in the Debug Perspective in Eclipse

In the toolbar area (highlighted in Figure 3.22), a number of functions are provided to control the way that you step through the code (e.g., line-by-line, stepping over method calls, returning from a method, and so forth). For the most part, the instrumentation layer is pure Eclipse, so all the basic debugging rules apply here. For more information about the available functions, we recommend that you read through the Eclipse help documentation, which can be accessed by selecting HELP • HELP CONTENTS in the top-level menu bar.

3.4.2 Profiling Java Web Applications

Another useful tool in the SAP HCP toolset is the *SAP JVM Profiler*. This tool is used to build an analysis profile of a running JVM (which is the backbone of an

SAP HCP instance) and pinpoint performance bottlenecks. In this section, we'll observe how the SAP JVM Profiler can be used to identify segments of code that consume inordinate amounts of memory, I/O resources, and so on.

Prerequisites for Using the SAP JVM Profiler

As the name suggests, the SAP JVM Profiler is built on top of SAP's proprietary version of the JVM, called SAP JVM. Here, SAP went above and beyond the requirements of the default JVM specification to include first-class support for collecting performance traces from a running JVM instance.

Although SAP JVM is used by default in cloud-based SAP HCP instances, it's technically possible to run the SAP HCP local runtime using any compliant JVM implementation. However, if you plan on running the SAP JVM Profiler on your local SAP HCP instance, then you must configure that instance to utilize the SAP JVM. For this reason (and others), we strongly recommend that you standardize around the SAP JVM so that you can keep your SAP HCP instances as consistent as possible. If you skipped over this step when you originally installed the SAP HCP SDK, then you can reconfigure your environment after the fact by using the steps described in Chapter 2, Section 2.3.3.

Working with the SAP JVM Profiler

Similar to the debugger tool we explored in Section 3.4.1, the SAP JVM Profiler is a server-based function that can be controlled from within the SERVERS view in the Eclipse IDE. As you can see in Figure 3.23, we can control the SAP JVM Profiler by right-clicking on a server node and choosing the appropriate menu options (e.g., RESTART IN PROFILE). Once again, you'll want to be careful not to disturb other users when profiling shared SAP HCP instances.

Once the server node is (re)started in profile mode, we can launch the SAP JVM Profiler by opening up the PROFILING perspective in Eclipse. By default, this perspective will bring up the VM EXPLORER view shown in Figure 3.24. From here, we can drill into the running profile by double-clicking on the record in the VM EXPLORER table.

Figure 3.23 Starting the SAP JVM Profiler in the Eclipse IDE

Figure 3.24 Accessing the Profiling Perspective in Eclipse

This will bring up the profiler dashboard shown in Figure 3.25. Within this dashboard, you can turn on various types of traces by simply clicking on the links in the AVAILABLE ANALYSES panel (Figure 3.25). For example, if you wanted to trace long-running methods in the code, then you might activate the Performance Hotspot Analysis by clicking on the corresponding PERFORMANCE HOTSPOT ANALYSIS link.

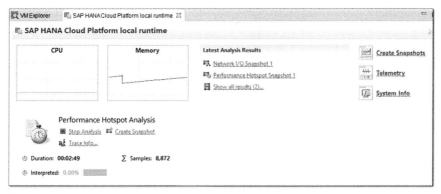

Figure 3.25 Starting an Analysis Session

Once the analysis starts, the dashboard will adjust to include running analysis information as well as controls for stopping the analysis, taking periodic snapshots, and so forth. While this is running, you can switch over to your browser and run through various application scenarios so that slow-running processes are captured in the analysis. Then, once you're finished, you can return to the analysis view and click on the STOP ANALYSIS link to stop the analysis (see Figure 3.26). Finally, after the profiler collects the results, you should see a new analysis results link show up in the LATEST ANALYSIS RESULTS panel (Figure 3.26).

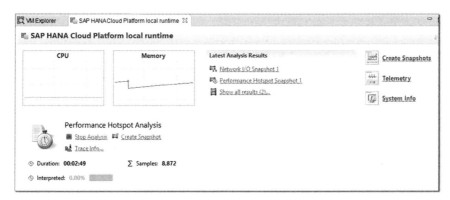

Figure 3.26 Monitoring an Analysis in the Profiling Perspective

Depending on the type of analysis you create, the analysis results view will naturally look a little different. For example, in Figure 3.27, you can see the analysis overview for a Performance Hotspot Analysis session that we created. Here, various statistical measures are organized into categories that make it easy to find what you're looking for.

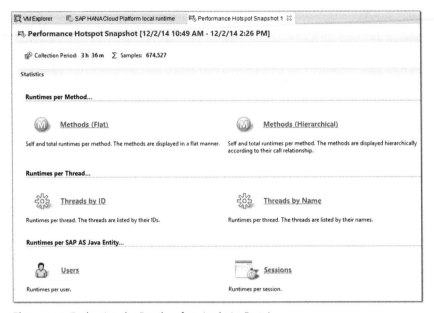

Figure 3.27 Evaluating the Results of an Analysis: Part 1

As you drill in further, you can see various summarizations of the data, such as the method runtimes summary shown in Figure 3.28. Here, functions are provided to sort, group, and filter the data as needed. You also have the ability to export the results to Microsoft Excel and other desktop file types.

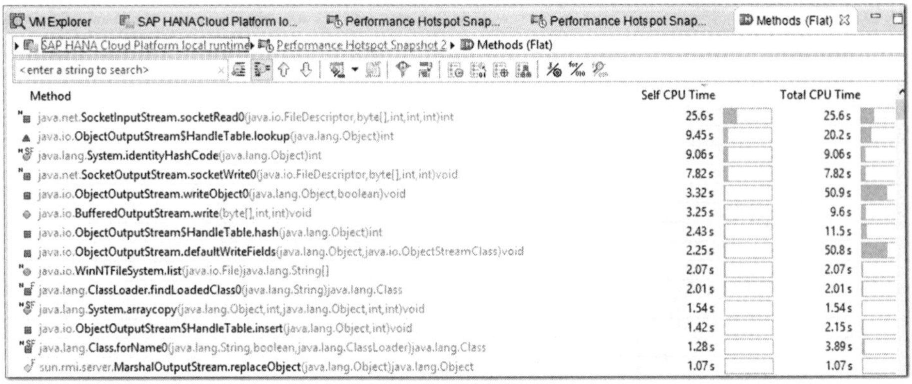

Figure 3.28 Evaluating the Results of an Analysis: Part 2

3.5   Next Steps

Hopefully, this brief introduction to Java application development helped you get a sense for how Java-based web applications are built on SAP HCP. Although we'll be expanding on many of these concepts in subsequent chapters, our treatment will be much more focused on particular topics of interest (e.g., persistence or the consumption of cloud services). Therefore, if you're new to Java or need further resources to help you get started, here are some recommended titles to take a look at:

- Java introduction:
  - *The Java Programming Language, 4th Edition* (Arnold, Gosling, Holmes, Addison-Wesley, 2005)
  - *Thinking in Java, 4th Edition* (Eckel, Prentice Hall, 2006)
- Servlets and JSPs
  - *Java Servlet Programming, 2nd Edition* (Hunter, Crawford, O'Reilly, 2010)
  - *JavaServer Pages, 3rd Edition* (Bergsten, O'Reilly, 2009)
- Enterprise JavaBeans
  - *Enterprise JavaBeans 3.1* (Rubinger, Burke, O'Reilly, 2010)

In addition to the standard Java SE and EE APIs, we'd also encourage you to explore the various open-source frameworks designed to simplify Java application development, such as Spring MVC. You can generally find excellent resources related to these frameworks online.

Finally, another valuable resource to consider when approaching application development is the various sample applications included with the SAP HCP SDK. There, you will find many useful examples that can be used as a template for carrying out common development tasks.

3.6   Summary

In this chapter, you learned some of the basics of Java application development on SAP HCP. Collectively, the skills obtained in this chapter will serve as a foundation for approaching more advanced topics as we progress throughout the book. In general, we think you'll find that all SAP HCP applications, regardless of their complexity, originate from the same humble beginnings. From here, we'll just keep adding layers as you learn how to consume cloud services and perform more complex tasks.

In the next chapter, we'll take this show on the road by showing you how to deploy your Java applications on SAP HCP. Along the way, we'll explore key software logistics concepts that you should be mindful of when developing real-world SAP HCP applications.

In order to develop production-quality SAP HCP applications, we need to have the necessary tools and processes in place to manage the software development lifecycle from start to finish. In this chapter, we'll look at some of the tools and processes you can use to manage and deploy Java-based SAP HCP applications.

4   Managing and Deploying Java Applications

In the previous chapter, we observed how the SAP HCP tools make it easy to develop, deploy, and test Java-based web applications from within the Eclipse IDE. In the early phases of development, these tools provide us with everything we need to get the job done. However, as we progress a little bit further along in the software development lifecycle, matters become much more complicated.

With that in mind, this chapter will consider how to develop a software logistics infrastructure for SAP HCP development. Although the focus in this chapter will be primarily on Java-based development, many of the concepts and tools introduced will also apply towards the development of other types of SAP HCP applications (e.g., HTML5 applications). Indeed, regardless of the language you use to develop SAP HCP applications, you'll find that SAP has provided an open environment that makes it possible to take advantage of just about any logistics tool available on the market. This allows organizations to easily tailor SAP HCP development to align with corporate standards and best practices.

4.1   Overview

Let's face it: Software logistics is one of the more boring topics in the world of software engineering. For many developers, the mere mention of the subject evokes images of piles of red tape, tedium, and nasty emails from development managers trying to keep everyone in line. Still, despite its bad rap, software logistics is not something to be taken lightly. After all, without the proper methods and procedures in place, we might inadvertently cause application outages, data corruption, or various other mistakes that can cost organizations dearly.

Even if you're lucky enough to be the master of your own little corner of the SAP HCP universe, keeping track of all the source code files that accumulate over time is not a trivial task. For developers working in larger organizations, this problem is compounded by the fact that development tasks are often split up among developers around the globe. Here, it's vital that the developers have some sort of centralized repository to keep track of the various artifacts being created and shared among team members. We'll explore some options for creating such repositories in Section 4.3.

In addition to keeping track of source code, there are several other logistical issues of similar importance for us to think about: application builds, transports, and long-term support. To put these concerns into perspective, consider the software development lifecycle diagram depicted in Figure 4.1. In this (simplified) diagram, we can observe the high-level stages of the software development process.

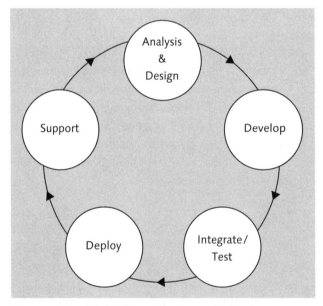

Figure 4.1 Simplified Software Development Lifecycle

In the simple examples we've considered thus far, our focus has been primarily on the initial development phase. As you can see in Figure 4.1, the next major phase in the lifecycle is the integration/testing phase. In this phase, the goal is to integrate our source code into a deployable application (e.g., as a WAR file) and install it on a test environment so that end users/testers can run through more elaborate test scenarios. The complexity of this task depends on multiple factors:

▸ **Landscape differences**
Various organizations may choose to configure their SAP HCP landscapes in different ways. Some organizations might have dedicated consolidation/test instances, whereas others may prefer to run tests using local instances and/or trial landscape-based instances.

▸ **Application complexity**
For simple Java-based web applications, we've seen how easy it is to create a WAR file from within the Eclipse IDE. On the other hand, large, multi-module applications can be much more difficult to build and deploy. Here, multiple steps are usually needed to complete the build.

▸ **Environmental differences**
Depending on the aforementioned landscape differences, we could also have to account for environmental differences. For example, as we'll learn in Chapter 6, the setup required to consume SAP HCP services can be very different when working with local instances versus remote cloud instances.

Although we can't avoid such complexities, there are tools out there that can automate and streamline this process. We'll explore the use of a couple of tools in this space in Section 4.4.

After the integration/testing phase is completed, we're ready to move on to the deployment phase, in which we deploy our application(s) to a productive SAP HCP instance. In Section 4.2, we'll learn how the SAP HCP tools make it fairly easy to perform this task. However, much like the integration/testing phase, this step could be complicated by environmental differences and the like.

Perhaps even more challenging is the typical "division of labor" requirement that many organizations have in place that prevents developers from deploying their own applications. Logistically, this can be challenging, because most administrator types aren't accustomed to jumping into the Eclipse IDE and assembling or deploying code. For this reason (and others), it often makes sense to employ the use of a tool that provides for automated and continuous integration. We'll consider these concepts in further detail in Section 4.4 and Section 4.5, respectively.

4.2   Deploying Java Applications

In order to understand how software logistics works within the SAP HCP landscape, it's helpful to start by looking at the end game: application deployment. Then, once you understand how applications are deployed, you'll have a better sense of how the rest of the logistical pieces fall into place.

In this section, we'll learn various techniques for deploying Java-based web applications. Here, we'll differentiate between local deployments and deployments to a remote SAP HCP cloud instance. Along the way, we'll take a look at ways of monitoring deployments and at techniques for implementing application logging or tracing so that you can see what's going on behind the scenes.

4.2.1   Deployment Using the Eclipse IDE

As we (briefly) observed in Chapter 3, it's pretty easy to deploy Java-based web applications from within the Eclipse IDE. This process is streamlined by the built-in server management capabilities provided by the Eclipse *Web Tools Platform* (WTP). Among other things, Eclipse WTP includes extensions for out-of-the-box server integration with a variety of Java EE-compliant application servers: Apache Tomcat, JBoss, and more. With the installation of the SAP HCP Tools plug-ins, this list of servers is expanded to include SAP HCP server types.

In this section, we'll learn how to configure SAP HCP server nodes and how we can use those server nodes to deploy applications using Eclipse WTP.

Creating Server Nodes

You can see the list of servers configured within your Eclipse IDE by opening the SERVERS view (highlighted in Figure 4.2). If this view is not visible in your IDE configuration, you can access it via the menu option WINDOW • SHOW VIEW • OTHER.... Then, in the SHOW VIEW popup window, expand the SERVER node, select the SERVERS view, and click on the OK button.

As you can see in Figure 4.2, the toolbar on the SERVERS view contains a number of useful functions that can be used to start or stop a server instance, turn on debugging mode, and so forth. These same functions can also be accessed from within a given server node's context menu, as shown in Figure 4.3. Within this context menu, you'll also find a series of deployment-related functions that make it easy to deploy or undeploy applications directly within the console.

Figure 4.2 Accessing the Servers View in the Eclipse IDE

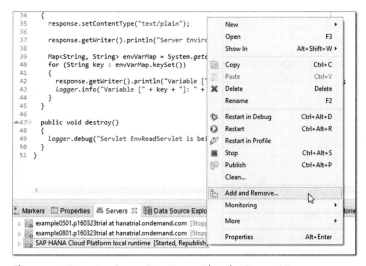

Figure 4.3 Accessing Server Functions within the Servers View

As is the case with most things in Eclipse, server nodes can be created in a couple of different ways. Within the SERVERS view itself, you can create a new server node by right-clicking somewhere in the view whitespace and choosing the NEW • SERVER context menu option, as shown in Figure 4.4.

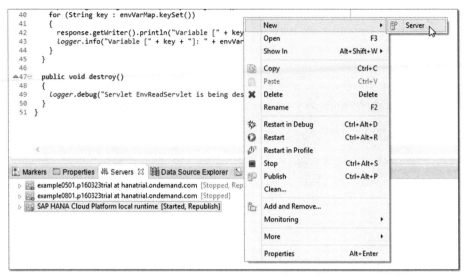

Figure 4.4 Creating a New Server Node in the Servers View: Part 1

This will bring up the New Server dialog window shown in Figure 4.5. From here, you can expand the SAP folder to locate the configured SAP server types. As you can see in Figure 4.5, you can choose from among the following different SAP HCP server types:

▶ Java EE 6 Web Profile Server
This server type points to a local runtime environment based on the Java EE 6 Web profile. Note that this server type is only available if the corresponding SAP HCP SDK has been downloaded and installed.

▶ Java Web Server
This server type points to a local runtime environment based on the Java Web Server profile. Note that this server type is only available if the corresponding SAP HCP SDK has been downloaded and installed.

▶ Java Web Tomcat 7 Server
This server type points to a local runtime environment based on the Java Web Tomcat 7 profile. Note that this server type is only available if the corresponding SAP HCP SDK has been downloaded and installed.

▶ SAP HANA CLOUD PLATFORM

This server type points to a cloud-based SAP HCP server instance. Here, you can configure access to customer or partner account instances and to trial account instances.

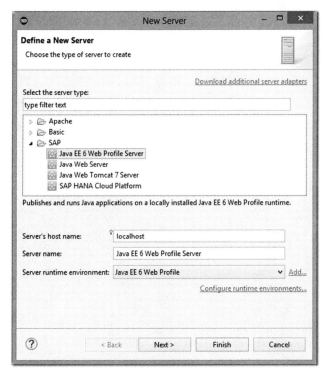

Figure 4.5 Creating a New Server Node in the Servers View: Part 2

As you can see in Figure 4.5, there's not much that we have to configure when defining a server node based on one of the local runtime profiles. Simply provide the server host name (which will generally be the default `localhost`), the server's name, and the target server runtime environment.

Cloud-based server nodes, on the other hand, require a little bit more work. Here, we're not really creating a server instance per se but rather a *connection* to a particular cloud instance. To specify *which* cloud instance, we must plug in the target server URL in the LANDSCAPE HOST field. As you can see in Figure 4.6, Eclipse has conveniently filled in the URL to the trial landscape on our behalf. You can configure the default URL that pops up here within the Eclipse PREFERENCES window shown in Figure 4.7.

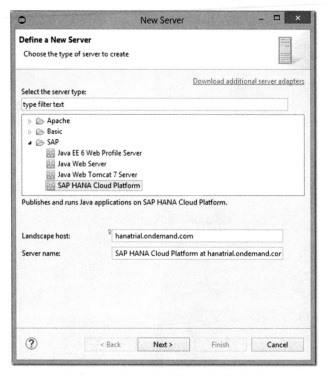

Figure 4.6 Defining a Cloud-Based Server Node: Part 1

The other alternative for creating server nodes is to create them as part of an Eclipse run configuration, as demonstrated when we created our first Java-based web application in Chapter 3. To refresh your memory on this process, this is achieved by right-clicking on a project node or an executable application artifact (e.g., a Servlet or JSP) and selecting the RUN AS • RUN ON SERVER menu option, as shown in Figure 4.8.

Figure 4.7 Defining a Cloud-Based Server Node: Part 2

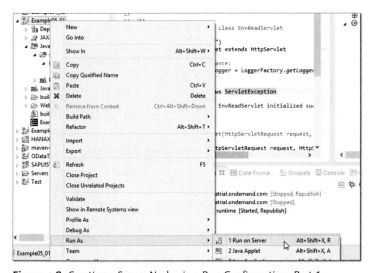

Figure 4.8 Creating a Server Node via a Run Configuration: Part 1

From here, you'll be presented with the RUN ON SERVER dialog box shown in Figure 4.9. Within this screen, you can configure an SAP HCP server node instance, just as you would if you were creating it directly from within the SERVERS view.

Figure 4.9 Creating a Server Node via a Run Configuration: Part 2

We'll defer a detailed description of what happens next in the RUN ON SERVER wizard for the "Deploying Applications to a Server Node" section, in which we'll look at how to deploy applications. For the purposes of this discussion, we simply wanted to show you how to create server nodes. Whether you decide to create server nodes within the SERVERS view or in ad hoc fashion within the RUN ON SERVER wizard is strictly a matter of preference. Both options get you to the same place. From here, deployment is a snap.

Deploying Applications to a Server Node

Once a server node is configured, we can utilize standard Eclipse WTP functions to facilitate deployment. Here, once again, we have a couple of options for carrying out this task.

While you're interactively developing and testing your application, you'll probably prefer to deploy your applications in ad hoc fashion by using the aforementioned RUN ON SERVER wizard. This wizard can be launched by executing the following steps:

1. Right-click on the top-level project node of the project you want to deploy or on an executable application artifact (e.g., a Servlet or JSP) contained within.

2. In the context menu that pops up, select the RUN AS • RUN ON SERVER menu option (Figure 4.8).

3. This opens the RUN ON SERVER dialog box shown in Figure 4.10. From here, you have the option of defining a new server node (as described in the previous section) or selecting an existing one. Choose the appropriate option, and click on the NEXT > button to continue.

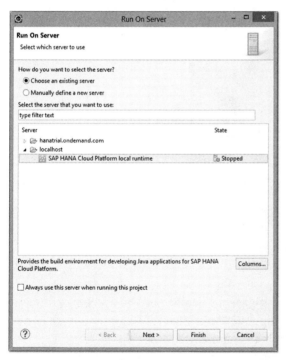

Figure 4.10 Deploying from within the Eclipse IDE: Part 1

4. If the selected server node points to a cloud-based SAP HCP instance, then the next step will require you to specify a name for the application you're deploying. As you can see in Figure 4.11, this step also requires that you specify account credentials that will be used to connect to the instance during deployment. Click on the NEXT > button to continue.

Figure 4.11 Deploying from within the Eclipse IDE: Part 2

5. In the next step, choose the project resources you want to add or remove from the server (see Figure 4.12).

6. With the resources set, you can trigger the deployment by clicking on the FIN-ISH button. At this point, the Eclipse WTP plug-ins will kick in and work in conjunction with the SAP HCP tools to communicate with the target server node and perform the deployment. If all goes well with the deployment, you should see the web application loaded into the internal Eclipse browser. We'll take a look at what to do when a deployment fails in Section 4.2.3.

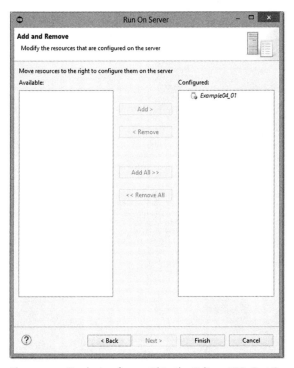

Figure 4.12 Deploying from within the Eclipse IDE: Part 3

Another place you can trigger deployment is from within the aforementioned SERVERS view. Here, the deployment steps are as follows:

1. Within the SERVERS view, select the target server node, right-click, and choose the ADD AND REMOVE... menu option (see Figure 4.13).

2. This will bring up the ADD AND REMOVE... dialog box shown in Figure 4.14. If this screen looks familiar, it's because it's almost completely identical to the ADD AND REMOVE step for the RUN ON SERVER wizard shown in Figure 4.12. Within this screen, we can stage the addition or removal of applications via the provided ADD > and < REMOVE buttons. Click on the FINISH button to initiate the deployment.

Figure 4.13 Triggering Deployment from within the Servers View: Part 1

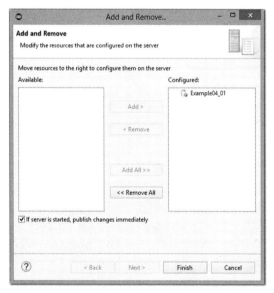

Figure 4.14 Triggering Deployment from within the Servers View: Part 2

Synchronizing Changes with the Server

After an application is initially deployed, the Eclipse WTP toolset will track changes that are made to projects and keep tabs on which applications need to be redeployed. You can see this highlighted in the SERVERS view in Figure 4.15. Here, for example, you can see that project EXAMPLE04_01 has been marked as dirty and needs to be redeployed (or republished).

Figure 4.15 Publishing Changes to Applications: Part 1

To republish applications from within this view, right-click on the target server node and choose the PUBLISH menu option. This will retrigger deployment behind the scenes and then update the status of the server and application in the SERVERS view when complete. As you can imagine, this feature can be quite handy when you're in the early code-deploy-test-repeat stages of development.

4.2.2 Deployment Using the Console Client

In the previous section, we learned how easy it is to deploy applications from within the Eclipse IDE. However, there will be times when deployment through Eclipse may not be desirable or even feasible. Some examples of these situations include the following:

▶ **Deployments to controlled environments**
When deploying to productive instances or even controlled QA instances, many organizations will have policies in place that ensure that deployments are carried out by administrators instead of developers. Although such administrators could certainly install the Eclipse IDE and corresponding SAP HCP tools to perform such deployments, most admins will prefer to use an external deployment tool. This is especially the case for admins who are uninitiated in the ways of Eclipse and Java development.

▶ **System copies or builds**
For more complex landscapes, there might be situations in which code needs to be deployed en masse as part of a system copy or build. In these cases, automation of deployment is essential.

▸ **Integration with external build tools**

For organizations that utilize standard build tools (e.g., Apache Maven), it's important to be able to incorporate the deployment step into those tools.

For these reasons (and many others), SAP provides a command-line tool called the *Console Client*, which can be used to perform administrative tasks, such as deployment from the command line. In this section, we'll see how this tool can be used to facilitate deployments.

Getting Started with the Console Client

Before we begin looking at how the Console Client is used to facilitate deployments, let's first take a moment to understand what it is and what it brings to the table from an administrative perspective. In a nutshell, the Console Client is an executable file that launches a command prompt in which we can issue various commands to interact with an SAP HCP server instance. In this regard, it serves the same purpose as the command (DOS) prompt in MS Windows or the terminal in Unix, Linux, or Mac OS systems.

For the most part, the Console Client is the command-line analog of the UI-based instrumentation tools provided in the Eclipse IDE and online SAP HCP Cockpit. This is to say that there are commands provided to perform most basic administrative tasks, such as starting and stopping server instances, maintaining accounts, triggering deployments, and so on. Aside from being convenient for admin types who prefer to work via a command prompt, this feature opens up all kinds of opportunities for automation via shell scripts and so on.

To access the Console Client, open a command prompt and navigate to the TOOLS subdirectory of your SAP HCP SDK installation folder. Within this directory, you'll find an executable file called neo.bat (Windows) or neo.sh. From here, you can launch commands via the syntax illustrated in Listing 4.1.

```
$ neo <command name> <mandatory parameters> [optional parameters]
```
Listing 4.1 Syntax for Executing a Command within the Console Client

> **Note**
>
> Alternatively, you can add the Console Client executable to your OS' path variable so that you can launch the client from anywhere.

For example, if we wanted to know the status of an application on an SAP HCP cloud instance, then we might issue the status command, as illustrated in Listing 4.2.

```
$ neo status --account p1234567 --application example0401
           --host hanatrial.ondemand.com --user abc@123.com
```
Listing 4.2 A Sample Command Test

As you can imagine, keying in all the parameters required to issue particular commands can become quite tedious if you spend a great deal of time within the Console Client. Recognizing this, SAP lets you externalize some of the parameters that you use over and over again (i.e., user name, account name, and landscape host) in a .properties file. That way, rather than having to key in these properties for each command, you can simply issue the command using a syntax like the one shown in Listing 4.3.

```
$ neo <command name> [properties] <properties file location>
```
Listing 4.3 Simplifying Commands Using Properties Files

If you're interested in learning more about some of the various commands offered by the Console Client, we highly recommend that you take a look at the CONSOLE CLIENT • CONSOLE CLIENT COMMANDS section of the SAP HANA Cloud Documentation available online at *http://help.hana.ondemand.com*. There, you will find a complete list of supported commands and their call syntax. There's also a link to a video tutorial that demonstrates how to interact with the client.

Triggering a Local Deployment

Triggering a deployment to a local SAP HCP instance using the Console Client is generally a three-step process:

1. Use the install-local command to perform a one-time installation of a local server instance within the *<SDK installation folder>/server* directory.

2. Generate WAR files for the application(s) that you want to deploy.

3. Use the deploy-local command to hot deploy the target WAR file(s).

Strictly speaking, the first step in the local deployment process is an optional one. Internally, the Console Client assumes that the local server instance it's controlling is contained within the <SDK INSTALLATION FOLDER>/SERVER directory. If you prefer to install the server elsewhere or would rather just use the same default local server instance defined within the Eclipse IDE, then you can use the `--location` argument to specify the server's home directory. Better yet, you can use a .properties file to specify this up front and save yourself some redundant keystrokes.

Once you sort out which local server instance you wish to deploy to, the next step is to get your hands on the WAR file(s) that correspond with the application(s) you want to deploy. Within the Eclipse IDE, this can be achieved by right-clicking on the root node of your web project and selecting the EXPORT • WAR FILE menu option, as shown in Figure 4.16.

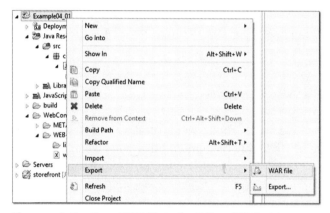

Figure 4.16 Creating a WAR File in the Eclipse IDE: Part 1

This will open up the EXPORT dialog box (Figure 4.17). Here, all you have to provide is the directory and file name for the generated WAR file; then, click on FINISH. If you look closely at Figure 4.17, you'll also notice that there's an option for optimizing the archive for the SAP HANA Cloud server runtime. It's generally a good idea to keep this default setting unless you have a very compelling reason not to.

To kick off the deployment process, open up a command prompt, and navigate to the *<SDK installation folder>/tools* directory. Then, if it's not started already, you'll want to start up your local server instance by using the `start-local` command, the syntax of which is illustrated in Listing 4.4.

```
neo start-local [--location <target server directory>]
```
Listing 4.4 Starting Your Local Server Instance via the Console Client

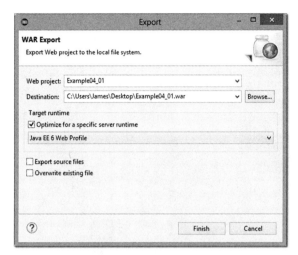

Figure 4.17 Creating a WAR File in the Eclipse IDE: Part 2

After the server is up and running, you can trigger the deployment by using the deploy-local command, the syntax of which is illustrated in Listing 4.5. If all goes well, the Console Client will return with a message indicating that the application was deployed successfully. From here, you can test your results by opening the application in a web browser. Unless you explicitly changed the port configuration during the server installation process, the URL will be of the form *http://localhost:8080/path/to/your/application*.

```
neo deploy-local --source c:/users/james/desktop/example04_01.war
                 [--location <target server directory>]
```
Listing 4.5 Triggering a Local Deployment via the Console Client

Triggering a Remote Deployment

To a large degree, the process of deploying to the cloud using the Console Client is quite similar to the one used to perform local deployments. Here, we collect our WAR file(s) as demonstrated in the previous section and then use the deploy command to trigger the deployment. The syntax for this command is demonstrated in Listing 4.6.

```
neo deploy --host <landscape_host> --account <account_name>
           --application <application_name>
           --source <path_to_war_file>
           --user <email_or_user>
```
Listing 4.6 Syntax for Invoking the deploy Command

Figure 4.18 shows how this plays out at the command prompt. Here, we're deploying an application called EXAMPLE0401 to our trial account hosted on *hanatrial.ondemand.com*. As is the case with all Console Client commands, we could have externalized these parameters in a .properties file. However, for demonstration purposes, we thought it would be helpful to see the parameters entered on the screen.

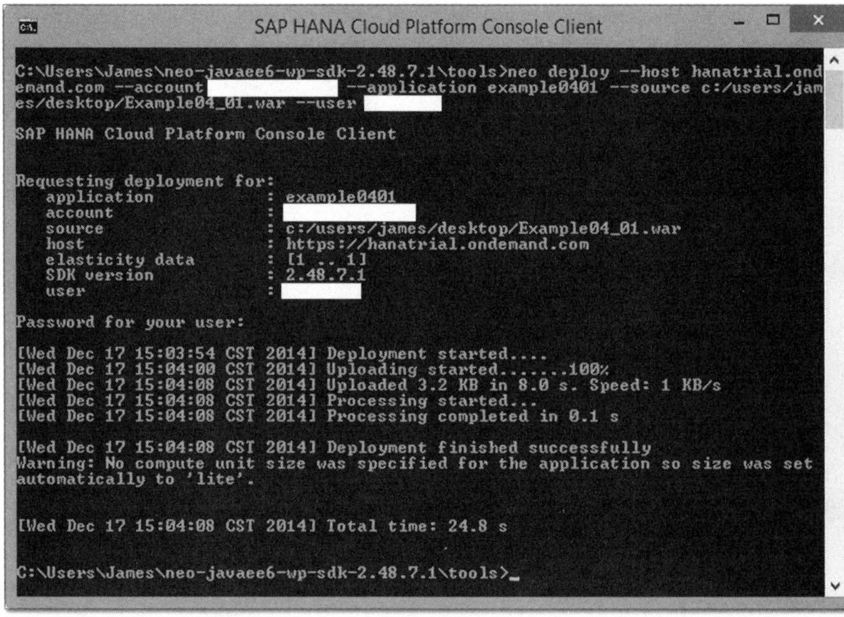

Figure 4.18 Triggering a Remote Deployment via the Console Client

As you can see in Figure 4.18, once the `deploy` command is issued, the Console Client will ask for the password of the user account that's being used to facilitate the deployment. Assuming the credentials match, the deployment process will ensue, and if all goes well you'll end up with the DEPLOYMENT FINISHED SUCCESSFULLY message, which indicates that the deployment is complete. Next we'll look at steps you can take if the deployment doesn't go as planned.

4.2.3 Monitoring Deployments

On occasion, the deployment process may fail, leaving you wondering where things went wrong. Here, both the Eclipse IDE and Console Client will rarely provide you with more than just a generic "your deployment failed" message. From here, it's up to you to do some digging and figure out where things went wrong behind the scenes. In this section, we'll consider some practical steps for trouble-shooting such occurrences.

Troubleshooting Local Deployment Errors

Whenever a local deployment fails, the first place to look is within the <SERVER_DIRECTORY>/LOGS folder. Here, you'll find a file called ljs_trace.log, which contains the detailed trace messages created by the server during the deployment process. Naturally, the nature of the trace messages will vary greatly depending on the type(s) of errors that have occurred. Still, as you can see in Figure 4.19, there's generally quite a bit of information to work with: information messages, stack traces, and so forth.

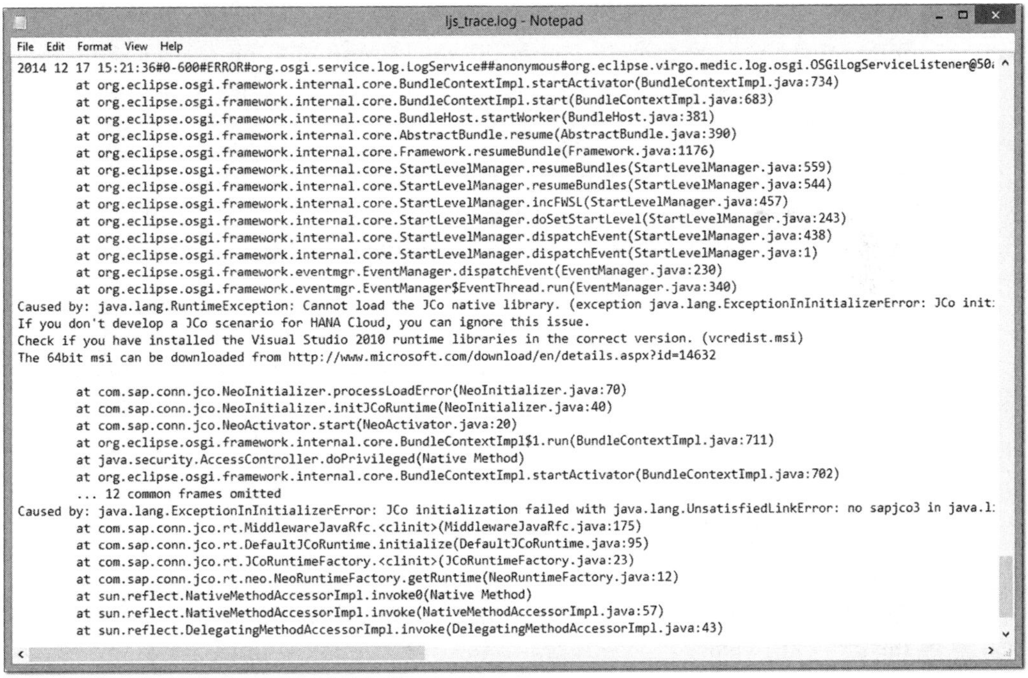

Figure 4.19 Investigating Deployment Errors in the ljs_trace.log File

Often, you can paste the root of an exception message into your favorite search engine and find a number of threads that explain the nature of the problem and the appropriate course of remediation. Here, because the SAP HCP local runtime is based on the same codebase as Apache Tomcat and Eclipse Equinox/Virgo, you have the luxury of expanding the scope of your search to include sites and message threads that are not specific to SAP.

If the nature of the error condition is not so obvious, then the next option is to remove the application, strip it down, and then begin putting the pieces back incrementally until you can pinpoint the error. This can be achieved by performing the following steps:

1. If the server didn't crash, then you'll need to stop it. This can be achieved by using the toolbar functions of the SERVERS view in Eclipse or the Console Client's `stop-local` command.

2. Once the server is stopped, you'll want to open up the server installation directory and navigate to the WEBAPPS folder. From here, find the archive folder for your application and delete it.

3. Next, you'll want to make a copy of the faulty application and begin stripping out any elements in the application copy that you think may be contributing to the error.

4. Once the application copy is ready, you can restart the server and deploy the stripped-down version of the application. If the deployment works, then you can incrementally replace the elements you removed from before in a strategic fashion and retry the deployment.

5. Finally, after several iterations of this, you should be able to locate the faulty element and remove it. If you're lucky, maybe the application will just work, and perhaps the error condition was an anomaly to begin with; stranger things have happened.

Troubleshooting Cloud Deployment Errors

In order to troubleshoot cloud deployment errors, you must open up the SAP HCP Cockpit and locate the application logs. This can be achieved by performing the following steps:

1. From the SAP HCP Cockpit landing page, select the JAVA APPLICATIONS link in the CONTENT panel.

2. In the DETAILS panel, click on the target application's link in the NAME column.

3. This will cause the DETAILS panel to be replaced with an application details screen like the one shown in Figure 4.20. From here, you can locate the application's log files by scrolling down to the MOST RECENT LOGGING panel, which contains a list of the application's log files.

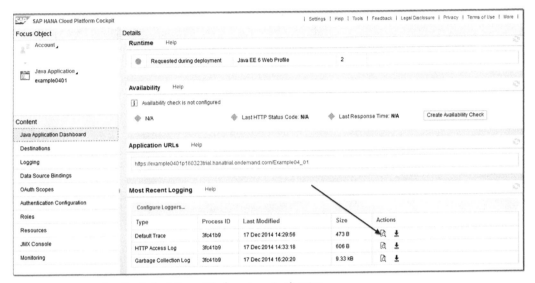

Figure 4.20 Accessing the Default Trace File for a Java Application

4. Any deployment issues that might have cropped up will be logged within the default trace log file (indicated by an arrow in Figure 4.20). You can access this log via the action links contained within the ACTIONS column. Here, you have the option to view the log file online or download it to your local machine. For demonstration purposes, consider the former option.

5. When you click on the SHOW link, the log file will show up in a separate window or tab in your browser, as shown in Figure 4.21. Here, you can scroll through each log entry, perform criteria-based searches, and so forth.

6. Once you find the log entries that describe the error condition, you can research the error condition online and iteratively try to rework the code, as described in the previous section. If the deployment error proves to be severe, you can stop or delete your application by using the functions in the STATE panel within the Java Application Dashboard. After correcting the problem, you can redeploy the application and try again.

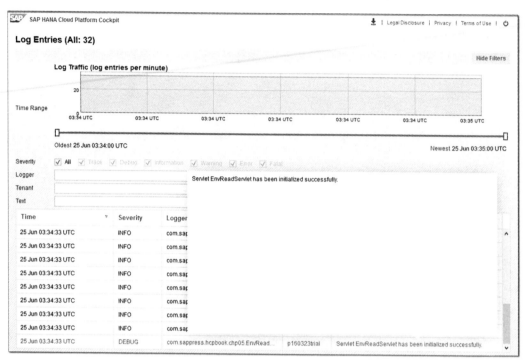

Figure 4.21 Viewing the Default Trace File in the SAP HCP Cockpit

4.2.4 Logging and Tracing Concepts

Sometimes, an application may deploy, but there could be resource-related issues that prevent it from actually launching. In these situations, it can be useful to be able to write out a series of trace messages that provide clues about what went wrong. As it turns out, SAP HCP makes logging and tracing with Java applications a snap. In this section, we'll look at what's required to make this happen.

Getting Started with the Simple Logging Façade for Java API

Simplified logging and tracing access for SAP HCP Java applications is provided via the *Simple Logging Façade for Java* (SLF4J), which, as the name suggests, is a façade or abstraction on top of a number of Java-based logging frameworks, such as log4j, the `java.util.logging` package, and so on. Java applications can access the SLF4J API without having to add in specialized references or copy third-party JAR files into the WEB-INF/LIB folder.

The code excerpt contained in Listing 4.7 demonstrates how a logger handle can be obtained using the `org.slf4j.LoggerFactory` factory class. Note that we defined this handle using the `static` modifier in Java in order to reduce resource consumption. Alas, there's no real advantage to defining logger handles at the instance level.

```
...
import org.slf4j.Logger; import org.slf4j.LoggerFactory;

public class EnvReadServlet extends HttpServlet
{
  // Create a logger instance:
  private static Logger logger =
    LoggerFactory.getLogger(EnvReadServlet.class);
  ...
}
```
Listing 4.7 Obtaining a Logger Reference Using SLF4J

Once an `org.slf4j.Logger` instance is defined, we can use it to create log and trace messages via the various output methods described in Table 4.1. Note that each of the methods described have multiple overrides that allow you to call them using different types of arguments. For example, you can call the `error()` method using a string, a `java.lang.Throwable`, or so on. You can find a complete listing of supported methods and their signatures in the SLF4J online help documentation, available online at *www.slf4j.org*.

Method Name	Description
debug()	This method is used to output messages useful for debugging logic errors and so on.
error()	This method is used to output any sort of error messages that might occur, including exceptions.
info()	This method is used to output informational messages as needed.
trace()	This method is used to output trace messages, which are useful in determining code sequencing, tracing program logic, and so on.
warn()	This method is used to output warning messages.

Table 4.1 Output Methods of the org.slf4j.Logger Interface

The code excerpt contained in Listing 4.8 demonstrates how these methods are used in code. Here, we're using the `debug()` method to track the Servlet lifecycle and the `info()` method to output server environment variables (e.g., server host). As you can see, the content here can be pretty much whatever we want it to be. Of course, it's best to not get carried away, as I/O-related performance issues can begin to creep in if we're not careful.

```
public class EnvReadServlet extends HttpServlet
{
  // Create a logger instance:
  private static Logger logger =
    LoggerFactory.getLogger(EnvReadServlet.class);

  @Override
  public void init() throws ServletException
  {
    logger.debug("Servlet EnvReadServlet has been initialized.");
  }

  protected void doGet(HttpServletRequest request,
                       HttpServletResponse response)
    throws ServletException, IOException
  {
    response.setContentType("text/plain");

    response.getWriter().println(
      "Server Environment Variables:\n\n");

    Map<String, String> envVarMap = System.getenv();
    for (String key : envVarMap.keySet())
    {
      String msg =
        "Variable [" + key + "]: " + envVarMap.get(key);
      response.getWriter().println(msg);

      logger.info(msg);

    }
  }

  public void destroy()
  {
    logger.debug("Servlet EnvReadServlet is being destroyed.");
  }
}
```

Listing 4.8 Writing Logging and Tracing Messages via SLF4J

Accessing and Configuring Log Files

Log and trace messages such as the ones illustrated in Listing 4.8 can be viewed via the same default trace files described in Section 4.2.3. There is one caveat here, however. By default, the effective logging level for a particular logger defaults to ERROR. This means that log messages having a lower effective logging level (e.g., INFO or DEBUG) won't show up unless we configure the effective logging level accordingly.

What does this mean? In the case of the default ERROR logging level, only messages having ERROR-level severity will be added to the log. If we were to change the logging level to WARN, then both warning messages and error messages would show up. If we dialed the logging level up one more level to INFO, then we would see information messages in addition to warning and error messages. If we simply wanted to see all messages regardless of severity, then we could just set the effective level to ALL.

The value in having such configurability is that we can dynamically adjust the logging levels on an as-needed basis. For example, in a production environment, we would probably set the logging level to ERROR so that we wouldn't incur all the overhead of writing out trace or debug messages and so on. However, if we were assigned a particularly complex defect, we might turn the logging level up for a time in order to troubleshoot the problem. As you can imagine, this is a very nice feature, because it gives us the ability to quickly obtain more information about an application error without having to touch the source code.

Performance Tip

Performance wise, we should point out that there is some minimal overhead associated with calling a log method, even in situations in which the effective log level filters out the message from the log. You can eliminate this overhead by using the various is<logging_level>Enabled() Boolean methods of the org.slf4j.Logger interface. The typical usage looks like this:

```
if (logger.isDebugEnabled())
  logger.debug("Debugging message...");
```

Because many developers already feel that logging statements clutter up the code, it's up to you as to whether or not you want to escape every log message with an if statement. For more details and other useful performance tips, check out the SLF4J FAQ page, available online at *www.slf4j.org/faq.html#logging_performance*.

Configuration wise, there are several places you can go to adjust the effective logging level for an application:

▸ Within the Eclipse IDE, you can configure loggers by double-clicking on the target server in the SERVERS view and then navigating to the LOGGERS tab, as shown in Figure 4.22. Note that this configuration panel is available for local server instances and cloud-based instances; the process is the same in both cases.

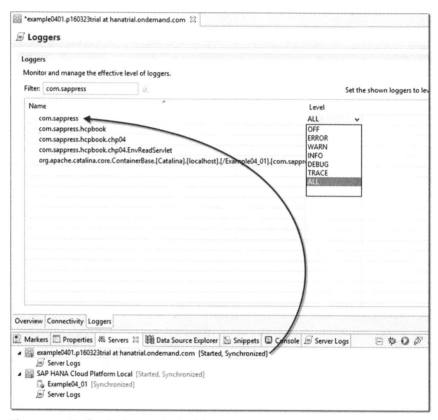

Figure 4.22 Configuring Loggers in the Eclipse IDE

Within the LOGGERS table, you can search or scroll through the list to find the target logger instance that you want to configure. Once you find the logger you're looking for, you can use the dropdown list in the LEVEL column to specify the effective level of a logger. As you can see in Figure 4.22, you can configure the effective level of a logger at the class level or at the package level. The advantage of package-level configuration is that the settings propagate down to the lower-level packages and classes automatically. On the other hand, if you need to be precise in your configuration, then you can choose to simply configure the class itself or a subpackage.

▸ For applications deployed in the cloud, you can also configure the effective level of loggers within the SAP HCP Cockpit. To access this configuration option, simply open up the Java application dashboard for your application and click on the CONFIGURE LOGGERS... link, shown in Figure 4.23. This will open up the dialog box shown in Figure 4.24.

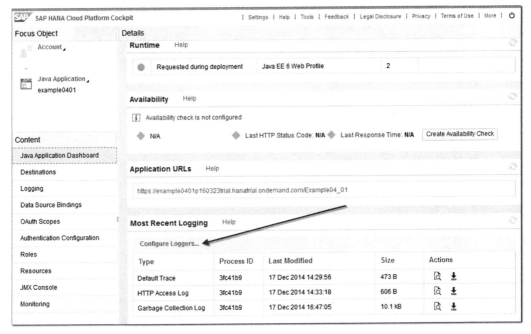

Figure 4.23 Configuring Logging in the SAP HCP Cockpit: Part 1

▸ As you can see, this UI is almost identical to that of the Eclipse IDE and can be used in the exact same way to configure the effective logging level of applications or packages.

▸ The third option for configuring logging levels is to use the `set-log-level` command of the Console Client. For more details on this option, check out the online help documentation available online at *http://help.hana.ondemand.com.*

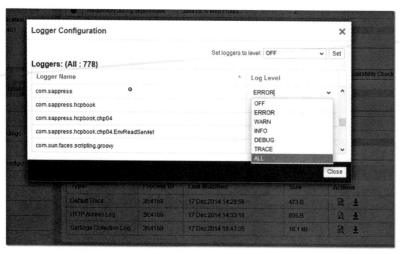

Figure 4.24 Configuring Logging in the SAP HCP Cockpit: Part 2

4.3 Source Code Management

One of the really great things about SAP HCP is its openness. From the use of industry standard libraries and APIs to the open Eclipse platform, developers are essentially free to use any tools at their disposal to build cloud-based applications. This openness also extends to the selection of source code management (SCM) tools. Here, development teams are free to work with most any SCM tool available on the market: Git, Subversion, Perforce, and many more.

Although this is great news for development teams, it does make the job of writing a book like this much more difficult. Indeed, even if we wanted to, there's no way we could reasonably cover all of the possible SCM tools that could be used to manage the source code of SAP HCP applications. That being said, our approach in this section will be to demonstrate source code management concepts using one of the more prominent SCM tools used in this space: *Git*. This choice is by no means meant to be prescriptive. Rather, we simply wanted to provide you with a practical example as we demonstrate how to manage the source code of your SAP HCP applications from within the Eclipse IDE.

For the most part, the concepts we'll review in this section will generally apply towards the use of other SCM tools. Much of this overlap is made possible by the core Eclipse framework, which defines a basic interface for integrating with various repository types. With this basic infrastructure in place, the prospect of hooking up Eclipse to your SCM tool of choice generally involves little more than installing a repository provider plug-in (if it's not installed already).

4.3.1 Introduction to Git and GitHub

At this point, we've already established that Git is an SCM tool. However, for many, Git is much more than just another SCM tool. Git was developed by Linus Torvalds (the creator of Linux) from the ground up as a distributed SCM tool with the goal of simplifying the coordination of Linux kernel development with developers across the world. Particular emphasis was placed on speed, distributed development, and efficient handling of large projects.

Again, it is not our intent to prescribe the use of Git (or any other SCM tool, for that matter) in this book; however, it bears mentioning that Git usage has increased exponentially in the past couple of years, and its footprint continues to grow. As of the time of writing, this growth has also extended to SAP HCP, as Git has been selected as the repository of choice for HTML5 applications (a subject we'll consider in Chapter 7). For these reasons, we would recommend that you at least familiarize yourself with Git so that you have a general sense for how it's used. If you're looking for more in-depth coverage, we recommend *Version Control with Git, 2nd Edition* (Loeliger, McCullough, O'Reilly, 2012).

Although it is certainly possible to install and maintain Git repositories in various configurations on-premise, many organizations have begun to enlist web-based hosting services such as GitHub due to their relative low cost and value-add services for project management. For the purposes of our demonstration, we'll be using a GitHub-based repository to give you a feel for what distributed development looks like with Git.

4.3.2 Getting Started with EGit

Though there are many ways to interface with Git, our focus in this section will be on access from within the Eclipse IDE using the EGit repository provider. If you followed along with the Eclipse installation steps described in Chapter 2, then EGit should be installed already. If you're unsure about this, you can verify the installation by opening the HELP • ABOUT ECLIPSE menu option and looking for the Eclipse EGit feature (see Figure 4.25). If EGit isn't installed, then you can quickly install it by opening the HELP • INSTALL NEW SOFTWARE... menu option and plugging in the EGit update site (*http://download.eclipse.org/egit/updates*, as shown in Figure 4.26).

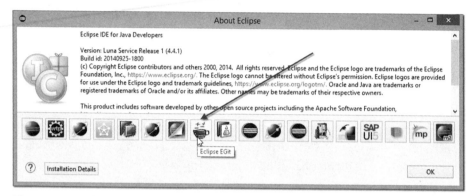

Figure 4.25 Verifying Installation of the EGit Team Provider in Eclipse

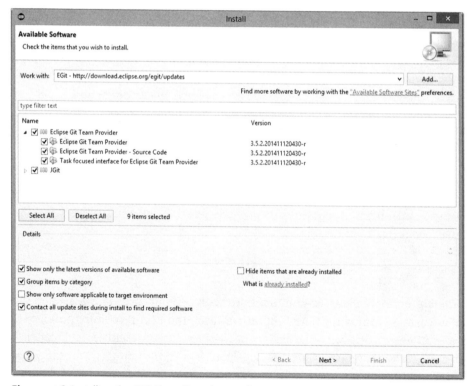

Figure 4.26 Installing the EGit Team Provider in Eclipse

After EGit is installed, it's generally ready to use straightaway. However, you may want to take note of the default settings before you get started and perhaps apply a few tweaks here and there. These settings are maintained from within the Eclipse PREFERENCES under TEAM • GIT. As you can see in Figure 4.27, the attributes maintained here determine where repositories are stored locally, how connections are established, and so on.

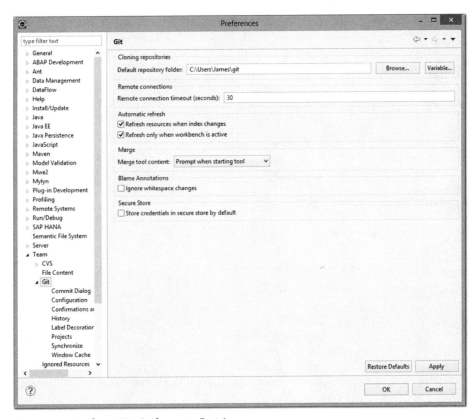

Figure 4.27 Verifying EGit Preferences: Part 1

Whether or not you choose to adjust the default EGit preferences, it's a good idea to at least take a moment to define your Git user profile. As you work with EGit, this profile will be used to annotate changes made to repositories so that other users know who changed what. As you can see in Figure 4.28, these settings are established in the TEAM • GIT • CONFIGURATION section of the Eclipse PREFERENCES.

You can configure your personalized settings in the USER SETTINGS tab by clicking on the ADD ENTRY... button.

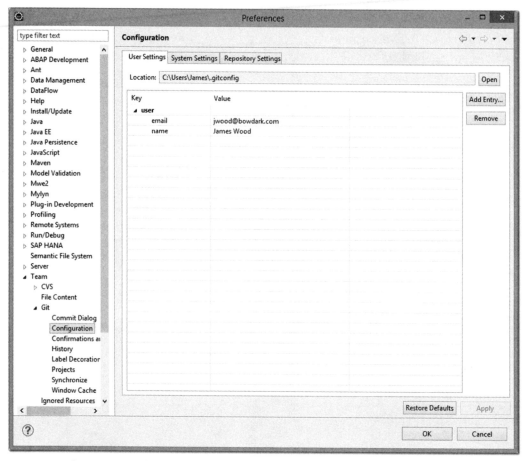

Figure 4.28 Verifying EGit Preferences: Part 2

4.3.3 Defining a Git Repository on GitHub

Now that we've got the basic Eclipse setup steps out of the way, we're ready to proceed with our demonstration. This starts with the definition of a Git *repository*. From a Git perspective, a repository is basically a database that contains all of the information Git needs to keep track of the history of a project. Whenever we kick off a new development project, creating or locating an appropriate Git repository is generally the first step in the process.

To demonstrate how this works, we'll create a new repository on GitHub. This can be achieved in a matter of minutes by logging onto *https://github.com* and clicking on the NEW REPOSITORY link (Figure 4.29).

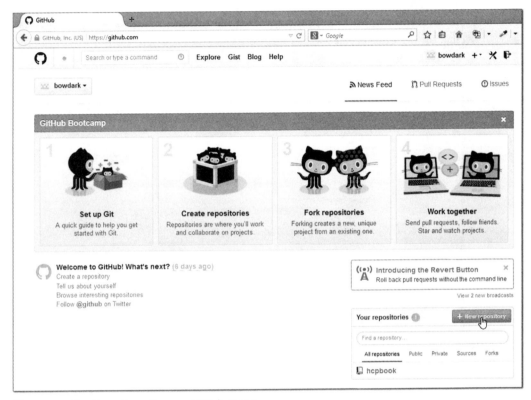

Figure 4.29 Creating a Repository on GitHub: Part 1

Setting Up a GitHub Account

If you wish to follow along with this demonstration, you can create a free trial account by following the sign-up link on the GitHub home page. After you create your trial account, we would recommend that you step through the GitHub Bootcamp tutorial to see how GitHub works and some of the various client-based tools you can download to simplify and/or automate certain Git-related tasks.

This will open up the repository creation page shown in Figure 4.30. As you can see, there's not much to specify up front other than the repository name, its description, and its overall visibility. For the purposes of our demonstration, we chose to name our repository hcpbook. Because we want to expose our repository to readers around the world, we also chose to make our repository visible to the public. Most development organizations will prefer the private visibility option for security reasons. In any case, once these basic parameters are in place, we can click on the CREATE REPOSITORY button to confirm our selections.

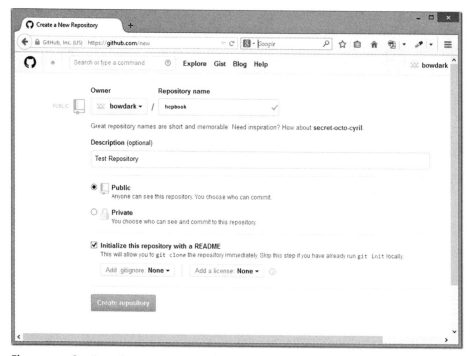

Figure 4.30 Creating a Repository on GitHub: Part 2

After the repository is created, we can navigate to an overview screen that allows us to browse the contents of the repository online, look at prior versions, and so on. Because we're going to want to eventually manage this repository within Eclipse, we'll want to copy the repository's clone URL by clicking on the COPY TO CLIPBOARD function in the right-hand actions panel (highlighted in Figure 4.31). In the next section, we'll see how this URL is used to synchronize the repository with Eclipse.

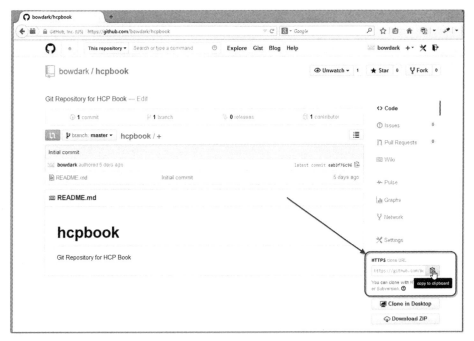

Figure 4.31 Editing Repositories within GitHub

4.3.4   Cloning a Git Repository in Eclipse

Once our Git repository is established, the next step is to create a copy of the repository on our local machine. In Git terminology, this process is achieved by *cloning* the repository. As the term suggests, this operation creates a complete snapshot of the target repository, copying the latest and greatest version of source code artifacts as well as all previous versions all in one fell swoop. With all this information in context, we have everything we need to unplug ourselves from the remote repository and work independently on project development tasks.

In order to clone our sample repository within Eclipse, we first need to enable the GIT REPOSITORIES view (Figure 4.32). This can be achieved by opening up the WINDOW • SHOW VIEW • OTHER… menu option, expanding the GIT folder, and choosing the GIT REPOSITORIES view. While we're at it, it's also a good idea to enable the GIT STAGING view, because we'll be spending quite a bit of time there as well.

145

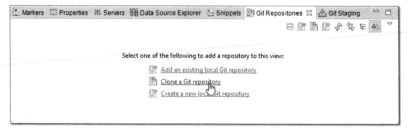

Figure 4.32 Cloning a Git Repository in Eclipse: Part 1

From within the GIT REPOSITORIES view, the steps to clone a Git repository are as follows:

1. To kick off the clone process, trigger the appropriate view function. If you're accessing the GIT REPOSITORIES view for the first time, then you can start the process by clicking on the CLONE A GIT REPOSITORY link highlighted in Figure 4.32. Otherwise, you can click on the CLONE A GIT REPOSITORY button 🖼 in the toolbar of the GIT REPOSITORIES view.

2. This will open the CLONE GIT REPOSITORY wizard shown in Figure 4.33. In the first step, specify the source Git repository that you plan to clone. In Figure 4.33, you can see that Eclipse has automatically picked up the clone URL that you copied to your clipboard via the GitHub repository editor page.

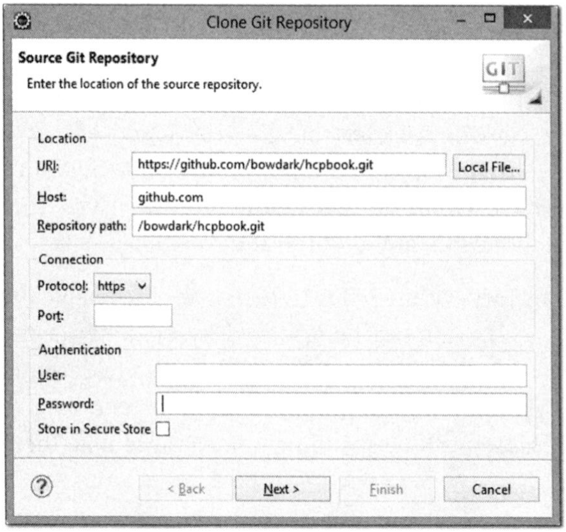

Figure 4.33 Cloning a Git Repository in Eclipse: Part 2

If the URL's not in your clipboard, you can simply key it into the URI field manually. Click on NEXT > to continue.

3. In the next step, you can specify settings that influence how the repository is copied. Most of the time, you can accept these default settings, as they're generally correct. One setting of note here though is the IMPORT ALL EXISTING PROJECTS AFTER CLONE FINISHES checkbox (see Figure 4.34). Whenever this checkbox is selected, any Eclipse projects that are contained within the repository will be automatically brought into the local Eclipse workspace. As you can imagine, this setting can be very convenient whenever developers are cloning repositories with the intent of enhancing or changing preexisting projects. Once you confirm your selections, click on the FINISH button to kick off the cloning process.

Figure 4.34 Cloning a Git Repository in Eclipse: Part 3

After the cloning process is completed, we basically have an empty repository on our hands. In the next section, we'll learn how to copy project resources into this repository so that we can share them with the rest of the development team.

4.3.5 Adding Projects to Change Control

In order to demonstrate how project resources are added to a Git repository, let's see what it takes to check the web project that we've been working on in this chapter into version control. Using EGit, the steps required here are as follows:

1. Select the target project that you want to share, right-click on it, and then select the TEAM • SHARE PROJECT... context menu option (Figure 4.35).

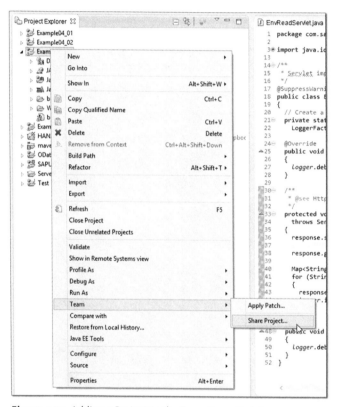

Figure 4.35 Adding a Project to the Repository: Part 1

2. This will open the SHARE PROJECT dialog box shown in Figure 4.36. Here, note that you have the option to share your project with a number of repository providers other than Git. Therefore, if your organization is, say, a Subversion shop, then you could plug in a Subversion repository provider, and the experience would be largely the same. Click on NEXT > to continue.

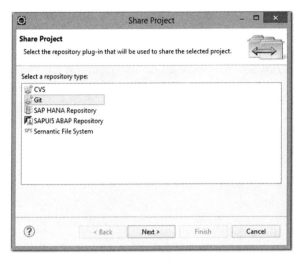

Figure 4.36 Adding a Project to the Repository: Part 2

3. In the next step, choose the target Git repository to which want to synchronize your project (see Figure 4.37). Once you confirm the source and target locations, you can click on FINISH to check the project into change control. At this point, the project directory and all its files will be moved from the source directory into the Git repository directory so that the files can be managed by Git.

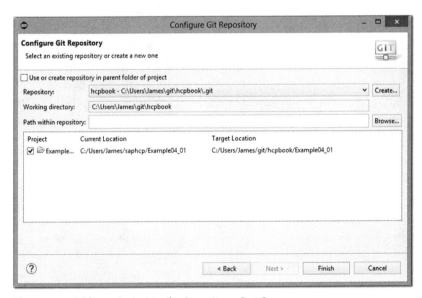

Figure 4.37 Adding a Project to the Repository: Part 3

4. As soon as the project is shared, you'll notice some subtle differences in the way the project is visualized in the PROJECT EXPLORER. As you can see in Figure 4.38, each project artifact is now annotated with icons and tags that illustrate its status within the repository. This is a convenient way of keeping track of in-flight changes as you're modifying and/or enhancing the project. Aside from these minor UI changes, it's basically business as usual from an Eclipse perspective.

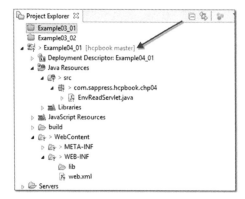

Figure 4.38 Visualization Differences for Shared Projects in Eclipse

4.3.6 Checking in Changes

In order to maintain the integrity of artifacts within the repository, Git does not automatically commit changes to the database. Indeed, when we shared our project with Git, all we really did was place the project files in a directory that Git happens to care about. At this point, Git is generally aware of the files' existence but chooses to ignore them until someone comes along and explicitly tells it to start tracking specific files. In Git terminology, such a command moves the files into the repository *staging area* (or index).

Once a file is moved into the staging area, it's ready to be committed to the repository database. Of course, even at this point we could still decide to change our mind and revert the file. This two-phase commit protocol ensures that changes to files don't ever accidentally make their way into the database; if a change gets added, it's because someone explicitly staged it and then pulled the trigger to commit it after the fact.

To see how this works, let's take a look at how we would perform an initial check-in of our sample web project. For this task, we'll want to open up the GIT STAGING view shown in Figure 4.39. Here, on the left-hand side of the view, we can see two listboxes:

▶ UNSTAGED CHANGES

In the UNSTAGED CHANGES listbox, we have a list of files that are contained within the Git repository directory but are not yet tracked within Git. Git is certainly aware of the presence of these files, but it doesn't do anything with them until we explicitly tell it to.

▶ STAGED CHANGES

This listbox contains artifacts that have been moved to the staging area of the Git database. In order to add, update, or remove files from Git, we must first stage the changes within the staging area.

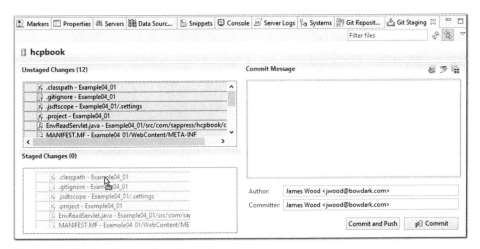

Figure 4.39 Staging Changes for a Commit

As you can see in Figure 4.40, the process of staging or unstaging changes within EGit is as simple as dragging files back and forth between these two listboxes. Once we're satisfied with the changes in the staging area, the next step is to trigger a *commit*. In the GIT STAGING view, this can be achieved by keying in a brief COMMIT MESSAGE and then clicking on the COMMIT AND PUSH button (see Figure 4.40). This action will force Git to commit the changes added to the staging area and push them out to the repository database hosted on GitHub.

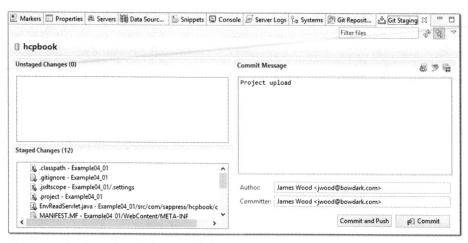

Figure 4.40 Issuing a Commit for a Set of Changes: Part 1

In the PUSH RESULTS dialog box shown in Figure 4.41, we can see that our (initial) commit has been added to the default master branch as expected. In a nutshell, this confirmation is telling us that the operation was successful and that we have a new version (or snapshot) of the repository.

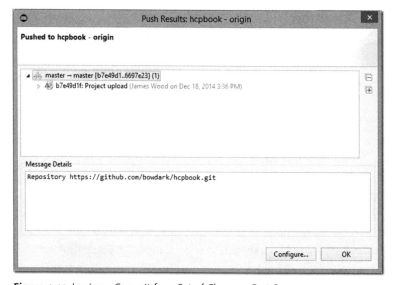

Figure 4.41 Issuing a Commit for a Set of Changes: Part 2

Over time, a repository will accumulate a number of commits or snapshots that can be used as logical points to revert a project back to a stable release or to fork the project into different branches so that developers can work on different versions of the project simultaneously.

From here, additional changes to the project are handled in largely the same way as we demonstrated here with the initial commit. For example, if other developers want to check out the project and make some changes, they would basically just clone the latest commit from the GitHub repository, stage their changes, and then commit them back to the repository using the steps outlined in this section.

For the most part, about the only thing that can go wrong in all of this is if two or more developers try to check in conflicting changes to the same artifact. Fortunately, Git is quite adept at detecting such collisions and will cancel the commit until the conflicts are reconciled and the changes are merged. Then (and only then) can the new version of the file be checked into the repository.

4.3.7 Where to Go From Here

Hopefully, this brief demonstration helped paint a picture for what source code management looks like in the SAP HCP development space. Obviously, we're painting in broad strokes here, because there are quite a few options for maintaining source code versions. Indeed, you don't have to use an SCM tool at all; some organizations that are just getting started with cloud application development may prefer to store source code on a network file share for a while until they come up with a better long-term strategy.

Whether you end up using Git or some other tool, the main takeaway from this section is that it's important to have a plan for keeping track of source code beyond merely storing it in your local Eclipse workspace. Backup reliability issues aside, trust us when we say that having no real plan for source code management is a recipe for disaster.

4.4 Build Automation with Apache Maven and Ant

In Section 4.2.2, we touched on the fact that many organizations have policies in place that prevent developers from deploying their own code into production. In practice, these policies usually also stipulate that developers can't even build their own code. After all, putting such checks and balances in place does a company little good if a developer is able to manipulate the build and sneak malicious code into a file that gets deployed indiscriminately by system administrators.

The downside and potential risk of establishing such policies is that it places the burden of application builds squarely on the shoulders of resources who many not know anything about the applications they're building. Indeed, knowing what you now know about source code management and deployment from within the Eclipse IDE, it's pretty plain to see that checking out code and performing a build is not a task that can be performed by just anyone.

To address these kinds of concerns, many companies elect to utilize build automation tools. Using these tools, administrators can quickly and easily build even the most complex of applications right from the comfort of their favorite command-line interface (CLI). In this section, we'll take a brief look at what it takes to implement such builds.

4.4.1 Getting Started with Apache Maven

The first build automation tool we'll take a look at is arguably the most popular one in the Java development space: *Apache Maven*. In the upcoming sections, we'll try to explain what Maven is and how it can be used to automate Java application builds. For brevity's sake, we can't really get into a thorough treatment of Maven within the context of this book. Instead, our goal will be to simply paint a picture of what Maven-based project development looks like. For a more detailed treatment of Maven, we highly recommend *Maven: The Definitive Guide, 2nd Edition* (Sonatype Company, O'Reilly, 2014).

What is Apache Maven?

According to Webster's dictionary, a *maven* is defined as one who is experienced or knowledgeable, an expert, or even a freak. As it relates to software project management and, more specifically, project builds, Apache Maven is a software package that certainly lives up to its name. This is to say that Maven is freakishly adept at performing automated builds with little or no supervision.

How is Maven able to achieve this? Unlike other build automation tools, the basic unit of configuration in Maven is not a build script. Instead, Maven utilizes a special XML configuration file called a *Project Object Model* file (or POM file). Within a POM file, our goal is to build a conceptual model of our project. Here, we can specify (among other things) the following:

▸ A unique identifier for the project, complete with the target version number

▸ Descriptive details about the project, the involved participants, and so on

▸ Defined dependencies to other projects or libraries

Noticeably absent here are low-level build details, such as which folder to copy source code from, compilation details, and so on.

The reason we can (generally) avoid having to specify these details is because Apache Maven subscribes to the motto of "convention over configuration." This is to say that it's rather opinionated about how builds are supposed to work. For example, rather than forcing developers to specify where source code resides each and every time, Maven conventionally assumes that source code resides in THE SRC/MAIN directory underneath the project root folder. Of course, these rules aren't set in stone; Maven will allow you to override such settings if you absolutely want to. However, the more we play along, the more Maven is able to intuit build details on our behalf.

Another major advantage of following convention is that it allows us to leverage a wide array of plug-ins developed within the community to perform specific tasks. Besides the more obvious compile and archive plug-ins, we can find useful plug-ins to generate project documentation, capture source code metrics, and execute unit tests. Within the SAP HCP development space, SAP provides a Maven plug-in that can be used to invoke Console Client commands from within a project build. You can view details about this plug-in online at *https:// help.hana.ondemand.com/mavenSite/index.html*.

Ultimately, the use of Maven leads to consistency in project maintenance. Projects take on a similar look and feel, and this generally makes it easier for developers to navigate through the project artifacts and find what they're looking for. From an administrative standpoint, Maven takes a lot of the guesswork out of project builds. Admins don't have to manipulate build scripts, download shared libraries, or do any sort of up-front prep work, because Maven is generally able to handle these tasks on its own. Even if admins don't know anything about the project they might be building, they can generally build it in a matter of seconds by simply typing in the command `mvn install` at their command prompt.

Working with Maven in Eclipse

Although Apache Maven is a standalone tool that can be downloaded and run from the command line, for SAP HCP development we'll generally prefer to interact with it from within the Eclipse IDE. If you followed along with the IDE installation instructions described in Chapter 2, then you should find that Maven is included with your Eclipse installation.

The Maven plug-ins in Eclipse allow you to create Maven projects in one of two ways. You can either create a Maven project from scratch or you can convert an existing project into a Maven project after the fact. Which approach you take in the course of your normal development is a matter of preference. However, because most SAP HCP tutorials are predicated on the use of the Eclipse Dynamic Web project, we thought it would be more beneficial to demonstrate how to convert existing projects since that will be the more typical scenario. The steps are as follows:

1. Select the project you wish to convert, right-click on it, and select the CONFIGURE • CONVERT TO MAVEN PROJECT menu option, as shown in Figure 4.42.

2. This will open the CREATE NEW POM dialog box shown in Figure 4.43. Here, you must enter your Maven "project coordinates" by specifying the group/artifact ID and version number. Collectively, these attributes uniquely identify your project within the Maven repository. This in turn allows other projects to create defined dependencies to your project down the line. Aside from these key attributes, you need to specify the packaging type and provide a meaningful name for your project. As you can see in Figure 4.43, we selected the packaging type WAR, because we're converting a Dynamic Web project that will ultimately generate a WAR file.

3. Once all of the POM details are specified, click on the FINISH button to complete the project conversion process.

Figure 4.42 Converting an Eclipse Project to a Maven Project: Part 1

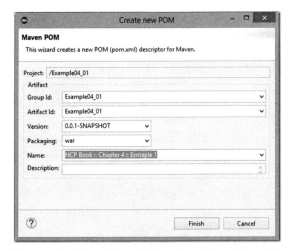

Figure 4.43 Converting an Eclipse Project to a Maven Project: Part 2

After the dust settles on the project conversion process, you'll notice that not much has changed from an Eclipse perspective. Indeed, the only real visible difference within the PROJECT EXPLORER view is the addition of a file called pom.xml. This is, not surprisingly, the project's POM configuration file. We'll look into the contents and purpose of this file in further detail in the next section.

Maintaining the Maven POM File

By default, the POM file generated by Eclipse is insufficient for building the project. Indeed, as you can see in Listing 4.9, aside from some build-specific details derived via the Maven plug-in, there's not much there.

```
<project xmlns...>
  <modelVersion>4.0.0</modelVersion>
  <groupId>Example04_01</groupId>
  <artifactId>Example04_01</artifactId>
  <version>0.0.1-SNAPSHOT</version>
  <packaging>war</packaging>
  <name>HCP Book :: Chapter 4 :: Example 1</name>

  <build>
    ...
  </build>
</project>
```
Listing 4.9 An Excerpt of the Generated pom.xml File

Notably absent in the generated POM file are the project dependencies. For instance, in our example, we're building a Dynamic Web project based on the Java Servlet and SLF4J APIs. In order to build our project, we need to tell Maven where to go to find the corresponding libraries.

To add these dependencies to our POM, we can either use the graphical editor provided on the DEPENDENCIES tab or key in the appropriate XML markup in the pom.xml source code. For the purposes of our demonstration, we chose the former approach, as shown in Figure 4.44. Here, in the SELECT DEPENDENCY dialog box, simply plug in the coordinates of the project or library you wish to define a dependency to, specify the scope of the dependency (PROVIDED in this case), and click on the OK button. Listing 4.10 shows the finished product for our sample project.

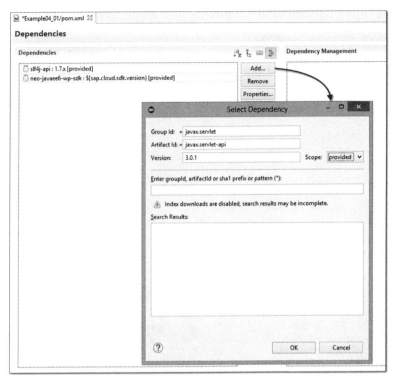

Figure 4.44 Adding Dependencies to the POM

```
<project...>
  <modelVersion>4.0.0</modelVersion>
  <groupId>Example04_01</groupId>
  <artifactId>Example04_01</artifactId>
  <version>0.0.1-SNAPSHOT</version>
  ...

  <dependencies>
    <dependency>
      <groupId>org.slf4j</groupId>
      <artifactId>slf4j-api</artifactId>
      <version>1.7.2</version>
      <scope>provided</scope>
    </dependency>
    <dependency>
        <groupId>com.sap.cloud</groupId>
        <artifactId>neo-javaee6-wp-api</artifactId>
        <version>${sap.cloud.sdk.version}</version>
        <scope>provided</scope>
    </dependency>
```

```
    <dependency>
        <groupId>javax.servlet</groupId>
        <artifactId>javax.servlet-api</artifactId>
        <version>3.0.1</version>
        <scope>provided</scope>
    </dependency>
  </dependencies>

  <build>
    <plugins>
      <plugin>
        <groupId>org.apache.maven.plugins</groupId>
        <artifactId>maven-war-plugin</artifactId>
        <configuration>
          <webXml>WebContent\WEB-INF\web.xml</webXml>
        </configuration>
      </plugin>
    </plugins>
  </build>
</project>
```

Listing 4.10 Revised POM File with Dependency Definitions

Understanding the Maven Repository Concept

Looking at the POM file contained in Listing 4.10, you might be wondering where we came up with the precise group/artifact IDs and versions. Unfortunately, this is not an exact science and requires a little bit of explanation.

Historically, one of the challenges of implementing automated builds has been figuring out how to keep track of library dependencies. Developers have traditionally had to come up with clever ways of attaching library folders to their projects so that they'd be available at build time.

In keeping with the "convention over configuration" motto, Maven defines such dependencies in more abstract terms. Because every project in Maven defines within its POM a unique project ID, Maven can use these coordinates to create a library index within its global repositories. At build time, the group/artifact ID and version specified in <dependency> elements provide Maven with a key for fetching the specified libraries from a remote repository and seamlessly incorporating them into the build.

At configuration time, we can use this same information to scan through the Maven repositories and search for the libraries we need to specify our project dependencies. One useful site for performing such searches is *www.mvnrepository.com*. This site provides a flexible search engine that allows you to search for libraries using group/artifact IDs and even free-form text descriptions.

In order to increase portability even further, you can adjust your user settings file attached to your Maven installation to include custom properties, such as the

${sap.cloud.sdk.version} property we used to obtain the target version of the Java EE 6 API. By not hard-coding this value, we can easily pass our project off to other developers who might need to configure a different version matrix.

Normally, you can adjust your user settings by editing the settings.xml file contained in the .M2 subfolder of your home directory. You can verify the exact path from within the Eclipse PREFERENCES by expanding MAVEN • USER SETTINGS. From here, browse to the settings.xml file specified in the USER SETTINGS input field. Custom properties can be added by adding XML markup underneath the settings/profiles/profile/properties element in the XML.

Once all of the requisite project dependencies are defined, we can trigger a build from within Eclipse by right-clicking on the pom.xml file and choosing the RUN AS • MAVEN INSTALL menu option, as shown in Figure 4.45.

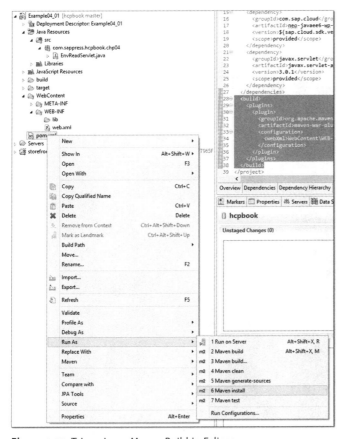

Figure 4.45 Triggering a Maven Build in Eclipse

When you run this for the first time, you'll notice in the CONSOLE output that Maven carries out quite a few steps up front to pre-fetch needed plug-ins, libraries, and the like. Again, the great thing about Maven is that it's (generally) able to do all of this on its own.

Using Maven from the Command Line

For admin types who prefer to run Maven from the command line, the build process essentially consists of two steps:

1. First, the admin needs to download the project folder from some source code repository (e.g., Git) to his or her local machine.

2. Once the source code is downloaded, the build can be kicked off by opening up a command prompt, navigating to the project folder, and entering the command `mvn install`, as shown in Figure 4.46. This, of course, assumes that some version of Maven has been installed on the user's local machine.

Figure 4.46 Running a Maven Build from the Command Line

4.4.2 Working with Apache Ant

Before Apache Maven came into prominence, the de facto build tool in the Java community was *Apache Ant*. To a large degree, Ant is a Java-based version of the popular make tool used to perform builds in the C/C++ communities. That is, Ant provides a runtime environment for executing build scripts.

In this section, we'll take a brief look at how such build scripts are constructed and how they're used to automate builds. For more information on the Apache Ant project, we would point you in the direction of the project documentation online at *http://ant.apache.org*.

Understanding the Ant Build Model

Unlike Maven, Ant makes no real assumptions about how a project is structured or how it is to be built. Instead, it provides us with an empty canvas that we can use to define each and every detail of a build: where source code is extracted from, how we invoke the Java compiler, how a Java archive file is built, and so on. Such details are specified in an XML build file called build.xml.

Listing 4.11 contains an example Ant build file that is used to build our sample project. Even if the exact syntax of the build file is new, you can generally gather what's going on in the file based on the descriptive XML element names. First, we specify various build properties, then we have a series of *targets*, which are basically executable steps within an Ant build file. Using the depends attribute of the <target> element, we can daisy-chain steps together to define the build sequence—for example, clean, then init, followed by compile, and then finally dist.

```
<project name="Example04_01" default="dist" basedir=".">
  <!-- Set global properties for this build -->
  <property environment="env" />
  <property name="src.dir" location="src" />
  <property name="classes.dir"
       location="WebContent/WEB-INF/classes" />
  <property name="lib.dir" location="WebContent/WEB-INF/lib" />
  <property name="war.dir" location="WebContent" />
  <property name="cloud.host" value="hanatrial.ondemand.com" />
  <property name="app.name" value="example0401" />


  <path id="class.path">
    <fileset dir="${env.HCP_SDK_HOME}/repository/plugins">
```

```
      <include name="**/*.jar" />
    </fileset>
    <fileset dir="${lib.dir}">
      <include name="**/*.jar" />
    </fileset>
  </path>


  <target name="init" depends="clean">
    <tstamp/>
    <mkdir dir="${classes.dir}" />
  </target>


  <target name="compile" depends="init"
   description="Compile the source files">
    <!-- Compile the java code from ${src} -->
    <javac srcdir="${src.dir}" destdir="${classes.dir}">
      <classpath refid="class.path" />
    </javac>
  </target>


  <target name="dist" depends="compile"
   description="Generate the WAR file">
  <!-- Create the WAR file -->
    <jar jarfile="${ant.project.name}.war"
         basedir="${war.dir}" />
  </target>


  <target name="clean" description="Clean up previous builds">
    <!-- Cleanup prior builds -->
    <delete dir="${classes.dir}" />
  </target>
  ...
</project>
```

Listing 4.11 An Example Ant Build File

The targets themselves are defined using a series of Ant tasks that carry out the steps needed to perform a particular build task. Looking at the excerpt contained in Listing 4.11, you can see that we're using a number of standard Ant tasks to add and remove directories, compile Java code, and build the final WAR file. Ant provides most of the major tasks you would need for a typical build out of the box. However, if you need a more customized task, then you can either create your own or utilize the exec task to call out to an external program or script.

When working with SAP HCP application builds, this task provides us with the hooks we need to invoke Console Client commands, for example.

As you play around with Ant, you'll find that it's generally possible to define a basic template for the build.xml file that merely has to be tweaked a bit each time you reuse it (e.g., different project names, different archive files, etc.). Such a copy-and-paste approach might not be quite as convenient as Maven, but it sure beats having to rewrite the build script from scratch each time out.

Triggering Builds

Much like we observed with Maven, Ant builds can be triggered from within the Eclipse IDE or via the command line. Within Eclipse, you can trigger a build by right-clicking on your BUILD.XML file and selecting the RUN AS • ANT BUILD menu option. From the command line, you simply need to navigate to the directory where the build.xml file is contained and execute the `ant` command.

4.5   Continuous Integration with Jenkins

The next step in the evolution of software logistics is *continuous integration* (CI). As the name suggests, CI is about streamlining the integration process and avoiding the costly rework associated with integration conflicts. In effect, CI forces developers to address such conflicts up front so that integration problems get resolved well before they spiral out of control.

In practice, CI is implemented using a tool that monitors the project's source code repository (e.g., Git). Whenever changes are checked into the repository, the CI tool will react by automatically building and testing the application. If the build or test fails, then the associated developer(s) will be notified straightaway, and any integration conflicts that show up can be resolved in short order. Such instantaneous feedback ensures that the project doesn't stray too far off course over time.

In this section, we'll take a brief look at how you can implement CI within the context of your SAP HCP application development using one of the more popular CI tools in the Java development space: *Jenkins*.

4.5.1   Introducing Jenkins

Jenkins (formerly known as *Hudson*) is an open-source CI tool written in Java. In addition to performing the core CI tasks described earlier in this section, Jenkins also comes equipped with many value-add features, including the following:

- Integration with many code quality analysis tools
- Extensive reporting capabilities that project managers can use to track the overall health of software projects
- Integration with test tools and the capacity for performing test coverage analysis
- A robust job scheduler tool
- External integration via REST APIs

Plus, with its wide following in the software community, there's a vast number of useful plug-ins to make it easy to connect with various SCM tools, build tools, and so on. You can find out more information about these features and others via the project website at *http://jenkins-ci.org*. Another useful resource here is *Jenkins: The Definitive Guide* (Smart, O'Reilly, 2011).

4.5.2   Installing Jenkins on SAP HCP

For the most part, Jenkins is very easy to install and configure. Indeed, if all you're doing is performing a local installation, then you can download the appropriate installation package from the project website and be up and running in a matter of minutes. However, when it comes to installing Jenkins on SAP HCP, matters become slightly more complicated. This is because Jenkins is designed to store the various artifacts it creates at the file system level. Because we don't have access to a file system from within SAP HCP, a workaround is required to allow Jenkins to operate smoothly on SAP HCP.

Fortunately, SAP has provided just such a workaround and uploaded it to GitHub so that developers can create an SAP HCP-compatible Jenkins distribution. The solution effectively reroutes any file-based I/O to the Document Service that we'll be covering in Chapter 6. You can find more information about this project online at *https://github.com/SAP/cloud-jenkins*. There, in addition to the project source code, you'll also find a link to an excellent blog post on SCN written by the lead developer on the project (the great Mr. Stephan Weber).

That being said, the basic steps for a cloud-based Jenkins installation are as follows:

1. Use Git to download (clone) the SAP Cloud Jenkins project. This can be achieved by logging onto the SAP Cloud Jenkins project site at *https://github.com/SAP/cloud-jenkins*, copying the clone URL, and performing the steps described in Section 4.3.

2. After the project files are downloaded, you can build the installation file using Maven. For specific details about this build, we would direct you to the aforementioned SCN blog, as it describes which Maven repository specific artifacts are stored in and so on.

3. Once the Maven installation is complete, you'll find that a WAR file has been created that can be used to deploy Jenkins onto SAP HCP. This file can be deployed via any of the methods described in Section 4.2.

4. After Jenkins is deployed, you can start it just like any other Java application from within the SAP HCP Cockpit. However, before you begin using it, there are a few post-installation steps that need to be carried out in order to configure its use within your SAP HCP account. Because the nature of these steps varies depending on whether you're deploying Jenkins on a trial account versus a customer account, we would once again refer you to the aforementioned SCN blog, as it provides you with the details you would need for your specific scenario.

4.5.3 Moving toward Continuous Integration

Once Jenkins is up and running, the next step is to begin configuring build jobs. Such jobs can be created by clicking on the NEW JOB link, as shown in Figure 4.47. This will launch a wizard that allows you to specify important job details, such as the following:

▶ PROJECT BUILD TYPE
Here, we tell Jenkins what kind of project we're building. As you can see in Figure 4.47, we have several options to choose from here: free-style projects, Maven projects, and so forth.

▶ SCM INTEGRATION
At this step, we specify how Jenkins will connect to the project's source code repository. Here, Jenkins provides plug-ins that allow us to connect to most any SCM system.

▶ BUILD TRIGGERS/SCHEDULE DETAILS

Once we configure the connection to the SCM repository, we can specify the build triggers and/or scheduling details that determine when the build job is triggered.

▶ BUILD STEPS

At this step, we tell Jenkins how we want it to build our project. Here, we can add Maven/Ant build steps and more.

▶ POSTBUILD ACTIONS

Finally, after the build steps are in place, we have the option of specifying one or more postbuild actions. Such actions might include the publishing of Java-Docs or unit test results, report generation, email notifications, and so on.

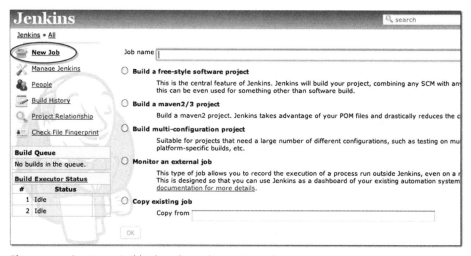

Figure 4.47 Creating a Build Job in the Jenkins UI Console

Once our job definition is configured, Jenkins will assume responsibility for builds and ensure that applications stay in sync. This frees developers and admin types up to focus on more important issues, such as application functionality and performance.

4.6   Summary

In this chapter, we covered the ins and outs of Java-based software logistics in the SAP HCP development landscape. You started this journey by learning about the various options for Java-based application deployment and what to do when deployments go wrong. From here, we looked at some different techniques for source code management and build automation. Finally, we showed how these tools can be leveraged towards the implementation of continuous integration scenarios.

Collectively, the tools and techniques described in this chapter should provide you with the foundation you need to organize the vast number of development objects created during the course of SAP HCP application development. We'll also see many of these concepts on display in later chapters, when we approach software logistics for native SAP HANA and HTML5 applications on SAP HCP.

In the next chapter, we'll shift gears a bit and take a look at native SAP HANA application development concepts.

One of the more compelling features of SAP HCP is its support for native SAP HANA development in the cloud. In this chapter, we'll take a look at these capabilities and learn how to develop new applications on this platform.

5   Developing Native SAP HANA Applications

In its relatively short lifespan, SAP HCP has experienced a number of significant transformations. From the early days in 2011 when SAP HCP went by the name SAP NetWeaver Cloud (or NEO), to the mature solution that's emerged today, we've certainly seen a lot of new features come along in the last several years.

One of the more notable additions to the SAP HCP toolset arrived in late 2013, when SAP first announced (limited) support for native SAP HANA development in SAP HCP. It was at this point that SAP HCP transcended from a generic PaaS solution with a feature set similar to other leading PaaS solutions of the time (e.g., the Google App Engine and Amazon Web Services) into something that's truly unique within the industry. After all, there's really no other platform out there that compares with SAP HANA.

In this chapter, we'll take a look at what it takes to develop native SAP HANA applications on SAP HCP. Although we won't realistically be able to cover all of the tools and services provided as part of the SAP HANA platform, our goal is to sufficiently cover the basics so that you understand enough about how SAP HANA technology is integrated into SAP HCP that you'll be able to leverage other SAP HANA-specific resources to fill in the gaps where needed. Indeed, once you get a feel for how SAP HANA technology is integrated into SAP HCP, we think that you'll find the cloud-based development experience to be very similar to the on-premise experience. If you already have experience developing native SAP

HANA applications on-premise, then you'll find the transition to development in the cloud to be quite straightforward.

Note

While this chapter explores the possibilities for native SAP HANA development using the free SAP HCP developer accounts, keep in mind that—although quite flexible—free accounts have some features restricted. For example, you do not get full database administrator rights (you're only able to manage your schemas) and you can't install software distribution units (SDUs).

To get a full-featured SAP HANA instance, you need a commercial SAP HCP account, which is typically equipped with a dedicated SAP HANA instance. This enables software developers to develop multi-tenant cloud applications and leverage all the features in subsequent SAP HANA releases (while still making local decisions on what to share and what to isolate between different tenants).

5.1 Overview

Back in Chapter 2, we touched on the positioning of SAP HANA technology within SAP HCP. We identified two primary usage scenarios:

- **Basic database access**
  In this scenario, the SAP HANA database is used as the backend database for applications developed using general-purpose languages, such as Java. Here, the SAP HANA database plays a role that's similar to those of other SAP HCP-supported databases, such as SAP MaxDB. *Eclipse*

- **Full-scale native SAP HANA development** *WB Dev workbench*
  In this scenario, applications are developed from the ground up using native SAP HANA development objects, such as server-side JavaScript files, analytic views, stored procedures, and so on. These applications are deployed onto a virtualized SAP HANA instance that's included with an SAP HCP account. The basic architecture for this type of application is illustrated in Figure 5.1.

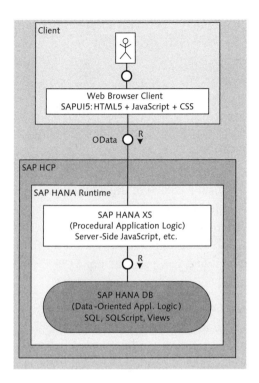

Figure 5.1 Basic Architecture of an SAP HANA Native Application

In this chapter, our focus will be on the development of native SAP HANA applications (we'll cover the basic database access scenario in Chapter 6). You'll learn how to set up a (trial) SAP HANA XS instance, create new SAP HANA XS applications, and deploy the finished product. As we move through the material, we'll endeavor to keep this introduction gentle enough so that you can follow along even if you're new to SAP HANA development. Having said that, though, we should point out that this chapter is by no means meant to be a thorough treatment of SAP HANA development concepts. For this, there are a variety of resources you can pull from, including the following:

- *SAP HANA: An Introduction, 3rd Edition* (Berg, Silvia, SAP PRESS, 2014)
- *Implementing SAP HANA, 2nd Edition* (Haun et al., SAP PRESS, 2015)
- *Introduction to Software Development on SAP HANA* (an online introductory course to SAP HANA development hosted on SAP's openSAP learning platform, available online at *https://open.sap.com/courses/hana1-1*)

- *Next Steps in Software Development on SAP HANA* (a continuing course on open-SAP exploring more advanced SAP HANA-related development topics, available online at *https://open.sap.com/courses/hana2*)
- The SAP HANA Developer Guide (available online at *http://help.sap.com/hana_platform*)

Introducing the Bookstore Sample Application

In order to demonstrate how SAP HANA development objects come together to create full-scale web applications, throughout the course of this chapter we'll be developing an application via which users can browse through a bookstore's catalog, search for books, and find out more information about a particular title. This simple demo app will allow us to model and load data into a custom database schema, expose the data via OData services, and consume it from SAPUI5 and server-side JavaScript.

You can find all of the application's source code in the book's source code bundle, available for download from *www.sap-press.com/3638*. We've also included a series of CSV files that we'll use to populate the data model with some sample data. If you're new to SAP HANA development, we'd strongly urge you to browse through the source code as you read through this chapter, as doing so will help you get a better sense for the big picture.

5.2 Getting Started

In just a moment, we'll roll up our sleeves and start getting our hands dirty with SAP HANA application development tasks. However, before we get started, there are a few administrative tasks that we need to take care of. In this section, we'll review these tasks and show you how to set up your local machine for SAP HANA development.

5.2.1 Creating a Trial SAP HANA Instance

When developing SAP HANA XS applications in the trial landscape, the first thing we need to do is create a *trial SAP HANA instance*. Such trial instances are abstractions of a normal SAP HANA instance and represent a logical grouping of schemas and tables, repository objects, users, and so forth. SAP uses this abstraction to split a physical SAP HANA instance hosted on SAP HCP into lots of little trial-account-specific partitions in order to conserve resources. The ramifications of all this from a development perspective are twofold:

1. The shared instance that we are provided within the trial landscape comes with some built-in restrictions and limited access rights. As you might expect, these restrictions were put in place to ensure the isolation of data and users within the shared SAP HANA instance.

2. For technical reasons, the up-front setup of a trial instance is a prerequisite for the development of SAP HANA XS applications in the trial landscape.

> **Note**
>
> You can find specific details about the limitations and restrictions of the trial SAP HANA instances in the SAP HCP help documentation available online at *http://help.hana.onde-mand.com*. Browse to the section titled "Using a Trial SAP HANA Instance."

Even though the behind-the-scenes details related to trial instances are quite complex, the process of setting up an instance in the SAP HCP Cockpit is relatively straightforward:

1. From the SAP HCP Cockpit landing page, navigate to the HANA INSTANCES tab.

2. Click on the NEW TRIAL INSTANCE link to reveal the NEW TRIAL INSTANCE panel shown in Figure 5.2.

3. Give your new instance a name (we called ours hcpbook), and click on the SAVE button to create the instance.

Figure 5.2 Creating a Trial SAP HANA XS Instance in the SAP HCP Cockpit

5.2.2 Working with Eclipse and the SAP HANA Tools

When developing SAP HANA XS applications, we have the choice of working with two different development environments: the familiar Eclipse IDE introduced in Chapter 2 and the new SAP HANA Web-Based Development Workbench (also known as the Web IDE—but not to be confused with the other web IDEs discussed in Chapter 7 and Chapter 10). In this section, we'll take a look at how to set up the Eclipse IDE for SAP HANA development in the cloud.

Setting up the SAP HANA Tools

In order to be able to connect to SAP HANA instances and create SAP HANA-specific development artifacts in Eclipse, we must install a series of plug-ins that are collectively referred to as the *SAP HANA Tools*. The SAP HANA Tools plug-ins can be installed onto a preexisting Eclipse instance or a clean Eclipse installation. When performing SAP HANA development in the cloud, we recommend installing the SAP HANA Tools alongside the SAP HCP Tools and other SAP HCP-related plug-ins so that all of the relevant cloud-based development functions are there in one place.

If you followed along with the installation instructions outlined in Chapter 2, Section 2.3.1, then you should already have the SAP HANA Tools plug-ins installed on your local Eclipse instance. Otherwise, we'd recommend that you reread through that section and/or consult the installation guide available online at *https://tools.hana.ondemand.com/#hanatools*.

What about SAP HANA Studio?

If you have experience developing on the SAP HANA platform already, then you might be wondering how the Eclipse IDE instance that we've set up for SAP HCP relates to the standalone SAP HANA Studio tool. As it turns out, there's really not much difference functionality wise. This is because SAP HANA Studio is basically just a prepackaged Eclipse installation that includes the aforementioned SAP HANA Tools by default.

If you already have SAP HANA Studio installed on your local machine, then you can certainly use it in lieu of the Eclipse IDE instance described here; both IDEs work the same. We just standardized the examples in this book around a generic Eclipse instance based on the assumption that SAP HCP developers would prefer to work in the same IDE used for the rest of their SAP HCP development.

Establishing a Connection to a Remote SAP HANA Instance

Once the SAP HANA Tools are installed, we're ready to launch Eclipse and connect to the remote SAP HANA instance that we're going to be developing against. Whether this is a trial instance or a customer instance, the procedure for setting up a connection is the same:

1. Switch to the SAP HANA ADMINISTRATION CONSOLE perspective in Eclipse.

2. In the SYSTEMS view shown in Figure 5.3, right-click on the whitespace and select the ADD CLOUD SYSTEM... menu option.

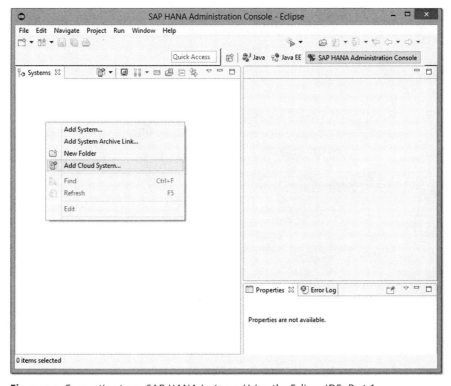

Figure 5.3 Connecting to an SAP HANA Instance Using the Eclipse IDE: Part 1

3. At this point, you'll be prompted with the ADD SAP HANA CLOUD PLATFORM SYSTEM dialog box shown in Figure 5.4. Plug in the appropriate LANDSCAPE HOST, ACCOUNT NAME, and logon credentials in order to connect to the target SAP HANA instance. Click on the NEXT > button to continue.

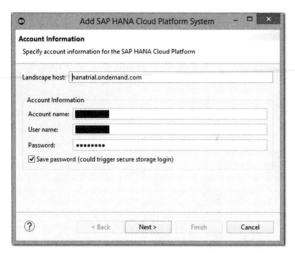

Figure 5.4 Connecting to an SAP HANA Instance Using the Eclipse IDE: Part 2

4. At the next step shown in Figure 5.5, you have the option of choosing between instances configured on a trial account or productive instances. Here, select the trial instance you created in Section 5.2.1.

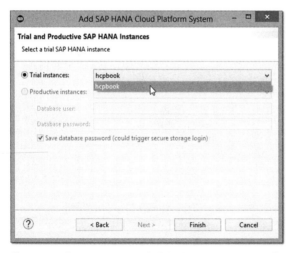

Figure 5.5 Connecting to an SAP HANA Instance Using the Eclipse IDE: Part 3

5. Confirm your selection by clicking on the FINISH button. At this point, Eclipse will connect to the remote SAP HANA instance and create a system node underneath the SYSTEMS view.

Organizing Repository Content into Subpackages

In Section 5.3, we'll begin creating custom SAP HANA artifacts in Eclipse. However, before we head down this path, it's a good idea to spend some time up front determining how we want to organize our development objects. After all, if you dumped everything into the root package, it would eventually become rather difficult to determine what's what.

Within the SAP HANA Repository, you can group related development objects into *packages*. Besides providing a neat folder structure, packages also allow you to assign relevant permissions to development objects at a macro level (similar to access control lists in operating systems or content repository systems). The details around this and other logistics-related concepts are described at length in the SAP HANA help documentation.

For the purposes of our demonstration, we'll be creating a single subpackage underneath the `hcpbook` (trial) instance we created in Section 5.2.1. This can be achieved by performing the following steps:

1. From the same SYSTEMS view you used to establish your repository connection in the previous section, expand the CONTENT folder down to the package that matches up with the SAP HANA instance you created in Section 5.2.1.

2. Once you find the target folder/package, right-click on it and select the NEW • PACKAGE... menu option, as shown in Figure 5.6.

3. In the NEW PACKAGE dialog box shown in Figure 5.7, specify a name for your new package and an optional description. Note that the name you give to the package must be fully qualified. If you wanted to name the subpackage `book-store`, then you would need to qualify the name with the relevant parent packages (e.g., `{account_name}.hcpbook.bookstore`).

179

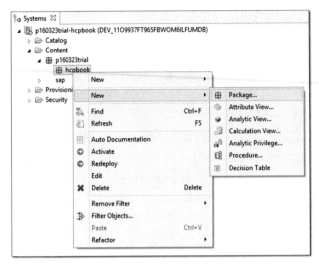

Figure 5.6 Creating a Subpackage: Part 1

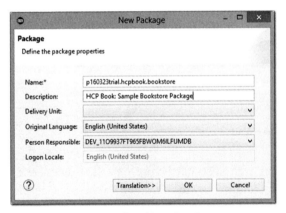

Figure 5.7 Creating a Subpackage: Part 2

4. Once you're satisfied with your selection, click on the OK button to create the subpackage.

Depending on the complexity of the application(s) you're building, it might make sense to create additional subpackages to organize specific model objects, utilities, and so forth. As you build out your package hierarchies, it's worth noting that the SAP HANA Repository's fairly forgiving if you end up making mistakes. In these situations, you can reorganize package hierarchies and move relevant development objects around as needed.

Setting up a Repository Workspace

Even though Eclipse maintains a live connection to the remote SAP HANA Repository, it's important to note that changes you make to artifacts in Eclipse will be applied *locally*. This is to say that the files will be maintained in a directory on your local machine, and you'll need to periodically synchronize these files with the remote SAP HANA Repository.

Rather than having to coordinate these changes on our own, the SAP HANA Tools make it possible for us to track these changes within a *repository workspace*. In the upcoming sections, we'll find that repository workspaces greatly simplify the task of checking in updates to the SAP HANA Repository.

To set up a repository workspace in Eclipse, perform the following steps:

1. Switch to the SAP HANA DEVELOPMENT perspective in Eclipse.

2. From the REPOSITORIES view shown in Figure 5.8, right-click on your remote system connection and select the CREATE REPOSITORY WORKSPACE menu option.

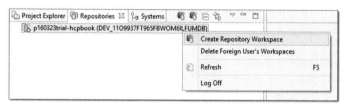

Figure 5.8 Creating a Repository Workspace: Part 1

3. In the CREATE NEW REPOSITORY WORKSPACE dialog box shown in Figure 5.9, assign your workspace a name and a root directory location. The latter refers to a directory on your local machine where you'll store all of your repository-related objects during development.

4. Once all of the proper settings are in place, click on the FINISH button to create the workspace.

For now, that's all there is to it. A little bit later on, we'll see how this repository is used to track SAP HANA XS project artifacts and perform remote activations in the SAP HANA Repository.

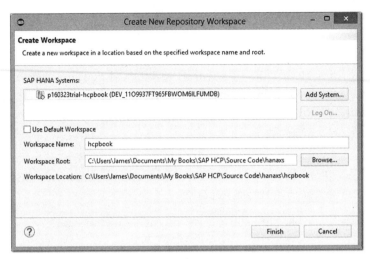

Figure 5.9 Creating a Repository Workspace: Part 2

5.2.3 Working with the SAP HANA Web-Based Development Workbench

Although most SAP HANA developers these days prefer to work in the more mature Eclipse IDE, it's important to note that Eclipse is not the only game in town when it comes to native SAP HANA development. As we noted in Section 5.2.2, SAP also provides a web-based development environment called the *SAP HANA Web-Based Development Workbench*. This web-based tool can be used to directly access and edit development objects within a remote SAP HANA Repository.

Unlike the Eclipse IDE, the SAP HANA Web-Based Development Workbench requires no up-front installation. Indeed, to launch the tool, all we have to do is open up the workbench URL in a browser. You can find the workbench URL on the HANA INSTANCES tab in the SAP HCP Cockpit, as shown in Figure 5.10.

Figure 5.11 shows what the workbench editor screen looks like within a browser window. Here, we can browse through the contents of the remote SAP HANA Repository and create new folders or packages and even SAP HANA XS applications. In the latter case, we have the option of creating SAP HANA XS applications in reference to template projects that predefine a lot of common source files that we'd normally have to create by hand. For this reason, many developers prefer to kick off development projects in the web-based workbench and then switch over to Eclipse for the more in-depth development tasks.

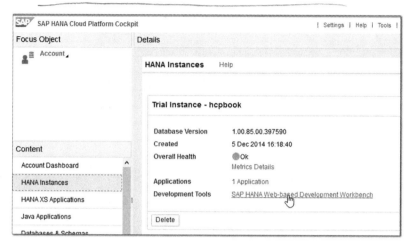

Figure 5.10 Launching the SAP HANA Web-Based Development Workbench

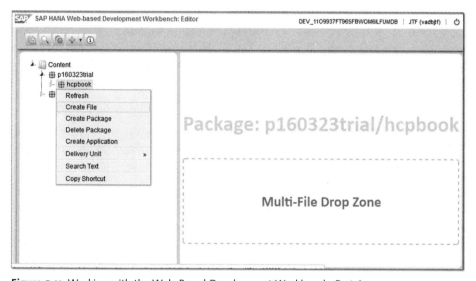

Figure 5.11 Working with the Web-Based Development Workbench: Part 1

As you can see in Figure 5.12, the web-based workbench has some built-in source code editor features, such syntax highlighting, work protection, and so on. As of the time of writing, the capabilities are more or less on par with most common text editor tools, but the feature set is expanding all the time.

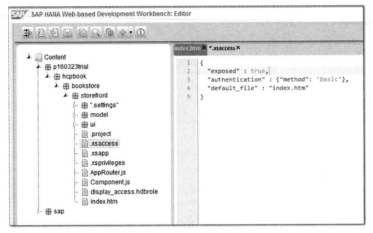

Figure 5.12 Working with the Web-Based Development Workbench: Part 2

When working with the web-based workbench, one of the nice things you'll notice is that you don't have to sync up your changes with the SAP HANA Repository. This is because the workbench maintains a live connection with the SAP HANA Repository itself. As you can imagine, this feature can come in handy whenever administrators need to perform emergency updates and the like.

Throughout the remainder of this chapter, we'll be focusing our attention on the Eclipse IDE, because it offers a more streamlined approach to the development of our sample bookstore application. However, as time permits, we would encourage you to play around with the web-based workbench and explore some of the features it brings to the table. SAP has indicated that it will continue to expand on the feature set of the web-based toolset over time so that eventually there will be parity between the web-based workbench and the Eclipse IDE.

5.3   Creating an SAP HANA XS Project in Eclipse

Now that we've prepared the Eclipse IDE for SAP HANA development (Section 5.2.2), we're ready to begin developing our sample application. From a logistics perspective, this starts with the creation of an SAP HANA XS project in Eclipse. To set up a new SAP HANA XS project, perform the following steps:

1. Open the SAP HANA DEVELOPMENT perspective.

2. From the REPOSITORIES view, expand your package structure and right-click on the BOOKSTORE subpackage you created in Section 5.2.2. This will open up the context menu shown in Figure 5.13. Select the NEW • PROJECT... menu option to create a new project.

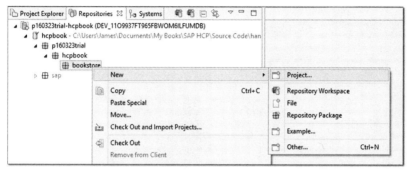

Figure 5.13 Creating an SAP HANA XS Project in Eclipse: Part 1

3. In the NEW PROJECT dialog box shown in Figure 5.14, open the SAP HANA folder, and select the XS PROJECT type. Click on the NEXT > button to continue.

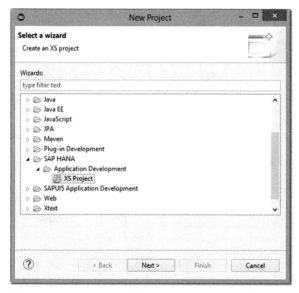

Figure 5.14 Creating an SAP HANA XS Project in Eclipse: Part 2

4. This will open the NEW XS PROJECT dialog box shown in Figure 5.15. Give your project a name (we called ours STOREFRONT) and a location on your local machine where all of the project artifacts will be stored. It's important that you map to the same folder you used to create your repository workspace back in Section 5.2.2. That way, you can let Eclipse worry about tracking all the various artifacts that you'll be creating within your project.

bookstore

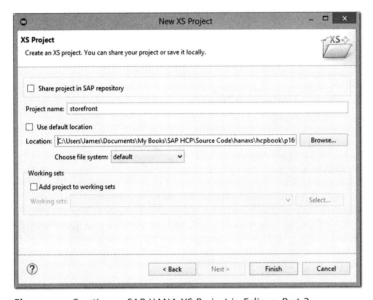

Figure 5.15 Creating an SAP HANA XS Project in Eclipse: Part 3

5. Once the relevant settings are in place, click on the FINISH button to create the project.

Linking the Project with the Repository Workspace

Before we move on from project creation, there's one final housekeeping item that you need to take care of: you need to formally share or link your project with the repository workspace you created in Section 5.2.2. The steps required to achieve this are as follows:

1. Right-click on the newly-created SAP HANA XS project and select the TEAM • SHARE PROJECT... menu option, as shown in Figure 5.16.

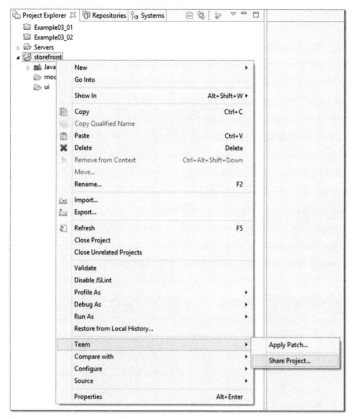

Figure 5.16 Setting Up Sharing with the SAP HANA XS Project: Part 1

2. This will open the SHARE PROJECT dialog box shown in Figure 5.17. At this step, you're prompted to select a repository type. Choose the SAP HANA REPOSITORY type and click on NEXT >.

3. If you set up your SAP HANA XS project correctly, then you'll end up at the confirmation screen shown in Figure 5.18. This screen is essentially confirming the fact that the project's contents are already stored in the selected repository workspace, so no further action is required. To confirm the changes, click on the FINISH button.

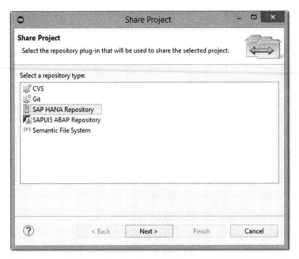

Figure 5.17 Setting Up Sharing with the SAP HANA XS Project: Part 2

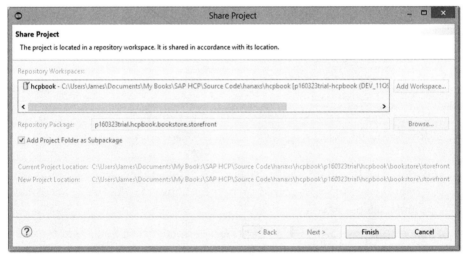

Figure 5.18 Setting Up Sharing with the SAP HANA XS Project: Part 3

5.4 Building the Application Data Model

In this section, you'll start building out your application's data model. Here, we'll start with the definition of the database tables that will store your bookstore data.

Then, once these tables are configured, we'll look at ways of exposing this data to the client tier.

5.4.1 Defining a Persistence Model Using Core Data Services

As a fully SQL-compliant database, it's fairly easy to create your application's database tables from the SQL command line using the data definition language (DDL). However, as it turns out, SAP HANA provides several alternatives for defining tables that greatly simplify logistics as you promote your application(s) through the system landscape. In essence, these alternatives call for the creation of SAP HANA-specific metafiles, which define tables in logical terms. Whenever we deploy these metafiles to the SAP HANA Repository, SAP HANA uses the metadata to automagically create the corresponding physical tables on our behalf. If you're familiar with the ABAP programming environment, this behavior is similar to transparent table definitions in the ABAP Data Dictionary.

These days, an emerging standard for defining tables or views in SAP HANA is *Core Data Services* (CDS). Conceptually, you can think of CDS as an SAP HANA-specific metalanguage that allows us to define reusable types, entities, views, and so forth in a generic manner. For our purposes, we'll be using CDS to build out the table schema shown in Figure 5.19. This simple model introduces a pair of entities (Books and Authors) that are linked by an association table (BookAuthors).

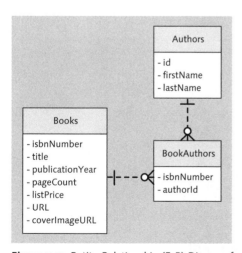

Figure 5.19 Entity-Relationship (E-R) Diagram for Bookstore Data Model

To create the data model shown in Figure 5.19 using CDS, you must create a new DDL source file within your project. This can be achieved by performing the following steps:

1. Within the SAP HANA XS project folder, create a subfolder in which all of your model-related objects will be stored. In our project, we called this subfolder MODEL. This folder can be created by right-clicking on the project folder in Eclipse and selecting the NEW • FOLDER menu option.

2. With the subfolder created, create the DDL file by right-clicking on the subfolder and selecting the NEW • OTHER... menu option. This will open the NEW dialog box shown in Figure 5.20. From here, the target object type is contained within the SAP HANA • DATABASE DEVELOPMENT folder structure. Click on the NEXT > button to continue.

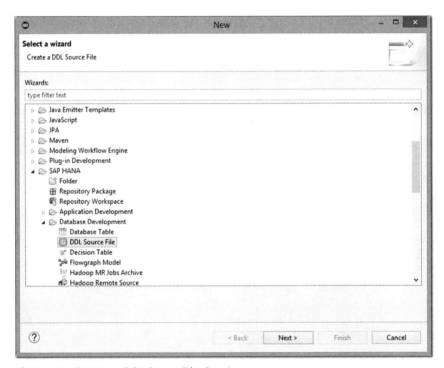

Figure 5.20 Creating a DDL Source File: Part 1

3. On the next screen (shown in Figure 5.21), give your file a name (Bookstore-Model.hdbdd) and click on the FINISH button to create the artifact.

Figure 5.21 Creating a DDL Source File: Part 2

Listing 5.1 contains the CDS content we used to create the bookstore data model. Although a thorough coverage of the CDS syntax used in this excerpt is beyond the scope of this book, it's not too difficult to figure out what's going on here. Basically, the three tables we want to define based on the E-R diagram contained in Figure 5.19 are represented as entity types. Aside from the entities themselves, we have a reusable type called ISBN and a view called BookAuthorsView, which we'll use later on to query the authors associated with a given book.

```
namespace {account_name}.hcpbook.bookstore.storefront.model;
                              ins     package      proj
@Schema: '_SYS_BIC'
context Bookstore {
  type ISBN: String(13);

  type AmountType {
    amount: Decimal(5,2);
    currencyCode: String(3);
  };
```

```
entity Books {
  key isbnNumber: ISBN;
  title: String(100);
  publicationYear: Integer;
  pageCount: Integer;
  listPrice: AmountType;
  URL: String(255);
  coverImageURL: String(255);
};

entity Authors {
  key id: Integer;
  firstName: String(50);
  lastName: String(50);
};

entity BookAuthors {
  key isbnNumber: ISBN;
  key author: Association to Authors;
};

define view BookAuthorsView as SELECT FROM BookAuthors {
  isbnNumber,
  author.firstName,
  author.lastName
};
};
```

Listing 5.1 Defining the Bookstore Data Model Using CDS

Note

For more information about CDS and various syntax options defined within the specification, we highly recommend that you download a copy of the *SAP HANA Core Data Services (CDS) Reference* available online at *http://help.sap.com/hana_platform*.

5.4.2 Exposing the Data Model as an OData Service

As we noted in Section 5.1, the user interface for our bookstore application will be based on SAPUI5 technology. From an integration perspective, this means that we'll have to expose our data model via some kind of REST-based service. Because SAPUI5 is ideally suited to consume OData-based services, let's take a look at what it takes to expose our data model as an OData service.

As it turns out, SAP HANA makes it absurdly easy to expose the data model we built in Section 5.4.1 as an OData service. For this, we use the XS OData object type, which defines an abstracted syntax for mapping tables or views from the SAP HANA database to entities within an OData service definition.

To create an XS OData file, right-click on your MODEL folder and select the NEW • XS ODATA FILE menu option, as shown in Figure 5.22. Then, in the NEW XS ODATA SERVICE dialog box shown in Figure 5.23, assign your service file a name (BookstoreService.xsodata) and click on the FINISH button.

Figure 5.22 Creating an XS OData File: Part 1

Listing 5.2 contains an excerpt of the XS OData file we created for our sample application. Here, the {namespace} token refers to the same namespace we used to define the entities/views in the CDS file we created in Section 5.4.1. The as "{Entity_Name}" portion of the markup assigns selected tables or views to entities within the OData service definition file. Aside from the entity definitions themselves, we also mix in an association between the Books and BookAuthors entities so that our SAPUI5 application will be able to navigate this association to read the authors associated with a selected book at runtime.

Figure 5.23 Creating an XS OData File: Part 2

```
service namespace "hcpbook.bookstore" {
  "{namespace}::Bookstore.Books"
    as "Books" navigates ("Book_Authors" as "Authors");

  "{namespace}::Bookstore.BookAuthorsView"
    as "BookAuthors" key ("isbnNumber","firstName","lastName");

  association "Book_Authors" principal "Books"("isbnNumber")
    multiplicity "1"
    dependent "BookAuthors"("isbnNumber") multiplicity "*";
}
```

Listing 5.2 Example XS OData File

Although there is a bit of a learning curve up front with the SAP HANA XS OData file syntax, the major takeaway from all this is that we can develop a read-only OData service on top of an SAP HANA-based persistence model in just a few lines of code. Where needed, we can also expand the scope of our service to perform other CRUD operations (e.g., create, update, and delete) via custom exits written in SAP HANA's proprietary SQLScript language or server-side JavaScript. The details behind all this are contained within the *SAP HANA Developer Guide*.

5.4.3 Consuming the Data Model from Server-Side JavaScript

Although OData-based access will be the preferred method of data consumption for our SAPUI5 application, it's worth noting that the SAP HANA programming model also offers another alternative for exposing the data model to the client tier: server-side JavaScript.

In the book's source code bundle, you'll find a file called booklist.xsjs, which demonstrates how to fetch data from the Books table using a SQL query and then return the results in an HTML table. Conceptually, you'll find that the syntax/flow here is similar to that of a Java Servlet/JSP (see Listing 5.3). This is to say that the server-side JavaScript file is an HTTP addressable object that can be used to serve up all kinds of content: HTML, XML, JSON, and so forth. For more information on server-side JavaScript, please consult the *SAP HANA Developer Guide*.

```
// Build the HTML5 output string:
$.response.contentType = "text/html";
var output =
  '<!DOCTYPE html><head><meta charset="UTF-8">' +
  '<title>HCP Book: HANA XS App Demo</title></head><body>' +
  '<table><thead><tr><th>ISBN Number</th><th>Title</th>' +
  '<th>Year Published</th><th>Page Count</th></thead>';

// Fetch the book catalog from the Books table:
var sql =
  "SELECT * FROM " +
  "\"_SYS_BIC\".\"{account}.hcpbook.bookstore.storefront.model" +
  "::Bookstore.Books\"";
var conn = $.db.getConnection();
var pstmt =
  conn.prepareStatement(sql);
var rs = pstmt.executeQuery();

while (rs.next()) {
  output += '<tr>';
  output += '<td>' + rs.getString(1) + '</td>';
  output += '<td>' + rs.getString(2) + '</td>';
  output += '<td>' + rs.getString(3) + '</td>';
  output += '<td>' + rs.getString(4) + '</td>';
  output += '</tr>';
}
```

```
rs.close();
pstmt.close();
conn.close();

// Display the results:
output += '</table></body></html>';
$.response.setBody(output);
```
Listing 5.3 Server-Side JavaScript Example

5.5   Developing the Application UI

With the OData service created in Section 5.4.2 in tow, the development of the user interface with SAPUI5 was unremarkable in that we didn't have to introduce any SAP HANA-specific content. Indeed, if you browse through the book's source code bundle, you'll find that the UI we created contains SAPUI5 content as per usual.

This is illustrated in Figure 5.24, where you can see how we've defined lots of SAPUI5-related content files inside of our SAP HANA XS project in a folder called UI. The HTML bootstrap file (index.htm) is stored at the project root level.

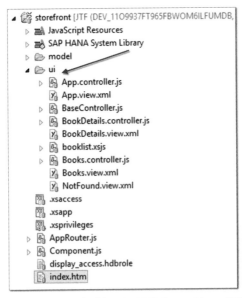

Figure 5.24 Embedding SAPUI5 Content in an SAP HANA XS Project

Within the SAPUI5 content itself, all the resource references are pretty well self-contained. The only notable items here worth mentioning from an SAP HANA perspective are the location of the SAPUI5 library files and the target OData service.

In Listing 5.4, you can see that the SAPUI5 core library file is being loaded from a relative URL */sap/ui5/1/resources/sap-ui-core.js*. Here, the *1* represents the latest-and-greatest version of the SAPUI5 library that's deployed on the SAP HANA XS engine. As long as our applications point here, we needn't worry about amending resource links in the long run.

```
<!DOCTYPE html>
<html>
  <head>
    <meta http-equiv="X-UA-Compatible" content="IE=edge" />
    <meta http-equiv="Content-Type"
          content="text/html;charset=UTF-8" />

    <script src="/sap/ui5/1/resources/sap-ui-core.js"
            id="sap-ui-bootstrap"
            data-sap-ui-libs="sap.m"
            data-sap-ui-theme="sap_bluecrystal">
    </script>
    ...
</html>
```

Listing 5.4 Accessing the SAPUI5 Library from an SAP HANA XS Application

To access the OData service, simply plug in the relative path to the XS OData file created in Section 5.4.2 (e.g., `/model/BookService.xsodata`). As you might expect, this implies that we can access the OData service directly in a browser by prepending the physical path of our SAP HANA XS application to the relative URL of the XS OData file. We'll explain how to run these kinds of tests in Section 5.6.

For brevity's sake, we don't really have more to say about the nitty-gritty details of the SAPUI5 content here. If you're interested in learning more about SAPUI5 technology, we'd recommend that you take a look at *Getting Started with SAPUI5* (Antolovic, SAP PRESS, 2014). You can also find a wealth of information in the official SAPUI5 documentation available online at *https://sapui5.netweaver.ondemand.com/sdk*.

5.6   Finishing Touches

With the bulk of the heavy lifting out of the way, there are just a few finishing touches needed to finish our sample application. In this section, we'll take a look at several important descriptor files that are used to configure our application for external use.

5.6.1   Creating the Application Descriptor File

The first descriptor file we'll be looking at is the main application descriptor file. This file must be present in order to deploy our SAP HANA XS application. To create the application descriptor file within your sample project, perform the following steps:

1. Right-click on the project root node and select the NEW • FILE menu option, as shown in Figure 5.25.

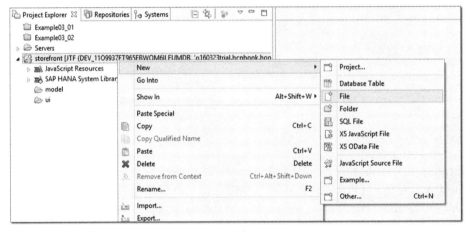

Figure 5.25 Creating the Application Descriptor File: Part 1

2. This will open the NEW wizard dialog box shown in Figure 5.26. Within this dialog box, you can initiate the creation of the file by expanding the SAP HANA • APPLICATION DEVELOPMENT folders and selecting the XS APPLICATION DESCRIPTOR FILE node. Click on NEXT > to continue.

3. On the confirmation screen shown in Figure 5.27, create the application descriptor by clicking on the FINISH button. Note that you don't have to specify the name of the file; the wizard has taken care of this for you automatically.

Figure 5.26 Creating the Application Descriptor File: Part 2

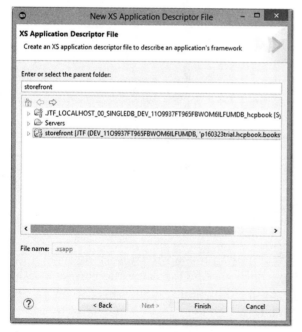

Figure 5.27 Creating the Application Descriptor File: Part 3

After the application descriptor creation wizard completes, you'll notice that a new file called .xsapp is created within the root folder. If you open up this file in a text editor, then you'll find that it's completely empty—and that's exactly as it should be. According to the SAP HANA help documentation, this file is intended to be empty (at least for the time being).

5.6.2 Defining the Application Access File

The next descriptor file that we'll be looking at is the application access file. This file can be created using the same procedure we demonstrated for the .xsapp file in Section 5.6.1; the only difference is that you'll want to select the XS APPLICATION ACCESS FILE option when kicking off the file creation wizard (see Figure 5.28).

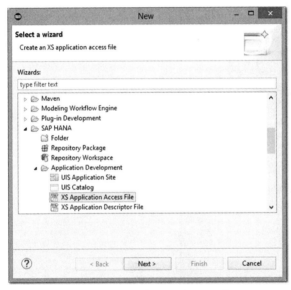

Figure 5.28 Creating the Application Access File

Much like the .xsapp application descriptor file described in Section 5.6.1, the generated application access file (which goes by the name .xsaccess) is initially empty. This time, though, there is some content that we'll want to fill in. In particular, we want to specify the following:

▶ Because SAP HANA XS applications are hidden from public view by default, we want to set the `exposed` attribute to `true` so that we'll be able to access the application externally (e.g., via a web browser).

▶ To enforce some measure of security, we'd like to turn on basic or form-based authentication so that users have to log in before accessing the SAP HANA XS application.

▶ To make it easier to launch the application, we specify index.htm as the application's default content file. That way, users can navigate to the application root, and the SAP HANA XS engine will load the landing page automatically.

Listing 5.5 shows how we're specifying these attributes for our sample application. As you can see, the .xsaccess file utilizes a JSON-based syntax based on simple name–value pairs. You can find the complete syntax diagram for this file in the online help documentation.

```
{
  "exposed" : true,
  "authentication" : {"method": "Basic"},
  "default_file" : "index.htm"
}
```
Listing 5.5 Defining the Application Access File

5.6.3 Defining a Security Role for Display Access

When developing production-quality SAP HANA XS applications, we must formulate a comprehensive security model that ensures that every aspect of our application is secure. Here, we might need to define a series of roles and privileges that determine the scope of access offered to particular sets of users.

In order to support all of the various requirements that might crop up within a particular development project, the SAP HANA security model is very granular, allowing us to define many different types of privileges. However, for the purposes of our demo application, we'll be working with only one type of privilege: the *application privilege*. This privilege type is used to provide application-level access to end users.

To create our application privilege within our SAP HANA XS application, we create a new file called .xsprivileges. As you can see in Listing 5.6, this file also utilizes JSON to specify one or more privileges. Each privilege record consists of a `name` attribute and a `description` attribute. For the purposes of our demo application, we created a generic privilege called `Basic` that we'll assign to any authorized users.

```
{ "privileges" :
    [ { "name" : "Basic",
        "description" : "Default User Privilege" } ]
}
```

Listing 5.6 Defining a Simple Application Privilege for the Demo Application

Although the SAP HANA security model allows us to assign privileges directly to users, the preferred method of delivery is via a *role assignment*. Therefore, once we create our privilege file, the next step is to create a new role definition. This is achieved by performing the following steps:

1. Right-click on the project root folder and select the New • Other menu option.

2. In the New dialog box shown in Figure 5.29, select the SAP HANA • Database Development • Role option. Click on Next > to continue.

Figure 5.29 Defining a Security Role: Part 1

3. On the confirmation screen, give your role a name and click on Finish (Figure 5.30). For our demo, we created a role called `display_access`. As the name suggests, this role will be used to provide basic display access to our application to end users.

Figure 5.30 Defining a Security Role: Part 2

Once the wizard completes, we'll end up with an empty file called {role_ name}.hdbrole. Listing 5.7 demonstrates the syntax needed to fill in the role details. Here, the role is defined via the initial `role` clause. The `{acct}` token refers to the target SAP HCP account, and the package is the fully qualified package used to define the role (e.g., `hcpbook.bookstore.storefront`). Within the role definition itself, we assign the application privilege we created in this section to the role, as well as some object privileges that will allow users to query entries from our bookstore data model. The latter is needed to process the OData requests from the SAPUI5 client application.

```
role {acct}.{package}::display_access {
  application privilege: {acct}.{package}::Basic;
  catalog sql object "_SYS_
BIC"."{acct}.{package}.model::Bookstore.Books": SELECT;
  catalog sql object "_SYS_
BIC"."{acct}.{package}.model::Bookstore.Authors": SELECT;
  catalog sql object "_SYS_
BIC"."{acct}.{package}.model::Bookstore.BookAuthors":
    SELECT;
  catalog sql object "_SYS_
BIC"."{acct}.{package}.model::Bookstore.BookAuthorsView":
    SELECT;
}
```

Listing 5.7 Defining a Display-Only Role for the Demo Application

For now, that's all we have to define. In the next section, you'll learn how to deploy this role and assign it to end users.

5.7 Deployment and Testing

Now that we've created all of the relevant repository artifacts that make up our sample application, we're ready to deploy our application and start testing it. In this section, we'll see how these tasks are performed using the Eclipse IDE and SAP HCP Cockpit tools.

5.7.1 Activating the SAP HANA XS Project

As we noted in Section 5.3, all of the source code artifacts created during the development process in the Eclipse IDE are initially saved to a workspace folder on your local machine. Therefore, before you can test your SAP HANA XS application, you must first synchronize the contents of this workspace folder with the remote SAP HANA Repository.

If you followed along with the SAP HANA XS project setup steps outlined in Section 5.3, then all of the necessary plumbing should be in place to trigger this synchronization process. Here, you can utilize the repository workspace created in Section 5.2.2 to open the remote SAP HANA Repository connection and sync the files. Within the Eclipse IDE, this task is carried out as follows:

1. Right-click on the SAP HANA XS project root folder and select the TEAM • ACTIVATE ALL… menu option, as shown in Figure 5.31.

2. This will open the ACTIVATE INACTIVE OBJECTS dialog box shown in Figure 5.32. From here, select or deselect the artifacts you wish to sync, and then click on the OK button to trigger the activation. At this point, the files will be copied to the remote SAP HANA Repository and, if there are no syntax errors, activated.

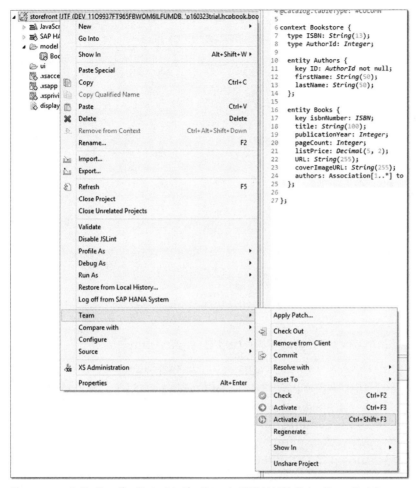

Figure 5.31 Activating the Project in the Remote SAP HANA Repository: Part 1

Note that this same process would be used to perform incremental sync-ups whenever you're unit testing the application and applying defect corrections. Or, if you prefer, you can perform one-off activations by right-clicking on a particular repository file and activating it directly.

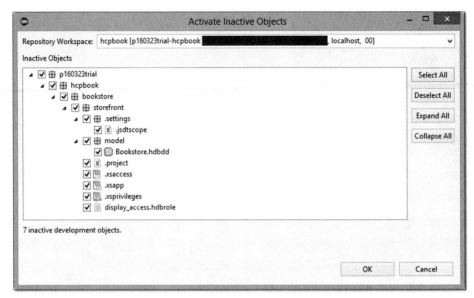

Figure 5.32 Activating the Project in the Remote SAP HANA Repository: Part 2

5.7.2 Assigning the Display Role to a User Account

Once your SAP HANA XS project is activated, you should see several new objects installed in the SAP HANA Repository: the tables and views we defined in Section 5.4, the SAP HANA XS application itself, and so forth. Included in this list of repository artifacts is the security role we created in Section 5.6.3. Before you can test your SAP HANA XS application, you need to assign this role to the user account(s) you want to use to test the application.

To perform this role assignment, you must execute a stored procedure within the target SAP HANA instance. When working with an SAP HCP trial account, the steps required to execute this procedure are as follows:

1. Within the Eclipse IDE, open the SAP HANA DEVELOPMENT perspective, and switch over to the SYSTEMS tab.

2. Select the connection node for your remote SAP HANA instance, and click on the SQL button in the top-level toolbar (see Figure 5.33).

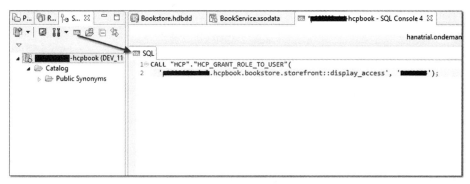

Figure 5.33 Assigning the Display Role to a Test User

3. This will open the SQL CONSOLE window shown on the right-hand side of Figure 5.33. Within this editor, you'll want to build the call to the HCP_GRANT_ROLE_TO_USER procedure, using the syntax contained in Listing 5.8.

4. Once you've crafted your CALL procedure statement, click on the EXECUTE button <image id inline> to perform the assignment.

```
CALL "HCP"."HCP_GRANT_ROLE_TO_USER"(
  '{acct_name}.{pkg_name}::{role_name}',
  '{user_name}');
```

Listing 5.8 Granting the Display Role to an End User

If you're working with a customer or partner account, the role assignment process is similar to that of the trial account but calls for the use of a different set of stored procedures. You can find details regarding which procedures to call and the specific call syntax in the SAP HANA Security Guide, available online at *http://help.sap.com/hana_platform*.

5.7.3 Importing Test Data

After the role assignments are complete, our bookstore application is officially open for business. However, because the tables we created are empty, the application doesn't really do all that much. Therefore, to get things up and running, we need to load our data model with some test data.

Although there are many ways of accomplishing data loads in SAP HANA, one convenient option is to use the data import wizard included with the SAP HANA

Tools plug-ins installed in the Eclipse IDE. Here, we have the option of uploading test data from CSV files, Excel files, and so forth.

For the purposes of our demonstration, we've included a series of CSV files with the book's source code bundle (downloadable from *www.sap-press.com/3638*) that you can use to prepopulate the bookstore data model with some sample data. To import these files into your custom bookstore schema, perform the following steps:

1. Within the Eclipse IDE, open the SAP HANA DEVELOPMENT perspective, and select the FILE • IMPORT... menu option from the top-level menu bar.

2. This will open the IMPORT dialog box shown in Figure 5.34. From here, expand the SAP HANA CONTENTfolder and select the DATA FROM LOCAL FILE option. Click on NEXT > to continue.

Figure 5.34 Importing Test Data from Eclipse: Part 1

3. In the next step, you'll be prompted to select the target SAP HANA system you want to upload the data to (see Figure 5.35). Select the target system, and click on NEXT >.

Figure 5.35 Importing Test Data from Eclipse: Part 2

4. Select the source CSV file that you want to upload and the target table where you want to land the data. As you can see in Figure 5.36, this step also allows you to specify the field delimiter, ranges of records within the file to upload, and so forth. For our purposes, we'll choose the default file encoding, the default record delimiter (comma), and the IMPORT ALL DATA checkbox, because we want to pull in all the test data contained in the source file in one go. Click on the NEXT > button to continue.

5. In the MANAGE TABLE DEFINITION AND DATA MAPPINGS step (Figure 5.37), map the fields from the source CSV file to the corresponding fields in the target table. Because the test files are fully populated, you can select the ONE TO ONE menu option highlighted in Figure 5.37 to automatically map the fields. As the mapping(s) are being defined, you can preview the import in the bottom panel of the IMPORT dialog box (see Figure 5.37). Once all the mappings are in place, click on the FINISH button to kick off the import process.

Figure 5.36 Importing Test Data from Eclipse: Part 3

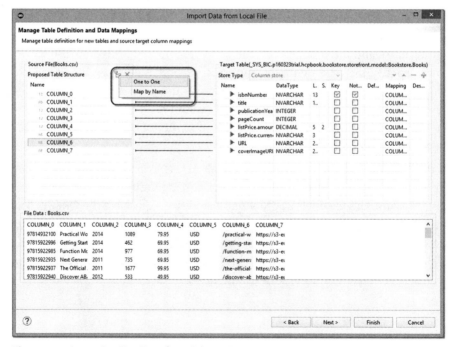

Figure 5.37 Importing Test Data from Eclipse: Part 4

6. Once you get the hang of this process, you'll want to repeat it for each of the three entities we created in Section 5.4. In the source code bundle, you'll find that the source CSV files match up with the names of the entities themselves, so the import process should be pretty straightforward.

5.7.4   Launching the Application

Finally, all of the pieces are in place to test our sample application. To view the finished product, log onto the SAP HCP Cockpit, and click on the HANA XS APPLICATIONS tab. Then, in the HANA XS APPLICATIONS dashboard shown in Figure 5.38, you can launch the application by clicking on the application URL contained in the URL column.

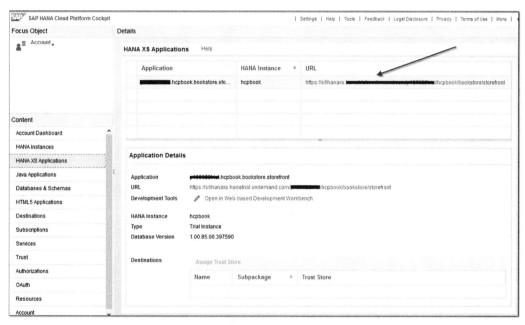

Figure 5.38 Launching an SAP HANA XS Application from the SAP HCP Cockpit

Whenever the application launches, we'll initially be directed to the familiar SAP ID Service log on screen. As you may recall from Section 5.6.2, this authentication prompt is a result of the authentication configuration we applied to our application's .xsaccess file. After successfully authenticating, we finally arrive at the application main screen, shown in Figure 5.39.

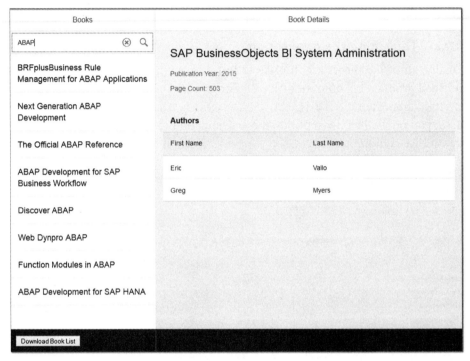

Figure 5.39 Testing the Bookstore Application in a Desktop Browser

Because our bookstore application is based on the `sap.m` library within the SAPUI5 framework, the look and feel will vary somewhat whenever we launch the application in a desktop browser versus, for example, a mobile device. For example, the screenshots contained in Figure 5.40 and Figure 5.41 illustrate what the bookstore application looks like on an Android device.

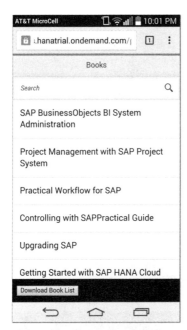

Figure 5.40 Testing the Bookstore Application using a Mobile Device: Part 1

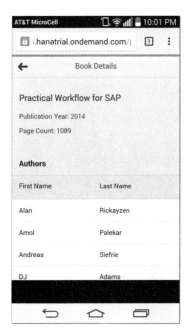

Figure 5.41 Testing the Bookstore Application using a Mobile Device: Part 2

As you play around with the application, we'd encourage you to open up your browser's developer tools console and watch the XS OData service call traffic being executed behind the scenes. For example, in Figure 5.42, you can see how the bookstore application issued a pair of requests to the OData service whenever we selected a particular title within the Books list. When troubleshooting data or connection issues, this trace information can be very useful in getting to the bottom of code or configuration defects.

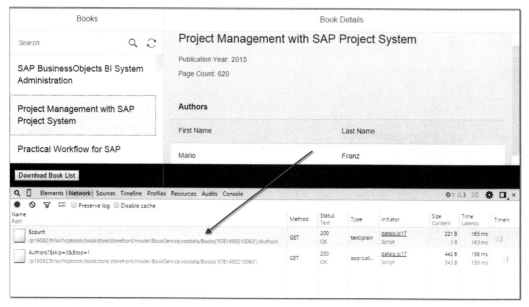

Figure 5.42 Tracing OData Calls to the XS OData Service

5.8   Summary

In this chapter, we were able to demonstrate some of the ins and outs of native SAP HANA development on SAP HCP. You learned how to create and deploy SAP HANA XS applications and to test them end to end. With these skills in tow, you should be able to consult various SAP HANA-specific development resources to fill in the gaps in your knowledge and start building industrial-strength SAP HANA applications in the cloud.

As we wrap up this discussion, we should note that the SAP HANA programming model is and should be considered a first-class citizen within the set of programming models supported by SAP HCP. Although SAP HANA does naturally lend itself towards the creation of data-centric, analytical applications, all of the pieces are in place to develop general-purpose applications as well. Of course, whether you choose to leverage SAP HANA in this capacity remains a matter of preference.

In the next chapter, we'll focus our attention on some of the key enablement services provided with SAP HCP. There, you'll learn how to utilize these services to implement application persistence, external connectivity, and much more.

Building industrial-strength cloud applications calls for more than just a runtime environment. Real-world applications need to have a reliable persistence layer, access to external or on-premise data sources, and occasionally a content repository. In this section, we'll learn about the core services SAP HCP provides to satisfy these requirements.

6   Consuming Cloud Services

In Chapter 3, you learned how to create some basic web applications using the Java programming model. We emphasize the term basic here because, when you think about it, these applications were lacking some of the essential features common to production-quality applications: persistence, access to external resources or APIs, and so forth. In this chapter, we'll look to fill in these gaps by exploring the core cloud-based services offered to SAP HCP applications.

6.1   Overview

Given the relatively advanced nature of the material we're about to cover, we decided that a simple technical overview of the cloud services and their corresponding APIs was inadequate for really wrapping your head around what these services can do. Therefore, to better demonstrate these capabilities, we decided to create a fully functional Java web application that approximates something that you might create in the real world. Here, we show you not only how the services are consumed, but also how the services fit into the larger picture of cloud-based application development.

Although this demonstration is purposefully intended to be Java-centric, it's important to keep in mind that the same basic concepts introduced in this chapter generally apply for SAP HANA XS applications, too. Aside from the obvious syntactical differences between Java and server-side JavaScript, we think that you'll find that the usage patterns are basically the same.

Before you begin reading this chapter, we'd encourage you to download the book's source code bundle (*www.sap-press.com/3638*) and import the sample application for this chapter into your local Eclipse instance. Although we'll cover each related topic in depth, we think that you'll benefit greatly by cross-referencing the concepts covered in the book with their application in the sample code.

Part of the criteria for building our demo application was to find an application domain that would give us an opportunity to see how the various cloud-based services are utilized in a real-world setting. After careful consideration, we ended up choosing an application that typically pushes the envelope from a requirements perspective: *incident management*. Here, we're talking about a general-purpose application businesses might use to record incidents that might occur within the company (e.g., an employee slips on a wet floor).

Without digressing too much into domain-specific minutiae, we purposefully designed our incident management application to include the following features:

▶ Support for detailed incident recording so that we can demonstrate complex entity relationships in the Java Persistence API (JPA; see Section 6.2.3)

▶ Support for dynamic queries, which allow us to show how the JDBC API can be used within the Persistence Service (see Section 6.2.4)

▶ Support for loading on-premise data from an SAP Business Suite system using Remote Function Call (RFC) functions (see Section 6.3.3)

▶ A call to a RESTful web service hosted on the Internet (see Section 6.3.4)

▶ An email function that shows how the Connectivity Service can be used to communicate with email providers (see Section 6.3.5)

▶ The upload and retrieval of attachment documents (see Section 6.4)

Along the way, we'll also touch on other features, showing you how the various pieces fit together from an application perspective.

The model diagram contained in Figure 6.1 illustrates the high-level entity model for the incident management application. Here, we have an Incident entity that stores individual incident records and a number of supporting entities that keep track of details such as where the incident occurred, who were the involved persons, and what attachments exist. We'll use this data model as a reference when we look at how to create the application's database schema in Section 6.2.

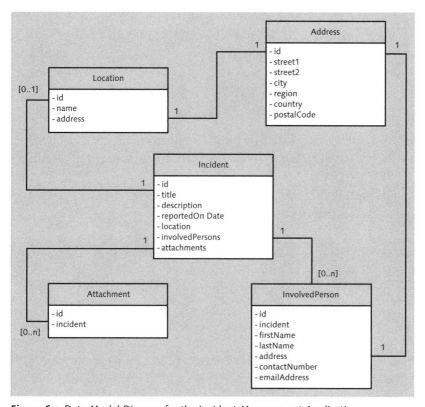

Figure 6.1 Data Model Diagram for the Incident Management Application

For simplicity's sake, we chose to keep the UI layer pretty plain, based on a handful of simple Servlets and JSPs. This design choice was made for illustrative purposes so that we could focus our attention on the application layer. Once you get a feel for how the various cloud-based services contribute to the development of the business layer of a Java web application, we think that you'll find the exercise of replacing this basic UI layer with something more appropriate (such as SAPUI5) to be rather straightforward.

6.2   Using the Persistence Service

Enterprise applications, perhaps more so than any other class of applications, depend heavily on having a reliable and accessible persistence layer. Indeed, the bonds between an enterprise application and its underlying database are usually so tight that most enterprise applications can't even be launched if the database is unavailable. Recognizing this critical requirement, SAP designed SAP HCP from the ground up to include first-class support for persistence in relational databases. This support is provided in the form of a core service called the *Persistence Service*.

6.2.1 Conceptual Overview

In the Java world, the Persistence Service is an abstraction layer built into the Application Runtime Container that provides access to virtualized databases hosted in the cloud. As such, it plays more of a behind-the-scenes role, taking care of low-level technical details such as database backup and recovery, load balancing and scaling, connection management, and so forth.

> **Note**
>
> For SAP HANA XS applications, there's no real need for a separate persistence service, because SAP HANA XS applications naturally have a direct connection to the backend SAP HANA database.

The architectural diagram contained in Figure 6.2 illustrates how the Persistence Service fits into the Application Runtime Container. Here, you can see how database access is abstracted using the industry-standard JPA and JDBC APIs. From a development perspective, this is huge; it allows Java developers who are already comfortable working with these APIs to jump in and begin consuming the Persistence Service right away.

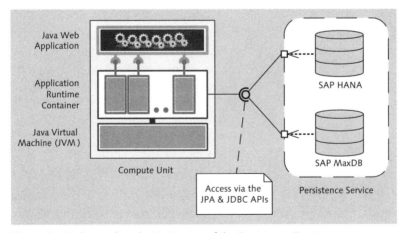

Figure 6.2 Understanding the Positioning of the Persistence Service

As of the time of writing, the Persistence Service supports only two database platforms: the SAP HANA database and SAP MaxDB. Which platform you choose is a matter of preference; you can opt for the raw power of SAP HANA or the economic efficiency of SAP MaxDB. Depending on the complexity of your application, you might decide to mix and match instances. In the next section, we'll see that SAP HCP makes it very easy to set up schemas on either of these database platforms and bind them to new or existing Java applications.

6.2.2 Managing Database Schemas

As we mentioned in the previous section, the Persistence Service provides a layer of abstraction that sits on top of virtualized database instances hosted within the cloud. From a conceptual point of view, the basis of this abstraction is the so-called *database schema*.

Within SAP HCP, *database schemas* are logical databases associated with a particular SAP HCP account. Put a different way, you can think of database schemas as being the cloud-based equivalent to database instances you might stand up for on-premise solutions. As such, setting up database schemas is an important first step for implementing persistence scenarios within SAP HCP.

With that in mind, in this section we'll look at how schemas are created and linked with Java web applications. This will set the stage for exploring persistence scenarios from a programmer's point of view in Section 6.2.3 and Section 6.2.4.

Creating Database Schemas

Within SAP HCP, database schemas are created in one of three ways:

▶ Interactively via the SAP HCP Cockpit

▶ Using the `create-schema` command of the Console Client

▶ Automatically during the application deployment process

In order to understand what's involved in the creation of a database schema, let's take a look at what it takes to create a schema within the SAP HCP Cockpit. As you can see in Figure 6.3, this task can be performed by opening the DATABASES & SCHEMAS tab and clicking on the NEW toolbar button contained within the DATABASES & SCHEMAS table. This will reveal the NEW DATABASE/SCHEMA panel shown in the lower half of the screen in Figure 6.3. Here, there are only two attributes that you must specify:

- ▸ SCHEMA ID
  For the schema ID, you must assign an ID that uniquely identifies the schema within the SAP HCP account. The ID value must start with a letter and can contain letters, numbers, and the special characters . and -.

- ▸ DATABASE SYSTEM
  As you can see in Figure 6.3, the DATABASE SYSTEM attribute allows you to specify which supported database type you wish to utilize in your schema definition: SAP HANA or SAP MaxDB.

Figure 6.3 Creating a Schema in the SAP HCP Cockpit

Noticeably absent in the creation process are some of the typical installation and configuration parameters used to set up a physical database instance: host name, port, disk allocation, and so forth. Within SAP HCP, all of these low-level details are abstracted away by the Persistence Service. This allows you to create a database schema in a matter of seconds as opposed to the days or weeks it might take to get a database instance set up on-premise.

For the most part, the creation of a schema using the Console Client follows what we demonstrated via the SAP HCP Cockpit (e.g., using the `create-schema` command). However, the automatic creation process is a different story entirely. During the application deployment process, the system will automagically create a schema if the application does not have a schema bound to it whenever it is deployed or started for the first time. Although we've sort of glossed over this fallback behavior up until now, you can find evidence of this by looking in the SAP HCP Cockpit, as shown in Figure 6.3. There, you'll find implicitly defined schemas created for the demo applications we created in earlier chapters. The naming convention for these autogenerated schemas is {account}.{application_name}.web.

Although the dynamic schema creation is an innate behavior within SAP HCP itself, you can at least determine which database type you want the system to select for you during the creation process by clicking on the CHANGE button in the toolbar of the DATABASES & SCHEMAS table, as shown in Figure 6.4. Here, you can choose the default database type within the correspondingly named DEFAULT DATABASE dropdown list.

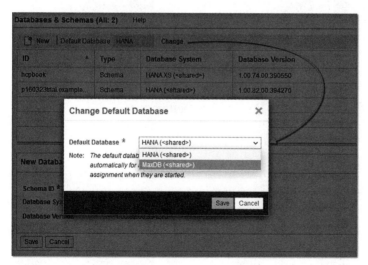

Figure 6.4 Setting the Default Database for Automatic Schema Creation

Binding Schemas with Java Applications

Initially, database schemas are just empty partitions void of any data or table definitions. In order to put a database schema to work, you need to *bind* the schema with a Java web application. This step allows you to utilize the JPA or JDBC APIs to create tables and fill them with data.

Much like the schema creation process, schemas can be bound either explicitly or implicitly. You can explicitly bind a database schema to an application using the SAP HCP Cockpit or the Console Client via the `bind-schema` command. In the SAP HCP Cockpit, you can bind schemas within the same DATABASES & SCHEMAS tab used to create schemas in the first place. Here, simply select the target schema in the DATABASES & SCHEMAS panel at the top of the main content area, and then create a binding by clicking on the NEW BINDING button in the lower-level schema editor panel. This brings up the NEW BINDING dialog box shown in Figure 6.5.

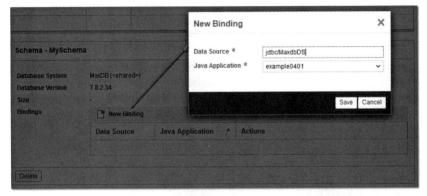

Figure 6.5 Creating Application Bindings in the SAP HCP Cockpit

Here, there are two main attributes that must be configured:

▸ DATA SOURCE
In order for your Java application to be able to address and access a binding, you must assign the binding a data source name. As you can see in Figure 6.5, the naming convention for data sources aligns with the typical JNDI naming convention used to create JDBC data sources—that is, `jdbc/{DataSourceName-InCamelCase}`. In Section 6.2.4, you'll see how this name allows you to define JDBC data sources as resources within your Java web application's web.xml file. The name can also be used to allocate data sources using dependency injections.

▸ JAVA APPLICATION
In the JAVA APPLICATION dropdown list, select the target application that you wish to define the binding for. This list is automatically populated based on the Java applications that are currently deployed within the account (active or otherwise).

In addition to the two main attributes described previously, bindings to productive SAP HANA instances also require that we specify database user credentials so that we can bind to the instance with a user account that has the appropriate permissions to access catalog objects within the target SAP HANA database schema. More information can be found on this step in the online help documentation underneath the section entitled "Binding Productive SAP HANA Instances to Applications."

Schemas are implicitly bound in cases in which a database schema is created implicitly during the application deployment process, as described in the previous section. Here, the autogenerated schema becomes the "default" data source for the application being deployed. To remove this default data source binding, you must open up the target Java application in the SAP HCP Cockpit and select the DATA SOURCE BINDINGS subtab. Within the main content area, you can delete the schema binding by finding the target data source and clicking on the DELETE button, as shown in Figure 6.6. Here, options are also provided to create new bindings or navigate to the corresponding schema definition.

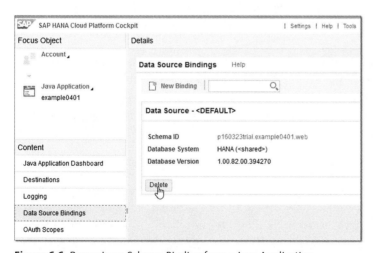

Figure 6.6 Removing a Schema Binding from a Java Application

Working with Multiple Schemas

Most of the time, Java applications are bound to a single database schema. However, that doesn't mean that a given application can't be bound to more than one schema at a time. Indeed, as you can see in Figure 6.7, it's possible for a Java application to be bound to many schemas across database types.

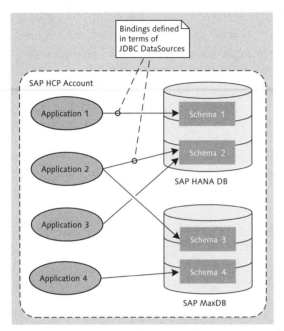

Figure 6.7 Understanding the Relationship between Applications and Schemas

This leads to all kinds of interesting scenarios. For example, if multiple applications happen to share the same set of database entities, then you might define a single schema and point (bind) each of the corresponding applications to it, or you might define one or more schemas to store reusable entities and then create custom ones for specific application requirements.

Sharing Schemas between Accounts

As you can see in Figure 6.7, the relationships between Java applications and database schemas are normally defined within the context of an SAP HCP account. However, we should point out that it's technically possible to share schemas between accounts if you so desire (though as of the time of writing, this feature is only available for database schemas defined using the SAP HANA DB). For more details about the security-related steps required to grant this access, please read through the online help documentation in the section entitled "Accessing Schemas Across Accounts."

How does all this mixing and matching of schemas work at the application level? To some extent, these questions will be answered as we explore the JPA and JDBC APIs in Section 6.2.3 and Section 6.2.4, respectively. However, the short answer here is that you can use the JNDI-based data source names created as part of a schema binding definition in JNDI lookups to fetch the various data sources from the JNDI context of the Java EE application container. This step can be performed declaratively in deployment descriptors or interactively using the JNDI API at runtime.

6.2.3 Working with the Java Persistence API

According to the SAP HCP online help documentation, the JPA is "considered the standard approach for developing applications for the SAP HANA Cloud Platform." Therefore, even if you're a nonconformist and prefer to write your own SQL, it's important to at least have a basic understanding of how persistence scenarios are implemented using the JPA—a concept we'll attempt to tackle in this section. If nothing else, this knowledge will at least help you understand how to troubleshoot JPA-based applications delivered by SAP and/or other developers.

JPA Overview

For developers that may be new to the JPA, it's helpful to take a moment to understand what it is exactly. At a high level, JPA is a Java API that makes it easy for developers to implement *object-relational mapping* (ORM). What is ORM? As the name suggests, ORM is a technique for synchronizing data stored in objects with relational database tables. Here, Java objects and database rows become equivalent representations of the same data, and operations performed on a Java object are automatically reflected in the database and vice versa.

From a development perspective, the advantage of using an ORM tool over performing such translations by hand is that developers don't have to cross over from the object-oriented (OO) world into the procedural world of SQL and relational databases. Besides saving time, this technique also makes the code much more flexible and readable.

Figure 6.8 illustrates the role that the JPA plays in implementing an ORM scenario. Here, we can see that the JPA consists of two parts:

▶ **Interface/API layer**
At the interface layer, the JPA provides Java developers with a generic library that can be used to define, search for, and manipulate entities. The classes and

interfaces that make up this library are contained within the `javax.per-sistence` package, which is available in both the Java SE and Java EE APIs.

▶ **Implementation/provider layer**
The low-level database translations and operations are performed within the implementation (or provider) layer. Here, an external JPA persistence provider delivers the functionality required to synchronize data from relational database tables into Java objects and vice versa.

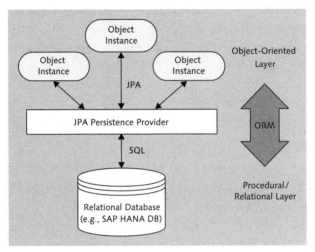

Figure 6.8 Understanding ORM and the Purpose of JPA

From a historical perspective, the current version of the JPA (2.1 as of the time of writing) represents the culmination of countless previous attempts to implement ORM in the Java world. As such, JPA incorporates many of the important lessons learned from previous attempts at ORM standardization, such as EJB 2.x and JDO. The upshot of this from a developer's perspective is that the API is considerably less intrusive than prior approaches. In the upcoming sections, we'll see this characteristic on display quite a bit.

Object-Relational Mapping Concepts in JPA

Within the JPA, the Java classes that correspond with database tables are called *entities*. Here, the instance attributes of entity classes are mapped to table columns, as illustrated in Figure 6.9.

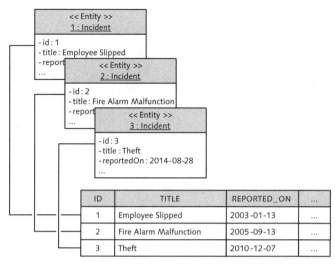

Figure 6.9 Visualizing the ORM of Entities

When it comes to creating entities within the JPA, pretty much any Java class (or *Plain Old Java Object* [POJO]) can be used. This is to say that you don't have to inherit from an API-specific class or even implement an interface with lots of call-back methods you rarely use. With the JPA, you need only inject the class with the `javax.persistence.Entity` annotation, as demonstrated in Listing 6.1.

```
import javax.persistence.Entity; @Entity

public class Incident {
  private String title;
  ...
}
```

Listing 6.1 Defining an Entity Using JPA

Once your entity classes are defined (or identified in the case of preexisting classes), the next step is to map them to relational database tables. For this task, you generally have one of two options. You can describe attribute-to-column mappings using annotations, or you can specify the mapping outside the code using XML deployment descriptors. Both approaches get you to the same place, so which method you choose is largely a matter of preference. For the purposes of this book, though, our focus will be on the annotation-based approach, as it's by far the most popular within the community.

Listing 6.2 demonstrates the annotation-based approach for an entity called `Address`. In this example, you can see how you can use the `javax.persistence.Table` annotation to map the entity to a specific table name (`ADDRESSES`). Similarly, the `javax.persistence.Column` annotation allows you to map instance attributes to specific columns in the target table. For specifying constraints, there are annotations such as the `javax.persistence.Id` annotation, which identifies the `id` attribute as the primary key for your `Address` entity.

```
@Entity @Table(name="ADDRESSES")

public class Address {

    @Id
    @Column(name="ADDRESS_ID")

  private String id;
  private String street;
  private String city;
  ...
}
```

Listing 6.2 Implementing ORM Using Annotations

> ### Understanding the JPA's Use of Convention over Configuration
>
> As you can imagine, the mapping process can become quite tedious whenever you're dealing with complex database schemas containing many entities. Fortunately, the JPA has some built-in intelligence that allows you to skip over the mapping step in many cases. For example, if you look closely at the `Address` entity in Listing 6.2, you'll notice that there are no annotations attached to the `street` and `city` attributes. By omitting these details, we're effectively telling the JPA persistence provider that these attributes match up with table columns having the same name and data type. For newly developed database schemas, you can even go so far as to let the JPA persistence provider create the underlying database tables for you in reference to the mapped entities. This is a classic example of how the JPA uses the "convention over configuration" technique to minimize development time.

In addition to the annotations used to configure individual entities, the JPA also contains a number of annotations that can be used to specify relationships between entities. The code excerpt in Listing 6.3 provides a sample of this with the `Incident` entity class. Here, we're using the `javax.persistence.OneToOne` and `javax.persistence.OneToMany` annotations to describe one-to-one and one-to-many relationships with the `Location` and `InvolvedPerson` entity types, respectively. Using these annotations (and their corresponding attributes), you can specify foreign key relationships, relationship cardinalities, cascading behaviors (e.g., delete all children whenever the parent is deleted), and so forth.

```
public class Incident {
  @Id
  private String id;
  @Basic
  private String title = "";
  ...
  @OneToOne(cascade=CascadeType.PERSIST)
  @JoinColumn(name="LOCATION_ID", referencedColumnName="ID")

  private Location location = new Location();

  @OneToMany(mappedBy="incident", cascade={CascadeType.ALL})

  private List<InvolvedPerson> involvedPersons =
    new ArrayList<InvolvedPerson>();
  ...
}
```

Listing 6.3 Defining Relationships between Entities

After all of the relevant entities are defined, the next step is to group them all together in something the JPA calls a *persistence unit*. Persistence units are defined within a specialized XML file called persistence.xml. This XML file provides the JPA with a logical grouping of entity classes and with lower-level database configuration details.

Listing 6.4 illustrates the basic anatomy of a persistence.xml file. Here, configuration details are organized into specific sections:

1. Within the `<persistence-unit>` element, you must specify the name of your persistence unit and the transaction type. In managed environments such as SAP HCP, the *Java Transaction API* (JTA) option will be used by default.

2. Next, use the `<provider>` element to inform the JPA which persistence provider you plan to use. Here, you must plug in the fully qualified class name of a JPA persistence provider class. In the example shown in Listing 6.4, we've proposed the popular EclipseLink persistence provider. EclipseLink is generally the preferred persistence provider used within SAP HCP.

3. Although not depicted in Listing 6.4, the next element in the persistence schema is the optional `<jta-data-source>` element. Within this element, you

can specify the target JTA data source that you want to use to define your persistence unit. Here, the data source name is defined in terms of the JNDI data source name assigned whenever a schema binding is created. If this element is omitted, then the default data source for the application is used implicitly.

4. The next section is used to identify the entity classes that will be included in the persistence unit. Here, you have the choice of plugging in the fully qualified class names of annotated entity classes or pointing to a separate XML-based ORM mapping file. In the former case, this listing is usually optional, because most persistence providers are able to detect the presence of entity classes automagically.

5. Lastly, within the `<properties>` element, you can specify custom properties that configure the JPA persistence provider, the underlying JDBC-based data source, or both. In the example file contained in Listing 6.4, we've specified a custom property of the EclipseLink persistence provider called `eclipselink.ddl-generation`. This property coerces EclipseLink into automatically creating database tables based on the defined entities contained within the persistence unit at deployment time. As you can imagine, this property comes in quite handy when it comes time to transport applications.

```
<persistence>
  <persistence-unit name="examplePU" transaction-type="JTA">
  <provider>
    <!-- Class name of persistence provider -->
    org.eclipse.persistence.jpa.PersistenceProvider
  </provider>

  <!-- Entity Classes/ORM Mapping Files Section -->
  <class>com.sappress.hcpbook.chp06.Persistence.Incident</class>
  <class>...</class>
  <!--<mapping-file>META-INF/orm.xml</mapping-file>-->

  <!-- Custom Properties Section -->
  <properties>
    <property name="eclipselink.ddl-generation"
              value="create-tables" />
  </properties>
</persistence>
```

Listing 6.4 Defining a Persistence Unit

As you can imagine, this brief introduction barely scratches the surface with regards to the myriad of ORM options available within JPA. For a more comprehensive reference, we highly recommend that you pick up a copy of *Java Persistence with JPA 2.1* (Yang, Outskirts Press, 2013). You can also find details concerning specific annotation types in the Java EE 6 API documentation online at *http://docs.oracle.com/javaee/6/api*.

Manipulating Entities Programmatically

In terms of development effort, mapping entities for use within the JPA is by far the hardest part. Once the entities are defined, JPA makes it easy to access and manipulate entity instances at runtime. Here, you need only obtain a `javax.persistence.EntityManager` instance, and you're off and running.

Within a managed environment like SAP HCP, `EntityManager` instances are normally obtained via dependency injection inside of a stateless session bean, as shown in Listing 6.5. This approach allows you to take advantage of the *container-managed persistence* (CMP) capabilities of the Java EE application container. Here, you allow the application container to manage the lifecycle of the entity manager and the transactions you perform against it.

```
import javax.persistence.EntityManager;
import javax.persistence.PersistenceContext;

@Stateless
@LocalBean
public class IncidentBean {
  @PersistenceContext   private EntityManager em;
  ...
}
```

Listing 6.5 Obtaining a JPA Entity Manager Instance via Injection

Because injection ensures that the `EntityManager` instance is created during the bean-allocation process, you can begin using it to perform CRUD operations in EJB business methods right away. For example, in Listing 6.6, you can see how we're using the `persist()` method of the `EntityManager` interface to create a new incident record. In this scenario, the `Incident` instance (which is basically just a POJO) was instantiated using the `new` operator and populated via a series of setter methods, just like any other Java object. When passed to the `persist()` method, though, the `Incident` instance becomes a *managed entity instance*—at least for the duration of the JTA transaction spawned by the EJB container. After the `addIn-cident()` method completes, the JTA transaction is automatically committed, and the entity instance becomes "detached." This is to say that the `Incident` instance effectively becomes a normal object that can be passed around via different application layers without fear of thread safety or transactional integrity issues.

```
public class IncidentBean {
  public Incident addIncident(Incident incident) {
    return em.persist(incident);
  }
}
```

Listing 6.6 Creating Entity Records Using the JPA

After an entity record is created, you can update it using the `merge()` method of the `EntityManager` interface, as shown in Listing 6.7. As the method name suggests, this method effectively *merges* the state of the passed entity object with the persistence context.

```
public class IncidentBean {
  public Incident updateIncident(Incident incident) {
    return em.merge(incident);
  }
}
```

Listing 6.7 Updating Entity Records Using the JPA

To delete an entity record, you can use the `remove()` method of the `EntityManager` interface. However, as you can see in Listing 6.8, there is a twist to calling this method. Before you can remove a detached entity, you must first merge it into the persistence context. Therefore, first you merge the entity using `merge()`, and then you can simply pass the result on to `remove()`.

```
public class IncidentBean {
  public void removeIncident(Incident incident) {
    em.remove(em.merge(incident));
  }
}
```

Listing 6.8 Deleting Entity Records Using the JPA

When it comes to fetching entity instances, you have one of two options:

▶ If you happen to know the primary key of the target entity record, you can use the `find()` method of the `EntityManager` interface to look it up.

▶ For more advanced lookups, you can utilize a SQL-like query language called *JPA Query Language* (JPQL) to process queries.

Listing 6.9 demonstrates how the `find()` method is used to lookup an entity record by its primary key. Here, you must pass in two parameters: the entity class and the primary key, which can be of any object type in order to support composite keys.

```
public class IncidentBean {
  public Incident getIncidentById(String id) {
    return em.find(Incident.class, id);
  }
}
```

Listing 6.9 Fetching an Entity Record via Its Primary Key

If you have the primary key of an entity in hand, then the `find()` method is by far the easiest and most efficient way to go. More often than not, though, you probably won't know the primary key. This is particularly true of database schemas that utilize the autogeneration of keys. In these scenarios, you can create ad hoc queries using JPQL to find entity records based on alternative selection criteria. For example, in Listing 6.10, you can see how we're using JPQL to search for incident records created from a given date up until now. Here, you can use the `createQuery()` method of the `EntityManager` instance to define the query and then parameterize the query and execute it. Notice that the result set comes back as a series of entities wrapped up in a `java.util.List` collection. Naturally, the entities within the collection are detached and can be passed between different application layers as needed.

```
public class IncidentBean {
  public List<Incident> getIncidentsByDate(Date fromDate) {
    TypedQuery<Incident> query =
      em.createQuery("SELECT i FROM Incident i WHERE " +
                     "i.ReportedOn BETWEEN ?1 and ?2",
                     Incident.class);
    query.setParameter(1, fromDate);
    query.setParameter(2, new Date(System.currentTimeMillis()));
    return query.getResultList();
  }
}
```

Listing 6.10 Using JPQL to Search for Entity Records

For the most part, this is pretty much all there is to JPA development using CMP. Because the EJB container takes care of data source and transaction provisioning, you can simply use the API methods of the `javax.persistence.EntityManager` interface to perform CRUD operations and not concern yourself with low-level details, such as record locking and so on. Of course, if you ever have a need to take control over such details, then there is an alternative to CMP: *application-managed persistence* (AMP).

With AMP, you are responsible for obtaining a data source reference, binding it with an entity manager, and managing transactions. Why would you want to do this? One of the most common reasons developers choose to go with AMP is because their SAP HCP Application Runtime Container is based on the Java Web profile and they don't have access to an EJB container. In this scenario, the model layer for a Servlet/JSP application is based solely on POJOs, and AMP is the only game in town. If you find yourself in this boat, then you can find detailed step-by-step instructions for implementing AMP in the online help documentation, underneath the section entitled "Using Application-Managed Persistence."

Working with JPA in Eclipse

Now that you have a sense for how the JPA works on a conceptual level, let's see how we can apply these concepts to implement persistence scenarios in Java web applications. We'll begin our analysis by looking at what it takes to incorporate CMP into a Dynamic Web project in Eclipse via the following steps:

1. For the most part, the project creation process starts off as per usual. However, at the first project wizard screen (shown in Figure 6.10), you have to make sure that the target runtime points to the default SAP HANA CLOUD setting and that the DYNAMIC WEB MODULE VERSION dropdown list is set at version 3.0. The latter setting ensures that the project is based on the Servlet 3.0 and Java EE 6 standards that are necessary for JPA integration.

Figure 6.10 Creating a JPA-Enabled Project in Eclipse: Part 1

2. After the DYNAMIC WEB MODULE VERSION is selected, modify the project configuration by clicking on the MODIFY... button, shown adjacent to the CONFIGU-
   RATION dropdown list in Figure 6.10. This will open the PROJECT FACETS dialog
   box shown in Figure 6.11. Here, select the JPA checkbox to incorporate the JPA
   facet into your Dynamic Web project.

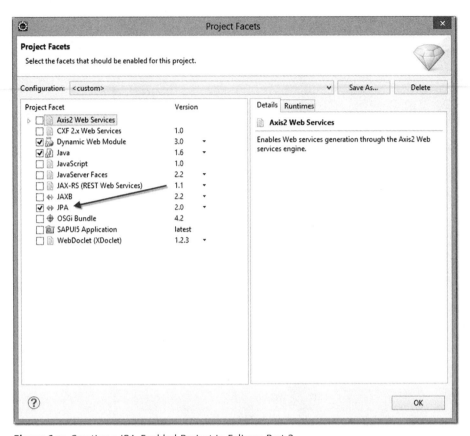

Figure 6.11 Creating a JPA-Enabled Project in Eclipse: Part 2

3. Once the JPA project facet is in place, continue to step through the project creation wizard by clicking on the NEXT > button. For the most part, you can accept the defaults, just like you would for any other Dynamic Web project. However, when you get to the JPA FACET step, there are a few more properties that you'll need to configure (refer to Figure 6.12):

❶ In the PLATFORM dropdown list, choose the appropriate JPA provider for your application. Within the SAP HCP landscape, EclipseLink is the library of choice, so ensure that the default ECLIPSELINK 2.4.x/2.5.x value is selected, as shown in Figure 6.12.

❷ In the JPA IMPLEMENTATION section, select the DISABLE LIBRARY CONFIGURATION option from the dropdown list. This option allows you to explicitly determine which JPA implementation library gets added to the classpath—

something that's needed when deploying to the SAP HCP environment. Here, plug in the proper EclipseLink library file to ensure that proper support is provided for the SAP HANA database.

❸ In the PERSISTENT CLASS MANAGEMENT section, select the DISCOVER ANNOTATED CLASSES AUTOMATICALLY radio button so that Eclipse will automatically detect entity classes defined using annotations.

Figure 6.12 Creating a JPA-Enabled Project in Eclipse: Part 3

Once the JPA facet is fully configured, click on the FINISH button to create the project.

Figure 6.13 shows what the completed project looks like. Here, there are three JPA-related elements that you need to define and configure:

1. Underneath the JPA CONTENT node (shown in ❶), you can find the default persistence.xml file created by the Eclipse project creation wizard. Within this file, you need to configure your JPA persistence unit and any database-specific properties that are relevant for your project.

2. To create the entity classes, simply create your Java source files in the SRC folder (shown in ❷) underneath the JAVA RESOURCES node as per usual. Here, you can also define the stateless session beans that will be used to proxy the JPA persistence access at runtime.

3. Finally, you need to copy the EclipseLink library into the WEBCONTENT/WEB-INF/LIB folder (shown in ❸) so that it will be available on the application classpath at runtime. You can download this library from the EclipseLink downloads page online at *www.eclipse.org/eclipselink/downloads*. From the landing page, you'll want to click on the link to download the installer ZIP file for the target EclipseLink release (2.5.x as of the time of writing). After you unpack the ZIP file, you can find the eclipselink.jar file in the *jlib* directory of the archive bundle. From here, you can copy and paste the file within the PROJECT EXPLORER view in Eclipse or via the file system.

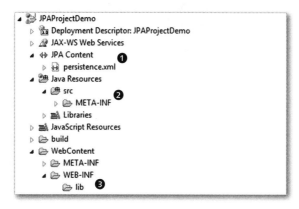

Figure 6.13 Configuring CMP with JPA in a Dynamic Web Project

If you look at the sample project included for this chapter in the book's source code bundle (downloadable from *www.sap-press.com/3638*), you can see how we've built out the JPA-based persistence model for our incident management application within the `com.sappress.hcpbook.chp06.persistence` package. There, you'll find entity classes that match up with the entities we identified in the data model diagram shown in Figure 6.1. We've also defined a couple of stateless session beans that are used to manage the persistence context.

During the deployment process, EclipseLink will automatically create tables in reference to the entities defined within the project. (Note: This generation process only happens the first time the application is deployed. In other words, the database isn't dropped and recreated each time the application is redeployed.) This behavior is defined via the custom EclipseLink schema-generation properties configured within the persistence.xml file (which can be found in the src/META-INF folder of the project). Once the application's deployed, you can launch the app and begin accessing the persistence context right away. As we noted earlier, this is made possible by the dynamic database schema allocation functionality of the Persistence Service.

Exposing JPA Entities as OData Services

In addition to providing the methods we need to perform basic CRUD operations on entities, the `javax.persistence.EntityManager` interface also exposes a method called `getMetamodel()` that can be used to introspect a persistence unit and fetch metadata about its defined entities. Although this sort of functionality may not be interesting to the average developer, it does provide all kinds of interesting capabilities for developers of reusable persistence frameworks.

One such framework that's of keen interest to SAP HCP developers is the *Apache Olingo* framework. This framework provides a collection of Java libraries that can be used to build and consume OData services. Included in this library collection is the Olingo OData JPA Processor library, which makes it easy to expose a JPA model as an OData service.

To demonstrate how to use the Olingo JPA Processor library, let's take a look at how you would create an OData service on top of the incident data model that we've been working on in this section. Here, the steps are as follows:

1. Download the OData Processor library and some open-source companion libraries needed to create the service. The simplest way to get all of the required libraries in one fell swoop is to open the Olingo downloads page at *http://olingo.apache.org/download.html* and download the Olingo OData reference scenario package. Within this package, you should find a file called olingo-odata2-jpa-processor-ref-web-2.x.x.war. If you unpack the lib folder in this WAR file, you'll find all of the JAR files you need to get started. For the purposes of this demonstration, simply copy these files over into the /WEB-INF/lib/folder of your web project.

2. Once all of the relevant libraries are on the classpath, the next step is to create a custom class that inherits from the `org.apache.olingo.odata2.jpa.processor.api.ODataJPAServiceFactory` class. Here, you need to override the

initializeODataJPAContext() method that Olingo uses to link with the target JPA persistence unit. You can see how we implemented this class in the sample application by looking at the ODataServiceFactory class of the com.sappress.hcpbook.chp06.persistence package. Here, the only real trick was to figure out how to supply the ODataJPAContext instance with a javax.persistence.EntityManagerFactory instance. Because the sample application uses CMP, we had to introduce a JPAUtilities class to store an EntityManagerFactory loaded from a faceless Servlet called BootstrapServlet that gets loaded at startup.

3. Once you define the OData service factory, you have everything you need to set up the service. For this final task, simply open up the web.xml file and configure a Servlet class that was included in the libraries that were copied over in step 1: org.apache.cxf.jaxrs.servlet.CXFNonSpringJaxrsServlet. Listing 6.11 contains an excerpt of the web.xml file contained within the sample application. With minimal configuration, Olingo has everything it needs to bootstrap the service.

```
<web-app>
  ...
  <servlet>
    <servlet-name>IncidentODataProviderServlet</servlet-name>
    <servlet-class>
      org.apache.cxf.jaxrs.servlet.CXFNonSpringJaxrsServlet
    </servlet-class>
    <init-param>
      <param-name>javax.ws.rs.Application</param-name>
      <param-value>
        org.apache.olingo.odata2.core.rest.app.ODataApplication
      </param-value>
    </init-param>
    <init-param>
      <param-name>
        org.apache.olingo.odata2.service.factory
      </param-name>
      <param-value>
        com.sappress.hcpbook.chp06.persistence.ODataServiceFactory
      </param-value>
    </init-param>
    <load-on-startup>2</load-on-startup>
  </servlet>
  ...
  <servlet-mapping>
    <servlet-name>IncidentODataProviderServlet</servlet-name>
    <url-pattern>/IncidentProcessing.svc/*</url-pattern>
```

```
        </servlet-mapping>
        ...
    </web-app>
```

Listing 6.11 Exposing an OData Service Using Apache Olingo

To test the finished product, open the sample application, and click on the TEST ODATA SERVICE link shown in Figure 6.14. This will open the OData service document. From here, you can test the service from within your web browser or via any number of freeware OData client and test tools available online.

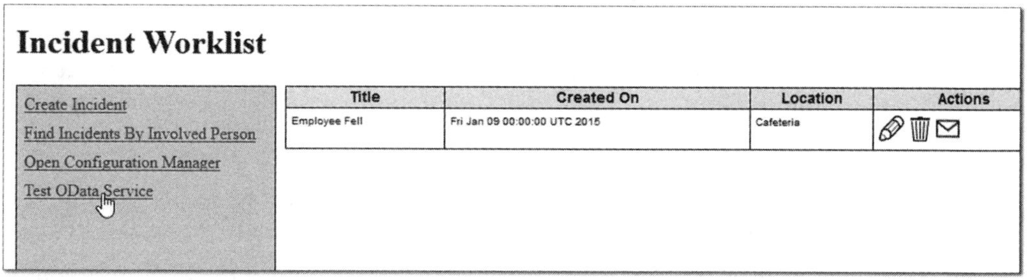

Figure 6.14 Testing the Incident OData Service

> **Limitations of the Apache Olingo Type System**
>
> As of the time of writing, the Apache Olingo project is working on providing support for the OData 4.0 standard. During this transition period, we should point out that there are certain limitations with the Olingo type system that you should be aware of. In general, the current version of the library does not support all of the various data types that you can use to define entity attributes in the JPA. This is particularly the case with primitive types or temporal types, such as the java.sql.Date or `java.sql.Time` types.

6.2.4 Working with Java Database Connectivity

Despite its ease of use, the JPA approach to persistence does have a certain amount of overhead associated with it from a technical point of view. For application scenarios focused on processing a handful of objects at a time, this tiny amount of bloat may go unnoticed. On the other hand, if you're building reporting or analytics applications, even the tiniest bit of overhead can have significant impacts on application performance.

For these reasons, and others, SAP allows you to take more direct control over the data access process using the familiar *Java Database Connectivity* (JDBC) API. In this section, we'll learn how to incorporate JDBC-based persistence scenarios into Java web applications.

Getting Started with JDBC

If you haven't worked with JDBC before, then a brief introduction is in order. Logistically, the core classes and interfaces that make up the JDBC API are contained within the `java.sql` and `javax.sql` packages of the Java SE library. As you browse through these packages, you'll notice that roughly 90% of the API is defined using interfaces. This design choice was made in order to separate the core JDBC interface from implementation details specific to various database vendors (e.g., Oracle vs. Microsoft SQL Server). The lower-level implementation details are provided in the form of a vendor-specific JDBC driver library packaged as one or more JAR files.

Within a managed environment such as SAP HCP, database connections are abstracted in the form of a `javax.sql.DataSource` object, which is normally allocated using injection techniques within a Servlet or EJB component. From here, you can obtain a database connection, prepare a statement, and execute your queries or updates in procedural fashion.

> **Note**
>
> The alternative here would be to manually lookup the data source within the Java EE container's JNDI context using the data source name provided as part of the schema binding definition, as described in Section 6.2.2.

To demonstrate how this works, let's look at how we implemented a slightly more advanced query from within our incident management application. Here, within our `IncidentBean` EJB façade, we defined a business method called `getIncidentsByInvolvedPerson()`. This method uses the JDBC API to build a dynamic query that incorporates fuzzy search logic to make it easier to search for incidents by involved persons. An excerpt of this method is contained within Listing 6.12.

```
@Stateless
@LocalBean
public class IncidentBean {
    @Resource(mappedName="java:comp/env/jdbc/DefaultDB")
    private javax.sql.DataSource dataSource;
    ...
    public List<Incident> getIncidentsByInvolvedPerson(
```

```
      String firstName, String lastName)
  throws java.sql.SQLException
{
  java.sql.Connection conn = null;
  List<Incident> incidents = new ArrayList<Incident>();

  try
  {
    // Build the dynamic SQL query to fetch the incidents:
    StringBuffer query = new StringBuffer();
    String fname = ((firstName == null) ? "" :
      firstName.replaceAll("\\*", "%"));
    String lname = ((firstName == null) ? "" :
      lastName.replaceAll("\\*", "%"));
    ...
    query.append(
      "SELECT i.id, i.title, i.reportedon, i.reportedat " +
        "FROM incident AS i INNER JOIN involvedperson AS p ");
    query.append("ON i.id = p.incident_id ");
    ...

    // Create a database connection:
    conn = dataSource.getConnection();

    // Create a statement object to encapsulate the query:
    PreparedStatement ps =
      conn.prepareStatement(query.toString());

    if (! fname.equals("")) {
      ps.setString(1, fname);
    if (! lname.equals(""))
        ps.setString(2, lname);
    }
    else {
      if (! lname.equals(""))
        ps.setString(1, lname);
    }

    // Execute the query:
    ResultSet rs = ps.executeQuery();

    // Copy the results into DTOs to be transferred to
    // the frontend:
    while (rs.next()) {
      Incident incident = new Incident();
      incident.setId(rs.getString(1));
      incident.setTitle(rs.getString(2));
      incident.setReportedOn(rs.getDate(3));
      incidents.add(incident);
    }
```

```
      }
      finally
      {
        // Always remember to release the connection to
        // conserve resources!!!
        if (conn != null) {
          try { conn.close(); } catch (SQLException se) {}
        }
      }
      return incidents;
    }
    ...
}
```

Listing 6.12 Consuming the Persistence Service Using the JDBC API

As you can see in Listing 6.12, the JDBC approach to database access is highly procedural:

1. Use the `getConnection()` method of the injected `javax.sql.DataSource` to create or obtain a database connection. In a managed environment like SAP HCP, connections are pooled in such a way that the performance overhead with this step is minimized.

2. Create an instance of the `java.sql.Statement` interface, which is the rough JDBC equivalent of a database command-line prompt. In the code excerpt contained in Listing 6.12, we used the `java.sql.PreparedStatement` subinterface, because it provides for optimizations such as statement caching and precompilation. As the basis for our `Statement`, we provided a dynamically generated SQL `SELECT` statement.

3. To process the query, we used the `executeQuery()` method of the `java.sql.Statement` interface. If you look at the JavaDoc for this interface, you can find a number of other `execute()` methods that can be used to process DML statements and so on.

4. The result of the query is returned in the form of a `java.sql.ResultSet` object. This object provides a cursor that can be used to scroll through the data. Here, you can access selected columns using the plethora of getter methods included within the interface definition.

5. Once you're done with your queries, it's important to close out the connection using the `close()` method of the `java.sql.Connection` handle. Note that within a managed environment like SAP HCP, this method name is a bit of a

misnomer, in that you're not actually closing the connection. Instead, you're basically just returning the connection instance to the connection pool.

Most JDBC access scenarios look rather similar to the one depicted in Listing 6.12. Of course, depending on your scenario, you might batch multiple statements together within a logical unit of work (LUW), but the same general process flow will apply regardless.

Configuring Data Sources

In Section 6.2.2, we described how it's technically possible for a given Java application to reference multiple database schemas. Knowing what you now know about JDBC `DataSource` objects, you can probably guess how this is achieved at the application level. Here, you use the JNDI-based data source names associated with the various schema bindings as a key for fetching the corresponding `javax.sql.Data-Source` objects bound within the JNDI context of the Java EE container.

To put all this into perspective, let's consider a Java application that uses two data sources that are bound as `jdbc/MainDS` and `jdbc/AltDS`, respectively. In order to reference these data sources from within your Java application, you must use the `<resource-ref>` element of the web.xml file to define resource references to the schema bindings created using the same JNDI data source names (see Listing 6.13).

```
<web-app>
  ...
  <resource-ref>
    <res-ref-name>jdbc/MainDS</res-ref-name>
    <res-type>javax.sql.DataSource</res-type>
  </resource-ref>
  <resource-ref>
    <res-ref-name>jdbc/AltDS</res-ref-name>
    <res-type>javax.sql.DataSource</res-type>
  </resource-ref>
</web-app>
```
Listing 6.13 Defining JDBC Data Source References in the web.xml File

Once the resource references are defined within the web.xml file, you can use them to look up the corresponding data sources in one of two ways: manually using the JNDI API or via injection using the `javax.annotation.Resource` annotation. Both techniques are demonstrated in the code excerpt contained in Listing 6.14.

```
public class DataSourceTest extends HttpServlet {
  private DataSource mainDataSource;

  @Resource(name="jdbc/AltDS")
  private DataSource altDataSource;

  private void initMainDataSource()
  {
    try
    {
      javax.naming.InitialContext ctx =
        new javax.naming.InitialContext();

      mainDataSource = (DataSource)
        ctx.lookup("java:comp/env/jdbc/MainDS");
    }
    catch (Exception ex)
    {
    }
  }
  ...
}
```

Listing 6.14 Working with Multiple Data Sources in a Java Web Application

Advantages of Using JDBC vs. JPA

When compared to the ease of use afforded by the JPA, there's really no getting around the fact that JDBC-based persistence scenarios are tedious to implement. Having said that, though, there are many reasons that it might make sense to utilize a JDBC approach to persistence. Some of these reasons include the following:

▶ **Minimized resource utilization**
  In many situations, the JPA pulls back more information from the database than you might need. For example, in the simple query scenario demonstrated in this section, we only pulled back selected columns from the Incident and Involved-Person entities. This use of SQL projection reduced the memory footprint of the query results considerably. When you imagine a productive system with thousands of records, you can see that this reduction in memory footprint can have significant impacts on application performance. Suffice to say that there are times when you really want to exert control over what gets queried and when.

▶ **Compatibility with legacy or third-party applications/frameworks**
Because SAP HCP is fully Java EE compliant, there may be cases in which you want to deploy preexisting applications or frameworks based on JDBC. Here, there's no need to reinvent the wheel with JPA.

▶ **Access to database-specific features**
In cases in which performance is critical, it might make sense to use JDBC as a mechanism for implementing *database pushdown* techniques. Here, for example, you might utilize the SQLScript language of the SAP HANA database to create stored procedures that bundle together related database operations in close proximity to the data. You can then access these stored procedures using the JDBC API at runtime to minimize the amount of data exchanged over the network and take advantage of the raw calculation power of the SAP HANA database engines.

Of course, there's no reason why you can't mix and match techniques as needed. For example, you can use the JPA for defining your entity model and handling basic CRUD operations and then pick and choose the places in which you might want to utilize the JDBC API to improve performance.

6.2.5 Database Management Concepts

As you've seen throughout the course of this section, the Persistence Service takes care of most of the low-level database management tasks required for on-premise database instances. However, although you needn't worry about performing backups or (re)allocating disk space, there are certain administrative tasks that you need to perform from time to time. Therefore, in this section you'll learn how to perform some common administrative tasks for database schemas hosted in the cloud.

Accessing Database Schemas Remotely

For security reasons, database instances in the cloud are protected by a network firewall. This firewall is designed to prevent unauthorized access to sensitive data from the outside world. Although all this is of no concern to cloud-based applications running inside the firewall, it does present a bit of a challenge in situations in which you have legitimate need to access database instances remotely. Fortunately, SAP HCP makes it possible to establish secure database tunnels so that you can connect to remote database instances using familiar database tools provided in Eclipse and SAP HANA Studio.

If the target database schema is running on the SAP HANA database, then the simplest way to connect to the instance is to use the SAP HANA ADMINISTRATION CONSOLE perspective of SAP HANA Studio to create a cloud system connection. If you have the SAP HANA Tools plug-ins installed in your local Eclipse instance, then this connection can be established as follows:

1. Open the SAP HANA ADMINISTRATION CONSOLE perspective in Eclipse.

2. In the SYSTEMS view on the left-hand side of the page, right-click somewhere in the whitespace and choose the ADD CLOUD SYSTEM... menu option (Figure 6.15).

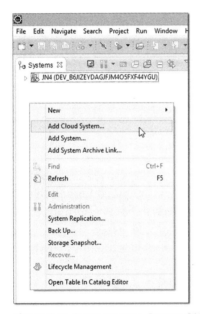

Figure 6.15 Connecting to a Remote SAP HANA Database Instance: Part 1

3. This will open the ADD SAP HANA CLOUD PLATFORM SYSTEM dialog box shown in Figure 6.16. Within this dialog box, specify the target landscape host (e.g., enter "hanatrial.ondemand.com" for trial accounts), the SAP HCP account name, and logon credentials to establish the connection. Click on the NEXT > button to continue.

Figure 6.16 Connecting to a Remote SAP HANA Database Instance: Part 2

4. After successfully authenticating, the next step will open a screen in which you can select the target database instance you wish to connect to. Here, the TRIAL INSTANCES or PRODUCTION INSTANCES dropdown lists will be filled with database schemas created under the selected SAP HCP account. Once you identify the target instance, click on the FINISH button to confirm your selection.

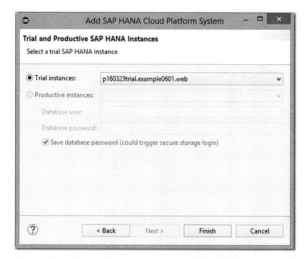

Figure 6.17 Connecting to a Remote SAP HANA Database Instance: Part 3

Once a system connection is established, you can use the built-in features of the SAP HANA Tools to perform all kinds of useful operations. For example, in Figure 6.18, you can see the context menu options associated with the INCIDENTS table that was created in reference to the Incidents entity introduced in Section 6.2.3. Here, options are provided to view and/or update the table definition, browse the table's content, and even perform imports or exports of the table data. If you prefer to access this data from an SQL command prompt, then you can open one by clicking on the SQL button in the SYSTEMS view toolbar (see Figure 6.18).

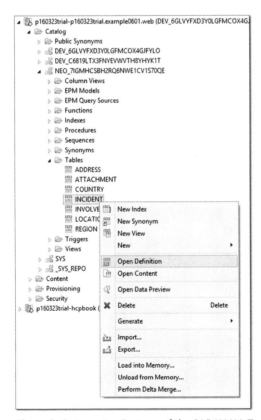

Figure 6.18 Accessing Features of the SAP HANA Tools in Eclipse

For general-purpose access to cloud-based database instances (including those based on SAP MaxDB), you can use the `open-db-tunnel` command of the Console Client to open a database tunnel on your local host. Listing 6.15 demonstrates the syntax required to run this command.

```
neo open-db-tunnel -h <host> -u <user> -a <account> --id <schema>
```
Listing 6.15 Opening a Database Tunnel Using the Console Client

Once the tunnel is opened, the Console Client will display an output window like the one shown in Figure 6.19. Here, you are provided with JDBC connection details that can be used to establish connections in JDBC-based tools or stand-alone load or test programs written in Java. While this session is open, you can use the database tunnel to connect to the target database schema.

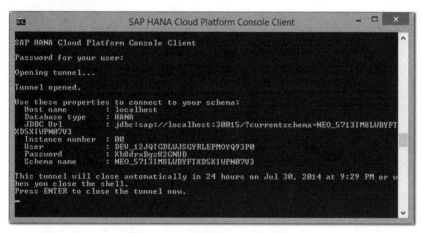

Figure 6.19 Creating a Database Tunnel Using the Console Client

To demonstrate how to utilize database tunnel connections for administrative purposes, let's take a look at how to set up a connection using the Eclipse *Data Tools Platform* (DTP). Here, the steps are as follows:

1. Open the DATA SOURCE EXPLORER view, as shown in Figure 6.20. This view is provided in conjunction with the Eclipse DTP and should be available by default in your Eclipse environment.

2. Within the DATA SOURCE EXPLORER view, create a new connection by right-clicking on the DATABASE CONNECTIONS node and choosing the NEW... menu option (Figure 6.21).

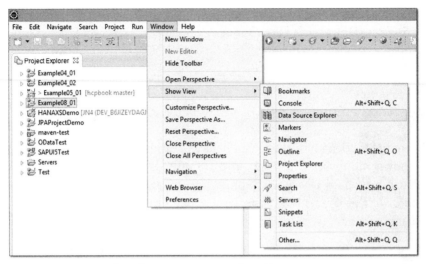

Figure 6.20 Opening the Eclipse Data Source Explorer View

Figure 6.21 Opening a Connection in the Data Source Explorer: Part 1

3. This will open the NEW CONNECTION PROFILE dialog box shown in Figure 6.22. Within this dialog box, there are a series of preconfigured connection profiles for popular databases, such as Oracle, IBM DB2, and so forth. In this case, we're primarily interested in the MAXDB option for connecting to SAP MaxDB instances and the GENERIC JDBC profile, which can be used to establish connections to SAP HANA instances. Aside from the profile selection, you must also specify a connection name and an optional description. After these parameters are set, click on the NEXT > button to proceed.

4. At the next screen (shown in Figure 6.23), choose the target JDBC driver, and plug in the connection parameters from the Console Client output window shown in Figure 6.19.

Figure 6.22 Opening a Connection in the Data Source Explorer: Part 2

Figure 6.23 Opening a Connection in the Data Source Explorer: Part 3

5. Once the parameters are set, click on the FINISH button to establish the connection.

Figure 6.24 shows what an established connection looks like in the Data Source Explorer view. Within this view, you can drill into the appropriate schemas and access catalog objects, as shown in Figure 6.25. The context menu options provided here allow you to perform similar operations to those demonstrated for the SAP HANA Tools earlier in this section.

Figure 6.24 Utilizing the Eclipse DTP to Access an SAP HANA Instance: Part 1

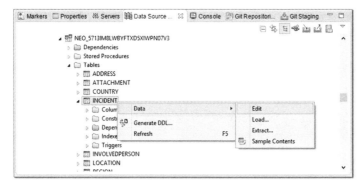

Figure 6.25 Utilizing the Eclipse DTP to Access an SAP HANA Instance: Part 2

Running SQL Traces

Whether you implement persistence scenarios using JPA, JDBC, or a combination of the two, the end result from a runtime perspective is that a series of SQL commands will be issued against the database instance(s) your Java applications are bound to. Sometimes, if you're not careful, the performance of these SQL commands at runtime may not be what you expect. For example, a query that performs well in a development environment might end up running rather poorly in production if the size of the target table grows exponentially. In these circumstances, it's important to be able to trace the performance of SQL commands so that you can identify performance bottlenecks.

Within the SAP HCP Cockpit, you can turn on a SQL trace via the logger configuration screens of the JAVA APPLICATION DASHBOARD, as described in Section 4.2.4 of Chapter 4. Here, the target logger is com.sap.core.persistence.sql.trace, as shown in Figure 6.26. By setting the LOG LEVEL to DEBUG or higher, you can immediately turn on the SQL trace for the selected Java application. Similarly, you can turn the SQL trace off by dialing the logging level back.

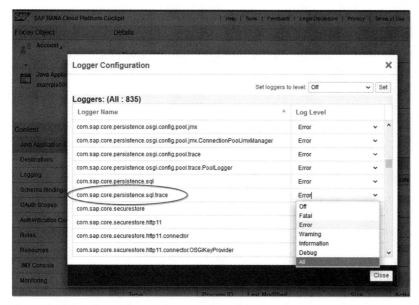

Figure 6.26 Turning on the SQL Trace in the SAP HCP Cockpit

Once the SQL trace is turned on, the default trace log will be filled with detailed information about JDBC data source or connection allocation and statement processing metrics. For example, in Figure 6.27, you can see how the trace shows a SQL command issued from within the incident management application. In addition to showing the actual SQL statement executed, the trace will also show the time it took the command to complete, the number of bytes transferred across the network, and so forth.

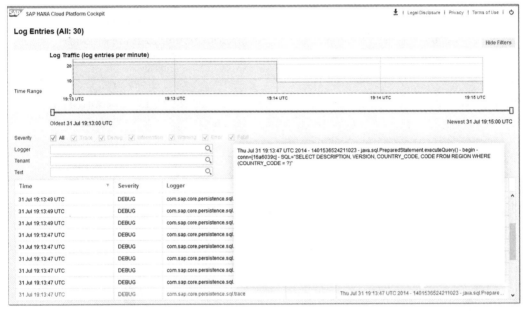

Figure 6.27 Browsing through SQL Trace Records in the Default Trace File

From a performance tracing or debugging perspective, one of the nice things about the SQL trace is that you can turn it on for any application at pretty much any time. This can be particularly handy in situations in which you might be troubleshooting third-party applications about which you know nothing. Here, if nothing else, you can at least determine which tables or queries are causing issues and backtrack from there.

Defining a Local Testing Environment Using Apache Derby

Most developers working in the SAP HCP environment prefer to carry out the early rounds of the code-test-repeat development cycle using the local runtime environment. Although this is certainly understandable, it does present a bit of a logistical challenge when implementing persistence scenarios. After all, it's not as if you can just quickly stand up an SAP HANA instance on your laptop. Instead, when working with the local runtime environment, you have to make do with something smaller and more lightweight: *Apache Derby*.

Apache Derby is a lightweight, open-source RDBMS written using pure Java. It's embedded by default in the SAP HCP local runtime environment, so there's nothing you have to do to install it. Indeed, if your application scenario is simple and you only use the default data source for persistence using JPA/JDBC, then Apache Derby can be used pretty much out of the box. However, if you plan on testing with multiple data sources and the like, then additional configuration is required.

This configuration can be carried out within the Eclipse IDE by opening up the SAP HCP local runtime configuration in the PROJECT EXPLORER view, shown in Figure 6.28. Within the CONFIG_MASTER • CONNECTION_DATA folders, the target configuration file is called CONNECTION.PROPERTIES. By default, this properties file will include configuration settings for a "demo" data source. You can use this template to create additional data sources as needed. The new data sources will show up after the server is restarted. From an application perspective, you can bind the new data sources as per usual.

> **Note**
>
> Technically speaking, it's also possible to configure data sources against other RDBMSs here (e.g., a local instance of MySQL). However, this approach is generally unsupported by SAP, so proceed at your own risk.

Figure 6.28 Configuring Data Sources for Use with Apache Derby

6.3   Using the Connectivity Service

Much like the SAP Composition Environment (CE) before it, SAP HCP is well-suited to building *composite applications* (also known as *XApps* or *mashups*) within the enterprise. Here, you can weave Internet-based services together with services hosted on-premise to create powerful application scenarios that may not have been previously possible for many organizations. From a technical perspective, the engine that makes all this possible within SAP HCP is the *Connectivity Service*.

In this section, we'll investigate the Connectivity Service and explain how it can be used to connect Java-based web applications to services hosted in different network segments using various application protocols. Along the way, you'll also have an opportunity to familiarize yourself with the SAP HANA Cloud Connector, which is used to establish a secure link between Java-based web applications and on-premise systems.

6.3.1   Conceptual Overview

What is the Connectivity Service? Much like the Persistence Service described in Section 6.2, the Connectivity Service is a built-in service of SAP HCP that provides web applications with the ability to connect to external Internet-based services and/or on-premise systems in a secure and reliable manner. Such connections are based on standardized protocols such as HTTP, RFC, SMTP, and POP3/IMAP.

Figure 6.29 illustrates the positioning of the Connectivity Service from the perspective of a Java web application running within an SAP HCP account. Here, Java applications can tap into the functionality of the Connectivity Service using an API provided with the SAP HCP SDK called the *Connectivity and Destination API*. (You can review the JavaDocs for this API online at *https://help.hana.onde-mand.com/javadoc/index.html*.) This API makes it possible to create connections in an abstract manner based on a Connectivity Service–specific configuration object called a *destination*. Within a destination definition, you can specify all of the parameters needed to establish a connection to an Internet-based or on-premise service (e.g., target host/port, security credentials, etc.). At runtime, the Connectivity Service will use these connection details to create a connection object and hand it back to the application. From here, the Java application can utilize the connection to access remote services, send or retrieve email messages, and so forth, just as it would if it were running on-premise. Behind the scenes, the Connectivity Service will step in as needed to broker connection requests, implement secure tunneling, and generally fill in the low-level technical requirements needed to ensure a seamless communication flow.

Figure 6.29 Understanding the Positioning of the Connectivity Service

Looking closely at Figure 6.29, you can see that calls to on-premise systems are brokered through a separate software component called the *SAP HANA Cloud Connector*. This software component establishes a secure SSL VPN tunnel between on-premise systems and an SAP HCP instance running in the cloud. Behind the scenes, the Connectivity Service works very closely with the Cloud Connector to establish connections to on-premise systems. From an application perspective, this is all conveniently abstracted behind the aforementioned Connectivity and Destination API.

In the upcoming sections, you'll see how these communication channels are established from a technical perspective. However, before we move on, we thought it might be useful to demonstrate some application scenarios that might call for the use of the Connectivity Service. We've highlighted some of the more common scenarios in Table 6.1. As you browse through this list, we should also point out that the Connectivity Service is not intended to be used as a general-purpose middleware. Instead, it's intended to be used for smaller, ad hoc service calls incorporated into composite applications and the like. For large-scale data loads and more advanced integration scenarios, we'd recommend that you take a look at *SAP HANA Cloud Integration* (SAP HCI), which is designed to handle such requirements. SAP HCI is covered in Chapter 10.

Service Location	Protocol	Description
Internet	HTTP(s)	Call a web service hosted by a third-party vendor on the Internet. An example of this is a REST-based service call to services provided by Yahoo!, Google, and others.
On-premise	HTTP	Call web services hosted on systems available on-premise. In SAP application scenarios, such services are often brokered through a product called *SAP Gateway*, which makes it easy to expose preexisting ABAP APIs as RESTful web services. Of course, use of SAP Gateway is not a hard requirement; it's possible to consume standalone RESTful services, SOAP-based services, and even services exposed on non-SAP systems.
On-premise	RFC	In this scenario, you use the Connectivity Service to invoke remote-enabled function modules on ABAP systems using the RFC protocol. Here, you can call custom RFC functions or preexisting RFCs/BAPIs as needed.
Internet	SMTP	In this scenario, you can use the Connectivity Service to connect to an external mail server using the SMTP protocol and send email messages.
Internet	POP3/ IMAP	In this scenario, you can use the Connectivity Service to connect to a mail server using either the POP3 or IMAP protocols to fetch email messages and process them. This feature could be used to implement a form of the *publish-subscribe* messaging pattern.

Table 6.1 Usage Scenarios for the Connectivity Service

6.3.2 Working with Destinations

The primary function of the Connectivity Service is to abstract low-level communication details from applications so that service calls are easier to implement. One of the ways the Connectivity Service pulls this off is in its use of *destinations*.

As we noted in the previous section, destinations provide a layer of indirection between an application and an external application or service. This layer of indirection makes it easier for the application to focus on invoking a service without having to worry about where the service resides (e.g., on-premise vs. the Internet).

Creating Destinations

From a configuration perspective, destinations can be established on several different levels:

- **Application level**
  If you need to establish a connection that's unique to a particular application, then you can configure a destination directly within the application definition.

- **Customer account level**
  If a connection might be reused across multiple applications, then you can configure a reusable destination at the customer account level (i.e., at the root of the SAP HCP Cockpit).

- **Subscription level**
  This level is defined in situations in which application subscription scenarios are configured, a topic that's beyond the scope of this book.

For the most part, the definition process is the same regardless of the level at which you choose to define your destination. The primary difference lies in where you go to define the destination (e.g., from the account dashboard or the application dashboard). If you're defining a destination at the application level, then you have the option of defining the destination directly within the Eclipse IDE. Otherwise, you can use the SAP HCP Cockpit or Console Client tools to configure destinations at all three levels.

Because destinations are normally managed within the SAP HCP Cockpit, we'll demonstrate the destination creation process within this tool. Here, you can access the destination editor screen in one of two ways:

- At the customer account level, you can access the editor by clicking on the DESTINATIONS link in the CONTENT panel (Figure 6.30).

- At the application level, you can access the editor by opening the target Java application and choosing the DESTINATIONS link from the CONTENT panel (Figure 6.31).

Figure 6.30 Configuring Destinations at the Customer Account Level

Figure 6.31 Configuring Destinations at the Application Level

In both cases, you end up at an editor screen containing a table control that allows you to create new destinations or edit, clone, or delete existing ones. To create a new destination, you can either create the destination from scratch by clicking on the NEW DESTINATION button or you can import a previously configured destination from a file using the IMPORT FROM FILE button. The latter scenario can be used to transport destinations between accounts using export/import semantics.

Figure 6.32 shows what the editor screen looks like when you click on the NEW DESTINATION button. Here, you're presented with a screen in which you must specify a unique name for the destination, the protocol type (e.g., HTTP, RFC, or MAIL), and the connection-specific parameters needed to connect to the target endpoint (e.g., host name/URL, port, security credentials, and so forth). If you're familiar with these application protocols, then most of the parameters will feel quite intuitive. However, if you need further clarification about a specific parameter type, you can find the documentation you're looking for in the SAP HCP Developer's Guide in the "Consuming the Connectivity Service" section and "Destinations" subsection.

Figure 6.32 Creating a Destination in the SAP HCP Cockpit

Depending on the nature of the authentication requirements, you also have the option of using the CERTIFICATES button to upload client certificates in the form of JKS files. The uploaded certificates can then be used in conjunction with the AUTHENTICATION property to define client certificate authentication, for example.

Given the myriad of connection options and scenarios supported by the Connectivity Service, it's simply not feasible to go over each and every configuration option here. However, in the upcoming case study sections, we'll take a look at some typical configuration scenarios so that you can see how the corresponding destinations are established at configuration time.

Accessing Destinations from Java Applications

Once a destination object is created, its connection details are encapsulated in an object that can be referenced using name-based lookup semantics at runtime (e.g., using JNDI for HTTP and Mail destinations and the `JCoDestinationManager` library for RFC destinations). From an application perspective, this means that you can use typical resource allocation techniques (such as JNDI lookups and resource injection) to allocate connection objects.

The code excerpt in Listing 6.16 demonstrates how the resource injection technique is used to create a `com.sap.core.connectivity.api.http.HttpDestination` object based on an HTTP destination called `GoogleGeocodeDest`. At runtime, whenever the `HttpDestination` object is injected, all of the configuration settings contained within the HTTP destination definition will be copied over with it. From here, you can use the `createHttpClient()` method to create an HTTP client request and invoke the target service.

```
@Stateless
@LocalBean
public class IncidentBean
{
    ...
    @Resource(mappedName="GoogleGeocodeDest")
    private HttpDestination geocodeDestination;
    ...
}
```

Listing 6.16 Using Resource Injection to Create an HTTP Destination

One of the really nice things about the Connectivity and Destination API is that it only introduces proprietary elements where necessary. For example, in the code excerpt in Listing 6.16, the `com.sap.core.connectivity.api` library is only there to provide a convenient way of accessing HTTP connection details, because this is not standardized within the Java SE or EE APIs. However, the connection request that's passed back is based on the HTTP libraries bundled with the Apache Http-Components project (formerly known as Apache Commons HttpClient). Therefore, if you've already built a RESTful client on top of the Apache library, you can easily incorporate it here without having to work through a lot of proprietary restrictions. In the case of RFC or Mail destinations, there's even less indirection, because you can use the destinations to allocate `com.sap.conn.jco.JCoDestina-`

`tionManager` and `javax.mail.Session` objects directly. From here on out, it's business as usual, using the SAP Java Connector (JCo) and `javax.mail` libraries.

6.3.3 Case Study: Calling On-Premise RFC Functions

Now that you've seen how the Connectivity Service is positioned from a conceptual point of view, let's switch gears and look at some practical examples of how it's used in Java applications. In our first demonstration, you'll see how to call RFC functions on an on-premise AS ABAP system.

Design Approach and Initial Setup

Figure 6.33 illustrates the mechanics of the RFC call that you'll be building. There are several steps required to implement the integration scenario:

1. First, you need to install the SAP HANA Cloud Connector somewhere on-premise. For the purposes of this demonstration, we'll assume that the SAP HANA Cloud Connector is installed on the same application server host as the AS ABAP system that we'll be calling the RFC function on.

2. Next, establish an SSL VPN tunnel between the SAP HANA Cloud Connector and the target SAP HCP account you wish to integrate with.

3. After the connection is established, the next step is to create a system mapping to the backend AS ABAP system and configure access control. Here, you must declare the RFC functions that you wish to expose to the target SAP HCP instance.

4. Finally, use the virtual system mapping (shown in ❸) as the basis for creating an RFC destination in the SAP HCP Cockpit. Within the application code, you can use this destination to obtain a JCo connection and invoke the target RFC functions.

5. To get things started, you must first install the SAP HANA Cloud Connector. Although this is a step typically performed by system administrator types, it's fairly easy to set up locally if you want to give it a try using a local SAP instance. Here, you basically just need to download the installation file for your OS via *https://tools.hana.ondemand.com/#cloud* and then either unpack the distribution or run the setup executable (Microsoft Windows). The SAP HANA Cloud Connector itself is rather small and takes minutes to install.

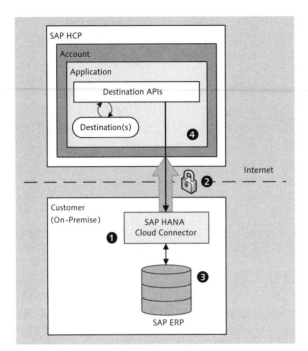

Figure 6.33 Configuring an On-Premise RFC Function Call

6. After the SAP HANA Cloud Connector is installed and started for the first time, you can access its administrative console by opening a browser window and navigating to *https://<hostname>:8443*. (Note that the actual port number can vary depending on how the connector is or was installed.) Here, you'll be taken through a series of postinstallation steps that configure your SAP HANA Cloud Connector administrative account and bind the SAP HANA Cloud Connector with your SAP HCP account in the cloud. Specific details for these steps are given in length in the SAP HANA Cloud Connector installation guide.

7. Once these settings are in place, you are finished with ❶ and ❷ from the overview diagram contained in Figure 6.33. Picking up with ❸, the next task is to configure a connection between the SAP HANA Cloud Connector and the backend AS ABAP system. Within the SAP HANA Cloud Connector administrative console, this task can be completed by opening up the ACCESS CONTROL link in the CONTENT pane and mapping an internal system. This can be achieved by clicking on the ADD... button, as shown in Figure 6.34.

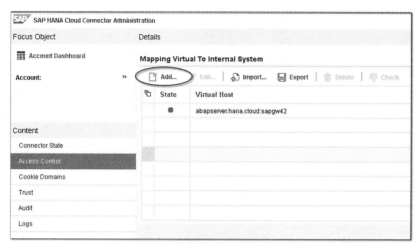

Figure 6.34 Mapping an Internal System in the SAP HANA Cloud Connector Admin Console: Part 1

8. This will open the ADD SYSTEM MAPPING dialog box shown in Figure 6.35. Within this dialog box, you can map your internal AS ABAP system to a virtual host and port that will be used to address the system within the cloud. The name of the virtual host you define here is completely arbitrary; you just need to have something tangible to bind to within your destination configuration.

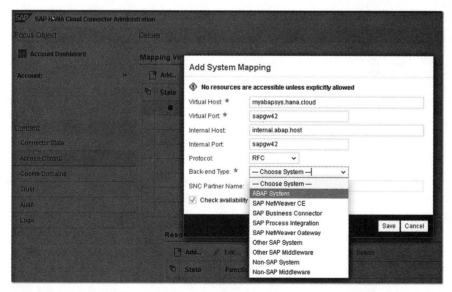

Figure 6.35 Mapping an Internal System in the SAP HANA Cloud Connector Admin Console: Part 2

9. After you create the system mapping, the next step is to specify the RFC or BAPI functions that you wish to expose to SAP HCP. As you can see in Figure 6.36, this can be achieved by clicking on the ADD... button in the RESOURCES ACCESSIBLE ON HOST panel at the bottom of the screen. Within the ADD RESOURCE dialog box, you have the option of specifying complete function names or function patterns (e.g., Z*). Which option you choose here depends on the level of security you wish to enforce. As a rule, it's highly recommended that you keep this locked down to just the functions that you actually plan to consume from the cloud.

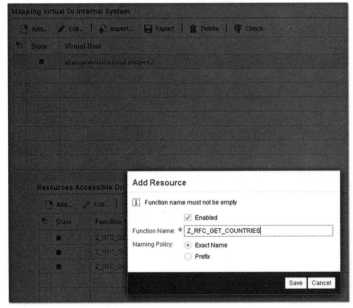

Figure 6.36 Mapping an Internal System in the SAP HANA Cloud Connector Admin Console: Part 3

With the internal system mapping complete, you can now turn your attention to configuring the RFC destination within SAP HCP Cockpit. For the purposes of this demonstration, we'll create our destination at the application level, though you could have just as easily created it at the customer account level. In any case, Figure 6.37 shows the finished product for an RFC destination named ABAPOnPremise. As you can see, the details you provide here are in line with what you might see in a jco.properties file or an RFC destination configured inside of an AS ABAP system (i.e., in Transaction SM59): application server host, client, system number, user name and password, and so on. In the case of the application server host/port properties, notice that we're using the virtual host/port configured within the system mapping defined in the SAP HANA Cloud Connector administration console. This is essential to establishing the connection, because the cloud instance has no visibility to the actual internal system host or port; everything's virtualized within the SAP HANA Cloud Connector.

Figure 6.37 Configuring an RFC Destination in the SAP HCP Cockpit

With your RFC destination in place, you're ready to begin incorporating RFC calls into your sample Java application. Therefore, next we'll get started with the coding portion of this exercise.

Calling RFC Functions within a Java Application

Because the RFC protocol is proprietary to SAP, you can't simply use a Java SE or Java EE API to invoke an RFC function. Instead, you must use a specialized connector library that SAP provides called the *SAP Java Connector* (JCo). In many respects, the JCo library is utilized in much the same way that you use the JDBC library to connect to database systems. Classes and interfaces are provided to create connections, build RFC function calls, parse through the results, and so on.

Within the context of SAP HCP, the JCo library is essentially built into the Connectivity Service. This means that you don't have to worry about bundling the library within your web applications or making sure that the library is on the application classpath at runtime. It also means that you don't have to worry about connection allocation like you would if you were using the standalone version of JCo. Here, instead of hard-coding the connection parameters or externalizing them in a jco.properties file, you can use the RFC destination object created in the SAP HCP Cockpit (or elsewhere) as the starting point for creating a connection object.

> **Note**
>
> The version of the JCo library installed on SAP HCP is stripped down from the standalone version. If you're familiar with JCo programming concepts, some notable items that are missing in the SAP HCP version of JCo include support for server-side programming, IDoc consumption, and dynamic connection configuration and allocation.

The code excerpt contained in Listing 6.17 illustrates the connection allocation process. Here, you use the `getDestination()` method of the `com.sap.conn.jco.JCoDestinationManager` class to fetch the JCo destination that matches up with the specified destination name. As you can see, the destination name you're using matches up with the one that you created within the SAP HCP Cockpit in the previous section. At runtime, the Connectivity Service will use this destination name as a key to fetch the configured destination properties and allocate a `com.sap.conn.jco.JCoDestination` object that represents the JCo connection to the backend. From here on out, it's JCo programming as per usual.

```
import com.sap.conn.jco.*;
@Stateless
@LocalBean
public class RfcProxyBean
{
```

```
private static final String DEFAULT_DESTINATION =
  "ABAPOnPremise";
public List<Country> getCountries()
  throws AbapException, JCoException
{
  try
  {
    JCoDestination jcoDest =
JCoDestinationManager.getDestination(DEFAULT_DESTINATION);
    ...
}
```

Listing 6.17 Creating a JCo Destination Object within a Java Class

The code excerpt in Listing 6.18 demonstrates how you can use the allocated `JCoDestination` object to invoke an RFC function. Here, you call a custom RFC function named `Z_RFC_GET_COUNTRIES`, provided with the book's source code bundle (downloadable from *www.sap-press.com/3638*). This simple function provides a listing of countries configured in the backend AS ABAP system.

```
public class RfcProxyBean
{
  public List<Country> getCountries()
    throws AbapException, JCoException
  {
    List<Country> countryList =
      new ArrayList<Country>();

    try {
      // Access the default JCo destination:
      JCoDestination jcoDest =
       JCoDestinationManager.getDestination(DEFAULT_DESTINATION);

      // Call Z_RFC_GET_COUNTRIES to fetch the country list:
      JCoRepository jcoRepository = jcoDest.getRepository();
      JCoFunction jcoFunction =
        jcoRepository.getFunction("Z_RFC_GET_COUNTRIES");

      jcoFunction.execute(jcoDest);

      // Copy the results into the country list:
      JCoTable tabCountries =
       jcoFunction.getTableParameterList().getTable("COUNTRIES");

      for (int row = 0; row < tabCountries.getNumRows();
           row++, tabCountries.nextRow())
        countryList.add(
```

```
                new Country(tabCountries.getString("LAND1"),
                        tabCountries.getString("LANDX")));
    }
    catch (AbapException ae) {
      throw ae;
    }
    catch (JCoException je) {
      throw je;
    }

    // Return the result set:
    return countryList;
  } // -- public List getCountries() -- //
}
```

Listing 6.18 Calling an RFC Function and Processing the Results

Within the incident management sample application we've been developing in this chapter, you use the Z_RFC_GET_COUNTRIES function to build out the country code selection list used to specify the incident location. This lookup is encapsulated inside of an EJB session bean called com.sappress.hcpbook.chp06.connectivity.RfcProxyBean. You can test this code out in the sample application by clicking on the OPEN CONFIGURATION MANAGER link from the application landing page (see Figure 6.38).

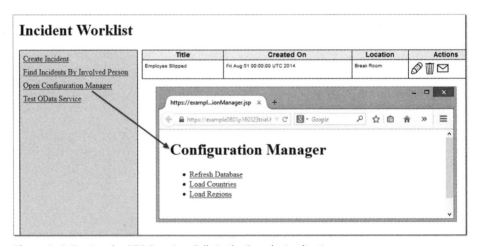

Figure 6.38 Testing the RFC Function Calls in the Sample Application

6.3.4   Case Study: Consuming a RESTful Web Service

For our next demonstration, we'll take a look at how to consume a RESTful web service hosted on the Internet. Although there are many useful services to choose from, we chose the Google Geocoding API, because it's easy to consume and also ties in well with our incident management application. Here, you'll use the API to lookup the precise geographic coordinates for an incident location.

Design Approach and Setup

Because Google's Geocoding API doesn't really deal with sensitive information, there's not much in the way of complex authentication requirements that you have to account for. In general, the only authentication token you have to pass to the service is an API key that you can create within your Google Account. For more information about how to set up this key, check out *https://developers.google.com/maps/documentation/geocoding/#api_key*. Once the key is created, you should be able to locate it within your Google APIs Console, underneath the API Access tab, as shown in Figure 6.39.

Figure 6.39 Finding the API Key for the Geocoding API Access

With your API key in hand, you essentially have everything you need to get started. Because you'll be using the Connectivity Service to broker the connection, you must create an HTTP destination to point to the API endpoint. Figure 6.40 shows the destination that we created. As you can see, we named the destination `GoogleGeocdeDest` and pointed it to the Geocoding API URL *https://maps.googleapis.com/maps/api/geocode/json*. Note that the PROXY TYPE is set to INTERNET, because this is to be an external call. If you were calling an API hosted on-premise, then you would have chosen the ONPREMISE option.

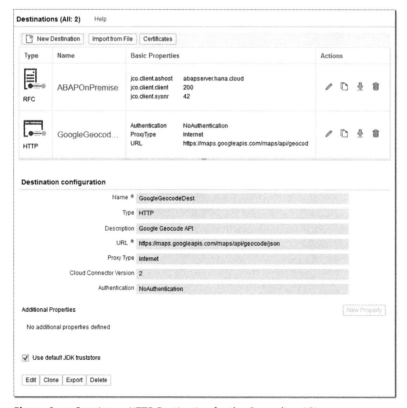

Figure 6.40 Creating an HTTP Destination for the Geocoding API

In this particular scenario, that's all the setup that's required. In more advanced scenarios, your job would be only slightly harder, in that you would likely have to configure more advanced authentication properties in order to support mutual authentication using certificates, OAuth/SAML assertions, and so on. Specific details for each of these authentication types are provided in the online help documentation.

Calling the RESTful Service within a Java Application

With your HTTP destination in place, the steps required to set up the call to the Geocoding API service within your incident management application are as follows:

1. Define a resource reference to the HTTP destination within the application's web.xml file:

```
<web-app>
  ...
  <resource-ref> <res-ref-name>GoogleGeocodeDest</res-ref-name>
    <res-type>com.sap.core.connectivity.api.http.HttpDestination
    </res-type>
  </resource-ref>
</web-app>
```

2. Use a dependency injection to allocate the HttpDestination object at runtime:

```
public class IncidentBean
{
    @Resource(mappedName="GoogleGeocodeDest")
    private HttpDestination geocodeDestination;
    ...
}
```

3. Use the createHttpClient() instance method of the HttpDestination class to obtain a reference to an org.apache.http.client.HttpClient instance. From here on out, you can use this HTTP client connection to invoke the service just as you would outside of SAP HCP.

For brevity's sake, we won't include the detailed HTTP request handling logic in this section. However, if you're interested in seeing how this works, check out the loadGeoCoordinates() method of the com.sappress.hcpbook.chp06.persistence.IncidentBean class. There, you can see how we're encoding the location address for transmission, parsing the JSON results, and storing the coordinate data inside of the Address entity object. You can test this feature from within the E<small>DIT</small> I<small>NCIDENT</small> screen by clicking on the G<small>ET</small> C<small>OORDINATES</small> link, as shown in Figure 6.41.

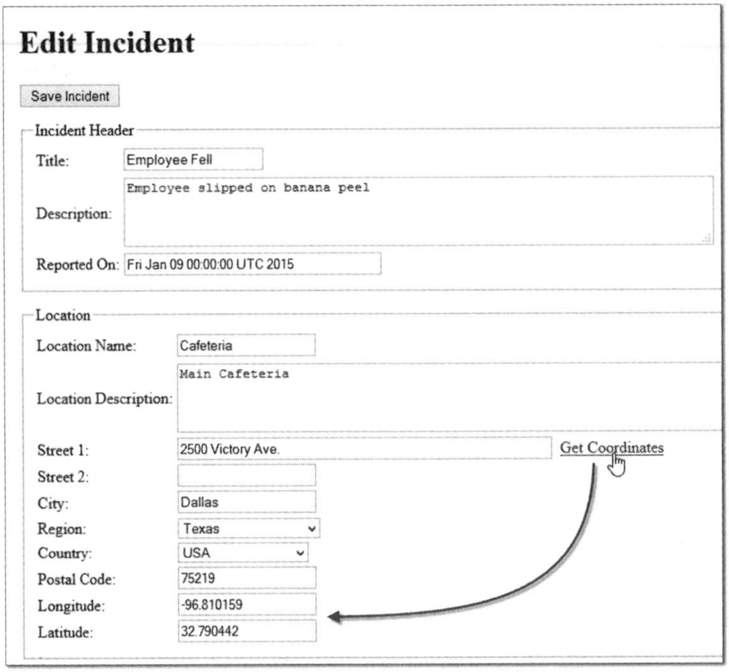

Edit Incident

Save Incident

Incident Header

Title: Employee Fell

Description: Employee slipped on banana peel

Reported On: Fri Jan 09 00:00:00 UTC 2015

Location

Location Name: Cafeteria

Location Description: Main Cafeteria

Street 1: 2500 Victory Ave. Get Coordinates

Street 2:

City: Dallas

Region: Texas

Country: USA

Postal Code: 75219

Longitude: -96.810159

Latitude: 32.790442

Figure 6.41 Triggering the Geocoding API Call within the Incident Editor

6.3.5 Case Study: Sending an E-Mail Message

In our last case study, we'll demonstrate how the Connectivity Service can be used to send email messages. Here, you'll enhance your incident management application to include a link that allows users to send incident notification messages to interested parties as needed.

Design Approach and Initial Setup

In many ways, the initial setup for this scenario mirrors the steps we demonstrated for the RESTful service call setup in Section 6.3.4. You basically need to collect the connection parameters for the mail server to which you wish to connect and then create a `Mail` destination to encapsulate these parameters. For the purposes of our demonstration, we'll be connecting to Google's Gmail server using the SMTP protocol.

Figure 6.42 shows the Mail destination that we configured for our sample scenario. As you can see, we've named our destination `Session` and assigned it the type `Mail`. Aside from these main properties, we've also specified a number of additional properties that are required to establish a connection to the target SMTP server: SMTP host and port, authentication parameters, protocol (SMTP), and so on.

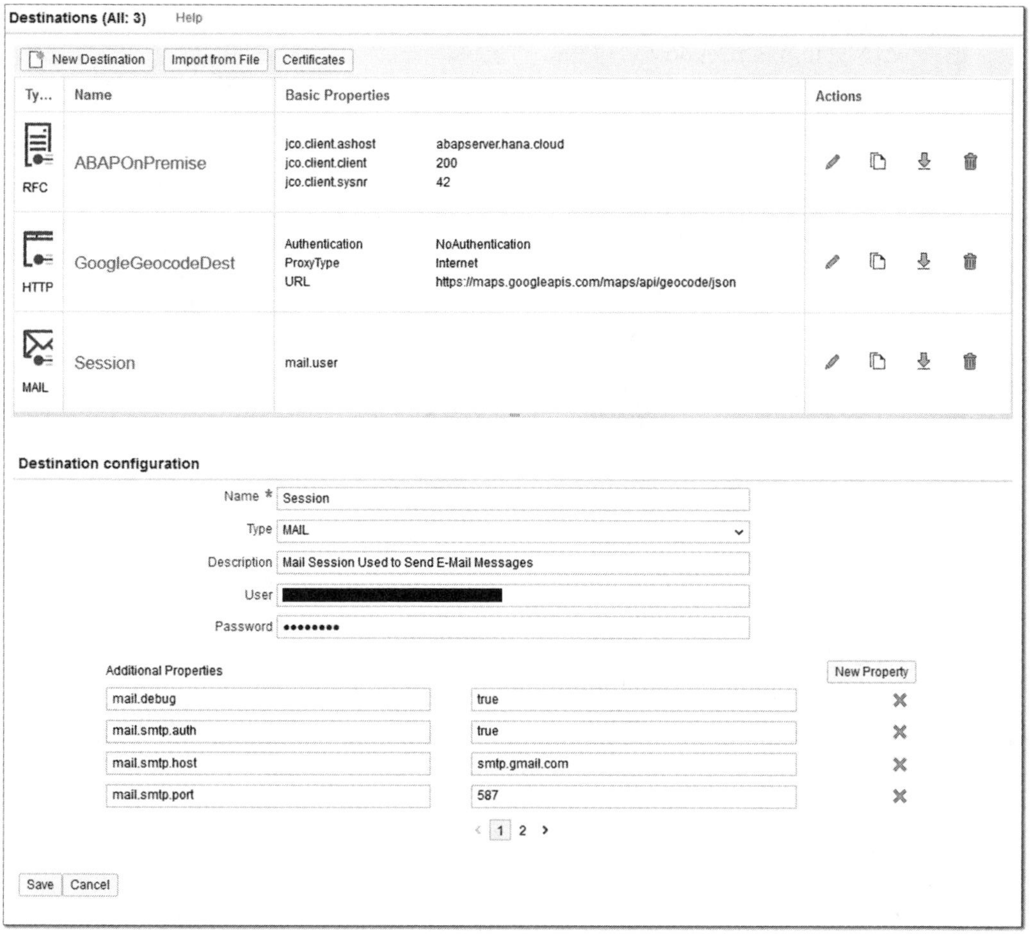

Figure 6.42 Creating a Mail Destination in SAP HCP Cockpit

Whenever the destination is saved, the parameters are used to create a `javax.mail.Session` object that gets stored in the Java EE container's JNDI context under the `mail/<Destination Name>` context path (e.g., `mail/Session` in our example). In the next section, you'll see how your Java applications can pick up this object and use it to send email messages.

Working with the javax.mail Library

Because the Connectivity Service takes the liberty of creating a `javax.mail.Session` object for us, the task of sending (or receiving) an email message is rather straightforward. The code excerpt contained in Listing 6.19 demonstrates this with a simple method called `sendMessage()` that can be used generically to send an email message to a particular recipient. The basic API call sequence is as follows:

1. First, the method creates a `MimeMessage` object that encapsulates the email message you'll be sending. This message instance is linked to the `Session` object that's loaded into context using the injection technique whenever the overarching EJB is instantiated.

2. Next, you bind the sender and receiver of the message and define the message subject line.

3. Then, because your sample scenario sends HTML-based messages, you create a MIME body part and append your HTML message payload to it.

4. Finally, you can use the `Session` instance to open up a connection and send the message. Here, the connection parameters specified in the Mail destination are used to connect to the target SMTP server used to transmit the message.

```
@Stateless
@LocalBean
public class EmailAgentBean
{

    @Resource(name="mail/Session")
    private Session mailSession;

    public void sendMessage(String sender,
                            String receiver,
                            String subject,
                            String body)
        throws MessagingException
    {
        Transport transport = null;

        try
        {
```

```
        MimeMessage message = new MimeMessage(mailSession);

        InternetAddress[] recipients =
          InternetAddress.parse(receiver);
        message.setFrom(new InternetAddress(sender));
        message.setRecipients(RecipientType.TO, recipients);
        message.setSubject(subject, "UTF-8");

        Multipart multipart = new MimeMultipart("alternative");
        MimeBodyPart htmlPart = new MimeBodyPart();
        htmlPart.setContent(body, "text/html");
        multipart.addBodyPart(htmlPart);
        message.setContent(multipart);

        transport = mailSession.getTransport();
        transport.connect();
        transport.sendMessage(message, message.getAllRecipients());
      }
      catch (Exception ex)
      {
        logger.error(ex.getMessage());
        throw new MessagingException(ex.getMessage(), ex);
      }
      finally
      {
        if (transport != null)
        {
          try
          {
            transport.close();
          }
          catch (MessagingException me) { }
        }
      }
    } // -- public void sendMessage() -- //
    ...
}
```

Listing 6.19 Sending an Email Message Using the javax.mail Library

You can test this functionality in the sample application by clicking on the EMAIL icon (the envelope) available in the ACTIONS column of the INCIDENT WORKLIST screen, as shown in Figure 6.43. If you run into issues, then you can turn on debugging for your Mail destination by setting the mail.debug property to true. The debug output will be provided by the System.out logger. You may have to tweak the log level of the logger to enable the log output to show up at runtime.

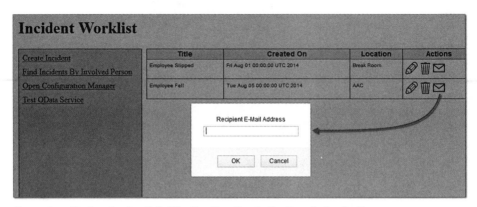

Figure 6.43 Testing the Email Notification Function in the Sample Application

6.4   Using the Document Service

In Section 6.2, you learned how to use the Persistence Service to store structured data in relational databases. By structured data, we're referring to data that is highly organized and predictable in nature. Such data fits nicely into two-dimensional tables and is easy to analyze using query languages, such as SQL.

Although many enterprise applications work pretty much exclusively with structured data, there are times when an application may also need to deal with raw, unstructured data, such as document attachments, social media feeds, and so on. Although you could technically store this raw data in the database along with everything else, to do so would be tantamount to stacking boxes in the archives closet; no one will ever see the data again. In order to be able to do productive things with this unstructured data, you need something more than just a simple data store. What you need is a *content repository*.

In addition to providing data storage capabilities, content repositories also provide several other important value-add features, including the following:

▶ Versioning
▶ Security using access control lists (ACLs)
▶ Indexing
▶ Advanced query and search capabilities

Collectively, these features allow you to get more out of your unstructured data.

Within SAP HCP, you can create content repositories using the *Document Service*. In this section, we'll take a brief look at the Document Service and some of the core features it has to offer.

6.4.1 Conceptual Overview

Within SAP HCP, the Document Service plays the role of content repository. It can be used to store and retrieve unstructured or semistructured data. Internally, this unstructured data can be enriched with various properties that help to classify the data and make it easier to mine later on.

Conceptually speaking, content within the Document Service is organized in much the same way that content is organized within a file system. You can organize files into a hierarchical folder structure that implicitly defines a content taxonomy. How you choose to organize this content is up to you; the Document Service doesn't really care one way or another.

Creating a Mock File System Using the Document Service

Although the Document Service is primarily intended for use as a full-scale content repository, it can actually be used as a mock file system whenever you have application scenarios that absolutely require the use of a file system. Such scenarios often crop up whenever you attempt to install third-party or legacy Java applications onto SAP HCP. Indeed, as you may recall from Chapter 4, the Cloud Jenkins project uses the Document Service to provide Jenkins with a file system that can be used to store configuration files and so on. Therefore, though widespread use of the Document Service in this capacity is probably not ideal, it's certainly possible.

In keeping with the openness of SAP HCP, the functionality of the Document Service is exposed using the industry standard *Content Management Interoperability Services* (CMIS) protocol defined by the OASIS consortium. Rather than building a protocol handler from scratch, SAP also standardized around the open-source OpenCMIS library provided by the Apache Chemistry Project. (For more information about the Apache Chemistry Project, check out *http://chemistry. apache.org*.) This library is automatically included in the classpath for SAP HCP applications, so there's nothing we have to do up front to install it. In addition to being easy to work with, the use of OpenCMIS makes it possible to reuse libraries and frameworks that can be used to synchronize content and so on.

6.4.2   Working with the OpenCMIS API

In order to understand how to tap into the functionality of the Document Service, it's helpful to take a look at how you can interact with it using the OpenCMIS API. Therefore, in this section, we'll show you how this API can be used to connect to a repository, add and remove content, and search for content after the fact. Once you grasp these concepts, it will be much easier to see how to exploit some of the value-add features of the Document Service within your application scenarios.

To guide this discussion, we would recommend that you open up the `Attach-mentProcessorBean.java` file contained within this chapter's source code bundle in the `com.sappress.hcpbook.chp06.document` package (downloadable from *www.sap-press.com/3638*). This session EJB is used within the incident management application to process attachments that are uploaded for particular incidents (see Figure 6.44). As such, it provides a fairly typical example of how the Document Service is used from an application perspective.

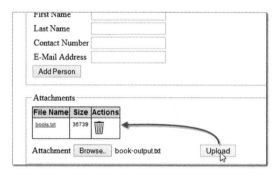

Figure 6.44 Working with Attachments in the Incident Editor Application

Establishing a CMIS Session

Before you can begin doing anything useful with the Document Service, you first need to establish a CMIS session. This session essentially connects you with the application-specific content repository that you wish to interact with.

The code excerpt contained in Listing 6.20 demonstrates how you can create a CMIS session using the OpenCMIS library. The code begins by looking up the core `com.sap.ecm.api.EcmService` service façade provided by the Document Service via the JNDI context. Although this service is managed by the Document Service, you do have to create a resource reference to it in the application's web.xml file.

```
import org.apache.chemistry.opencmis.client.api.*;

@Stateless
@LocalBean
public class AttachmentProcessorBean
{
  private static final String UNIQUE_NAME = "IncidentRepository";
  private static final String SECRET_KEY = "IncidentAttachments";

  private Session getCmisSession()
  {
    EcmService ecmService = null;

    try
    {
      InitialContext ctx = new InitialContext();
      ecmService = (EcmService)
        ctx.lookup("java:comp/env/EcmService");
      return ecmService.connect(UNIQUE_NAME, SECRET_KEY);
    }
    catch (NamingException ne)
    {
      throw new CmisRuntimeException(ne.getMessage(), ne);
    }
    catch (CmisObjectNotFoundException confe)
    {
      RepositoryOptions options = new RepositoryOptions();
      options.setUniqueName(UNIQUE_NAME);
      options.setRepositoryKey(SECRET_KEY);
      options.setVisibility(Visibility.PROTECTED);
      ecmService.createRepository(options);

      return ecmService.connect(UNIQUE_NAME, SECRET_KEY);
    }
  }
}
```

Listing 6.20 Establishing a CMIS Session within a Session Bean

Once you obtain a reference to the EcmService handle, you can use its connect()
method to connect to the target repository, which is keyed by two string tokens
described within the API as the *unique name* and *secret key*, respectively. Because
this call will fail the first time due to the fact that the repository in question does
not yet exist, the code is designed to catch exceptions of type CmisObjectNot-
FoundException so that you can create the repository on the fly as needed.

Creating and Removing Content within a Repository

Whenever a repository is initially created, it comes preassigned with a root-level folder. From this root-level folder, you can branch out by defining subfolders and filling them with documents. These operations are carried out using methods provided by the `org.apache.chemistry.opencmis.client.api.Folder` interface.

Listing 6.21 demonstrates how you can use the `createFolder()` method to create a new subfolder underneath the root folder called `MyFolder`. As you can see, the details of the folder itself are captured within a `java.util.Map` object that maps a series of property names to unique property values. Conceptually, you can think of these properties as tags that are assigned to the folder as it is stored within the repository. These same tags can be used in queries to locate specific pieces of content and so on.

```
Session session = getCmisSession();
Folder rootFolder = session.getRootFolder();

Map<String, String> folderProps =
  new HashMap<String, String>();
folderProps.put(PropertyIds.OBJECT_TYPE_ID, "cmis:folder");
folderProps.put(PropertyIds.NAME, "MyFolder");

Folder folder = rootFolder.createFolder(folderProps);
```
Listing 6.21 Creating a Folder within a CMIS Repository

To create new files, use the `createDocument()` method of the `Folder` interface. This overloaded method defines three main parameters:

▸ Much like the `createFolder()` method, you must pass a `java.util.Map` collection object to define the file's properties.

▸ The content of the file being created is passed in the form of an `org.apache.chemistry.opencmis.commons.data.ContentStream` object. This object surrounds a `java.io.InputStream` with additional file metadata, such as the file name, MIME type, and byte count.

▸ Because documents can exist in versions, you must specify the versioning state of the document at the outset. If desired, you also have the option of turning off versioning for the file.

Once the repository is filled with documents and folders, you can use the methods of the `org.apache.chemistry.opencmis.client.api.Session` interface to traverse through the repository and search for content. Here, if you happen to know the ID of the object you're looking for, you can use the `getObject()` method to fetch the object directly. Otherwise, you can search for the content in one of two ways:

▶ You can use the `Session` interface's `query()` method to search for the content using a SQL-like query language called CMISSQL. This query language allows you to search for documents based on their assigned properties (e.g., `cmis:name`, `cmis:createdBy`, etc.).

▶ If you don't know exactly what you're looking for, then you can recursively search through the folder structure using the `Folder` interface's `getChildren()` method.

Regardless of how you get our hands on the content, you can then manipulate it using methods provided by the `Folder` and `Document` interfaces. Within these interfaces, you'll find a number of overloaded methods that make it easy to update and remove content, create copies of files, work with version control, and more.

For more information about the kinds of operations that can be performed, we would highly recommend that you read through the help documentation provided online at *http://chemistry.apache.org*. Suffice to say that there's functionality here to perform just about any content management operation imaginable.

6.4.3 Consuming the Document Service Externally

Most of the time, the content stored within the Document Service is intended to be consumed directly by SAP HCP applications. However, that being said, there could be times when this content needs to be consumed externally. For example, it could be that you need to implement some form of content syndication between a cloud-based repository and a repository hosted on-premise, or, if you're building standalone HTML5 applications (which we'll cover in Chapter 7), then you might want to proxy document access to those applications.

Although you could build your own application to expose this content externally, it turns out that SAP has already provided a (mostly) fully functional Servlet class in the SAP HCP SDK for this purpose. The name of this class is `com.sap.ecm.api.AbstractCmisProxyServlet`. As the name suggests, this class provides a proxy (or bridge) between the CMIS provider (i.e., the Document Service) and CMIS clients. With this functionality in place, you can hook on popular tools such as the Apache Chemistry Workbench to remote repositories and consume the content as needed.

If you want, you can test this functionality out using the `com.sappress.hcp-book.chp06.document.CMISProxyServlet` class bundled with the incident management application. You can download the Apache Chemistry Workbench from the Apache Chemistry development tools page at *http://chemistry.apache.org/java/developing/tools/dev-tools-workbench.html*.

6.5 Summary

In this chapter, you were able to get your hands dirty with several core services provided as part of SAP HCP. These services go a long way towards rounding out Java application designs by providing developers with the tools they need to persist data and connect to external services within a cloud-based environment. Without these services, these tasks would be considerably more complicated and perhaps even out of reach for less experienced developers.

In the next chapter, we'll take a look at a fairly new application model that's been added to SAP HCP: the HTML5 application model. Here, you'll find that SAP HCP makes it easy to create lightweight HTML5 applications without having to deploy the HTML5 content through a server-side model, such as Java or SAP HANA XS.

This chapter introduces a relatively new addition to the list of programming models supported by SAP HCP: the HTML5 application model. As we'll learn, this application model makes it easy to rapidly develop and deploy lightweight HTML5 applications.

7   Developing HTML5 Applications

In the previous chapters, you learned how to create web applications using server-side programming models, such as the Java and native SAP HANA programming models. You explored various ways of exposing and/or generating HTML content and linking it with custom server-side components to create complex application scenarios.

Although it's nice to know that you have a complete portfolio of server-side components and services at your disposal whenever you need them, there are times when a more lightweight application model will suffice. For example, if the application you're building is merely a consumer of one or more REST-based services, then you can probably get away with building the application exclusively using client-side HTML5 content. This is where the SAP HCP HTML5 application model comes into play.

In this chapter, we'll introduce you to the HTML5 application model and show you how it can be used to develop lightweight web applications. Along the way, we'll also introduce you to the SAP Web IDE which, as the name suggests, is a web-based development environment that's optimized for the development of HTML5/SAPUI5-based applications.

7.1   Overview

As we noted already, the HTML5 application model is a lightweight model that allows developers to build HTML5-based applications. These applications consist solely of client-side HTML5-based resources, such as HTML, JavaScript, and CSS

289

source files. At runtime, this static content is served up to users via a shared dispatcher service that's built into SAP HCP.

The block diagram contained in Figure 7.1 highlights the primary elements that make up the HTML5 application model. To understand how these elements interact with one another, we must explore the application model from both design time and runtime perspectives:

► **Design time**
At design time, developers create and manage HTML5 applications using SAP HCP Cockpit. Whenever a new HTML5 application is created, an application-specific Git repository is created behind the scenes. Developers use this repository to upload and maintain the HTML5 application's resource files.

Runtime
At runtime, clients access the HTML5 applications through the aforementioned dispatcher service. This service fetches the HTML5 application content from the corresponding Git repository and sends it back to the client. If the application relies on data from REST-based services, then these calls are also brokered through the dispatcher service. You can utilize the Connectivity Service to broker access to REST-based services hosted externally or on-premise.

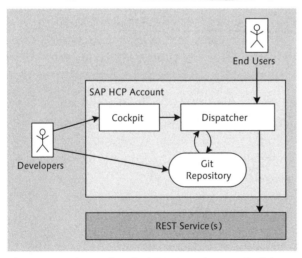

Figure 7.1 Understanding the HTML5 Application Model

If all this seems relatively straightforward, that's because it is. Indeed, aside from a few logistical items that we'll be addressing shortly, HTML5 application development consists of little more than uploading some HTML5 resource files to Git repositories hosted on SAP HCP. SAP purposefully gets out of the way, allowing developers to create the HTML5 content in whatever way they see fit and using the editor or IDE tool of their choice. In the next section, we'll see how all this works in practice.

7.2   Getting Started

Now that you have a general sense for how HTML5 applications work, we're ready to turn our attention towards more practical matters and see what it takes to create and deploy a brand-new HTML5 application. In the sections that follow, we'll walk you through this process step-by-step.

7.2.1   Defining a New HTML5 Application

As we noted in Section 7.1, HTML5 applications are managed within the SAP HCP Cockpit. To access the management console, click on the HTML5 APPLICATIONS tab from the main landing page. This will open a panel containing a table of HTML5 applications defined within your account. As you can see in Figure 7.2, controls are provided within this table to drill into application definitions and also start, stop, or delete applications as needed.

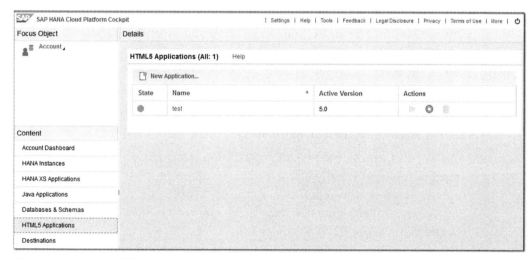

Figure 7.2 Managing HTML5 Applications in the SAP HCP Cockpit

To create a new application, simply click on the NEW APPLICATION… button in the table's toolbar. This will open the NEW HTML5 APPLICATION dialog box shown in Figure 7.3. Here, you're prompted to give your new HTML5 application a name. The naming rules are as follows:

▶ The name can only contain lowercase alphanumeric characters.

▶ The name cannot exceed 30 characters in length.

▶ The name must start with a letter.

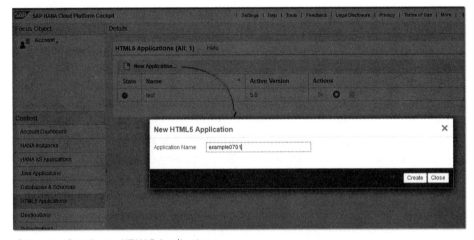

Figure 7.3 Creating an HTML5 Application

Once you confirm the name, you can go ahead and create the application by clicking on the CREATE button (see Figure 7.3). This causes several things to happen behind the scenes; the most notable is the creation of an application-specific Git repository in which the application artifacts will be stored.

7.2.2 Accessing the Git Repository

After the dust settles on the HTML5 application creation process, you will have an empty Git repository that you can use to start uploading your HTML5 application content. To access this repository, you need to drill into the application definition. As you can see Figure 7.4, this can be achieved by clicking on the link in the NAME column in the HTML5 APPLICATIONS table.

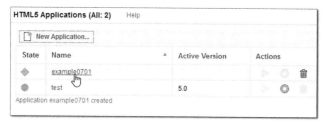

Figure 7.4 Accessing an HTML5 Application's Git Repository: Part 1

This will open the HTML5 application dashboard screen, which contains a general overview of the application state. To access the Git repository, navigate over to the DEVELOPMENT tab, as shown in Figure 7.5. From here, you can find the Git repository URL, which is of the form *https://git.{landscape_host}/{account_name}/{html5_app_name}*. Because you'll need to clone this repository in order proceed with development, it's a good idea to go ahead and copy this URL into your clipboard.

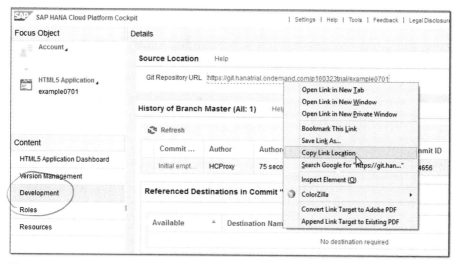

Figure 7.5 Accessing an HTML5 Application's Git Repository: Part 2

7.2.3 Working with the SAP Web IDE

Once you get your hands on an HTML5 application's Git repository URL, you can proceed with development in a lot of different ways. For instance, in Chapter 4, you learned how to use the EGit client built into the Eclipse IDE to clone a Git repository and manage repository resources, so if you wanted, you could develop the HTML5 content in Eclipse. Another option would be to use a command-line Git client to clone the repository and then develop the HTML5 content using a preferred editor tool, such as Adobe Dreamweaver, Mercury Editor, and so forth. The possibilities here are endless.

In addition to these usual suspects, SAP has recently introduced another editor option into the mix: the SAP Web IDE. The SAP Web IDE (formerly known as the SAP River RDE) is a 100% web-based IDE that requires no installation of custom components on your local machine.

Although a thorough treatment of the capabilities of the SAP Web IDE is beyond the scope of this book, here's a quick rundown of the functions and features that make it particularly appealing for the development of HTML5 applications:

▶ Excellent support for editing HTML5-based resources, including JavaScript code completion, intellisense for SAPUI5 development, and so on

▶ A built-in Git client that tracks changes to application resources and makes it easy to sync changes

▶ Wizards to create projects using templates and/or sample projects

▶ Real-time preview functions and support for mock data testing

Next, we'll show you how to utilize the SAP Web IDE to develop and maintain HTML5 applications.

Accessing the SAP Web IDE

From a technical perspective, the SAP Web IDE is made available to an SAP HCP account via a *subscription*. Subscriptions are used to grant access to applications hosted by an SAP HCP *provider account*. In the case of the SAP Web IDE, the provider account is sapwebide, an account hosted by SAP itself.

You can access this subscribed application within the SAP HCP Cockpit by clicking on the SUBSCRIPTIONS tab shown in Figure 7.6 and then on the link in the APPLICATION column of the SUBSCRIBED HTML5 APPLICATIONS table. This will open the HTML5 SUBSCRIPTION DASHBOARD screen shown in Figure 7.7. From there, you can launch the SAP Web IDE by clicking on the application URL.

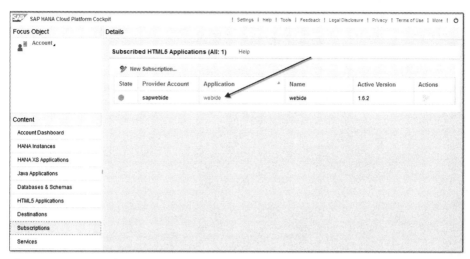

Figure 7.6 Accessing the SAP Web IDE: Part 1

Figure 7.7 Accessing the SAP Web IDE: Part 2

Alternatively, you can launch the IDE directly by plugging the application URL into a browser window. The URL syntax is *https://webide-{account_name}.dispatcher.{landscape_host}*.

In either case, once the IDE launches, you'll end up at a screen that resembles the one shown in Figure 7.8.

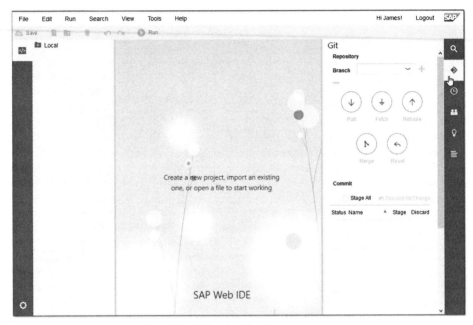

Figure 7.8 Opening up the SAP Web IDE for the First Time

Connecting to an HTML5 Application's Git Repository

Like many IDEs, the SAP Web IDE organizes the development artifacts you create into *projects*. Although it's technically possible to create projects in the local workspace, when developing HTML5 applications you'll want to ensure that your project resources are associated with the application's Git repository. To set this up, you need to clone the application's Git repository so that the SAP Web IDE's Git client can track changes to application resources. This can be achieved by performing the following steps:

1. From the top-level menu bar, select FILE • GIT • CLONE REPOSITORY, as shown in Figure 7.9.

2. This will open the CLONE REPOSITORY dialog box shown in Figure 7.10. Here, you'll want to paste the repository URL into the URL field in the LOCATION section. If you then tab over to the next field, you'll see that the screen parses out the URL and fills in the HOST and REPOSITORY PATH fields automagically. With

this information filled in, all that's left is filling in the USER and PASSWORD fields in the AUTHENTICATION section. In this section, you'll want to plug in your SAP HCP account credentials.

Figure 7.9 Cloning the HTML5 Application's Git Repository: Part 1

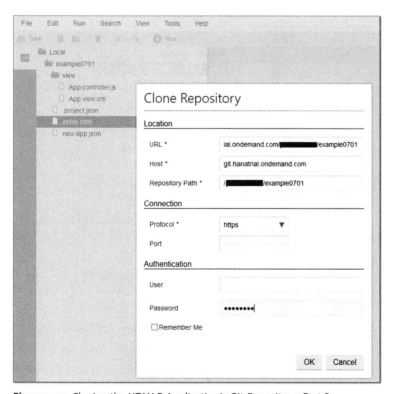

Figure 7.10 Cloning the HTML5 Application's Git Repository: Part 2

297

3. Once all of the parameters are set, you can complete the cloning process by clicking on the OK button. At this point, the SAP Web IDE will connect to the target Git repository and sync any content that might be there (it will be empty initially). When the dust settles here, you'll end up with a folder named such that it matches up with your HTML5 application name.

Creating Application Content

After you clone an HTML5 application's Git repository, you're ready to commence with the development of application content. To get things started, begin by creating a new project. The steps required here are as follows:

1. Right-click on the root folder created during the Git repository clone process and select the NEW • PROJECT FROM TEMPLATE menu option.

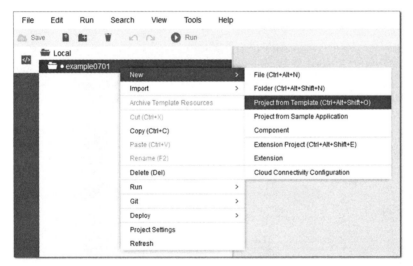

Figure 7.11 Creating a Project in the SAP Web IDE: Part 1

2. This will launch the NEW PROJECT wizard screen shown in Figure 7.12. From here, you can choose from among various templates that define different types of projects: SAPUI5 projects, SAP Fiori starter projects, mobile applications, and so forth. For the purposes of our demonstration, select the SAPUI5 APPLICATION PROJECT template. Once you select the appropriate template, click on the NEXT button to proceed.

Note

As of the time of writing, all of the available templates are based on the SAPUI5 framework. With that being said, please keep in mind that the selection of a particular template doesn't marry you to SAPUI5. If you like, you can delete the template content after the project is initially created and create regular HTML5-based content.

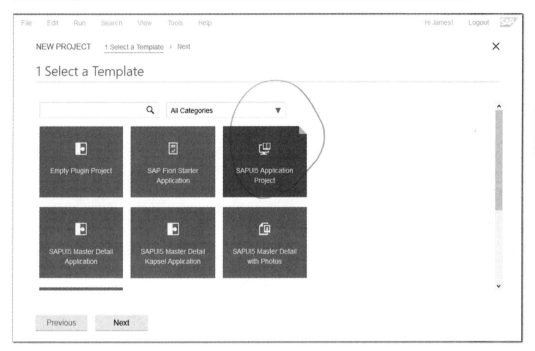

Figure 7.12 Creating a Project in the SAP Web IDE: Part 2

3. At the BASIC INFORMATION step shown in Figure 7.13, you'll need to enter a name for the project. We recommend plugging in the same project name you gave to the HTML5 application when you created it in the SAP HCP Cockpit. Click on NEXT to continue.

Figure 7.13 Creating a Project in the SAP Web IDE: Part 3

4. Depending on the type of template you selected, the next step will allow you to customize various project settings. Because you chose the SAPUI5 APPLICATION PROJECT template in this case, the customizing screen you arrive at (Figure 7.14) allows you to customize SAPUI5 application details. For the purposes of our demonstration, configure these details as follows:

   ▶ APPLICATION TYPE
     Choose DESKTOP.

   ▶ VIEW TYPE
     Choose XML.

   ▶ NAMESPACE.
     Enter "hcpbook.chp07.demo".

   ▶ VIEW NAME
     Enter "App".

   When you've finished, click on the NEXT button to continue.

5. At the CONFIRM step (Figure 7.15), you can confirm your selections and exit the project creation wizard by clicking on the FINISH button.

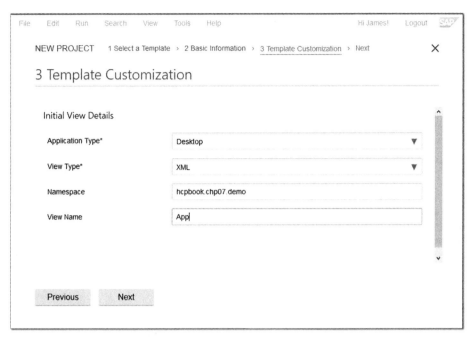

Figure 7.14 Creating a Project in the SAP Web IDE: Part 4

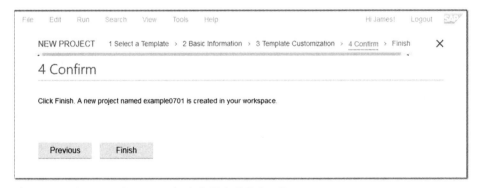

Figure 7.15 Creating a Project in the SAP Web IDE: Part 5

After the project wizard completes, you should see some default content show up in your application folder. From here, you can proceed with development by creating new files and/or editing some of the template files created via the project wizard. Depending on the type of file you're editing, content-specific syntax highlighting and tool-specific features will kick in automatically. For example, in Figure 7.16, you can see how the XML editor highlights XML markup. As you type in this editor, you'll find that the editor takes the liberty of autoclosing tags and highlighting syntax errors.

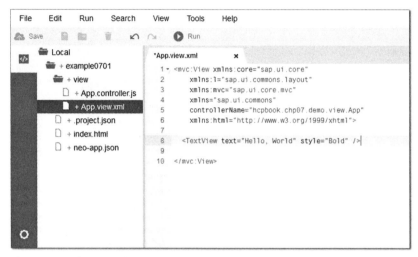

Figure 7.16 Editing Application Resources: Part 1

Figure 7.17 shows what the JavaScript editor screen looks like. Here, you can see the robust intellisense features of the IDE on display. You can access these features by placing your cursor in the desired location and then clicking on the Ctrl+Space keys simultaneously. If a syntax error occurs, then a little red square will show up at the line in which the error originates. You can find out more information about the nature of the error by hovering your mouse cursor over the red square.

At the end of the day, the SAP Web IDE works pretty much like any other IDE, so as you start playing around with it we think you'll find the experience to be pretty intuitive. However, if you find yourself getting stuck on something, rest assured that there are plenty of resources out there to help you on your way. Two of the more notable options include the various options contained within the HELP menu available within the IDE itself and the online help documentation available online at *https://help.hana.ondemand.com*. In the latter case, select the SAP WEB IDE link to be taken to the official help documentation provided by SAP.

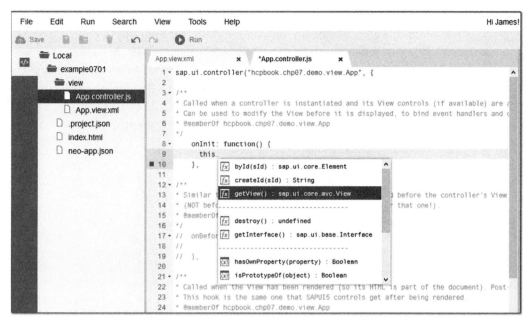

Figure 7.17 Editing Application Resources: Part 2

Running Local Unit Tests

During the course of the development cycle, you may want to periodically run some unit tests to verify that you're on the right track. Although you could check the content into Git and run the application from within your SAP HCP account, the SAP Web IDE provides a faster alternative: the built-in test tool.

Before you try to launch this tool, we'll have you add a bit of content to your template application so that you have something to test with. If you followed along with the project creation steps outlined in the previous section, then you should have a file in the VIEW folder called App.view.xml. Open this file and amend the XML, as highlighted in Listing 7.1. With this change, you should now see the text "Hello, World" show up on the application screen.

```
<mvc:View...>
  <TextView text="Hello, World" style="Bold" />
</mvc:View>
```

Listing 7.1 Creating Some Sample Content in the HTML5 Demo Application

With this change in place, you can run a test by selecting the application's index.html file and clicking on the RUN button in the application toolbar (see Figure 7.18). This will open the test tool shown in Figure 7.19. As you can see, one of the nice things about this test tool is that it allows you to preview the application at different resolution settings. This feature is very useful whenever you need to develop responsive web applications that should offer a consistent experience when accessed via tablets, mobile devices, and so forth.

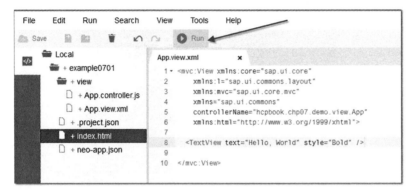

Figure 7.18 Testing the Application Locally: Part 1

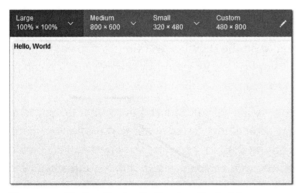

Figure 7.19 Testing the Application Locally: Part 2

Checking In Changes to the Git Repository

After you finish testing your application locally, the next step is to check the content in to the HTML5 application's Git repository. Before you can carry out this task, though, you need to configure your Git settings. This can be achieved by selecting TOOLS • GIT SETTINGS from the top-level menu bar. This will open up the GIT SETTINGS panel shown in Figure 7.20. Here, you need to specify a Git email address and user name to track the changes against.

> **Tip**
>
> The user name/email address you maintain in this section will be stored within your IDE preferences independent of any particular HTML5 application that you're working with. This means that you don't have to set up this information again for subsequent applications that you maintain using the SAP Web IDE.

Figure 7.20 Configuring Your Git Settings in the SAP Web IDE

To check in the changes, you need to open up the GIT view (that is, if it's not open already). You can access this view by selecting VIEW • GIT PANE from the top-level menu bar. As you can see in Figure 7.21, the Git client built in to the SAP Web IDE has been tracking all of the changes you've made to the cloned Git repository.

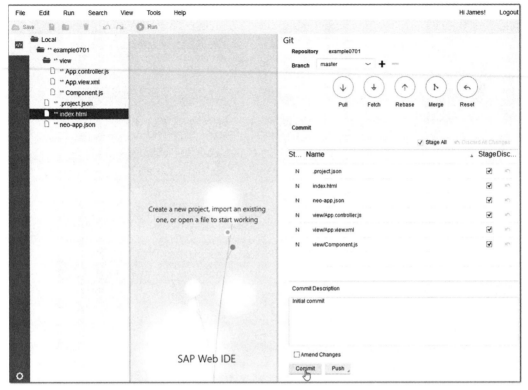

Figure 7.21 Working with the Git View

To check the changes into Git, you must perform the following steps:

1. Stage all the files that you want to check into the repository. You can stage each file individually, or you can choose the STAGE ALL checkbox to stage all of the files in one fell swoop.

2. Enter a commit description, and then click on the COMMIT button.

3. Push the changes up to the remote Git repository by selecting the PUSH • ORI-GIN/MASTER menu option. Here, once again, you'll be prompted to authenticate using your SAP HCP account, as shown in Figure 7.22.

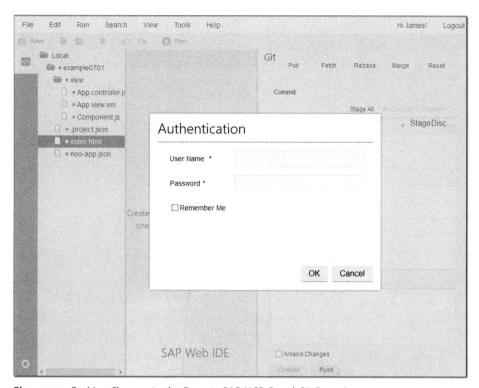

Figure 7.22 Pushing Changes to the Remote SAP HCP-Based Git Repository

7.2.4 Activating the HTML5 Application Content in the SAP HCP Cockpit

In the previous section, we concluded our demonstration of the SAP Web IDE development experience by showing you how to push the changes you made to your HTML5 application to the remote Git repository hosted on SAP HCP. Although this step takes care of synchronizing the content to SAP HCP, it doesn't activate the changes. In order to activate the latest and greatest changes, you must return to the SAP HCP Cockpit and perform the following steps:

1. From within the HTML5 application dashboard, click on the DEVELOPMENT tab. There, within the HISTORY OF BRANCH MASTER section, you can find the latest changes in the commit history (see Figure 7.23).

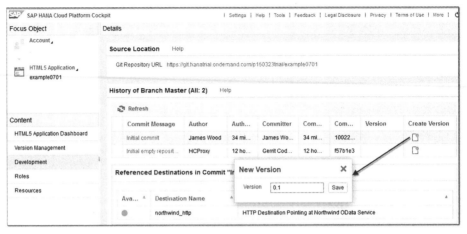

Figure 7.23 Managing Versions of the HTML5 Application

2. In order to bundle the changes together so that you can activate them, you need to create an application version. This is achieved by clicking on the CREATE VERSION button (see Figure 7.23). Then, in the NEW VERSION dialog box, you can assign a new version number, and click on the SAVE button to confirm the changes. In Git parlance, this version is defined in terms of a *tag*.

3. Once the version is created, you need to switch over to the VERSION MANAGEMENT tab and activate the newly created version in the AVAILABLE VERSIONS panel by clicking on the button with the matchstick icon (Figure 7.24).

Figure 7.24 Activating the HTML5 Application

From a conceptual point of view, this activation step represents the handoff between an HTML5 application's Git repository and the shared dispatcher service hosted by SAP HCP. Here, a version bundles together a specific snapshot of the application content and makes it easy for the dispatcher to know what content to load at runtime. Over time, you can accumulate multiple versions within the repository and revert backwards or forwards between versions as needed.

7.2.5 Testing the Finished Product

Now that you've activated the application in the previous section, you can test the finished product in several different ways:

▸ From the main HTML5 APPLICATION DASHBOARD tab, you can click on the APPLICATION URL link in the ACTIVE VERSION panel to launch the application.

▸ From the VERSION MANAGEMENT tab, you can launch any available version by clicking on the link in the VERSION column of the AVAILABLE VERSIONS panel (see Figure 7.25).

▸ You can access and/or bookmark the (active) version of the application by plugging in the direct application URL. Here, the URL syntax is *https://{html5_application_name}-{account_name}.{landscape_host}*.

Figure 7.25 Testing the HTML5 Application Using the SAP HCP Cockpit

Regardless of the path you take, the HTML5 application content will be served up via the SAP HCP dispatcher service, and you will test and/or debug the application using a web browser as usual.

7.3   Advanced Concepts

In Section 7.2, we showed you the basics of creating HTML5 applications within SAP HCP. Now that you're armed with this basic knowledge, we'll take a closer look at some advanced concepts that will help you round out your application designs.

7.3.1   Working with the Application Descriptor

Even though the HTML5 application model is primarily a client-side model, there are some server-side functions within the SAP HCP backend that you can leverage to influence the behavior of your applications. For example, in Section 7.3.3, you'll see how to use the Connectivity Service to broker connections to REST-based services that are hosted externally or on-premise. Similarly, in Section 7.3.4, you'll learn how to configure an HTML5 application's security on the backend.

In order to configure these kinds of features, you must fill out the HTML5 application's descriptor file. At runtime, the SAP HCP dispatcher service will use this descriptor file to determine when and where it should step in and influence the behavior of the application.

According to the HTML5 application model, the application descriptor file must be called neo-app.json and it must be made available at the root of the application's folder structure. As the .json file type suggests, the application descriptor content is specified using JSON notation.

Listing 7.2 contains the default application descriptor file created via the project creation wizard we reviewed in Section 7.2.3. Here, you can see that the project wizard defined several attributes for the HTML5 application:

▶ The welcomeFile attribute specifies the default HTML file to load whenever the application is loaded.

▶ The `routes` attribute specifies a couple of route definitions that the shared dispatcher service will use to map external resources (SAPUI5-related resources in this case) onto simple paths, such as `/resources`.

```
{
  "welcomeFile": "index.html",
  "routes": [
    {
      "path": "/resources",
      "target": {
        "type": "service",
        "name": "sapui5",
        "entryPath": "/resources"
      },
      "description": "SAPUI5 Resources"
    },
    {
      "path": "/test-resources",
      "target": {
        "type": "service",
        "name": "sapui5",
        "entryPath": "/test-resources"
      },
      "description": "SAPUI5 Test Resources"
    }
  ]
}
```

Listing 7.2 Sample neo-app.json Application Descriptor File

We'll be looking more closely at some of the other types of attributes you can specify in the upcoming sections. In addition to this overview, you can find a complete outline of the application descriptor file's schema in the SAP HANA Cloud Documentation available online at *http://help.hana.ondemand.com*. From the landing page, expand HTML5 APPLICATIONS DEVELOPMENT • DEVELOPER'S GUIDE • APPLICATION DESCRIPTOR FILE to access the detailed syntax diagram and overview.

7.3.2 Integrating SAPUI5 Content

Even though SAP HCP allows you to develop your HTML5 application content using the framework(s) of your choice, there are a lot of compelling reasons to standardize around SAPUI5. If you're working with the SAP Web IDE, then there's usually nothing you have to do to prepare for SAPUI5 development; the

SAP Web IDE handles all of this up front whenever you create development projects. On the other hand, if you're working with an external IDE, then there is a trick to incorporating SAPUI5 content into your applications.

For a variety of technical reasons, the preferred method of access to the SAPUI5 library files is through a shared service called `sapui5`. You can access this service within your HTML5 application by specifying a route definition in the application's deployment descriptor. The syntax for specifying such a route is demonstrated in Listing 7.3. Here, the `path` attribute indicates that any requests containing the `/resources` path will be processed by the `sapui5` service, which will serve up the SAPUI5 content dynamically.

```
{
  . . .
  "routes": [
    {
      "path": "/resources",
      "target": {
        "type": "service",
        "name": "sapui5",
        "entryPath": "/resources"
      },
      "description": "SAPUI5 Resources"
    },
  ]

  . . .
}
```

Listing 7.3 Defining a Route to the SAPUI5 Library in the Application Descriptor

Once you define a route in the application descriptor, you can use the configured path in your HTML markup, as shown in the excerpt contained in Listing 7.4. At runtime, whenever this HTTP request is triggered, the shared dispatcher service will proxy the request through the `sapui5` service and deliver the library content automagically.

```
<html>
  <head>
    <script src="resources/sap-ui-core.js"

            id="sap-ui-bootstrap"
            data-sap-ui-libs="sap.ui.commons"
            data-sap-ui-theme="sap_bluecrystal">
    </script>
    . . .
```

```
  </head>
  ...
</html>
```

Listing 7.4 Accessing the SAPUI5 Library via the Configured Route Definition

Aside from the upfront route setup, everything from here on out is SAPUI5 development as per usual. As you might expect, this transparency can come in handy whenever you need to port preexisting SAPUI5 apps or content into SAP HCP.

7.3.3 Accessing External Resources

Most of the time, the HTML5 applications that you develop on SAP HCP will need to consume data from RESTful services that are not directly accessible from the public Internet. Examples of the types of services you might want to access here include the following:

▶ OData services developed using other application models supported by SAP HCP, such as Java or SAP HANA XS

▶ RESTful services hosted by third-party partners or service providers

▶ On-premise services exposed via the SAP HANA Cloud Connector or SAP HANA Cloud Integration (SAP HCI)

To facilitate these kinds of requests, you can once again turn to the Connectivity Service that we covered in Chapter 6. In order to understand how this works, it's helpful to look at a demonstration that shows how all the pieces fit together. With that in mind, in the upcoming sections we'll walk you through a scenario in which you'll hook up an SAPUI5 application to a sample OData service called "Northwind" that's hosted on the official OData site. This service defines a handful of intuitive entity types, such as customers, sales order, and so on. You'll use these entities to create a simple application that allows users to scroll through a customer's sales orders.

Creating an HTTP Destination

To get things started, you first need to create an HTTP destination that points to your target OData service. As demonstrated in Chapter 6, this can be achieved by opening the SAP HCP Cockpit and clicking on the DESTINATIONS tab. From here, you can create a new destination by clicking on the NEW DESTINATION... button and filling in the details, as shown in Figure 7.26. For your convenience, we've also prepared a destination file in the book's source code bundle that you can upload called `northwind_http`. If you prefer to configure the destination manually, then you can do so by plugging in the service URL: *http://services.odata.org/ V3/Northwind/Northwind.svc.*

Figure 7.26 Defining an HTTP Destination Pointing to the Northwind Service

Defining a Route to the HTTP Destination in the Application Descriptor File

Once the HTTP destination is defined, the next step is to open your HTML5 application's descriptor file and create a route that binds a resource path to the destination. At runtime, the shared dispatcher service will use this route definition to determine when and where to reroute service requests through the Connectivity Service.

The descriptor excerpt contained in Listing 7.5 shows how to define a route that binds the HTTP destination with a resource path. As you can see, this route definition looks rather similar to the one you used to access the `sapui5` service.

However, in this case, the route target's `type` property is assigned the value `destination`, because you're pointing at an HTTP destination.

```
{
  ...
  "routes": [
    {
      "path": "/resources",
      "target": {
        "type": "service",
        "name": "sapui5",
        "entryPath": "/resources"
      },
      "description": "SAPUI5 Resources"
    },
    {
      "path": "/Northwind.svc",
      "target": {
        "type": "destination",
        "name": "northwind_http"
      },
      "description": "HTTP Destination to Northwind"
    }
  ],
  ...
}
```

Listing 7.5 Defining a Route to Point to the HTTP Destination

Using the Route Definition to Access the Backend Service

After you establish your route definition, you can use the configured resource path to proxy access the backend service. This is demonstrated in the SAPUI5 code excerpt contained in Listing 7.6. Here, you're creating an `sap.ui.model.odata.ODataModel` object to encapsulate access to the Northwind service. As you navigate through entities in the application, you can append various query options on the end of the relative `/Northwind.svc` path, just like you would if you were hitting the service directly via your browser. At runtime, the dispatcher service will translate these requests and proxy them through the backend service automatically.

```
sap.ui.core.UIComponent.extend("hcpbook.chp07.demo.Component", {
  ...
  init: function() {
    ...
```

```
    // Define the application's data model:
    var oModel =
      new sap.ui.model.odata.ODataModel("/Northwind.svc", true);
    this.setModel(oModel);
  }
});
```

Listing 7.6 Using a Route Definition in an SAPUI5 OData Model

7.3.4 Configuring Application Security

As you've observed throughout the course of this chapter, the bulk of HTML5 application content is static in nature. Although this simplifies the development process in many ways, it also introduces some challenges when it comes to application security. After all, if users can get their hands on the code, then they can glean insight into what's going on behind the scenes and potentially discover holes in security.

To prevent these kinds of vulnerabilities, you need to make sure that you lock down access to sensitive resources. This starts with determining who the user is (authentication) and then making sure that the user is authorized to access particular resources (authorization). With these two constraints in place, you can ensure that only authorized users can access HTML5 content and, by extension, the more sensitive resources (e.g., REST-based services) that the HTML5 applications access behind the scenes.

Within the HTML5 programming model, these kinds of checks are configured in the application descriptor file. Here, using a few lines of code, you can declaratively define the appropriate constraints. For example, Listing 7.7 shows how you can turn on authentication in an HTML5 application. Once this change is activated, users will have to log on with their SAP HCP user account in order to access the application.

```
{
  "authenticationMethod": "saml",
  "welcomeFile": "index.html",
  ...
}
```

Listing 7.7 Turning on Authentication in the Application Descriptor File

To protect access to particular resources (URLs), you need to define one or more *security constraints*. As you can see in Listing 7.8, a security constraint definition consists of a permission name, an optional description, and a list of (URL) paths that you want to protect. Here, we've defined a security constraint to prevent access to the application's deployment descriptor file. Because this file defines all of the security for the application, it's important that you prevent end users from browsing to this file.

```
{
  "authenticationMethod": "saml",
  ...
  "securityConstraints": [
    {
      "permission": "AccessApplicationDescriptor",
      "description": "Access application descriptor",
      "protectedPaths": ["/neo-app.json"]
    }
  ]
}
```

Listing 7.8 Defining Security Constraints

If you were just to define a security constraint like the one shown in Listing 7.8 and leave it at that, the only user(s) with authorization to browse to the neo-app.json file would be users within the SAP HCP account that have the built-in `AccountDeveloper` role. Although this is probably what you want for the deployment descriptor, most of the constraints that you define will point to resources that you want to expose on a wider scale. To provide this access to users, you must map these constraints to roles that you assign to end users. This can be achieved by performing the following steps:

1. Log on to the SAP HCP Cockpit and get into the target HTML5 application's dashboard, as demonstrated in Section 7.2.4. From here, navigate to the ROLES tab (Figure 7.27).

2. On the ROLES tab, you can define new roles and assign these roles to end users or user groups. To create a new role, click on the NEW ROLE... button shown in Figure 7.28. Here, you need only specify the role's name and then click on SAVE.

Figure 7.27 Defining a New HTML5 Application Role: Part 1

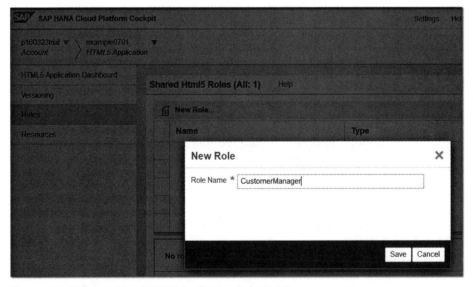

Figure 7.28 Defining a New HTML5 Application Role: Part 2

3. Once the role definition(s) are created, you can map application constraints to the roles by clicking back over to the HTML5 APPLICATION DASHBOARD tab and editing application permissions. As you can see in Figure 7.29, this is achieved by selecting the appropriate role in the ASSIGNED ROLE column for the target permission record.

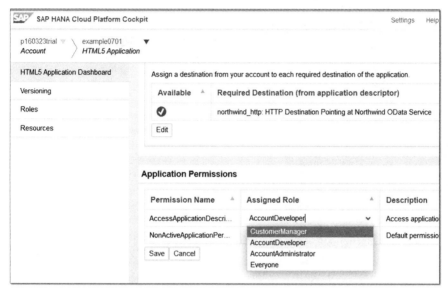

Figure 7.29 Mapping an Application Permission to a Role

4. After the application permissions are mapped to the appropriate roles, you can grant users access to these roles by assigning the roles to user accounts and/or user groups (refer back to Figure 7.27).

Collectively, the configuration options described in this section can go a long way towards locking down your applications. In Chapter 8, we'll look at ways of expanding on this and guarding against more advanced types of security attacks.

7.3.5 Putting It All Together

Now that you have a sense for how all the pieces fit together, let's take a look at the finished product, which is included in the book's source code bundle (downloadable from *www.sap-press.com/3638*). To import this content into the example application that you've been working on throughout the course of this chapter, perform the following steps:

1. Right-click on the top-level project folder and select the IMPORT • ARCHIVE menu option, as shown in Figure 7.30.

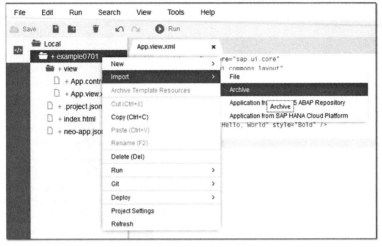

Figure 7.30 Importing the Sample Customer Project into the SAP Web IDE: Part 1

2. This will open the IMPORT ARCHIVE dialog box shown in Figure 7.31. Here, you'll want to click on the BROWSE… button to navigate to the Example07_01.zip file, which is included in the book's source code bundle. Click on the IMPORT button to kick off the import process.

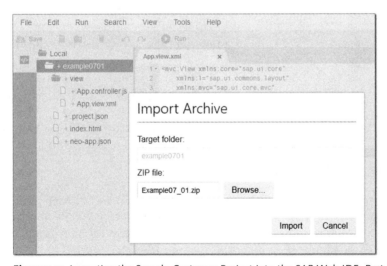

Figure 7.31 Importing the Sample Customer Project into the SAP Web IDE: Part 2

3. As the import runs, you'll encounter the confirmation dialog box shown in Figure 7.32. This dialog box is alerting you to the fact that the archive file contains files that will overwrite the current files you've defined in the application. You'll want to click on the OK button to proceed with the import.

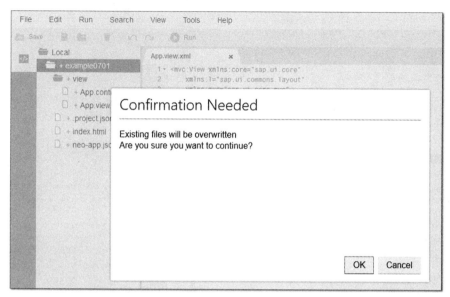

Figure 7.32 Importing the Sample Customer Project into the SAP Web IDE: Part 3

After the archive is imported, you'll see some new SAPUI5 content that displays relevant data from the backend OData service. To test this out, repeat the deployment steps outlined in Section 7.2.3 and Section 7.2.4. That is, you'll need to check in the revised code to the Git repository and activate the changes in the SAP HCP Cockpit.

Figure 7.33 shows the finished product in action in a browser window. As you test through the application, you can use the developer tools in the browser to monitor the network traffic and see the OData service calls happening behind the scenes. This is demonstrated in Figure 7.34.

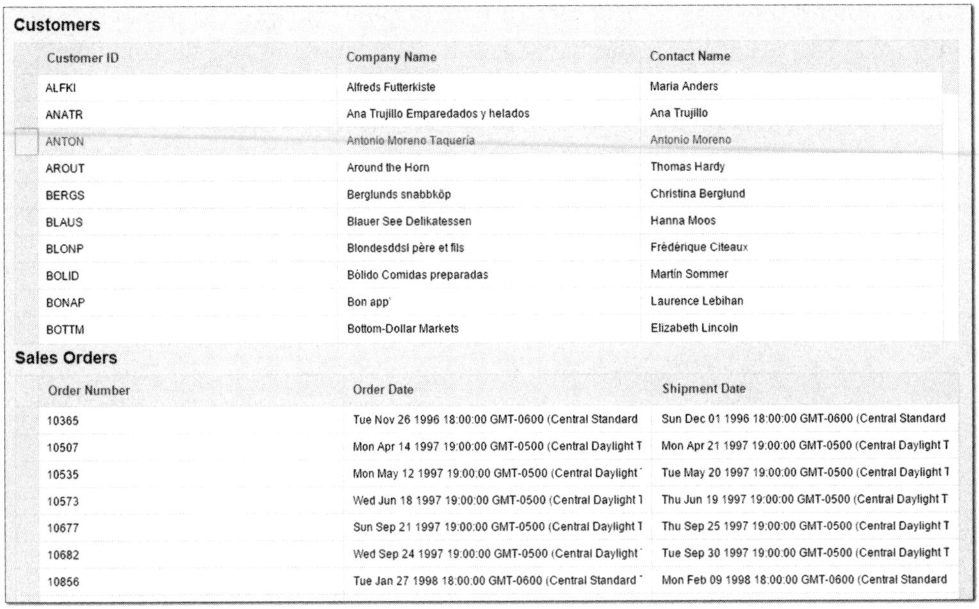

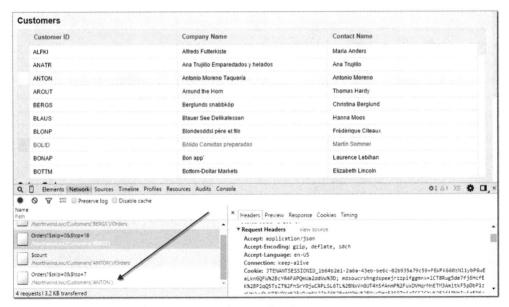

Figure 7.33 Testing the Customers Application: Part 1

Figure 7.34 Testing the Customers Application: Part 2

7.4   Summary

In this chapter, we showed you how to use the HTML5 application model to build lightweight, UI-centric applications. This application model, though less powerful than the Java and SAP HANA XS server-side models reviewed previously, offers tremendous benefits for customers looking to leverage in-house web development teams to create new applications or migrate existing applications to the cloud.

In the next chapter, we'll turn our attention to one of the most important topics in cloud-based application development: *security*. There, you'll find that SAP HCP has a number of useful tools and services that you can use to implement a holistic security model for your applications.

Despite the myriad of benefits associated with cloud computing, many businesses remain hesitant to jump on board the cloud bandwagon for one reason: security. Although some security concerns are perhaps unfounded, the fact remains that security threats are real and must be dealt with. In this chapter, we'll explain how to apply the appropriate security measures for SAP HCP applications.

8 Securing Cloud Applications

Within a given news cycle, it's not uncommon to find multiple reports of malicious attacks being launched against applications running in the cloud. As a result, it's not surprising that many organizations are more than a little hesitant to deploy enterprise applications that handle sensitive data to the public cloud. However, just because these attacks are so prevalent doesn't mean that we can't have secure applications running in the cloud; we just have to work at it a little bit more.

In this chapter, we'll take a look at some of the tools and services that you can use to secure applications running on SAP HCP. You'll find that SAP has blended security concepts from a variety of open standards (such as SAML and OAuth) to provide developers with a robust infrastructure for tackling even the most daunting of security requirements.

8.1 Overview

For years, most SAP landscapes have existed in isolation on-premise, being nested safely within the confines of a secure corporate firewall. Although such a setup doesn't eliminate security risks altogether, it certainly cuts down on the amount of time developers have to spend worrying about security concerns. Indeed, most SAP developers working in such environments rarely bother to protect against common security vulnerabilities because, quite frankly, the chances of such vulnerabilities being exploited inside the firewall are fairly low.

In the cloud, though, it's a completely different story. Here, you must adopt a holistic security model that ensures that every aspect of an application is protected against malicious attacks. Although the nature of this security model will change based on an application's requirements, there are generally three main issues that you must concern yourself with:

▸ **Authentication**
Authentication is all about verifying the identity of the user(s) that will be accessing your applications. In essence, you need to come up with a reliable way of determining if users are in fact who they say they are.

▸ **Authorization**
Once you determine a user's identity, the next step is to determine what functions the user is authorized to perform within the application. Here, the general rule of thumb is to limit a user's access to the functions that user needs to carry out his or her job on a daily basis—no more, no less.

▸ **Confidentiality and integrity**
As users navigate within an application, you need to make sure that the data being exchanged back and forth between the user and the application is transmitted securely. This means that no one can eavesdrop on the application's conversation. It also means that you must take steps to ensure that data packets are not tampered with as they travel back and forth between the client and server.

In the sections that follow, we'll explore the vast array of tools and services that SAP has provided with SAP HCP to address these key security issues. As you might expect, the way that these tools and services are utilized varies quite a bit between programming environments (e.g., Java vs. native SAP HANA). Therefore, because we cannot realistically cover each and every nuance of the environment-specific security models, we chose to develop the hands-on examples for this chapter using the Java programming language. This, of course, is by no means meant to be prescriptive; we simply felt that certain SAP HCP-related security concepts were easier to relate using Java.

Overall, our goal in this chapter will be to focus in on the main SAP HCP security concepts that apply across programming models. Once you grasp these concepts, we think that you'll find it fairly easy to relate them to your programming model of choice. To that end, we'll be sure to point out appropriate reference materials along the way that you can use to dig in and address specific requirements in further detail.

8.2 Introduction to Java EE Security Concepts

Even though most security concepts are universal in nature, the application of these concepts within a particular programming environment tends to vary quite a bit. Therefore, in this section, we'll set the stage for some of the Java-based examples we'll be developing later on in this chapter by examining the built-in features of the Java EE security model. As we progress through this chapter, you'll find that these basic features provide a foundation upon which SAP has implemented some of the more advanced security-related functions of SAP HCP.

8.2.1 Understanding the Java EE Security Model

When considering Java EE security concepts, it's important to recall that the Java EE specification was not designed with any particular application server in mind. In order to achieve this kind of portability, the writers of the Java EE specification defined a layer of abstraction that describes security implementation details in generic terms. Figure 8.1 highlights the basic elements that make up this abstract security model, and here you can identify the following:

▸ **Users**
Within the Java security model, users are referred to as *user principals*. According to the specification, user principals are identified by a unique *principal name* (i.e., user name) and can be authenticated using some form of authentication data. The specification has nothing to say about where these user principals are stored or how they're maintained; these implementation details are left up to the server vendor(s).

▸ **Roles**
Depending on the context, the term role within the Java EE security model can take on several connotations. In general, roles are meant to model the business roles performed by users. For example, when creating a purchasing application, you might define a `Buyer` role, a `Purchasing Manager` role, and so forth.

From a technical perspective, roles group together a series of related authorizations within a Java (web) application. For instance, the `Buyer` role mentioned previously would likely provide authorizations for accessing a purchase order maintenance application and related functions. In essence, the role would contain all of the authorizations that users operating in that business role need to perform their job. Functionally, roles can be used to define coarse-grained authorizations, fine-grained authorizations, or both.

At deployment time, users are mapped to specific roles using various features proprietary to a given Java server provider. Within SAP HCP, such assignments are normally defined within the SAP HCP Cockpit.

▶ **Groups**
Groups are used to simplify role administration for various user groups. For example, if a company has a large purchasing group, then it's possible that there might be many buyers. Therefore, rather than assigning the relevant buyer roles to each of those users, you can assign the roles to a Buyer group and then assign the users to that group. Not only does this save time up front, it also makes it easier to add or remove roles from that group of users down the road.

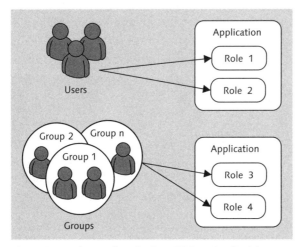

Figure 8.1 Understanding the Java EE Security Model

From a development perspective, you can utilize the elements of the Java EE security model in one of two ways:

▶ **Declaratively**
If your security requirements are sufficiently coarse-grained, you can utilize the web.xml deployment descriptor of Java web applications to declaratively

define security constraints based on user role assignments. Here, for example, you might define a security constraint that restricts access to a set of web resources (i.e., URLs) based on a user's role assignment(s). We'll show you how this is accomplished in Section 8.3.

▶ **Programmatically**
If you want to assert more conditional or fine-grained access control within your applications, then you also have the option of using functions of the Servlet and Java Authentication and Authorization Service (JAAS) APIs to check a user's authorizations within your application code. We'll explore these features in Section 8.4.

8.2.2 Technical Underpinnings

On the technical side of things, the Java EE security model is rounded out by implementation-specific features defined by server providers, such as SAP. To put these features into perspective, consider the technical overview diagram contained in Figure 8.2. Here, you can see that the Java EE security stack for web applications essentially consists of three main components:

▶ **Servlet/web container**
This container provides a secure environment for running Servlets/JSPs. From a security perspective, it's notable that the Java EE specification requires Java EE product providers to define access to Servlets/JSPs using both the HTTP and HTTPS protocols. This means that a Java EE implementation like SAP HCP provides out-of-the-box support for data encryption using the SSL/TLS protocols, satisfying the confidentiality and integrity security requirements described in Section 8.1.

▶ **Modular authentication /authorization based on JAAS**
As you can see in Figure 8.2, the Servlet container does not (generally) have direct connections to authentication/authorization providers. Instead, most Servlet containers delegate such requests to modules developed using JAAS. This layer of indirection shields developers from low-level security implementation details and also provides a unified API for implementing programmatic security requirements. We'll show you how this works in Section 8.4.3.

▶ **Authentication /authorization provider(s)**
At the bottom of the stack, you have one or more authentication or authorization providers, which provide capabilities around storing and maintaining

users, role assignments, and groups. In Section 8.5 and Section 8.6, you'll see how SAP HCP makes it possible for you to mix and match providers within SAP HCP itself, via third-party identity providers (such as the SAP ID Service), and even via preexisting providers managed on-premise.

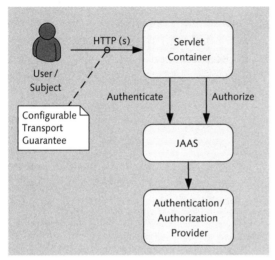

Figure 8.2 Elements of the Java EE Security Model for Web Applications

8.3 Implementing Declarative Security with Java

In Section 8.2.1, we noted that the Java EE specification supports a declarative security model in which the security mechanisms for an application are defined using the web.xml deployment descriptor. In this section, we'll take a look at what you can achieve using this declarative security model.

> **Note**
>
> As you read through this section, keep in mind that many of the concepts that we'll be describing here also generally apply to native SAP HANA applications and, to a lesser extent, HTML5 applications. For example, the roles and constraints that you define for Java applications in the web.xml deployment descriptor are comparable to the roles and privileges that you learned to create for native SAP HANA applications in Chapter 5. You'll also see similarities with the security constraints defined for HTML5 applications in the neo-app.json descriptor file (refer back to Chapter 7).

8.3.1 Configuring Authentication

According to the Java EE platform specification, all compliant Java web containers must provide some level of built-in support for authentication. Indeed, at a minimum, a server provider must include support for three authentication methods: HTTP basic authentication, HTTPS client authentication (i.e., client certificates), and form-based authentication. In the case of SAP HCP, there are quite a few other authentication methods in play as well.

For the most part, developers can tap into these built-in authentication methods by specifying the desired method within the web.xml deployment descriptor. This is achieved using the `<login-config>` element, as shown in Listing 8.1.

```
<web-app>
  ...
  <login-config>
    <auth-method>FORM</auth-method>
  </login-config>
  ...
</web-app>
```

Listing 8.1 Configuring the Authentication Method for a Java Web Application

In the web.xml excerpt contained in Listing 8.1, you can see how we've turned on form-based authentication within a web application. At runtime, this setting is processed as follows:

▸ If a user needs to authenticate for some reason (e.g., if the user tries to access a secure resource), then the form-based authentication method will be used.

▸ By default, the form that users use to authenticate is the default logon form provided by the SAP ID Service (Figure 8.3). You'll learn more about the positioning of the SAP ID Service in Section 8.5.

▸ If the user successfully authenticates, then details about the authenticated user will be stored in the Servlet request context.

In addition to the (default) form-based authentication method, SAP HCP also supports a number of other authorization methods. Table 8.1 contains a comprehensive list of the authentication methods supported by SAP HCP as of the time of writing. To incorporate a particular authentication method into your own Java web application(s), you simply plug in the appropriate authentication method name into the `<auth-method>` tag, as demonstrated in Listing 8.1. Of course, depending on the authentication method you choose, there may be additional steps required to configure authentication within your SAP HCP instance, on the client side, or both. For more information about the additional configuration steps required for a given authentication method, we recommend that you consult the SAP HANA Cloud Documentation available online at *https://help. hana.ondemand.com*.

Figure 8.3 Authenticating Using Form-Based Authentication

Authentication Method	Description
FORM	Within SAP HCP, this authentication method is used to configure form-based authentication using the Security Assertion Markup Language (SAML) 2.0 protocol. We'll explore this preferred method of authentication within SAP HCP at length in Section 8.5.
BASIC	This method enables authentication using HTTP basic authentication, as described in RFC 2617. This challenge-response scheme passes a user's logon credentials to the server in a base 64–encoded string embedded within an HTTP request header. On the server side, SAP HCP delegates the authentication request to the default identity provider (IdP) configured within the SAP HCP Cockpit. Normally, this implies that the request is processed by the SAP ID Service, but some customers may prefer to use an on-premise IdP instead. In any case, the use of basic authentication is not recommended, due to the fact that it's not as secure as the other supported authentication methods.

Table 8.1 Supported Authentication Methods of SAP HCP

Authentication Method	Description
CERT	This method makes it possible for users to log on using client certificates (e.g., X.509 certificates).
BASICCERT	This hybrid authentication method supports authentication with client certificates inside the corporate network and basic authentication outside the network.
OAUTH	This authentication method is used to secure web APIs using the OAuth 2.0 protocol. Here, clients authenticate by passing in an OAuth access token. We'll take a closer look at OAuth in Section 8.6.
SAML2	The behavior of this authentication method is identical to the FORM authentication method.

Table 8.1 Supported Authentication Methods of SAP HCP (Cont.)

8.3.2 Defining Security Roles and Constraints

Looking at the Java EE security model diagram in Figure 8.2, you can see that security roles are defined in the context of Java web applications. (In Section 8.5.3, you'll find that SAP HCP also allows you to define ad hoc security roles within SAP HCP Cockpit.) Within the web.xml deployment descriptor, security roles are defined using the <security-role> element, as demonstrated in Listing 8.2. Here, you can see that a role definition consists of a role name and an optional description.

```
<web-app>
  . . .
  <security-role>
    <description>Buyer Role</description>
    <role-name>buyer</role-name>
  </security-role>

  <security-role>
    <description>Manager Role</description>
    <role-name>manager</role-name>
  </security-role>
  . . .
</web-app>
```

Listing 8.2 Defining Security Roles in a Deployment Descriptor File

The granularity (or cut) of the roles that you define within an application is essentially up you; the Java EE specification doesn't have anything to say about how

333

roles are defined or used. Therefore, you can configure lots of tiny, fine-grained roles, several coarse-grained ones, or a mix of both.

After you define roles, the next step is to figure out how to use them to protect sensitive application resources. If your objective is to control access to particular URLs, then one way you can put your roles to work is by using them to declaratively define security constraints within the application's deployment descriptor. This approach is demonstrated in the web.xml excerpt contained in Figure 8.4. Here, you can interpret the XML markup as follows:

▸ The `<security-constraint>` element groups together a security constraint definition within the web.xml file. You can define as many `<security-constraint>` elements as you like.

▸ Using the child `<web-resource-collection>` element, you can define a series of web-based resources that you wish to protect. Such resources are identified using one or more `<url-pattern>` elements, which can point to specific Servlet or JSP URLs or to generic URLs matching some kind of wildcard pattern.

▸ Within a `<web-resource-collection>`, you can also specify the HTTP methods that you want to restrict access to (e.g., `GET` or `POST`).

Once you define `<web-resource-collection>`, you can determine the role(s) that are granted access to it using the `<auth-constraint>` element. As you can see in Figure 8.4, the role name(s) you specify in the `<role-name>` element here correspond with roles defined within the `<security-role>` element.

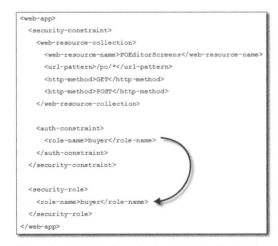

Figure 8.4 Defining Security Constraints in the Deployment Descriptor File

By using security constraints, you can effectively lock the front door to various application screens, preventing users from even navigating to pages or screens they're not authorized to see. This is great for situations in which the security requirements are black and white. However, there will be times when you have to account for situations in which users are granted partial access to web resources. For example, a user might be granted access to a particular page but restricted from seeing selected content areas that contain sensitive data. In Section 8.4.1, you'll learn how to handle more subtle security requirements like this using custom Java code.

8.3.3 Role Assignment in the SAP HCP Cockpit

Now that you've seen how to define security roles and constraints in the previous section, let's shift gears and see how roles are assigned to users within the SAP HCP Cockpit. This can be achieved by opening the SAP HCP Cockpit and clicking on the AUTHORIZATIONS tab. By default, this will open the AUTHORIZATION MANAGEMENT content page to the USERS subtab, as shown in Figure 8.5.

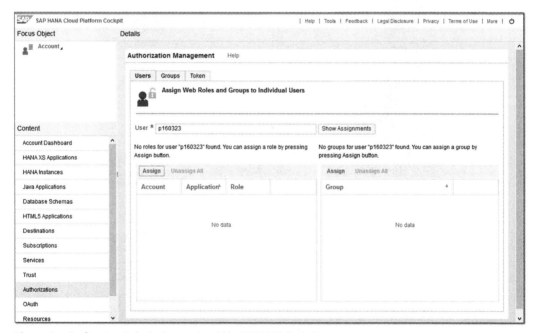

Figure 8.5 Performing Role Assignments within SAP HCP Cockpit

From the USERS subtab page shown in Figure 8.5, the steps required to perform user role assignments are as follows:

1. Select the user record that you want to maintain. This can be achieved by keying the target user account name into the USER field and then clicking on the SHOW ASSIGNMENTS button (see Figure 8.5).

2. In the roles table on the left-hand side of the page, add a new role by clicking on the ASSIGN button.

3. This will open the ASSIGN ROLES FOR USER... dialog box shown in Figure 8.6. Within this dialog box, pinpoint the target role by specifying the host SAP HCP account and the Java application that defines the role.

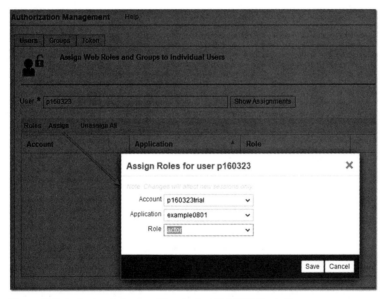

Figure 8.6 Assigning Roles to a User in the SAP HCP Cockpit

4. Complete the role assignment by clicking on the SAVE button.

Where Does SAP HCP Get Its User Accounts From?

As you're playing around with these role assignments, you might be asking yourself where the user accounts themselves are defined. Unlike many Java server implementations that utilize their own (proprietary) user store, SAP HCP is designed to work with user accounts that are maintained on external IdP systems. By default, SAP HCP uses the SAP ID Service as its primary IdP, though you can configure the use of other, additional

IdPs as well. We'll be exploring the implications of all this in greater detail in Section 8.5, but for now the primary takeaway of all this is that user accounts are defined outside of SAP HCP.

To simplify the role assignment process a bit further, SAP HCP also allows you to define custom *groups* that combine multiple roles together so that they can be assigned to particular classes of users in one go. For the most part, the process of assigning a user to a group is identical to the process used to assign roles. Of course, before you can do that, you have to first define the group(s) themselves.

Unlike user accounts, which are maintained within the external IdP, groups are defined within the context of an SAP HCP account in the SAP HCP Cockpit. From the top-level AUTHORIZATIONS tab page, you can get to the group editor by clicking on the GROUPS subtab (Figure 8.7).

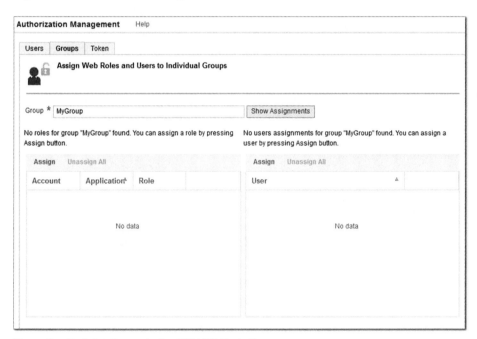

Figure 8.7 Defining Groups in the SAP HCP Cockpit

To create a new group record, simply plug the group name into the GROUP field and then click on the SHOW ASSIGNMENTS button. With the new group record staged, you can begin adding roles to the group using the roles table shown on the left-hand side of the group editor page (Figure 8.7). From here, you can add new roles to the group by clicking on the ASSIGN button. This triggers a similar popup window to the one shown in Figure 8.6 for user role assignments.

After a group is defined, you can begin assigning users in the user assignment panel on the right-hand side of the GROUPS tab page (see Figure 8.7) or from the USERS tab page shown in Figure 8.6. Both approaches get you to the same place, so which path you take is a matter of preference.

Even though groups make it easier to perform role assignments in bulk, there's no getting around the fact that such assignments still require a lot of administrative work whenever you're dealing with a large user base. With that in mind, in Section 8.5 we'll revisit the group assignment process and see how SAML can be used to automate group assignments.

8.4   Implementing Programmatic Security in Java

In the previous section, we demonstrated several techniques for declaratively specifying security constraints. Although these methods are effective for defining basic security constraints, they're not without their limitations. Indeed, if you want to implement conditional security logic and the like, then you're going to have to get your hands dirty with some custom Java code. In this section, we'll show you how to do just that.

8.4.1   Checking Authorizations Programmatically

In Section 8.3.2, you learned how to declaratively define security constraints that prevent unauthorized users from browsing to selected web resources. Although such a clear-cut approach to security is certainly desirable, there will be times when you need to provide users with conditional access to a web resource.

For example, imagine that you're building an employee directory application that allows employees within a company to look up information about their fellow employees. Within this application, suppose that there's an employee details page (perhaps written as a JSP) that displays basic employee contact information as well as more sensitive information, such as the employee's personal contact number, emergency contact, and so forth. Although every employee in the company should be able to access basic contact information, you need to restrict access to sensitive information to selected authorized users, such as the employee's HR manager.

To implement something like this using the declarative approach, you would have to end up creating multiple pages: one for end users and one for managers. As you can imagine, this sort of approach can become quite tedious from a maintenance perspective.

A more economical approach would be to create a single page and conditionally restrict access to particular content sections based on a user's role assignments. With Servlets/JSPs, you can implement such conditional logic using the Boolean `isUserInRole()` method of the `javax.servlet.HttpServletRequest` interface. This approach is demonstrated in the JSP code excerpt contained in Listing 8.3. Here, the `<div>` content contained within the JSP `<%...%>` scriptlet tags is only displayed if the user is mapped to the `manager` role.

```
<%@ page language="java"...%>
<!DOCTYPE HTML>
<html>
  <body>
    ...
    <div id="BasicData">...</div>
    <% if (request.isUserInRole("manager")) { %>
      <div id="PersonalData">...</div>
    <% } %>
  </body>
</html>
```

Listing 8.3 Programmatically Checking User Role Assignments

The code excerpt contained in Listing 8.4 shows how the same `isUserInRole()` method is used within a Java Servlet. Here, the method allows you to implement intelligent routing in a classic model-view-controller (MVC) architecture in which the Servlet plays the role of controller and JSP pages provide the view layer.

```
public class RoutingServlet extends HttpServlet
{
  protected void doGet(HttpServletRequest request,
                   HttpServletResponse response)
    throws ServletException, IOException
  {
    RequestDispatcher rd = null;
    if (request.isUserInRole("manager"))
    {
      rd = request.getRequestDispatcher("ManagerLaunchpad.jsp");
```

```
      rd.forward(request, response);
   }
   else
   {
      rd = request.getRequestDispatcher("EmployeeLaunchpad.jsp");
      rd.forward(request, response);
   }
 }
}
```

Listing 8.4 Using Programmatic Authorization Checks

8.4.2 Working with the User Management API

By default, the Java Servlet API provides two methods that you can use to determine the name of the user logged onto the application. Both of these methods are contained within the `javax.servlet.http.HttpServletRequest` interface, and they are called `getRemoteUser()` and `getUserPrincipal()`.

Although it's useful to be able to determine the user name of a logged-on user, there are typically other things that you'd also like to know about the user, including the following:

- ▸ Basic attributes of the user, such as the user's first and last name, email address, and so on
- ▸ The user's locale and preferences (e.g., country of origin, language spoken, etc.)
- ▸ The set of all roles and groups the user is assigned to
- ▸ The validity date of the user (if applicable)

Although the availability of much of this data is dependent on the capabilities of the underlying IdP, you can get your hands on the data that is available by using the SAP HCP User Management API contained within the `com.sap.secu-rity.um.*` package hierarchy.

> **Note**
>
> You can find a complete overview of the API functions available in the User Management API online at *https://help.hana.ondemand.com/javadoc/index.html*.

The code excerpt contained in Listing 8.5 demonstrates how to interface with the User Management API. Here, API access is provided through the `com.sap.secu-rity.um.user.UserProvider` interface, which can be used to look up information about a user. It should be noted that the user you query information about doesn't necessarily have to be the currently logged-on user; you could look up information about other users as well. In any case, once you have your hands on a `com.sap.security.um.user.User` instance, you can utilize its various getter methods to find out as much information about a user as is provided by the IdP.

```
import com.sap.security.um.user.User;
import com.sap.security.um.user.UserProvder;
import com.sap.security.um.service.UserManagementAccessor;
...
try {
  // Assumption: Only query the attributes for a logged-on user:
  if (request.getUserPrincipal() != null) {
    // Use the UserManagementAccessor factory to obtain an
    // instance of the UserProvider:
    UserProvider userProvider =
      UserManagementAccessor.getUserProvider();

    // Then, lookup the User record:
    User user =
      userProvider.getUser(request.getUserPrincipal().getName());

    // Enumerate the attributes assigned to the user:
    for (String attr : user.listAttributes) {
      response.getWriter().println(
        attr + " : " + user.getAttribute(a));
    }

    // List the user's role assignments:
    for (String role : user.getRoles()) {
      response.getWriter().println(role);
    }
  }
}
catch (Exception ex) { }
```
Listing 8.5 Working with the User Management API

Although the code excerpt contained in Listing 8.5 showed how to obtain a `User-Provider` instance via the `UserManagementAccessor` factory, there are actually a couple of other ways you can get your hands on this instance. One approach is to declare the `UserProvider` as a resource reference in the web.xml deployment descriptor, as shown in Listing 8.6. With the resource reference defined, you can look up the `UserProvider` in your application using a JNDI lookup.

```
<web-app>
  ...
```

```
    <resource-ref>
      <res-ref-name>user/Provider</res-ref-name>
      <res-type>com.sap.security.um.user.UserProvider</res-type>
    </resource-ref>
  </web-app>
```
Listing 8.6 Declaring the User Provider as a Resource Reference

Alternatively, if the SAP HCP instance you're working with is based on the Java EE 6 Web profile, then you can inject the `UserProvider` instance using the `@Resource` annotation, as shown in Listing 8.7.

```
@Resource
private UserProvider userProvider;
```
Listing 8.7 Injecting the UserProvider Instance

In addition to providing information about specific users, the `UserProvider` interface also contains a powerful search method called `searchUser()`, which can be used to search for users based on various types of search criteria. This feature can come in handy whenever you want to identify classes of users, for instance.

8.4.3 Working with the Authentication API

In Section 8.2.2, we mentioned that most Java EE server vendors prefer to externalize authentication and authorization handling logic to a series of modules built using JAAS. Although such details are typically abstracted from developers, this doesn't necessarily mean that developers can't get their hands on these modules to interface with this functionality directly.

Within SAP HCP, access to JAAS modules and callback handlers is provided in the form of the Authentication API contained in the `com.sap.security.auth.login`-package. Using this API, you can programmatically trigger a user login or logout as needed.

The code excerpt contained in Listing 8.8 demonstrates how you can use the Authentication API to dynamically trigger a form-based login in situations in which the user hasn't authenticated already. Here, the call to the `javax.security.auth.login.LoginContext` interface's `login()` method does the trick, temporarily rerouting the user to a form logon page like the one illustrated in Figure 8.3. After the user authenticates, the program picks up where it left off with the logged-on user information in tow.

```
import javax.security.auth.login.*;
import com.sap.security.auth.login.LoginContextFactory;

public class LoginServlet extends HttpServlet {
  protected void doGet(HttpServletRequest request,
                       HttpServletResponse response)
    throws ServletException, IOException
  {
    // Trigger a form-based login as necessary:
    if (request.getUserPrincipal() == null) {
      try {
        LoginContext ctx =
          LoginContextFactory.createLoginContext("FORM");
        ctx.login();
      }
      catch (LoginException le) {
        // TODO: Error handling...
      }
    }

    repsonse.getWriter().println("Hello, " +
      request.getUserPrincipal().getName());
  }
}
```

Listing 8.8 Triggering a Form-Based Login Using the Authentication API

To log a user out, simply call the `logout()` method of the `LoginContext` interface, as shown in Listing 8.9. That's pretty much all there is to it. However, if you're thinking of implementing a more elaborate logout scenario in your application, we would highly encourage you to read through the section entitled "Enabling Logout" in the SAP HANA Cloud Documentation (*https://help.hana.onde-mand.com*). There, you'll find lots of practical tips for incorporating this functionality into client-side JavaScript code.

```
import javax.security.auth.login.*;
import com.sap.security.auth.login.LoginContextFactory;

public class LogoutServlet extends HttpServlet {
  protected void doGet(HttpServletRequest request,
                       HttpServletResponse response)
    throws ServletException, IOException
  {
    try {
      LoginContext ctx =
        LoginContextFactory.createLoginContext();
      ctx.logout();
    }
```

```
catch (LoginException le) {
    // TODO: Error handling...
  }
 }
}
```

Listing 8.9 Logging a User Out via the Authentication API

8.4.4 Working with the Password Storage API

Although SAP HCP is designed to minimize the amount of sensitive user data you store on the platform itself, there may be times when you want to persist a piece of confidential data so that you can access it later on. For example, when you learn about the OAuth authorization protocol in Section 8.6, you'll find that authorization servers issue clients a couple of access tokens that can be used to obtain access to selected web resources. For the sake of convenience, it makes sense to store these access tokens in a secure location so that you can reuse them throughout the duration of their lifetime (which can span days or even weeks at a time).

Although you could technically store this information in a relational database table using the persistence service, it's preferable to store the data in something a bit more secure in the event that a malicious user obtains access to the system. Within SAP HCP, you can obtain access to a secure storage location using the Password Storage API.

The code excerpt contained in Listing 8.10 demonstrates how to work with the Password Storage API. As you can see in the code, you obtain access to this API via a JNDI lookup. This assumes that you've defined a resource reference in the web.xml deployment descriptor—something we'll look at in just a moment. Once you obtain your `PasswordStorage` instance, you can use its password-related methods to set, get, and delete a password as needed. Here, the password is referenced by some alias string that's unique within the password store.

```
import com.sap.cloud.security.password.*;

public class PasswordStorageServlet extends HttpServlet {
  protected void doGet(HttpServletRequest request,
                        HttpServletResponse response)
    throws ServletException, IOException
  {
    try {
      // Obtain a security access token, etc.
      String accessToken = ...
```

```
    // Obtain a refernce to the Password Storage API:
    InitialContext ctx = new InitialContext();
    PasswordStorage storage = (PasswordStorage)
      ctx.lookup("java:comp/env/PasswordStorage");

    // Define an alias that's used to reference the
    // stored token:
    String alias =
      request.getUserPrincipal().getName() + "_Token";

    // Store the token in the secure store:
    storage.setPassword(alias, accessToken.getBytes("UTF-8");

    // Refetch the token:
    String readToken =
      new String(storage.getPassword(alias), "UTF-8");

    // Delete the token from the secure store:
    storage.deletePassword(alias);
  }
  catch (Exception ex) {
  }
  }
}
```

Listing 8.10 Working with the Password Storage API

To access the Password Storage API from a JNDI lookup in your Java code, you must define a resource reference, as demonstrated in the web.xml excerpt contained in Listing 8.11.

```
<web-app>
  ...
  <resource-ref>
    <res-ref-name>PasswordStorage</res-ref-name>
    <res-type>
      com.sap.cloud.security.password.PasswordStorage
    </res-type>
  </resource-ref>
</web-app>
```

Listing 8.11 Adding the Password Storage API as a Resource Reference

8.4.5 Protecting Against Cross-Site Scripting Attacks

Cross-site scripting (XSS) is the name given to a class of vulnerabilities present in dynamic HTML-based web applications. Although the method(s) used by attackers tends to vary, the basic goal of an XSS attack is to figure out ways of injecting HTML and/or JavaScript markup in a web application in order to render it unusable, perform malicious operations, and so forth.

To guard against such attacks, it's good practice to filter any dynamically generated content through an output encoding library that sanitizes the data and protects against XSS vulnerabilities. Rather than having to build such a tool on your own, SAP provides a robust library in the SAP HCP SDK.

To incorporate this XSS output encoding library into your Java web application(s), perform the following steps:

1. Within the Eclipse PROJECT EXPLORER view, expand the WEBCONTENT/WEB-INF/ LIB folder, right-click on it, and select the IMPORT... menu option (Figure 8.8).

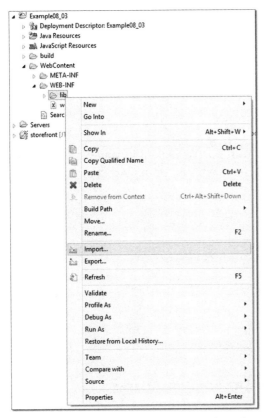

Figure 8.8 Importing the XSS Output Encoding Library: Part 1

2. In the IMPORT dialog box that pops up, expand the GENERAL folder and choose the FILE SYSTEM option, as shown in Figure 8.9. Click on the NEXT > button to continue.

Figure 8.9 Importing the XSS Output Encoding Library: Part 2

3. At the next screen, click on the BROWSE... button to open the IMPORT FROM DIRECTORY window shown in Figure 8.10. From here, navigate to the *repository/ plugins* subdirectory of your SAP HCP SDK folder and click on the OK button.

4. Scroll through the list of JAR files in the PLUGINS directory to find the COM.SAP.SECURITY.CORE.SERVER.CIS_1.X.Y.JAR archive file, as shown in Figure 8.11. Select the archive file and click on the FINISH button to import the library into your application.

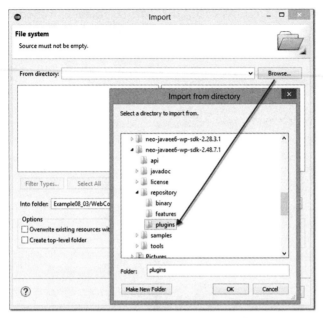

Figure 8.10 Importing the XSS Output Encoding Library: Part 3

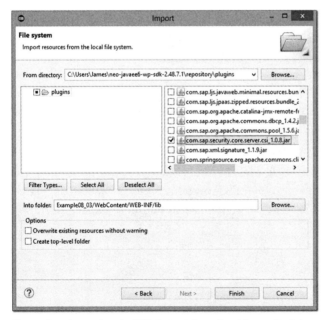

Figure 8.11 Importing the XSS Output Encoding Library: Part 4

Once the library's imported, you can access the XSS output encoding API by obtaining an instance of the `com.sap.security.core.server.csi.IXSSEncoder` interface, as demonstrated in the code excerpt contained in Listing 8.12. Here, you're obtaining this interface by calling the `getInstance()` factory method of the `com.sap.security.core.server.csi.XSSEncoder` class. With this instance in hand, you can encode content using the various `encode...()` methods, as shown in Listing 8.12.

```
import com.sap.security.core.server.csi.*;
...
try {
  IXSSEncoder encoder = XSSEncoder.getInstance();

  // Encode HTML markup:
  String rawHTML = ...
  String encodedHTML =
    encoder.encodeHTML(rawHTML).toString();

  // Encode JavaScript code:
  String rawJS = ...
  String encodedJS =
    encoder.encodeJavaScript(rawJS);
  ...
}
catch (UnsupportedEncodingException (uee) {
}
```

Listing 8.12 Using the XSS Output Encoding Library

You can find a comprehensive list of encoding methods defined in this library in the aforementioned API documentation. Here, you'll find methods for encoding HTML/XML, JavaScript, CSS, URLs, and more.

8.5 Authentication and Authorization with SAML 2.0

In Section 8.2.2, we touched on the fact that SAP HCP is capable of integrating with a wide array of authentication providers. Unlike other Java EE servers you may have worked with (e.g., the SAP AS Java), in which such features are considered "nice to have," it turns out that this capability is actually an essential part of the SAP HCP security infrastructure. This is because SAP HCP was designed from the ground up to not maintain any permanent user storage of its own.

Why take this approach, you might ask? If you consider the fact that most customers' biggest reservation about adopting cloud-based solutions is security, then it makes sense for SAP to remove as many potential security risks from the mix as possible. Using a federated approach to authentication reduces the threat of sensitive user information being compromised in the cloud. Plus, it also offers the added benefit of letting customers leverage preexisting IdP solutions they might have in-house.

In this section, you'll learn how to configure and leverage federated authentication using the industry-standard Security Assertion Markup Language (SAML) 2.0 protocol. This protocol is the primary protocol used by SAP HCP for the purposes of authentication and single sign-on (SSO).

8.5.1 SAML Overview

Before you begin looking at how to configure SAML-based authentication scenarios, it's helpful to understand a little more about what SAML is (and isn't). As its name implies, SAML defines an XML-based vocabulary that's used to exchange authentication and authorization data between parties. Within the vernacular, the negotiating parties are referred to as the *identity provider* (IdP) and *service provider*, respectively.

In addition to the XML-based messages it defines, the SAML 2.0 standard also specifies a series of protocols that describe how messages are exchanged between users, the IdP, and the service provider. The typical message flow for a SAML authentication request processed through SAP HCP is illustrated in Figure 8.12.

Within the flow diagram contained in Figure 8.12, you can observe the following:

❶ The process begins with a user attempting to access a secure web application hosted on the service provider. As you can see in Figure 8.12, SAP HCP plays the role of service provider in this scenario.

❷ Upon receipt of the request, the SAP HCP server determines via declarative constraints defined in the application's web.xml file that the user needs to authenticate before the server can decide whether or not the user is authorized to access the application. Assuming that the authentication method is set to FORM (refer back to Section 8.3.1), the request will be handed off to a JAAS-based login module. This module will generate a SAML authentication request (i.e., a SAML `AuthnRequest` message) and send it back to the user in an HTTP 302 redirect message.

❸ The browser then follows the redirect and forwards the SAML authentication request on to the SSO login page defined by the IdP. By default, this results in the user being routed to the login page of the SAP ID Service, as shown in Figure 8.3. Naturally, the look and feel of the page would be different if an alternative IdP is being used instead.

❹ Once the user fills in his or her user credentials and submits the login form, the login request is forwarded on to the IdP.

❺ Upon receipt of the login request, the IdP will process the request and return a SAML response message back to the user's browser.

❻ From here, the SAML response is forwarded on to the service provider, where it's unpacked to determine if the user was authenticated. Assuming the authentication is successful, then the web container will grant access to the target web application.

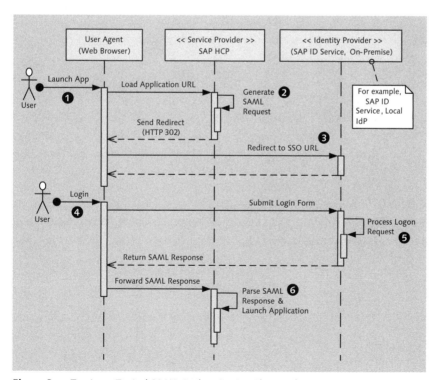

Figure 8.12 Tracing a Typical SAML Authentication Flow within SAP HCP

For the most part, developers don't really have to concern themselves with the intricacies of the authorization flow illustrated in Figure 8.12, because these details are handled automatically by the JAAS login module(s) of SAP HCP. With that being said, though, we should point out that a SAML response message contains more than just a flag indicating whether or not a user is authorized. The response message also contains a series of *assertions* (hence the name), which contain user attributes (e.g., first and last name, email address, telephone number, etc.), and sometimes authorization decision statements, which can be used to determine user authorizations. We'll explore some of the ways these attributes are used in Section 8.5.3.

8.5.2 Configuring Trusted Identity Providers

As we noted earlier, SAP HCP is configured by default to utilize the SAP ID Service as its trusted IdP. This SAP ID Service is the same one users use to access SCN and other SAP-related sites. Although this default IdP is suitable to get things up and running, most customers will prefer to connect with a preexisting IdP they already have in-house (e.g., Microsoft Active Directory Services). This IdP could be provided by a third party on the Internet or on-premise; it doesn't really matter one way or another to SAP HCP.

In order to leverage another IdP from within SAP HCP, you must configure a trust relationship between SAP HCP (which plays the role of a service provider) and the target IdP. To demonstrate how this works, let's take a look at how you can configure a trust relationship to the simplified (but fully SAML-compliant) IdP bundled with the local runtime environment included in the SAP HCP SDK. The configuration steps are as follows:

1. Open the SAP HCP Cockpit and access the TRUST tab. This will open the TRUST MANAGEMENT page shown in Figure 8.13. To create a new trust relationship, choose the CUSTOM configuration type in the CONFIGURATION TYPE dropdown list.

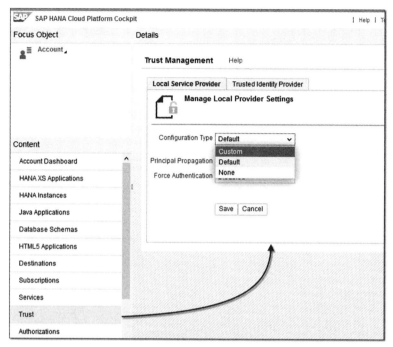

Figure 8.13 Configuring Access to a Local Identity Provider: Part 1

2. As soon as you select the custom configuration type, the screen will refresh itself to display details about the SAP HCP service provider (e.g., the provider name, its signing key and certificate, and so on). Although you have the option of overriding default values here, for now simply accept the defaults and click on the GET METADATA hyperlink (highlighted in Figure 8.14). This action will trigger the download of an XML file containing metadata about the service provider. (This metadata is encoded in an `EntityDescriptor` message, as defined by the SAML 2.0 standard.) For now, simply save the file locally so that you can use it a little bit later on.

3. On the IdP end of the exchange, you need to generate a metadata file containing information about the IdP. To perform this step, start up your local SAP HCP runtime and open a browser window to *http://{local_hcp_instance_host}:{port}/saml2/localidp/metadata*, as shown in Figure 8.15. Once again, you need to save the generated XML file so that you can import it in a later step.

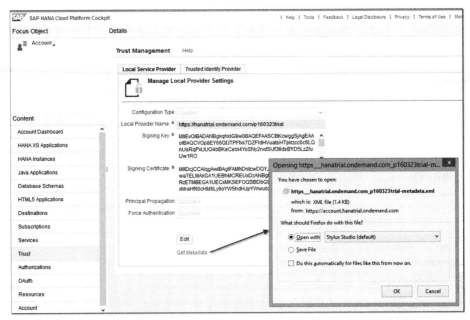

Figure 8.14 Configuring Access to a Local Identity Provider: Part 2

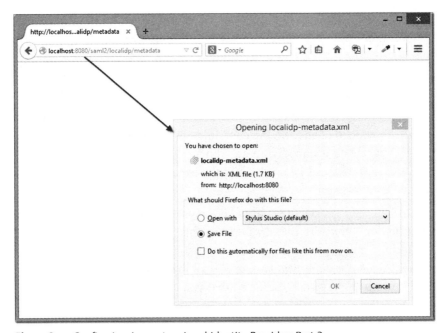

Figure 8.15 Configuring Access to a Local Identity Provider: Part 3

4. With the IdP metadata in hand, you can go back to the SAP HCP Cockpit and navigate to the TRUSTED IDENTITY PROVIDER subtab (Figure 8.16). Here, click on the ADD TRUSTED IDENTITY PROVIDER link to create the new trusted IdP configuration.

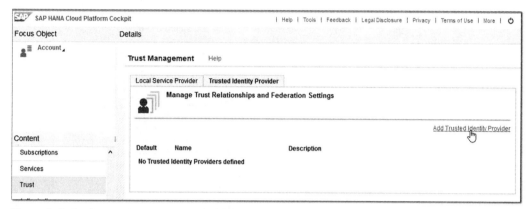

Figure 8.16 Configuring Access to a Local Identity Provider: Part 4

5. Figure 8.17 shows the popup box that opens whenever you go to create a new trusted IdP. Although there are a lot of attributes that have to be filled in to define a trust relationship, the good news is that you don't have to key in the attributes by hand. Instead, you can copy this information from the metadata file created in step 3 by clicking on the BROWSE… button adjacent to the METADATA FILE field and selecting the XML file generated by the local IdP. Once the attributes are copied over, you can save the trusted IdP configuration by clicking on the SAVE & CLOSE button.

6. The last step is to open the server configuration on the local IdP to plug in the metadata file generated by the SAP HCP service provider. This can be achieved by copying and pasting the XML file created in step 2 into the CONFIG_MASTER/COM.SAP.CORE.JPAAS.SECURITY.SAML2.CFG/LOCALIDP folder, as shown in Figure 8.18.

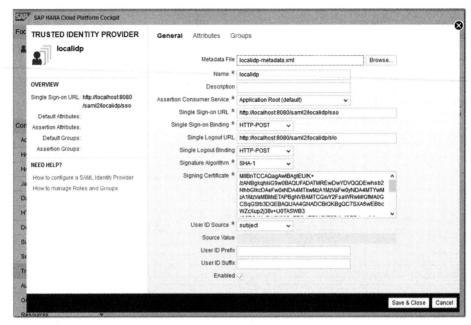

Figure 8.17 Configuring Access to a Local Identity Provider: Part 5

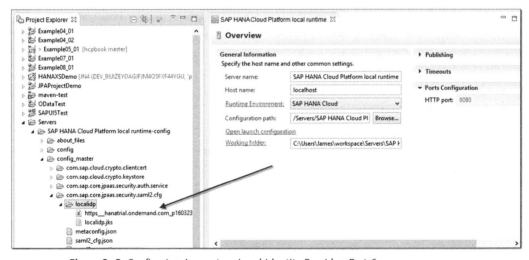

Figure 8.18 Configuring Access to a Local Identity Provider: Part 6

Once these configuration steps are in place, the changes will take effect immediately. To the end user, all of this will be transparent, save for the fact that the logon page will look a little bit different (see Figure 8.19).

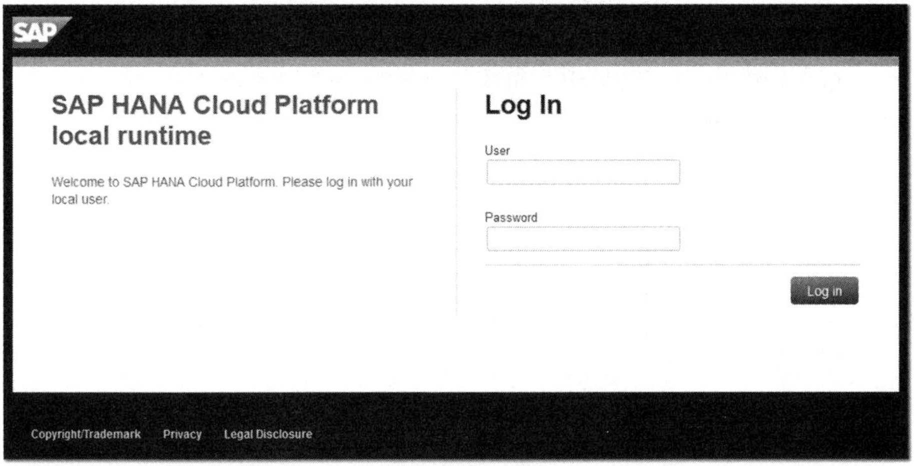

Figure 8.19 Accessing the SSO Logon Page of the SAP HCP Local Runtime

For the most part, the configuration steps required to establish a trust relationship with another SAML-compliant IdP are largely the same as the ones used to connect with the local test IdP. The primary differences lie in how you generate the IdP metadata and how you configure the trust relationship to the service provider from within the IdP itself. Fortunately, there are how-to guides available on SCN that describe IdP-specific requirements.

Before we move on, we should point out that it's technically possible to configure and run multiple IdPs simultaneously. In this scenario, you have a default IdP (of your choosing) and one or more alternative IdPs. At runtime, authentication requests will continue to be routed through the default IdP as usual. However, you can force authentication through one of the alternate IdPs by adding the query string parameter `saml2idp=<idp_name>` to the end of the application URL.

8.5.3 Implementing Assertion-Based Group Mapping

In Section 8.3.3, we observed just how tedious it can be to assign roles or groups to users—especially whenever you have lots of users to maintain. Fortunately, there's a simpler way. In this section, you'll learn how to use the assertion attributes returned in a SAML authentication response message to define flexible role or group assignments via mappings.

To get things started, let's take a look at some user master records on the local IdP you configured in Section 8.5.2. In Figure 8.20, you can see how we're creating a user record inside the SAP HCP local runtime's server administration page in Eclipse. Here, you specify the user ID and some basic contact information (e.g., first name, last name, and email address).

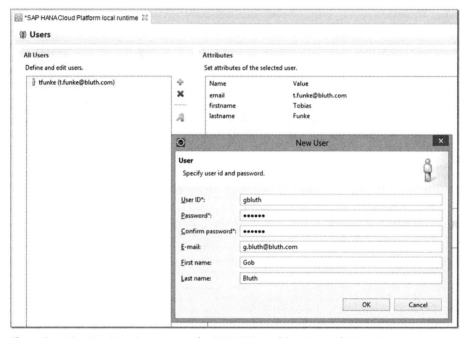

Figure 8.20 Creating User Accounts on the SAP HCP Local Runtime's IdP: Part 1

In addition to these default attributes, most IdPs also allow you to define custom user attributes as needed. For example, in Figure 8.21, you can see how we're creating a custom user attribute called skillset for the user record we created in Figure 8.20. Ultimately, our goal will be to use this attribute to determine which group(s) or role(s) the user should be assigned to.

In order to put our user attributes to work, we've prepared a sample application in the book's source code bundle called EXAMPLE08_01. This application defines two generic roles within its web.xml file: magician and actor (see Figure 8.22).

For now, we won't assign these roles to any of the users we created on our local IdP.

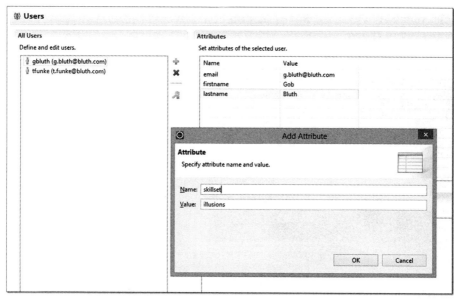

Figure 8.21 Creating User Accounts on the SAP HCP Local Runtime's IdP: Part 2

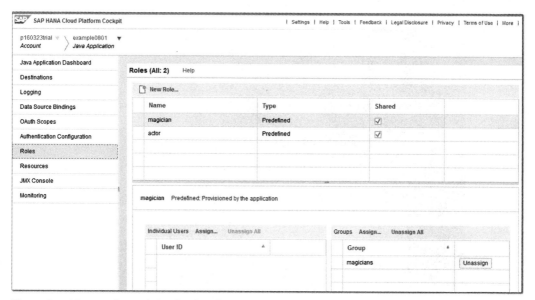

Figure 8.22 Viewing the Predefined Roles of the Sample Application

To make things even more interesting, we'll supplement the predefined roles deployed with the sample application with a new custom role called `manager`. Create this role by clicking on the NEW ROLE... button in the toolbar of the ROLES table contained within the ROLES tab of the JAVA APPLICATION DASHBOARD screen (Figure 8.22). Simply specify the role name and click on the SAVE button to create the role (see Figure 8.23).

Figure 8.23 Creating a Custom Role in the SAP HCP Cockpit

To simplify administration, consolidate these roles into group assignments, as shown in Figure 8.24. Momentarily, we'll show you how this additional step makes it easier to map users to their proper role assignments.

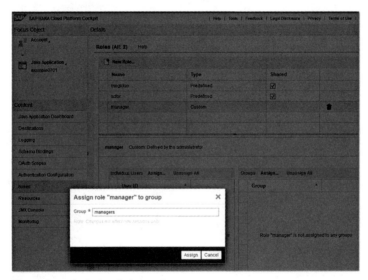

Figure 8.24 Assigning Roles to Groups

Once the group assignments are in place, the next step is to navigate over to the top-level TRUST tab of the SAP HCP Cockpit and configure assertion-based attribute mappings for your local IdP configuration. These mappings basically map assertion attributes coming back from the local IdP in a SAML response to attributes of the user principal object that you have access to via the User Management API (refer back to Section 8.4.2).

To create these mappings, you need to open the trust configuration for your local IdP and select the ATTRIBUTES subtab screen (Figure 8.25). From here, you can create assertion-based attributes by clicking on the ADD ASSERTION-BASED ATTRIBUTE link shown in Figure 8.25. Note that although the name of the ASSERTION ATTRIBUTE must align with the attributes defined in the IdP, you're generally free to call the corresponding PRINCIPAL ATTRIBUTE whatever you like. From a developer perspective, you just need to remember the names you choose, because these names will be what you use to access the attributes programmatically using the User Management API (refer back to Listing 8.5 for a refresher on how this works).

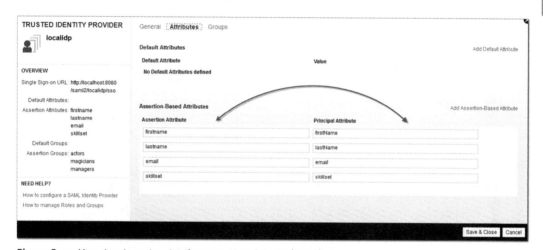

Figure 8.25 Mapping Assertion Attributes to User Principal Attributes

Finally, once the assertion-based attributes are in place, you can proceed with your group mappings by navigating over to the GROUPS tab. Here, you can define assertion-based group mappings by clicking on the ADD ASSERTION-BASED GROUP link shown in Figure 8.26. The mapping rules are configured as follows:

- ▶ In the GROUP column, specify the target user group that you want to map to.
- ▶ Then, in the next three columns, define mapping rule expressions by specifying the name of the assertion attribute in the first column, an operator in the second column, and the target value in the third column.

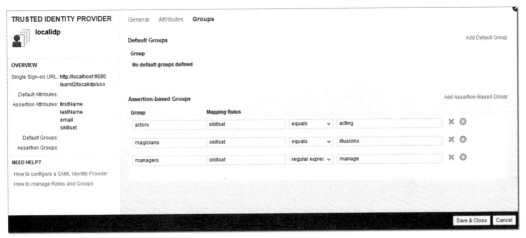

Figure 8.26 Applying Assertion-Based Group Mappings

Looking closely at Figure 8.26, you can see how we defined three different mapping rules. The first two rules utilize the EQUALS operator to build simple equality expressions. For example, in rule 1, we say that if the `skillset` assertion attribute is equal to `acting`, then the user should be mapped to the `actors` group. Similarly, in rule 2, we match the `illusions` skillset up with the `magicians` group. Rule three is slightly more complex, because we're using the regular expressions pattern language to match any user whose skillset contains the character sequence `manage` somewhere within it. This pattern would match the `managers` group with users having the `manager` skillset, `management` skillset, and so forth.

> **Further Resources**
>
> If you're not familiar with regular expressions, we highly recommend *Mastering Regular Expressions*, 3rd Edition (Friedl, O'Reilly, 2006).

> **Building Complex Mapping Rules**
>
> If needed, you can chain mapping rules together by defining a mapping rule and then clicking on the adjacent circular icon with the + sign on it. Any rules that you define using this approach are evaluated using the logical OR operator. That is to say that if you have a match on *any* of the expressions, then the user is assigned to the target group.

Once the mapping rules are in place, you can launch the sample application to see the role assignments in effect. As you play around with the application, notice how the programmatic role-based access checks cause the application to display messages tailored to the user's role assignments.

8.6   Protecting Web Resources with OAuth 2.0

If you spend much time on your smartphone or tablet, then you may have come to appreciate how convenient it is to be able to open an application without having to authenticate each and every time. Although you may not have given this behavior much thought before, rest assured that your mobile applications haven't discovered a loophole in security. Authentication and authorization checks are still being conducted behind the scenes; the only difference is that they're being carried out in a different and less intrusive kind of way.

The engine that makes all this work is the OAuth protocol. In this section, we'll explore this protocol and explain how to use it to protect web-based APIs or resources deployed on SAP HCP.

8.6.1   What Is OAuth?

In his book *Getting Started with OAuth 2.0* (O'Reilly, 2012), Ryan Boyd describes the OAuth protocol as being rather like those fancy new car keys that allow an owner to provide limited access to the car for valet attendants, children, and so forth. Using their smart keys, owners can grant a valet attendant the minimum amount of access the attendant needs to park the car. This is to say that the key will grant the valet access to drive the car (at a reasonable speed, of course), but restrict access to the trunk, glove box, and so on.

In the digital world, OAuth keys (or *tokens*) are designed to protect digital resources, such as personal data or account information. There are several key actors involved in the exchange:

▶ **Resource server**
The resource server is the server that hosts the data and resources being protected by OAuth. For the purposes of our discussion, the resource server is SAP HCP itself.

▶ **Resource owner**
The resource owner is the user who owns the rights to the data and resources hosted on the resource server.

▶ **Client**
In this context, the client refers to the application that's attempting to access data and resources on the resource server. This application could be, for example, a native mobile application or a web application.

▶ **Authorization server**
The authorization server is responsible for negotiating access between a client application and the resource owner. Whenever a client application wishes to obtain access to a particular resource, it must submit a request to the authorization server to obtain access. This request is in turn handed over to the resource owner, who ultimately gets to decide whether or not the request is granted.

To put these roles into perspective, let's consider a real-world example of a native mobile application utilizing a user's Google account to log a user in and access his or her account. In this scenario, the client application is the mobile app, the resource server is Google+, and the authorization server is Google's OAuth provider.

Whenever the resource owner (i.e., the user) attempts to log on to the mobile app for the first time, he or she will be prompted to log into his or her Google account. Once the user authenticates, he or she will then be presented with an authorization screen much like the one shown in Figure 8.27.

Looking at the authorization screen shown in Figure 8.27, you can see that Google+ is prompting the user to determine if he or she is willing to grant the client application access to his or her basic profile information, circles, and so on. If the user clicks on the SIGN IN button, then the request is verified and the client application will be granted an access token that grants access to perform the specific set of functions described on the authorization screen on the resource owner's behalf.

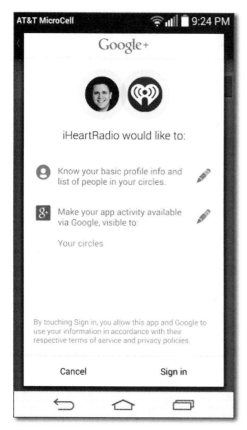

Figure 8.27 Using a Google Account to Authorize Access to a Mobile Application on a Mobile Device

Getting back to the valet example from earlier, this approval is rather like the car owner handing over the keys to the valet, in that the user is granting the client application the authority it needs to access the user's Google+ profile information. To the resource owner or the user, this is a convenience, because now the client application won't pester the user every time it needs to perform this task.

Before we wrap up this basic introduction to OAuth, there are several things we should point out about OAuth from a general security perspective:

1. Due to the presence of the mediating authorization server, a client application never gets its hands on the user's account credentials.

2. OAuth access tokens are designed to provide a client with the minimum amount of access it needs to do its job. Therefore, if a client is granted an access token to view basic information, it can't use this token to view other hidden data, modify data, and so on.

3. Normally, OAuth access tokens have an expiration date, which ensures that they don't become a long-term security risk.

4. OAuth access tokens can be revoked at any time to block access from particular clients and so on. This revocation process can be performed without disturbing the resource owner's account (e.g., by forcing the user to change his or her password).

Collectively, these principles lead to a very secure authorization protocol that offers the flexibility and convenience required by many modern application clients.

8.6.2 Understanding the OAuth Authorization Flow

Now that we've reviewed the basic concepts surrounding OAuth, let's narrow our focus a bit and consider how OAuth fits into the SAP HCP development landscape. Looking at the flow diagram in Figure 8.28, you can identify the positioning of OAuth-related components as they relate to SAP HCP. Here, you can observe the following:

▶ SAP HCP comes equipped with its own OAuth authorization server that can be used to process token requests and so on.

▶ SAP HCP also assumes the role of resource server, playing host to a number of web resources and APIs that you might want to provide with delegated access via OAuth. The SAP HCP Servlet/web container offers excellent support for OAuth-based security configurations.

▶ The SAP HCP authorization server components are able to delegate user authentication requests to any of the trusted SAML-based IdPs that might be configured within the landscape.

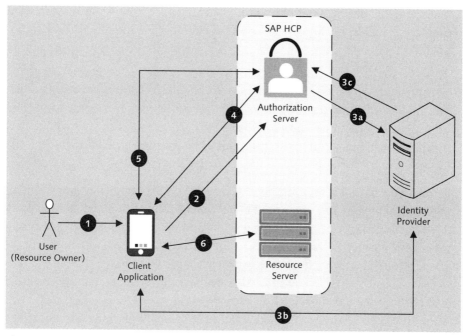

Figure 8.28 Tracing the OAuth Authorization Flow

With these basic components in place, you have everything you need to secure web resources hosted on SAP HCP using OAuth. To put this into perspective, imagine that you want to expose a REST-based API hosted on SAP HCP to external client applications. Following along with the flow diagram contained in Figure 8.28, you can see that the process flow works as follows:

1. The process begins with the user opening the client application.

2. If the client application doesn't have an access token on hand already, then its next step will be to submit an authorization request to the OAuth authorization server.

3. In order to process the authorization request, the authorization server must first establish the identity of the user who owns the resources the client application wishes to get its hands on. This authentication request is normally processed using the SAML protocol described in Section 8.5.

4. Once the user's identity is verified, the authorization server will then present the user with a prompt asking whether or not the user wishes to grant access to the resource(s) requested by the application.

367

5. Assuming the user decides to provide the client with access, the authorization server will invoke a callback service on the client, providing a temporary authorization code. The client will then exchange this authorization code for a more permanent access token.

6. Finally, with the access token in hand, the client application can begin accessing the target resources on the resource server by simply passing the access token in an HTTP request header. The resource server will use this token to perform the necessary authentication and authorization checks to access the resources.

Now that you have a sense for how the OAuth authorization flow works, we're ready to switch gears and take a look at how this process is implemented in practice. In the next two sections, we'll take a look at how to implement an actual scenario like the one illustrated in Figure 8.28. In Section 8.6.3, we'll get things started by looking at what it takes to expose a simple REST-based API built on top of a custom Java Servlet. Then, in Section 8.6.4, we'll show you how to consume this service from a client application running on the SAP HCP local runtime. You can find complete versions of the client and the server applications in the book's source code bundle (downloadable from *www.sap-press.com/3638*).

> **Note**
>
> Technically speaking, the OAuth protocol supports several other flow scenarios in addition to the one illustrated in Figure 8.28. However, as of the time of writing, not all of these scenarios are supported by the SAP HCP OAuth implementation. With that being said, for the purposes of our discussion in this section, we'll focus on the authorization code flow illustrated in Figure 8.28.

8.6.3 Securing Web Resources with OAuth

Tracing through the OAuth authorization flow depicted in Figure 8.28, you can see that most of the hard work happens up front on the client side. Here, a client must enter into a protocol handshake with the OAuth authorization server to obtain an access token. Once this token is obtained, clients can begin submitting requests to the resource server to access various web resources.

Because SAP provides a fully functional authorization server with SAP HCP, the scope of the server-side development is pretty much limited to securing the target web resources. From a Java development perspective, this can be achieved in one of two ways:

▸ **Declaratively**

With the declarative approach, web resources are protected by a Servlet filter class delivered with the SAP HCP SDK: `com.sap.cloud.security.oauth2.OAuthAuthorizationFilter`. This filter class can be configured in the web.xml deployment descriptor to intercept incoming HTTP requests and make sure that an OAuth access token is provided. In this way, the downstream web resources don't have to be modified to provide OAuth support.

▸ **Programmatically**

The alternative to the declarative approach is to utilize the various overloaded versions of the `isAuthorized()` method defined in the `com.sap.cloud.security.oauth2.OAuthAuthorization` class. Here, the web application resources themselves perform the authorization checks on the fly and must respond accordingly. For more information about this approach, we would recommend that you consult the SAP HCP API documentation online at *https://help.hana.ondemand.com/javadoc/index.html*.

Most of the time, it makes sense to utilize the declarative approach, because it offers a logical separation of concerns, so let's take a look at how this works. Listing 8.13 contains an excerpt of the web.xml deployment descriptor created for our contrived flight search API. (This is contained within the EXAMPLE08_02 application in the book's source code bundle, downloadable from *www.sappress.com/3638*.) Here, you can see that we've defined a custom Servlet class called `TravelAgentAPIServlet` and a corresponding Servlet filter definition based on the `OAuthAuthorizationFilter` class. The glue that links the filter with the Servlet resource is the `<url-pattern>` elements contained in the Servlet/filter definitions. Because the URL patterns match, the SAP HCP web container will automatically route incoming requests to this URL through the `OAuthAuthorizationFilter` class so that it can verify the presence of an OAuth access token. If no token is provided, then the request dies and the client never gets its hands on the protected web resource.

```
<web-app>
  <servlet>
    <servlet-name>TravelAgentAPIServlet</servlet-name>
    <servlet-class>
      com.sappress.hcpbook.chp08.TravelAgentAPIServlet
    </servlet-class>
```

```
  </servlet>
  <servlet-mapping>
    <servlet-name>TravelAgentAPIServlet</servlet-name>
    <url-pattern>/api/v1/flights</url-pattern>
  </servlet-mapping>
  <filter>
    <display-name>OAuth Scope for Flight Lookups</display-name>
    <filter-name>TravelAgentFlightsFilter</filter-name>
    <filter-class>
      com.sap.cloud.security.oauth2.OAuthAuthorizationFilter
    </filter-class>
    <init-param>
      <param-name>scope</param-name>
      <param-value>get-flights</param-value>
    </init-param>
    <init-param>
      <param-name>http-method</param-name>
      <param-value>get</param-value>
    </init-param>
    <init-param>
      <param-name>user-principal</param-name>
      <param-value>true</param-value>
    </init-param>
  </filter>
  <filter-mapping>
    <filter-name>TravelAgentFlightsFilter</filter-name>
    <url-pattern>/api/v1/flights</url-pattern>
  </filter-mapping>
</web-app>
```

Listing 8.13 Configuring the OAuth Authorization Filter in the web.xml File

Looking more closely at the filter definition contained in Listing 8.13, you can see that several initialization parameters are included:

▶ `scope`
This parameter is used to specify the OAuth scope that gets checked during the authorization processing. You'll learn what OAuth scopes are all about in just a moment.

▶ `http-method`
This optional parameter allows you to specify the HTTP method that you want to provide authorization for (e.g., GET in this case). If this parameter is omitted (as it frequently would be), then all HTTP methods would be checked indiscriminately.

▶ `user-principal`

This parameter determines whether or not the OAuth filter will map the resource owner's user ID upon successful authentication or authorization. If set to `true`, then you can get your hands on the user ID using the Servlet API as per usual.

Believe it or not, that's all you have to do, development-wise, to turn on OAuth-based authorization for your Java-based web resources. However, before you turn the resources over to clients, there is one last thing you have to configure on the server side of things.

After the application is deployed, you need to go into the SAP HCP Cockpit and configure one or more OAuth *scopes*. Conceptually, you can think of scopes as named authorizations that clients request access for from the OAuth authorization server. For example, in our flight API example, we've defined a single scope called `get-flights`, which is referenced in the web.xml file illustrated in Listing 8.13. This scope provides clients with access to look up flight information. If our API supported other flight operations, then we might have also defined scopes such as `create-flight`, `update-flight`, and so forth.

To define OAuth scopes for a Java application, simply open up the application dashboard and navigate to the OAUTH SCOPES tab page. From here, you can define as many scopes as you like by clicking on the NEW SCOPE button in the SCOPES table. This will bring up the form editor shown at the bottom of Figure 8.29. Within this form, you need to specify the scope ID and a long text description for the scope. In Section 8.6.4, you'll see that this description will be displayed on an SAP HCP-based authorization screen similar to the Google+ authorization screen depicted in Figure 8.27.

Ultimately, the scopes that get defined for an application are rather arbitrary and based on whims of the API provider. Scope-based authorizations could be coarse-grained or fine-grained; OAuth doesn't care one way or another. The only thing OAuth cares about is making sure that the scope IDs are configured according to specification.

Figure 8.29 Defining OAuth Scopes for Deployed Java Applications

8.6.4 Developing and Configuring OAuth Clients

With the server portion of our OAuth demo squared away, let's turn our attention now to the client application that will be consuming the flight query service. Here, although you may not plan to be in the business of developing client applications, it's helpful to at least understand how clients interface with your secured resources using OAuth. Plus, it also gives us an opportunity to see how clients are configured and maintained within the SAP HCP Cockpit.

To keep things simple, we decided to implement our client application as a server-side Java web application hosted on an instance of the SAP HCP local runtime. Of course, we could have just as easily developed this application using .NET technology, PHP, and so on. Indeed, one of the great things about OAuth is that it's an open standard that can be supported by just about any kind of client device imaginable.

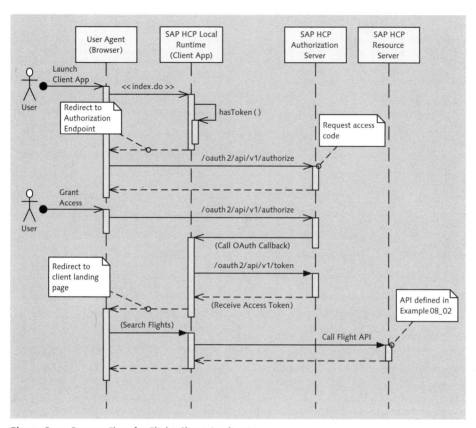

Figure 8.30 Process Flow for Flight Client Application

Figure 8.30 is a flow diagram that depicts the high-level process flow of the client application. Here, the process breaks down as follows:

1. Whenever the user launches the client application in his or her web browser or user agent, the first thing the client does is figure out whether or not it already has an OAuth access token on hand.

2. If it doesn't, then the user's browser will be redirected to the authorization endpoint of the SAP HCP authorization server with a request for an access code.

3. The authorization endpoint will first authenticate the user (using SAML) and then present a prompt to allow the user to determine whether or not he or she wishes to grant the client application access to the flight query service.

4. Assuming the user grants the request, control picks up on the SAP HCP authorization server, which generates an authorization code and invokes the OAuth callback URL provided in the original authorization request.

5. The OAuth callback service on the client application will receive the authorization code and invoke the token endpoint of the SAP HCP authorization server to exchange the authorization code for an access token.

6. After the access token is received, the client application will redirect the user's browser to the application start page where users can begin searching for flights.

7. Finally, whenever the user submits a flight query, the client will format the REST call and embed the access token in the HTTP request headers. If all goes well, then the flight API will respond with the desired flights, and the results will be parsed by the client application and displayed in the results list.

Looking closely at Figure 8.31, you can see that the client application interfaces with a couple of endpoints on the SAP HCP authorization server in order to obtain an OAuth access token. This raises the question: How do you know which URLs to hit when developing a client application? As is the case with most SAP HCP-related configuration items, you must go to the SAP HCP Cockpit to find out this information. From the main landing page, you can find the OAuth URLs by opening the OAUTH tab, as shown in Figure 8.31.

Figure 8.31 Accessing OAuth Authorization Server Endpoints

Because the OAuth URL syntax is predictable for any SAP HCP landscape, we implemented our client application in such a way that it only requires the SAP HCP account name and host as parameters; the fully qualified URLs are dynamically generated from there. You can see how this works in the EXAMPLE08_03 sample application by looking at the initialization parameters of the `ClientBoot-strapServlet` in the application's web.xml file.

> **Tip**
>
> In addition to the OAuth URLs, the OAUTH SETTINGS tab page also allows you to upload a custom logo image to apply customized branding on the OAuth authorization pages. For the purposes of our demo, we uploaded the SAP PRESS logo so that you can see how this impacts the look and feel of the authorization page.

Once the OAuth URLs are configured, you're almost ready to fire up your client application. However, before you proceed, there's one more configuration step that has to take place: you need to register your client with the OAuth authorization server. This registration process is required so that the authorization server has a tangible set of credentials to ensure the authenticity of incoming requests.

As you might expect, clients are registered via the CLIENTS subtab contained within the main OAUTH SETTINGS tab page (see Figure 8.32). To register a new client, you must specify some or all of the following attributes:

- NAME
  This mandatory attribute defines the client's name. The name must be unique within the SAP HCP instance.

- DESCRIPTION (optional)
  Here, you can specify a long-text description of the client.

- ID
  This attribute is generated by the SAP HCP Cockpit as the client's ID. This token will be used at runtime when an authorization request is submitted to the authorization or token endpoints.

- CONFIDENTIAL
  If this checkbox is selected, then you must fill in a password that will be exchanged at runtime in the authorization handshake. In OAuth parlance, this password is called the `client_secret`.

▶ REDIRECT URI

In this attribute, you must specify the OAuth callback URI that will be invoked at runtime. Although the OAuth protocol supports the exchange of this URI dynamically at runtime, the specification here helps reduce the risk of request forgeries.

▶ TOKEN LIFETIME

This attribute is used to define the lifetime (in days) of access tokens allocated to the client. If left blank, then the duration is infinite.

▶ REFRESH TOKEN LIFETIME

Although we've sort of glossed over this up to now, there are actually two tokens generated by the authorization server in response to an authorization request: an access token and a *refresh token*. Refresh tokens are used to (quickly) reacquire an access token in cases in which the old access token has expired.

With that being said, the REFRESH TOKEN LIFETIME attribute can be used to define the lifetime of a refresh token. If left blank, then the duration is infinite.

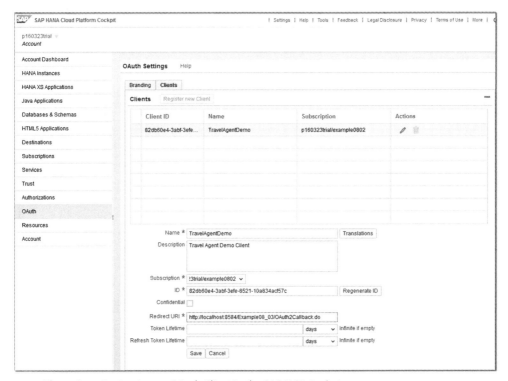

Figure 8.32 Registering an OAuth Client in the SAP HCP Cockpit

After the OAuth client is configured, you need to plug the generated client ID into the client application's web.xml file so that it can include the `client_id` attribute in authorization requests at runtime. From here, you can deploy the application and fire it up on your local SAP HCP runtime. As you can see in Figure 8.33, right off the bat you'll be prompted to authenticate and then authorize the client to look up flight information via the sample API created in the EXAMPLE08_02 application that's deployed on the cloud-based SAP HCP instance. Although this scenario's a bit contrived in that you're playing both the resource owner role and the resource provider role, it's not hard to imagine this authorization handshake playing out between, say, a mobile client and a web API that you've deployed on SAP HCP.

Figure 8.33 Authorizing the Sample Client to Look Up Flight Information

As soon as the client is authorized, the application redirects to the FLIGHT SEARCH page shown in Figure 8.34. From this page, you can submit various queries to the flight search API by filling in selection parameters and clicking on the Go button.

On the server side, you can manage the OAuth access tokens that are allocated by the authorization server by opening the SAP HCP Cockpit and clicking on the AUTHORIZATIONS tab. From the TOKEN subtab shown in Figure 8.35, you can view the access tokens that have been allocated and revoke them as necessary.

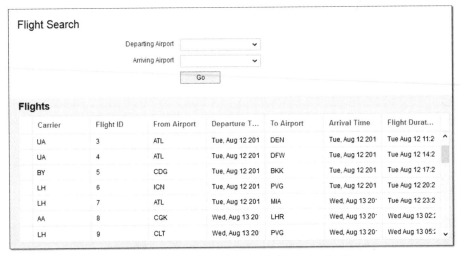

Figure 8.34 Accessing the Flight Service from the OAuth Client Application

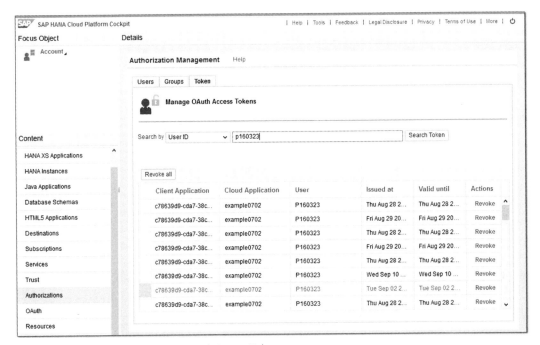

Figure 8.35 Managing OAuth Access Tokens

8.7   Summary

In this chapter, you learned various techniques for securing cloud applications. From SAML and OAuth to Java EE security concepts and SAP HCP APIs, it's plain to see that security has a lot of moving parts. Therefore, if nothing else, we hope that you'll take from this chapter one important lesson: Security development requires a holistic approach that encompasses all aspects of an application. Although this may seem overwhelming at first, we think that you'll find that the methods described in this chapter will fall into place quite naturally if you plan for security at the beginning of the development process. Otherwise, factoring for security after an application is built can be a very dicey proposition.

This chapter concludes our in-depth look at SAP HCP application development. From here on out, we'll broaden our focus a bit and look at some of the key enablement services supported by SAP HCP. In Chapter 9, we'll start by looking at SAP HANA Cloud Portal, a full-fledged portal service that can be used to build customer portal sites, mashups, and more.

PART III
Advanced Concepts

As we accumulate more than a handful of web applications, one of the primary logistical challenges we face is figuring out how to get our apps into the hands of the end users. In this chapter, we'll look at how to use SAP HANA Cloud Portal to streamline this delivery process.

9   Working with SAP HANA Cloud Portal

Up to now, the sample applications we've developed have existed in isolation. In practice, though, this will rarely be the case. Instead, the SAP HCP applications we create will normally become part of a larger suite of applications that users use in tandem to perform various job duties. Included in this suite of applications are custom-developed SAP HCP applications, applications leveraged from one of SAP's Software-as-a-Service (SaaS) offerings (e.g., SuccessFactors), and sometimes web applications from outside of the SAP landscape.

To the end user, it doesn't matter where these applications come from or how they're implemented; users just want a simple, streamlined interface they can use to get in and do their job. In these situations, we need a platform for consolidating application content so that we can provide users with a unified, role-specific access point. Within the SAP cloud landscape, we can utilize SAP HANA Cloud Portal to implement these requirements. In this chapter, we'll take a look at SAP HANA Cloud Portal and how it can be used to build beautiful mashup sites that seamlessly integrate various types of content.

9.1   Introduction

Before we start looking into the details of SAP HANA Cloud Portal, let's first take a moment to explain a little more about what it is (and isn't). In the sections that follow, we'll introduce you to SAP HANA Cloud Portal and its positioning in the SAP HCP landscape.

9.1.1 What Is SAP HANA Cloud Portal?

If you've worked with enterprise portal solutions in the past (e.g., SAP Enterprise Portal or Microsoft SharePoint), then you probably have a pretty good idea about what SAP HANA Cloud Portal is all about. For readers who are unfamiliar with portal concepts, though, some exposition is worthwhile.

In general, portal solutions like SAP HANA Cloud Portal are used to build *mashup sites* that provide centralized access to related applications or content. The use of the term "mashup" here is appropriate, because (as you can see in Figure 9.1) portal sites are aggregates that stitch together application content from here, there, and everywhere. To the end user, this is all abstracted behind the portal server, which fetches the relevant content from different locations and weaves it into consolidated HTML markup that clients access via their web browser as per usual.

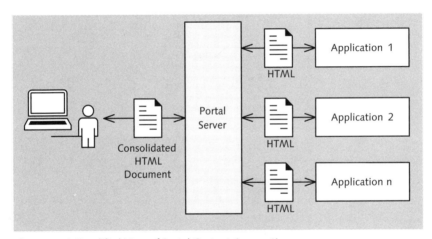

Figure 9.1 A Simplified View of Portal Content Aggregation

Now that we've established the basics of portal technology, we can turn our attention to SAP HANA Cloud Portal itself. According to the SAP help documentation, the SAP HANA Cloud Portal is defined as "a cloud-based solution for easy site creation and consumption with a superior user experience. Designed primarily for mobile consumption, it runs on top of SAP HANA Cloud and is built to operate with SAP HANA, for in-memory computing." Based on this definition, we can draw several important conclusions about SAP HANA Cloud Portal:

▶ From a software logistics perspective, we find that SAP HANA Cloud Portal is less a standalone application and more of an extension or service of SAP HCP.

▶ Because SAP HANA Cloud Portal is built on top of SAP HCP, it's able to easily integrate web applications deployed on the host SAP HCP platform. It's also able to leverage other functions of SAP HCP, such as security, theming, and so forth.

▶ Being "designed primarily for mobile consumption," SAP HANA Cloud Portal utilizes a lightweight content model based on responsive web design techniques. In and of itself, this doesn't guarantee a seamless experience across different form factors, but it certainly provides the foundation for heading in such a direction.

▶ In addition to delivering a "superior user experience," SAP HANA Cloud Portal is also focused on providing content administrator types with a simplified and rapid site development experience.

To summarize, we can say that SAP HANA Cloud Portal is a (lean) portal solution that's built on top of SAP HCP and positioned as a service that can be used to build mashup sites. If that seems overly simplistic, it's because it's supposed to be; the tool is meant to be easy to use and easy to consume.

> **SAP HANA Cloud Portal vs. SAP Enterprise Portal**
>
> If you've worked in the SAP software space for very long, then you might be wondering how SAP HANA Cloud Portal relates to SAP Enterprise Portal. The short answer here is that aside from the fact that they both fall under the heading of *enterprise portals*, the two solutions really have little to do with one another. SAP Enterprise Portal is a strictly on-premise portal offering that is best suited for integrating content within an intranet site; SAP HANA Cloud Portal is an extension of SAP HCP that embodies the concepts of a lean portal. This is to say that SAP HANA Cloud Portal offers a simpler, more lightweight content model that is easier to consume over the web using various device types.

9.1.2   Architectural Overview

In terms of functionality, SAP HANA Cloud Portal has all of the features you would expect from any lean portal product offering in the marketplace: a runtime container for content aggregation, a WYSIWYG (what you see is what you get) authoring environment, a host of enablement services and APIs, and lots of reusable content. However, as we noted in Section 9.1.1, instead of packaging these components as part of a standalone product offering, SAP decided to bundle them as a service of SAP HCP.

The block diagram in Figure 9.2 illustrates how all this plays out from a technical perspective. Here, you can see that the components and services of SAP HANA Cloud Portal are deployed right on top of SAP HCP itself. As you might expect, it is this close relationship that allows SAP HANA Cloud Portal to easily integrate application content and also leverage key enablement services, such as the Identity Service.

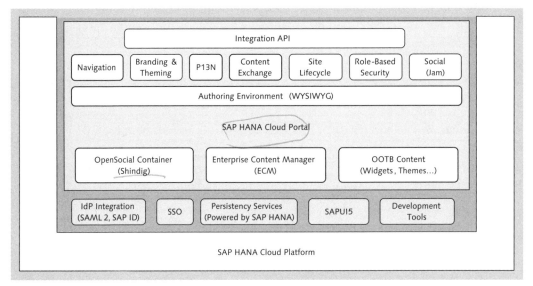

Figure 9.2 Positioning of SAP HANA Cloud Portal within SAP HCP

The engine that makes SAP HANA Cloud Platform go is the OpenSocial container depicted in Figure 9.2. At runtime, this container is primarily responsible for aggregating portal content and generating the consolidated site page that gets delivered to end users (see Figure 9.3).

If you compare the content flow diagram in Figure 9.3 with the more generalized flow diagram in Figure 9.1, you can see that the OpenSocial container plays the role of portal server within SAP HANA Cloud Portal. Instead of building this server from scratch, SAP elected to use the open source Apache Shindig container, which is the primary reference implementation for the W3C's OpenSocial specification (see the following boxed note).

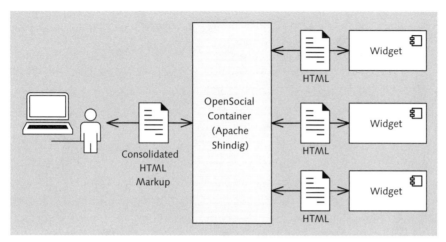

Figure 9.3 Understanding How Content Is Aggregated with OpenSocial

What Is OpenSocial?

OpenSocial is a W3C standard originally developed by Google with the goal of simplifying the development of social network applications (i.e., mashups). The specification defines the framework for building component containers, reusable UI components called *widgets*, and also provides a set of common APIs.

The unit of development within the OpenSocial framework is the aforementioned widget (or *gadget* in the Google parlance). Conceptually, you can think of widgets as thin wrappers or containers around some kind of HTML-based content. This container is defined in terms of an XML-based descriptor file that specifies details about where to load the HTML content from, which OpenSocial APIs the widget plans to use, and so forth.

At runtime, whenever users access portal sites, the incoming requests are funneled through the OpenSocial container, which dynamically generates HTML content for each of the embedded widget components and then weaves it together into a consolidated piece of HTML markup (see Figure 9.3). This approach offers several important benefits:

▶ It allows developers and portal admins to integrate content from just about anywhere. Indeed, as long as content is addressable via a URL from the OpenSocial container, it's pretty much fair game.

▶ The introduction of the specification XML allows developers to define dependencies to common libraries and APIs without having to worry about library versions, resource paths, and so on.

▶ The centralized OpenSocial container solves cross-domain issues that developers frequently encounter, because all requests (i.e., AJAX calls, etc.) end up originating from the same domain in the generated HTML.

> As of the time of writing, the OpenSocial specification has recently been incorporated into the W3C Social Web Working Group. As per the group's charter, this move is intended to help extend the reach of OpenSocial in the enterprise and also expand its scope. Over time, it's likely that we'll see these innovations find their way into SAP HANA Cloud Portal.

The block diagram in Figure 9.4 provides a closer look at how the OpenSocial framework is integrated into the SAP HANA Cloud Portal architecture. Here, in addition to the core Apache Shindig container, you can see that SAP HANA Cloud Portal also defines supplemental services that proxy requests from widgets to server-side resources (such as RESTful services), aid in the rendering of gadgets, and so forth. The gadget components are provided via one or more gadget providers. Much of the time, the only gadget provider in play is SAP HCP itself, but it's possible to integrate gadgets deployed on other SAP HCP accounts and even from an external server; it doesn't really matter one way or another to SAP HANA Cloud Portal.

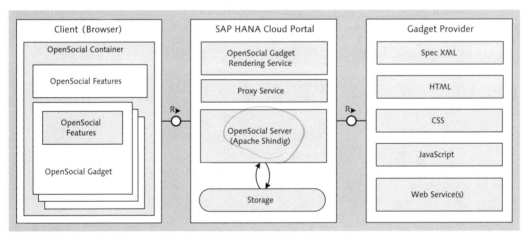

Figure 9.4 Content Flow for SAP HANA Cloud Portal

As we wrap up this architecture section, we recognize that you may have many questions about how all the various pieces of SAP HANA Cloud Portal's OpenSocial implementation fit together. Indeed, because many SAP developers may be encountering OpenSocial for the first time, there's a lot to wrap your head around early on. As we progress through this chapter and you have a chance to create a few widgets, we think that many of these concepts will begin to sink in organically. Fortunately, even if they don't, the great news is that SAP does such a good job of abstracting the technical underpinnings that you hardly even realize they're there 99% of the time. For developers, the focus is on creating widgets and laying out sites; Apache Shindig and SAP HANA Cloud Platform take care of the nitty-gritty technical details.

9.1.3 How Is SAP HANA Cloud Portal Used?

Now that you know what SAP HANA Cloud Portal is, you might be wondering what it's used for in the real world. The short answer is that SAP HANA Cloud Portal can be used for just about any requirement that calls for some kind of content aggregation. The list of content types that you can integrate includes the following:

▶ Custom-built web applications deployed on SAP HCP (e.g., Java, native SAP HANA, or HTML5 applications)

▶ SAP standard applications, such as those provided with SAP's newer SaaS offerings (e.g., SuccessFactors, Concur, etc.)

▶ Third-party applications and/or external web sites

▶ SAP Jam feeds

▶ Unstructured content (e.g., lists, documents, images, and videos)

▶ Custom-built widgets that round out the user experience and facilitate interapplication communication

By weaving these different content types together, you can provide users with a one-stop shop for performing related tasks. Although you could technically build such mashups from scratch, by using SAP HANA Cloud Portal you can take advantage of built-in features, such as site-wide branding and theming, prebuilt widgets, and a host of common APIs that allow you to implement certain site-wide functions in a portable and reusable manner.

You'll see many of these services and features on display in the upcoming sections, culminating in Section 9.4, in which we demonstrate the creation of a custom site definition that aggregates some of the content developed in earlier examples within the book. As you progress through the exercises, we would encourage you to think about how you might apply these concepts to real-world sites that you might want to develop in conjunction with your SAP HCP application development.

9.2 Understanding SAP HANA Cloud Portal's Content Model

Effective site design within SAP HANA Cloud Portal starts with an understanding of its underlying *content model*. Here, we're talking about the basic building blocks that make up a site definition: pages, widgets, and so forth. Collectively, these elements are used to organize portal content into a cohesive and intuitive site layout.

Figure 9.5 shows the primary elements that make up SAP HANA Cloud Portal's content model. As you can see, portal sites consist of the following:

- At the top of the hierarchy, there are *site definitions* that contain details about the site as a whole. Here, you can specify the site's theme (i.e., its look and feel), its structure, security settings, and more.

- The structure of a site is defined by assembling one or more *pages* into a page hierarchy. To a large degree, pages within the portal content model are analogous to the pages you would find in traditional web sites.

- The content area of pages is defined in terms of one or more OpenSocial widgets. The list of widgets to choose from here includes a number of out-of-the-box widgets, as well as third-party or custom widgets you import into the SAP HANA Cloud Portal content directory.

Looking at the model diagram depicted in Figure 9.5, it's pretty plain to see how all of the various pieces fit together. As a result, it can be tempting to jump right into the site designer tool and begin dropping in content. However, we'd encourage you to exercise some restraint and spend some time up front planning your site layout and collecting the relevant OpenSocial widgets. Because the name of the game with site design is to provide users with a simple and intuitive experience, it really pays to think about how best to organize your content within this content model.

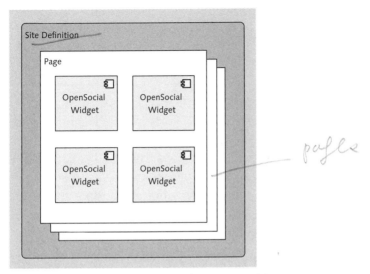

Figure 9.5 Basic Elements of the Portal Content Model

9.3 Developing Content for SAP HANA Cloud Portal

In the previous section, you learned that OpenSocial widgets make up the main content area of portal sites. From a development perspective, this implies that you have to package up every piece of content you plan to integrate into a portal site as an OpenSocial widget. In the sections that follow, we'll look at ways of achieving this using familiar SAP HCP development tools.

9.3.1 Creating OpenSocial Widgets

As we noted in Section 9.1.2, an OpenSocial widget is essentially a wrapper around a web application. In the simplest case, all it takes to transform a given web application into an OpenSocial widget is the inclusion of an XML deployment descriptor in the application's root folder. This XML descriptor file is referred to as the widget's *specification XML* (or *spec XML*).

Listing 9.1 contains a sample spec XML file that might be used to create a widget to display the SAP PRESS home page. As you can see, about the only thing going on with this markup is the specification of the widget's content in the correspondingly named <Content> element. This minimal information is all the Open-Social container needs to render the widget at runtime.

```
<?xml version="1.0" encoding="UTF-8"?>
<Module>
  <ModulePrefs title="Sample Widget" />
  <Content type="url" href="www.sap-press.com" />
</Module>
```

Listing 9.1 A Sample Spec XML File

Looking closely at the spec XML sample provided in Listing 9.1, you can see that the `<Content>` tag used to specify the widget's content has a `type` attribute that determines where the widget will be getting its content from. Although the example given in Listing 9.1 points to a URL, most of the custom widgets that you create will reference content contained somewhere within the hosting application itself.

In the next two sections, we'll demonstrate how this works by showing you how to create an OpenSocial widget out of an HTML5 application deployed on SAP HCP. Here, you'll create a widget to display the current temperature at a user's particular location. To keep things simple this first time out, we'll be sticking with plain HTML5 content. We'll then follow this up in Section 9.3.3 with some examples based on other SAP HCP application types.

Preparing for Widget Development in the SAP Web IDE

Technically speaking, the only OpenSocial-specific source code file that you'll be maintaining when building your custom widget components is the aforementioned spec XML file. Because you can edit this file using any text editor, you can develop OpenSocial widgets using just about any IDE or editor imaginable. Within SAP HCP, the list of options includes the Eclipse IDE and the SAP Web IDE.

Although you can't go wrong with either of these IDEs, there is an advantage to using the SAP Web IDE, because it includes an SAP HANA Cloud Portal-related plug-in that can be used to bootstrap the widget development process. With that in mind, you'll develop our simple weather widget using the SAP Web IDE so that you can see how this plug-in is used in practice.

To enable the SAP HANA Cloud Portal plug-in in your SAP Web IDE instance, select the Tools • External Plugins menu option from the top-level menu bar, and then turn on the sap.hcp.widget.plugin plug-in, as shown in Figure 9.6. Once you confirm your selection, click on the OK button to incorporate the widget into the IDE. From here on out, the widget will be enabled within the IDE at startup.

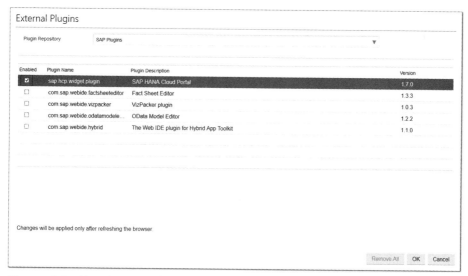

Figure 9.6 Enabling the SAP HANA Cloud Portal Widget Plug-in in the SAP Web IDE

Creating a Widget Component Using the SAP HANA Cloud Portal Widget Plugin

Once you have your SAP Web IDE set up, the process of creating your new widget component is almost identical to the HTML5 application creation process we reviewed in Chapter 7. As usual, we start by creating a new HTML5 application in the SAP HCP Cockpit and cloning the HTML5 application's Git repository within the SAP Web IDE tool. From here, you can then use the SAP HANA Cloud Portal widget plug-in to create the widget component by performing the following steps:

1. Create a new project by right-clicking on your HTML5 application's root folder and selecting the NEW • PROJECT FROM TEMPLATE menu option (see Figure 9.7).

2. This will open the NEW PROJECT creation wizard shown in Figure 9.8. At the initial step, choose the CLOUD PORTAL SAPUI5 STARTER WIDGET template type (highlighted in Figure 9.8). If you look closely here, you'll notice that there are a few other SAP HANA Cloud Portal-related template types to choose from. Click on the NEXT button to continue.

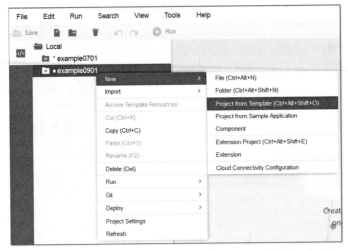

Figure 9.7 Creating an OpenSocial Widget from an HTML5 Application: Part 1

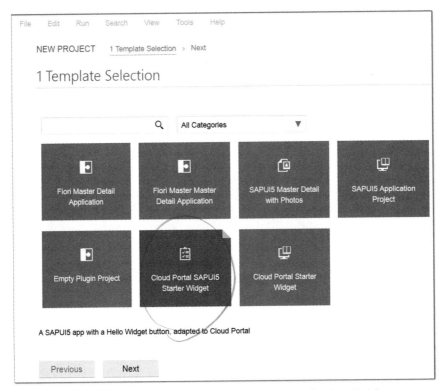

Figure 9.8 Creating an OpenSocial Widget from an HTML5 Application: Part 2

3. At the next step, give your project a name as usual (Figure 9.9) and proceed by clicking on the NEXT button.

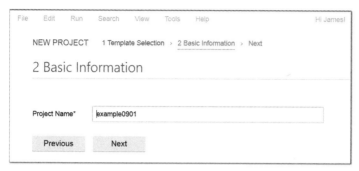

Figure 9.9 Creating an OpenSocial Widget from an HTML5 Application: Part 3

4. At the SELECT FEATURES step (Figure 9.10), choose all of the relevant OpenSocial features you want to include with your widget. We'll explore these features and their usage scenarios in Section 9.3.2.

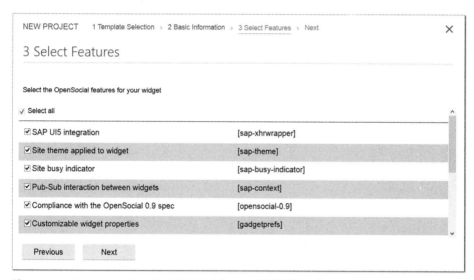

Figure 9.10 Creating an OpenSocial Widget from an HTML5 Application: Part 4

5. After you've selected the relevant OpenSocial features, you can proceed through the wizard and create the new project.

Once the dust settles on the project creation process, you'll notice that the wizard has created two main source code files that define your widget's content: an HTML file called index.html that contains the HTML5 markup and a spec XML file that contains the OpenSocial-specific module definition. Although you could certainly use these generated files as a baseline for starting your widget development, for the purposes of our demonstration we'll actually be overlaying these files with some predeveloped content included with the book's source code bundle (downloadable from *www.sap-press.com/3638*). That way, you can avoid having to wade through a lot of unneeded content and get to the heart of widget development.

To import the predeveloped weather widget content, perform the following steps:

1. Right-click on the project root folder and select the IMPORT • ARCHIVE menu option, as shown in Figure 9.11.

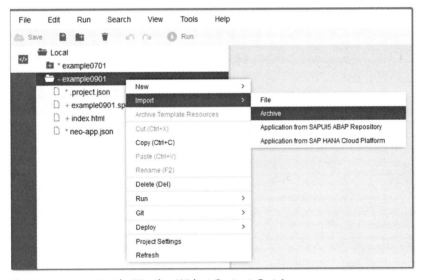

Figure 9.11 Importing the Weather Widget Content: Part 1

2. In the IMPORT ARCHIVE dialog box, browse to the example0901.zip file contained within the source code bundle, as shown in Figure 9.12. Click on the OK button to import the content.

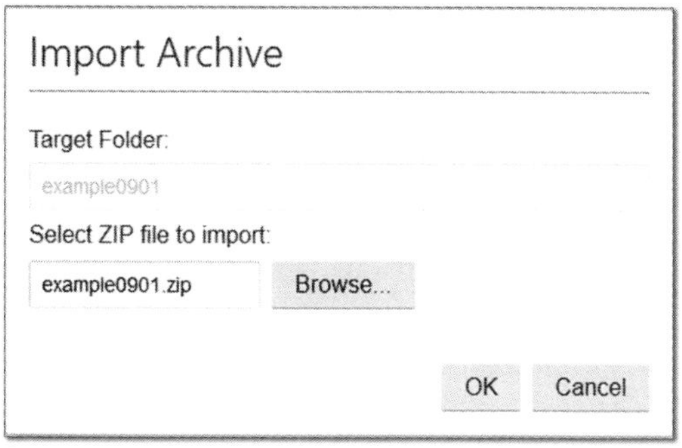

Import Archive
Target Folder:
example0901
Select ZIP file to import:
example0901.zip
Browse...
OK
Cancel

Figure 9.12 Importing the Weather Widget Content: Part 2

After the content is imported, you should see (among other things) two new files: weather.html and weather.spec.xml. With these files in place, you can delete the original HTML and spec XML files, because they're superseded by the imported files.

Developing the Weather Widget's Content

If you open the weather.html file that contains the weather widget's content, you'll find that it looks like pretty much any other HTML5 source file. Aside from the JavaScript script content (which we'll return to in Section 9.3.2), you'll find that the HTML `<body>` section consists of two `<div>` tags that are used to render the content shown in Figure 9.13. As you can see, the left-hand side of the content area shows the current temperature, whereas the right-hand side contains a REFRESH button, which allows users to refresh the current temperature value for their location.

eveloper | Report Content | Feedback
Hello James
Dallas: -0.6 °C

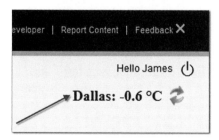

Figure 9.13 Demonstration of the Widget in Use in a Portal Site Definition

Listing 9.2 contains an excerpt of the weather.spec.xml file that defines the widget from an OpenSocial perspective. Looking at the highlighted `<Content>` element, you can see how you're pointing the OpenSocial container at the weather.html file containing the widget's content. The rest of the markup within this file configures the use of various SAP HANA Cloud Portal features—a topic that we'll pick up in Section 9.3.2.

```
<?xml version="1.0" encoding="UTF-8"?>
<Module>
  <ModulePrefs title="Weather Widget"
        description="HCP Book :: Chapter 9 :: Weather Widget">
    <Require feature="opensocial-0.9" />
    <Require...>
  </ModulePrefs>
  ...
  <Content type="html" href="weather.html"
        view="authoring, consumption, mobile, default" />
</Module>
```

Listing 9.2 The Spec XML File for the Weather Widget

9.3.2 Utilizing SAP HANA Cloud Portal Features

As we noted earlier, an important part of the OpenSocial specification is its support for reusable library APIs (or *features* in the parlance). These library APIs are based on JavaScript and provide solutions to the typical problems faced by widget developers.

Within SAP HANA Cloud Portal, you have access to core features defined by the OpenSocial specification and to a number of SAP HANA Cloud Portal-specific features. By standardizing around these features, you can develop widgets that are more lightweight and portable. This is an important feature when developing mashup applications that incorporate lots of different kinds of content. Here, even if the underlying technology stack is radically different between applications, developers can standardize around the OpenSocial or SAP HANA Cloud Portal features to implement interwidget communication, navigation, and so forth. Table 9.1 describes the SAP HANA Cloud Portal-specific features available as of the time of writing.

Feature	Description
Site Context (Pub-Sub) API	This API is used to implement interwidget communication using the familiar *publish-subscribe* integration pattern. Using this API, widgets can post messages to generic channels that interested widgets can register themselves as listeners for.
	Because of the decoupled nature of the message exchange, there's no hard-wiring that goes into setting up communication. This capability is particularly useful for SaaS vendors such as SAP that might need to broadcast events occurring within SuccessFactors applications, for example.
Context Object API	This API provides getter and setter methods around a bag-like data structure referred to as the *context object*. The context object is typically used for implementing shared data scenarios.
GadgetPrefs API	This API is used to implement personalization for widgets. Here, you can define custom properties that can be maintained by site administrators and/or end users when customizing a widget. The properties can be pretty much anything you come up with: the background color for the widget, locale information, and so forth.
Widget Navigation API	This API is used to implement dynamic navigation from a widget to a particular page within the site definition. Here, rather than hard-coding URLs, the navigation parameters are defined generically so that the navigation scenarios are 100% portable.
Widget Menu API	This API can be used to create custom menus within a widget.
Open Popup API	This API can be used to open up a widget view inside of a popup frame.
Widget Dynamic Height API	This API can be used to adjust the height of the widget. In particular, it can be used to define a widget's height in proportion with the surrounding content area.
Site Hierarchy API	This API can be used to introspect the page hierarchy within the current SAP HANA Cloud Portal site definition.
Login/Logout API	This API can be used to trigger login and logout requests within SAP HCP.

Table 9.1 SAP HANA Cloud Portal APIs for OpenSocial Widgets

Feature	Description
Busy Indicator API	This API can be used to show or hide a busy indicator whenever the widget performs a long-running task.
Custom Rich Text Editor API	This API can be used to dynamically create a Rich Text Editor widget.
Site Properties API	This API can be used to lookup properties that were defined by the site author within the overarching site definition. These properties can be used to initialize the widget content or perform other such tasks.

Table 9.1 SAP HANA Cloud Portal APIs for OpenSocial Widgets (Cont.)

Although a complete and thorough treatment of each and every SAP HANA Cloud Portal feature is beyond the scope of this book, our simple weather widget does incorporate several of these features in its design:

▶ To make our widget more customizable, we utilized the GadgetPrefs API to allow site administrators to specify the user location when embedding the widget so that users get a personalized temperature reading.

▶ Because our widget may be used in many different contexts, we're using the Dynamic Height API to dynamically calculate the height of the widget's content area.

▶ To make the widget appear more responsive to the end user, we're utilizing the Busy Indicator API to show the user that the widget is working whenever it goes and fetches the current temperature from its target REST-based service.

In order to utilize these features, you first have to formally *declare* your intentions to use these features within the spec XML file. As you can see in Listing 9.3, such declarations are specified within the `<ModulePrefs>` element using the highlighted `<Require>` element. The actual feature IDs are described within the SAP HANA Cloud Portal documentation available online at *https://help.hana.ondemand.com/cloud_portal/frameset.htm*. If you happen to know which features you wish to use up front, then this is something that the SAP HANA Cloud Portal widget plug-in of the SAP Web IDE can automate for you (as demonstrated in Section 9.3.1).

```
<?xml version="1.0" encoding="UTF-8"?>
<Module>
  <ModulePrefs title="Weather Widget">
```

```
    <Require feature="opensocial-0.9" />
    <Require feature="opensocial-jquery" />
    <Require feature="gadgetprefs" />
    <Require feature="sap-xhrwrapper" />
    <Require feature="sap-theme" />
    <Require feature="sap-busy-indicator" />
    <Require feature="sap-dynamic-height" />
  </ModulePrefs>
  ...
</Module>
```

Listing 9.3 Declaring Usages to SAP HANA Cloud Portal Features in the Spec XML File

At runtime, whenever the OpenSocial container evaluates the spec XML for your widget, it will use the set of `<Require>` elements to determine the appropriate JavaScript libraries to load into context for the generated widget markup. Because all of this is abstracted within the OpenSocial container, you needn't worry about loading libraries using HTML `<script>` tags and so on. Instead, you can simply start leveraging the relevant APIs in your code and assume that the library references will be supplied by the OpenSocial container at runtime.

This phenomenon is demonstrated by the HTML code excerpt contained in Listing 9.4. Here, notice how we're invoking the relevant APIs without any sort of initialization code. The scope of libraries made available to you here also extends to more generalized libraries, such as jQuery. Naturally, this makes your widget code much more portable over time, because library version management is handled within the OpenSocial container as opposed to the individual widget components.

```html
<!DOCTYPE html>
<html>
  <head>
    <meta charset="UTF-8">
    <title>HCP Book :: Chapter 9 :: Weather Widget</title>

    <script type="text/javascript">
      function init() {
        // Set the dynamic height of the widget:
        gadgets.sap.dynamicHeight.adjustHeight();

        // Register event handlers for the toolbar buttons:
        $("#linkRefresh").click(function() {
          getWeather();
        });

        // Load the current temperature into context:
```

```
        getWeather();
    }
    ...
    gadgets.util.registerOnLoadHandler(init);
  </script>
 </head>
 <body>
   ...
 </body>
</html>
```

Listing 9.4 Leveraging SAP HANA Cloud Portal Features in a Widget's HTML Content

The bulk of the heavy lifting for the weather widget is handled by a function called getWeather() that's triggered whenever the widget is initialized or refreshed. As you can see in Listing 9.5, the getWeather() function leverages the GadgetPrefs API to determine the user's preferred city and country and then utilizes those values to construct the service URL to a freely available REST-based weather lookup service hosted by OpenWeatherMap. Rather than call this service directly, the URL is passed to a separate callback function named callWeatherService() that's triggered via the Busy Indicator API. The results are then parsed by the parseWeatherResults() function, which copies the current temperature into the main HTML content area.

```
<!DOCTYPE html>
<html>
  <head>
    <meta charset="UTF-8">
    <title>HCP Book :: Chapter 9 :: Weather Widget</title>

    <script type="text/javascript">
      function init() {
        ...
        getWeather();
      }

      function getWeather() {
        // Fetch the target city/country to load weather
        // information for from the user preferences:
        var userPrefs = new gadgets.GadgetPrefs();
        var city = userPrefs.getPreference("City");
        var country = userPrefs.getPreference("Country");

        // Use this data to construct the service URL:
        var serviceUrl =
          "http://api.openweathermap.org/data/2.5/find?q=" +
          city + "," + country + "&units=metric";
```

```
        // Trigger the service and open up a busy indicator:
        gadgets.sap.busyIndicator.show(
          callWeatherService(serviceUrl), true);
      }

    function callWeatherService(serviceUrl) {
      // Trigger the service call:
      $.get(serviceUrl, parseWeatherResults);
    }

    function parseWeatherResults(data, status, xhr) {
      // Update the content area with the service call results:
      var userPrefs = new gadgets.GadgetPrefs();
      var city = userPrefs.getPreference("City");

      $("#weather").html(city + ": " +
          data.list[0].main.temp + " &deg;C");

      // Hide the busy indicator:
      gadgets.sap.busyIndicator.hide();
    }
    ...
    gadgets.util.registerOnLoadHandler(init);
  </script>
 </head>
 <body>
    ...
 </body>
</html>
```

Listing 9.5 Implementing the Weather Lookup Function

In Section 9.4.3, you'll see how site administrators can personalize your weather widget to pull the weather for a particular location. In the meantime, it's a good idea to go ahead and seed these parameters with reasonable defaults so that users have a good idea about what sort of data to fill in. As you can see in Listing 9.6, you can accomplish this within the spec XML file using the <UserPref> element.

```
<?xml version="1.0" encoding="UTF-8"?>
<Module>
  <ModulePrefs title="Weather Widget">
    ...
  </ModulePrefs>

  <UserPref name="City" display_name="City" datatype="string"
          default_value="Dallas" />
  <UserPref name="Country" display_name="Country"
```

```
             datatype="string" default_value="US" />

  <Content type="html" href="weather.html" />
</Module>
```
Listing 9.6 Defining Initial Values for the Weather Widget Preferences

Although we could have incorporated additional features into our widget's design, we hope that this simple demonstration gives you a general sense of what's possible with SAP HANA Cloud Portal features. The use of such features is not a hard requirement for widget development, but they're worth a look-see, especially if you find yourself creating lots of custom libraries for your widgets. Of course, having said that, we should point out that custom library development is not out-of-bounds with widget development. In some cases, it will make sense to blend custom or third-party libraries with SAP HANA Cloud Portal features and so on. The general rule of thumb here is just to utilize the standard features wherever possible.

9.3.3 Adapting Preexisting Web Applications

Now that you've seen how to adapt HTML5 applications (Section 9.3.1), you probably have a pretty good idea about how to adapt Java or native SAP HANA applications as OpenSocial widgets. Here, as was the case with HTML5 applications, you simply drop your widget's spec XML file in the application root folder and deploy the application as usual.

The only real trick to adapting preexisting applications is in dealing with cross-origin requests. For example, when adapting SAPUI5 applications, you may need to fetch the latest version of the SAPUI5 library from a *content delivery network* (CDN), or when calling a RESTful service, you might need to hit a URL endpoint hosted on a different server.

To address these issues, SAP provides an SAP HANA Cloud Portal-specific feature that provides access to an SAP HANA Cloud Portal proxy. From a development perspective, all you have to do to tap into this feature is define a reference to the sap-xhrwrapper feature, as demonstrated in Listing 9.7. Within the code itself, you don't have to modify URLs or filter them through some API function; the OpenSocial container will proxy the requests for you automagically.

```
<?xml version="1.0" encoding="UTF-8"?>
<Module>
```

```
<ModulePrefs title="Weather Widget">
  <Require feature="sap-xhrwrapper" />
  ...
</ModulePrefs>

<Content type="html" href="weather.html" />
</Module>
```
Listing 9.7 Accessing the SAP HANA Cloud Portal Proxy Feature

9.3.4 Adding a Widget to the Portal's Content Catalog

Once you finish development on your widget application, you'll want to publish it to the Content Catalog so that site designers can begin plugging the widget into site definitions. In general, widget publication is a straightforward and simple process that follows these steps:

1. Deploy the hosting application to SAP HCP as usual. For example, to deploy the weather widget developed in Section 9.3.1 and Section 9.3.2, simply deploy the HTML5 application using the same steps demonstrated in Chapter 7.

2. Once the application is deployed, open the SAP HANA Cloud Portal Authoring Space. You can get to this Authoring Space via the SAP HCP Cockpit by navigating to the SERVICES tab and clicking on the GO TO SERVICE link for SAP HANA Cloud Portal (Figure 9.14).

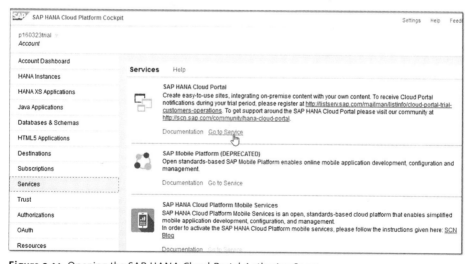

Figure 9.14 Opening the SAP HANA Cloud Portal Authoring Space

3. Within the SAP HANA Cloud Portal Authoring Space, widgets are maintained on the CONTENT tab. From this tab, you can add a new widget by clicking on the ADD WIDGET link shown in Figure 9.15.

Figure 9.15 Adding a Widget to the Content Catalog: Part 1

4. This will open the ADD WIDGET dialog box shown in Figure 9.16. Here, you must specify the widget's type (OpenSocial in this case), its name, an optional description and icon used to identify the widget, and, most importantly, the URL for the widget's spec XML file.

Figure 9.16 Adding a Widget to the Content Catalog: Part 2

5. Once all of the widget attributes are in place, click on the SAVE button to add the widget to the catalog.

After the widget upload process completes, you'll see your new widget available in the Content Catalog alongside all of the standard widget types provided by SAP. In the next section, you'll see how to put these widgets to work when we demonstrate how to create new site definitions.

9.4 Case Study: Building a Custom Portal Site

Once you accumulate the various widget components you plan to incorporate into your site definition, the process of developing the site itself is remarkably straightforward. To demonstrate just how easy this is, in this section we'll walk you through creating a site that presents a portfolio that showcases some of the sample applications you've developed on SAP HCP throughout the course of this book.

9.4.1 Creating a Site in the Site Directory

As you might expect, the first step in the site development process is the creation of the site itself. This task can be carried out within the SAP HANA Cloud Portal Authoring Space, which was briefly introduced in Section 9.3.4. Here, you have two options for creating new site definitions.

The first and most straightforward option is to create the site from scratch on the SITE DIRECTORY tab shown in Figure 9.17.

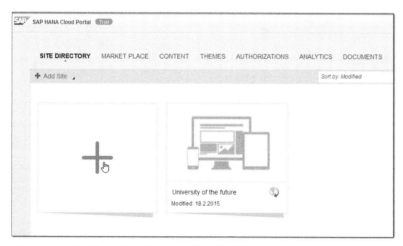

Figure 9.17 Creating a New Site Definition: Part 1

You can click on the tile with the big plus sign on it to create a new site definition. Once you click on this button, the tile will be refreshed to show the simple input form contained in Figure 9.18. Within this form, give your site a name and an optional description, and then click on either the SAVE button or the CREATE AND OPEN button to create the site.

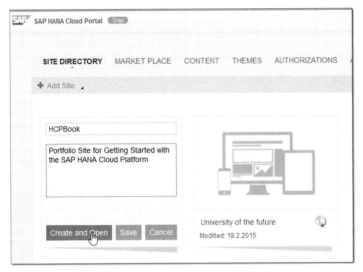

Figure 9.18 Creating a New Site Definition: Part 2

Figure 9.19 shows what your newly created site looks like whenever you create a site from scratch. As you can see, what gets created is essentially a shell of a site with a default theme and layout selected. Although you can change the default theme that gets selected within the THEMES tab, that's about the extent of the influence you have over the creation process. From here on out, you have to manually define all of the various content elements from within the Authoring Space.

The alternative to creating a site from scratch is to leverage one of the template sites provided on the MARKET PLACE tab within the Authoring Space. As you can see in Figure 9.20, there are a number of template sites to choose from, and more are being added all the time. To add one of these templates to the site directory, simply click on the GET THIS SITE button for the relevant site template, and then the site will be downloaded automatically.

Figure 9.19 Initial Site Definition Created by the Site Creation Wizard

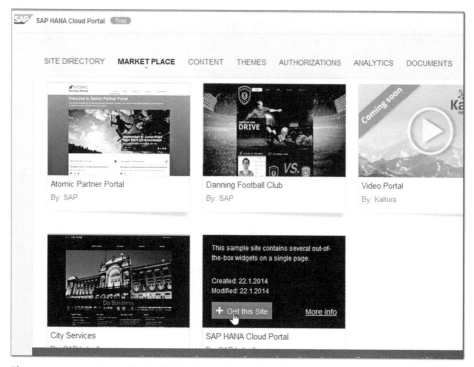

Figure 9.20 Importing a Site Definition from the Market Place

Regardless of the path you take to create a site, you can maintain the site from the SITE DIRECTORY tab by selecting the site and clicking on the EDIT button shown in Figure 9.21. This will open the site in a separate window, as was shown in Figure 9.19. From here, you can begin adding in new content or tailoring the template content as needed.

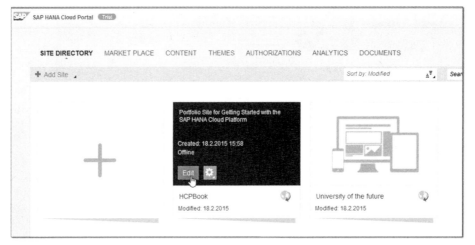

Figure 9.21 Editing a Site Definition

For the purposes of our case study, we'll be working off of a manually created site. Although you'll be adding content to this site soon enough, there are a few administrative tasks that you need to perform at the site definition level.

Configuring the Site Settings

First, you should review the site settings. This can be achieved within the Authoring Space by clicking on the toolbar button on the right-hand side of the page with the gear icon on it. This will open the SITE SETTINGS flyout panel shown in Figure 9.22. For this simple demo, leave the default settings intact, but it's worth taking a moment to review the types of settings you can configure:

▸ URL REDIRECT WHEN SITE IS DOWN
You can use this setting to redirect users to a different URL if the site is down or otherwise unavailable.

▶ WEB ANALYTICS

This setting allows you to capture site traffic analytics using web analytics services such as Google Analytics or SAP Web Analytics.

▶ SMARTPHONE-FRIENDLY SITE

If you need to maintain separate sites for different form factors (e.g., desktop vs. mobile), then you can use this setting to specify an alternative site that gets loaded whenever users access the site via a mobile device.

▶ SITE LANGUAGES

This setting can be used to maintain translations for the various languages that will be supported by the site.

▶ SITE PROPERTIES

This setting can be used to create properties (i.e., key-value pairs) that can be read by widgets using the Site Properties API (refer back to Section 9.3.2).

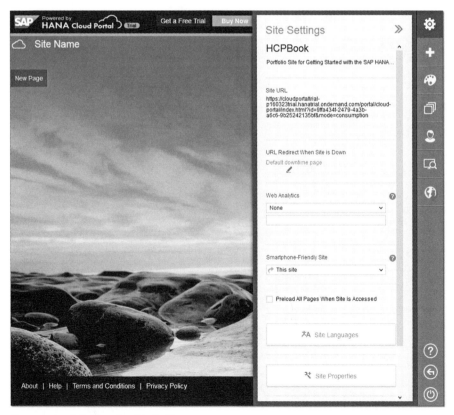

Figure 9.22 Adjusting the Site Settings

Defining the Site's Theme and Layout

Once you configure the overall site settings, the next thing you need to do is work on the site's *theming*. Here, we're talking about the site's look and feel in terms of color scheme, image background, and page layout. These settings can be configured by clicking on the toolbar button with the artist's palette icon on it (see Figure 9.23). Within the DESIGN SETTINGS flyout pane, you can adjust the site's look and feel in several different ways:

▶ In the WIDGET SETTINGS section, you can determine whether or not the widgets you embed will have a frame around them.

▶ In the PAGE TEMPLATES section, you can configure and/or maintain the (default) page template used for embedding pages within the site. These templates determine how content is organized within a page (e.g., as a three-column layout, etc.).

▶ In the THEMES section, you can select the site's *theme*. This selection determines the basic color scheme of the site, the background image, and so forth.

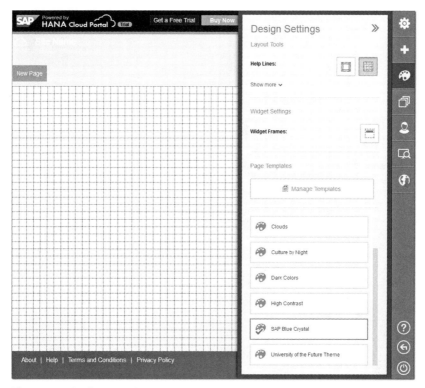

Figure 9.23 Configuring a Site's Design Settings

For the purposes of this case study, keep the default page template and change the theme to SAP BLUE CRYSTAL (the theme you normally see used in SAPUI5 applications). As you go to configure your site's theme, it's important to bear in mind that you're not limited to the out-of-the-box themes. If desired, you can also upload your own theme files to SAP HANA Cloud Portal. This can be carried out on the THEMES tab, as shown in Figure 9.24. Here, the theme elements are defined within the context of a LESS file (see the boxed note ahead) that gets uploaded into the theme catalog using the ADD THEME link.

Figure 9.24 Maintaining Themes within the SAP HANA Cloud Portal Authoring Space

---

What Is LESS?

LESS is a dynamic stylesheet language that's compiled and parsed into Cascading Style Sheets (CSS) content. If you're familiar with XSLT, then you can equate the relationship between LESS and CSS with the relationship between XSLT and XML. Compared with static CSS content, LESS provides developers with a programming context that can be used to automate certain tasks and speed up the design process.

LESS files can be edited using any text editor, though there are IDE plug-ins out there that provide a certain amount of syntax highlighting and code completion. For brevity's sake, we won't say more about LESS here. However, as an open standard, you'll find a wealth of resources online. Also, if you're looking for a quick deep dive into LESS, we recommend *LESS CSS Preprocessor How-To* (Libby, Packt Publishing, 2013).

Looking closely at the THEMES tab page (Figure 9.24), you'll notice that there is also a series of functions that allow you to edit and/or download existing themes. These functions are useful in situations in which you merely want to tweak one of the existing themes (e.g., changing the visualization of a button). Here, you can download the theme's LESS file, make the appropriate changes in a local text editor, and then upload the file as a new theme. This process is defined in further detail in the online help documentation.

Laying Out the Site's Masthead

With the basic site design and theming in place, you can next turn your attention to the configuration of the site's masthead area. For your sample site, you'll be configuring two items here:

▶ First, you'll replace the default SITE NAME title with a more appropriate title.

▶ Then, just for fun, you'll drop in the weather widget you created in Section 9.3.1 and Section 9.3.2 so that users can quickly see the weather conditions outside the office.

In order to carry out these tasks, you need to edit the page template used for your site (which is the standard template by default). This can be achieved by maneuvering your mouse over the masthead until you see the EDIT button shown in Figure 9.25 appear. After you click on the EDIT button, the look and feel of the editor will change to indicate that you're editing the page template.

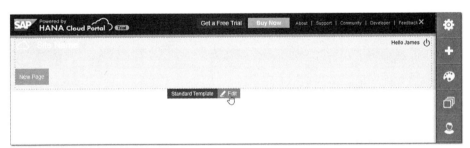

Figure 9.25 Editing the Site Masthead

To edit the site's title bar, perform the following steps:

1. Hover your mouse cursor over the SITE NAME text area until you see the gear icon shown in Figure 9.26 appear.

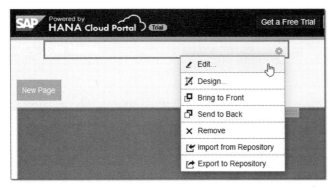

Figure 9.26 Editing the Site Title: Part 1

2. Clicking on the gear icon will open up a dropdown menu that contains a number of editing options. To change the text, select the EDIT… menu option, as shown in Figure 9.26.

3. This will open the text editor window shown in Figure 9.27. Here, plug in the new site text, change the text color to black, and click on the SAVE AND CLOSE button to save your changes.

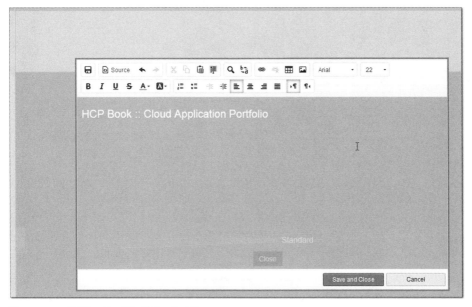

Figure 9.27 Editing the Site Title: Part 2

Because you already configured the weather widget in Section 9.3.4, dropping this widget onto the masthead is a snap. Perform the following steps:

1. Open the Content Catalog by clicking on the toolbar button with the plus (+) icon on it (see Figure 9.28).

2. In the CONTENT CATALOG flyout pane, scroll down to locate the weather widget (see Figure 9.28).

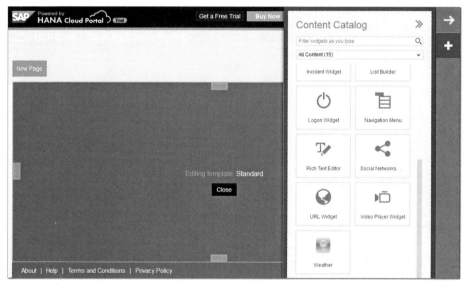

Figure 9.28 Adding the Weather Widget to the Masthead: Part 1

3. As you hover your mouse cursor over the widget, you'll find that the tile visualization changes to depict a grid like the one shown in Figure 9.29. This grid allows you to determine the placement of the widget within the page layout. Because you want to place the widget in the masthead area, click on that section in the grid to insert the widget.

4. Once the widget is placed on the masthead, you'll want to resize it and move it over to the right-hand side of the screen, as shown in Figure 9.30. This can be achieved using the drag handles that appear whenever you hover your mouse cursor over the widget.

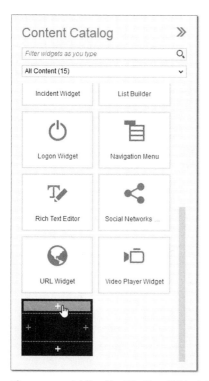

Figure 9.29 Adding the Weather Widget to the Masthead: Part 2

Figure 9.30 Adjusting the Placement of the Weather Widget

As you can see in Figure 9.30, the weather widget initially displays the temperature for the default location specified in the widget's spec XML. You can reconfigure this location by selecting the EDIT... menu option in the widget's SETTINGS menu. This will open the EDIT menu shown in Figure 9.31. Here, you can specify a new location and click on the OK button to confirm your selection. Internally, the weather widget will fetch the newly configured value using the GadgetPrefs API, as described in Section 9.3.2.

Figure 9.31 Editing the Weather Widget Preferences

9.4.2 Setting Up the Site's Page Hierarchy

With the site definition in place, you're now ready to begin laying out the site's *page hierarchy*. In this context, the term "page hierarchy" refers to the collection of pages you add to a site definition. For your portfolio site, you'll be creating three pages to showcase SAP HCP applications you've developed using the Java, SAP HANA XS, and HTML5 programming models. You'll also create some supplementary pages to show off built-in SAP HANA Cloud Portal functionality.

To create new pages within your site definition, access the Page Management flyout pane by clicking on the toolbar button with the collated pages icon on it. As you can see Figure 9.32, the sample site comes preequipped with a default page called New Page. Because a site definition must include at least one page definition at all times, you cannot delete this page.

To work around this limitation, you can simply rebrand the page by changing its label. This is achieved by clicking on the page definition in the Page Management pane, as shown in Figure 9.33. Here, in addition to changing the page label, you can also select an alternative page template and specify a *page alias*. These aliases are used by the Widget Navigation API to facilitate logical navigation scenarios between widgets and pages.

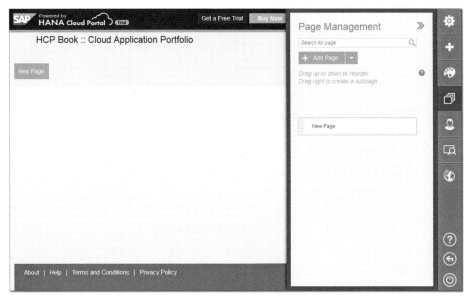

Figure 9.32 Accessing the Page Management Pane

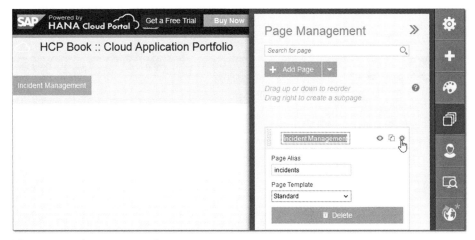

Figure 9.33 Editing a Page Definition

To define the other pages for your site, use the ADD PAGE button at the top of the PAGE MANAGEMENT pane, as shown in Figure 9.34. By clicking on this button, you end up with new page instances that you can edit in the same way that you edited the default page. Repeat this step three times to create the ONLINE BOOKSTORE,

CUSTOMER WORKLIST, and SCRATCH PAD pages shown in Figure 9.35. As you can see, each new page you create adds another tab in the site's navigation tabstrip.

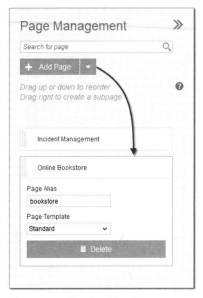

Figure 9.34 Creating New Pages

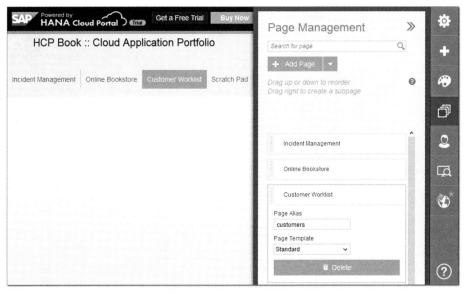

Figure 9.35 Building Out the Page Hierarchy

To round out the page hierarchy, add a link that can be used to find out more information about SAP HANA Cloud Portal. These links are created by selecting the dropdown menu on the ADD PAGE button and selecting the ADD LINK menu option (see Figure 9.36). This will open the editor pane shown in Figure 9.37. Here, we've plugged in the URL to the SAP HANA Cloud Portal content space on SCN: *http://scn.sap.com/community/hana-cloud-portal*.

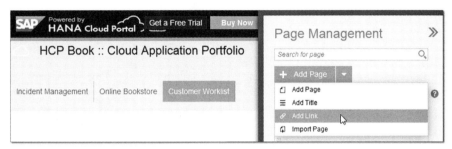

Figure 9.36 Adding a Link to the Page Hierarchy: Part 1

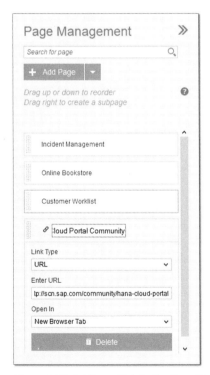

Figure 9.37 Adding a Link to the Page Hierarchy: Part 2

9.4.3 Adding Content to the Pages

Now that you have your pages in place, your site definition is really starting to round into form. At this point, you get to move onto the fun stuff: adding widget content to the pages. Here, you'll use a blend of standard and custom-delivered widgets to lay out the content areas of your pages.

Creating a Widget for the Java-Based Incident Management Application

Before you start editing the pages, you first need to create custom widgets for the SAP HCP applications that you want to showcase in your portfolio site. You'll start this process by creating a widget around the Java-based incident management application you created in Chapter 6. As you learned in Section 9.3.3, all that's required for this is the inclusion of a spec XML in the application's root folder (see Figure 9.38).

Figure 9.38 Adding a Spec XML File to the Incident Management Application

Listing 9.8 contains an excerpt of the spec XML file that we created for the Incident Management widget. Here, notice how the `<Content>` tag points to the JSP-based landing page for the application: `IncidentWorklist.jsp`.

```
<?xml version="1.0" encoding="UTF-8"?>
<Module>
  <ModulePrefs title="Incident Widget">
    <Require feature="opensocial-0.9" />
    <Require feature="opensocial-jquery" />
    <Require feature="sap-xhrwrapper" />
    <Require feature="sap-theme" />
    <Require feature="sap-dynamic-height" />
  </ModulePrefs>
```

```
<Content type="html" href="IncidentWorklist.jsp"
    view="authoring, consumption, mobile, preview, default" />
</Module>
```

Listing 9.8 Spec XML File for the Incident Management Widget

Once you redeploy the Java application, you'll see that SAP HANA Cloud Portal has detected the widget's spec XML and automatically created a new widget in the content catalog (see Figure 9.39).

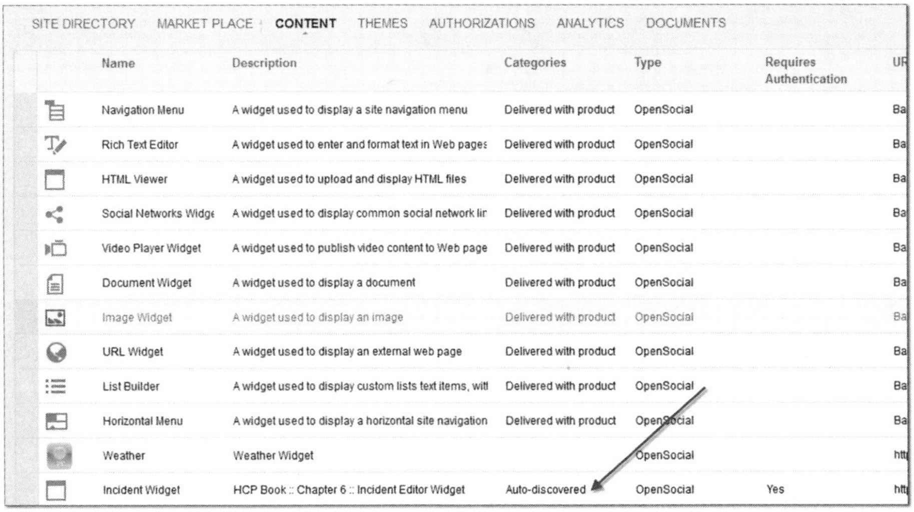

Figure 9.39 Finding Autodiscovered Widgets in the Content Catalog

Creating Widgets for SAP HANA XS and HTML5 Applications

As of the time of writing, the autodiscovery feature does not apply to applications developed using the SAP HANA XS and HTML5 programming models. Therefore, the widgets that you create for these applications will need to be manually created. Here, you basically repeat the steps outlined in Section 9.3.4, only this time you point at the application's URL in lieu of a spec XML file. Figure 9.40 shows the finished product for two widgets we created. As you can see, we created widgets to expose the SAP HANA-based online bookstore application created in Chapter 5 and the HTML5-based customer maintenance application created in Chapter 7.

Figure 9.40 Creating Widgets for the SAP HANA XS and HTML5 Applications

Embedding the Application Widgets

With your application widgets in place, you're ready to start building out the content areas of your pages. For the application-based pages, the steps required to drop in your application widgets are as follows:

1. Navigate to the page that you want to edit, and open up the CONTENT CATALOG pane via the toolbar button on the right-hand side of the page with the plus (+) icon on it.

2. Locate the target widget and drag it onto the page's content area (see Figure 9.41).

3. To resize the widget, you have two options: Use the drag handles surrounding the widget (see Figure 9.41) to move and resize the widget, or configure the widget to expand to match the size of the page's content area. In this case, opt for the latter approach by opening up the widget's design panel. This is achieved by selecting the DESIGN... menu option from the widget's menu bar (see Figure 9.42).

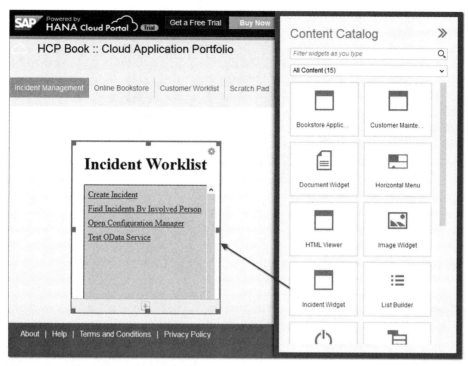

Figure 9.41 Adding an Application Widget to a Page: Part 1

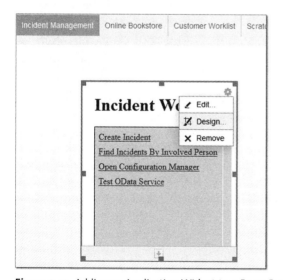

Figure 9.42 Adding an Application Widget to a Page: Part 2

4. This will open the DESIGN popup window shown in Figure 9.43. To expand the widget size, click on the SET AS FULL PAGE button.

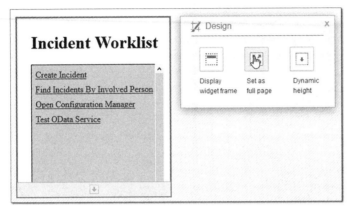

Figure 9.43 Adding an Application Widget to a Page: Part 3

Playing with Predelivered Widget Types

After you embed your application-based widgets, all that's left to configure, content-wise, is the SCRATCH PAD page that we created to demonstrate the capabilities of some of the SAP HANA Cloud Portal's out-of-the-box widgets.

The first widget you'll embed is the List Builder widget. As the name suggests, this widget type is used to create lists. For the purposes of this demo, create a THINGS TO WORK ON list that highlights some of the SAP HANA Cloud Portal-related technologies we've covered in the book. Figure 9.44 shows what the editor view looks like for this widget. As you can see, the editor view provides most of the text editing features common to word processing applications like Microsoft Word. Thus, it's a fairly simple task to touch up the list content.

The next widget you'll embed is the Video Player widget. This widget provides a nice container for displaying videos that might have been uploaded to YouTube, Vimeo, and so forth. As you can see in Figure 9.45, the only thing you have to specify when configuring this widget is the URL to the video you wish to display.

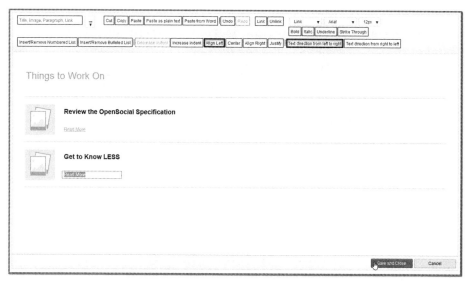

Figure 9.44 Adding a List to the Site

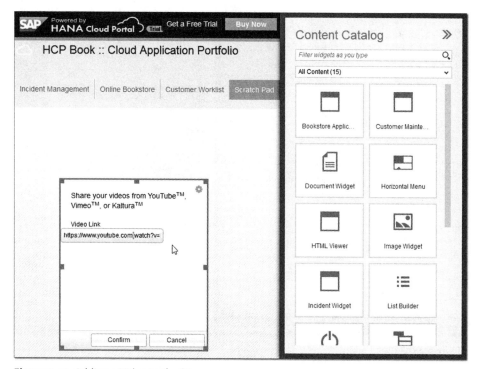

Figure 9.45 Adding a Video to the Site

Obviously, this simple demonstration barely scratches the surface of what some of these predelivered widget types can do. For more information about the widget types that are available and their specific capabilities, we recommend that you check out the online help documentation.

9.4.4   Publishing and Testing the Site

At this point, you've completed your content development and are ready to test out your site definition. Before you can test the site, though, you first have to *publish* it.

To publish a site, click on the toolbar button with the planet icon on it. This opens the PUBLISHING OPTIONS flyout pane shown in Figure 9.46. Here, simply click on the PUBLISH button to publish the site. Also worth noting on the PUBLISHING OPTIONS pane are the REVERT TO LAST PUBLISHED SITE and TAKE OFFLINE buttons. As the labels suggest, these buttons can be used to revert inadvertent changes and/or take down a site altogether.

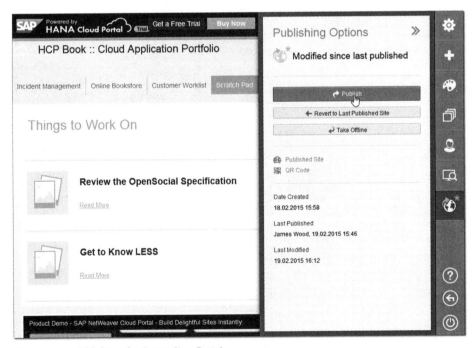

Figure 9.46 Publishing the Demo Site: Part 1

Whenever you click on the PUBLISH button, you'll be presented with the confirmation prompt shown in Figure 9.47. If you choose to proceed (by clicking on the PUBLISH button), then the latest-and-greatest version of the site will be published, and you should eventually arrive at the completion screen shown in Figure 9.48.

Figure 9.47 Publishing the Demo Site: Part 2

Figure 9.48 Publishing the Demo Site: Part 3

After the site is published, you can access it by clicking on the PUBLISHED SITE link in the PUBLISHING OPTIONS pane, as shown in Figure 9.49.

This will open the site in a separate browser window or tab, as shown in Figure 9.50. From here, you can click through the various pages and verify that all the content is showing up correctly. It's also a good idea to plug the site URL into other device types (e.g., tablets, phones, etc.) to see what the site looks like there. Because we didn't really tailor our demo site for mobile access, the spoiler alert here is that the site won't look fantastic on a small form factor, but that's a challenge for another day.

Figure 9.49 Launching the Published Site: Part 1

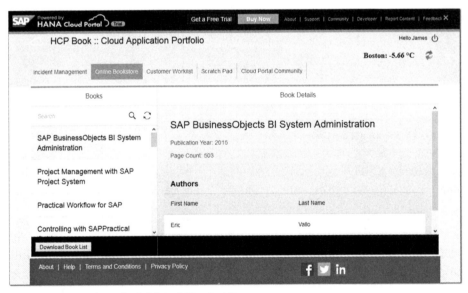

Figure 9.50 Launching the Published Site: Part 2

9.5   Next Steps

Despite being positioned as a service within SAP HCP, one could certainly make the argument that SAP HANA Cloud Portal is a product unto itself. Indeed, with so many powerful features, it's difficult to do SAP HANA Cloud Portal justice in an introductory chapter like this one. Still, we hope that we've provided you with a good enough foundation to take the next steps on your journey.

What are these next steps, you might ask? For developers, there's obviously an emphasis on learning the ins and outs of the OpenSocial standard for widget development, LESS for theming, and so forth. For the foreseeable future, though, it's also vitally important that developers learn their way around SAP HANA Cloud Portal's administrative tools. This is because the lines between content developer and content administrator will likely be blurred for a while as SAP HANA Cloud Portal matures.

The day-to-day administrative tasks are described in the online help documentation, underneath the section titled "SAP HANA Cloud Portal—User Guide." Within this guide, you can find details about how to configure site security, translate site content, and configure the use of standard-delivered widgets. Even if you never plan on performing an SAP HANA Cloud Portal administrative task, this is good knowledge to have, because it helps you develop *with* the platform instead of against it.

9.6   Summary

In this chapter, we provided you with a whirlwind introduction to SAP HANA Cloud Portal. As we observed, this SAP HCP service provides a rapid development environment for building mashup sites. As such, it's central to a lot of the extension application development that goes on in SAP HCP.

In the next chapter, we'll take a look at another useful service offering within SAP HCP: SAP HANA Cloud Integration (SAP HCI). Here, we'll see how this service can be used to build complex integration scenarios between applications hosted on the cloud and on-premise.

SAP HANA Cloud Integration is the cloud-based sister of SAP Process Integration. This chapter will show you what it's all about.

10 Introduction to SAP HANA Cloud Integration

One of the components provided as part of SAP HCP is SAP HANA Cloud Integration (SAP HCI). In this chapter, we'll introduce you to what this solution is (Section 10.1) and what it can be used for (Section 10.2). We'll then walk you through the main steps in setting up Eclipse (Section 10.3), which is the integrated development environment (IDE) we'll use in the example development scenario we present in this chapter. Once these basics are out of the way, we will dive into more detail in Section 10.4, which describes how to implement a simple scenario in which SAP HCI uses the SOAP adapter. Finally, although the focus in this chapter is using the Eclipse IDE for SAP HCI development, we'll conclude with a brief introduction to the other possible development environment: the web UI, also known as SAP HCI Spaces (Section 10.5).

10.1 Overview

Since the introduction of cloud computing technology, there has been a shift in the level of investment by organizations in software licenses. Organizations are rapidly moving from the concept of software ownership to software rental. As a consequence, SAP is also currently growing its cloud portfolio, with products from human resources (e.g., SuccessFactors), marketing, sales, service, procurement, supply chain management, and finance. We're convinced that this portfolio will continue to grow.

You might now be wondering about SAP's proposition to integrate this armada of cloud applications. Part of the answer lies in SAP's release and offering of SAP

HCI as its latest integration Platform-as-a-Service (iPaaS) for enterprise and B2B integration solutions.

SAP HCI is designed to handle data and process integration between cloud to cloud and from on-premise to cloud. It connects to applications, databases, and files, and also facilitates integration between SAP and non-SAP systems. Examples of applications it can connect to include SAP Business Suite, SAP Sales and Operations Planning (S&OP), and SuccessFactors. Examples of databases it can connect to include SAP HANA, Oracle, DB2, SQL Server, and MySQL.

SAP HCI comes in two flavors: SAP HCI for process integration and SAP HCI for data services. When SAP HCI is used for data services, it supports ETL (extract/transform/load) type integration by enabling the migration of data between on-premise and cloud applications. SAP HCI for process integration involves the creation of integration flows for end-to-end messaging and connectivity between on-premise and cloud solutions. (Note that the example in this chapter focuses on using SAP HCI for process integration purposes.)

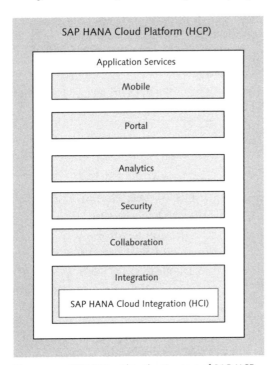

Figure 10.1 SAP HCI within the Context of SAP HCP

As Figure 10.1 depicts, SAP HCI is part of SAP HCP. SAP HCI can be categorized as the integration component of the application services block.

As opposed to SAP HCP, which enables customers and developers to build, extend, and run applications on SAP HANA in the cloud, SAP HCI is positioned as an integration platform or enterprise service bus (ESB) running on top of SAP HCP. From that perspective, the different applications provided by SAP HCP can be integrated together using SAP HCI.

In principle, SAP HCI has a separate license than SAP HCP. However, it is also possible to use it as part of your SAP HCP license. There are three main license editions: the application edition, the standalone integration platform edition, and the developer edition. This choice of edition creates the flexibility for customers to choose the model that best fits their needs. These three edition options are subscription based and can be described as follows:

▸ **Application edition**
This edition can be used by customers using other SAP Cloud applications, such as SAP Cloud for Customer, SuccessFactors, and SAP Financial Services Network (FSN). This edition comes equipped with prepackaged content and flows that can be used directly without deep technical knowledge. This content can be found from the web-based application known as the Integration Content Catalog. The Integration Content Catalog can be accessed via *https://cloudintegration.hana.ondemand.com*.

▸ **Standalone integration platform edition**
This is a version of SAP HCI that enables you to integrate any application into your landscape (including SAP and third-party applications). Within this context, there are two different levels: the SAP HCI standard and professional packages. The standard edition is the entry-level package. It has full integration capabilities but is limited in terms of the total amount of bandwidth that can be used per month. The professional package, on the other hand, caters for more bandwidth. The professional package has many more levels that customers can select from, depending on their needs.

▸ **Developer edition**
This edition is intended for SAP partners to develop custom applications, such as the Adapter Development Kit (ADK), integration flows, and other integration artifacts. This edition was released in early 2015.

10.2 Use Cases

At this point, you might be asking yourself how you will know in which situations SAP HCI might be applicable or relevant.

Imagine that you have a scenario that requires you to integrate two different applications that have been built on top of SAP HCP. You might be tempted to build direct connections between the different applications using homegrown solutions facilitated by the SAP HCP Connectivity Service. At first view, this might be an easy and quick solution, especially with fewer applications to connect. However, its disadvantages become visible as the organization's cloud application landscape becomes more complex and larger. The point-to-point approach forms a spider web of application connections, as shown in Figure 10.2. This connection spaghetti will keep growing exponentially as more systems are introduced into the landscape.

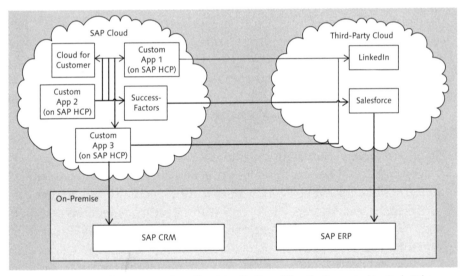

Figure 10.2 Point-to-Point Integration: Cloud Applications Directly Connected to Each Other

When using the point-to-point integration approach, each system is aware of the connection and message details of the system on the other side of the exchange. Every time a particular system changes or needs to be replaced, the impact will be felt by all other systems communicating with it. If a vulnerable security connection is discovered in one of the systems, then all applications currently connecting with it will need to be changed, adapted, and potentially be unavailable for a long time, all of which results in higher costs of development and maintenance in the long run.

That is where an ESB like SAP HCI comes to the rescue. SAP HCI eliminates and remedies the problems caused when using point-to-point integration by taking on the role of the central integration hub, which facilitates the routing and transformation of different structures of the systems involved in an integration, as shown in Figure 10.3.

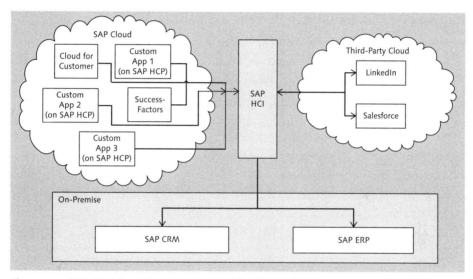

Figure 10.3 SAP HCI Integrates On-Premise and On-Demand Applications

SAP HCI is the glue that can hold cloud-based and on-premise applications together. SAP HCI integrates these applications in an easy and cost-effective way—especially for some specific scenarios, because it provides numerous prepackaged integration content choices for different SAP Cloud solutions.

Even though SAP HCI covers a wide range of use cases, the next section will only focus on few illustrative and more commonly used cases. The following cases can be considered:

▸ **Integrating with SAP Cloud for Customer**
Customers currently using the SAP Cloud for Customer solution can easily integrate it with an on-premise SAP CRM or SAP ERP solution via the prepackaged solution provided in SAP HCI.

- **Integrating SuccessFactors**

  Customers using the SuccessFactors platform can rapidly integrate it with an on-premise SAP ERP solution using the specific prepackaged solution provided in SAP HCI. Furthermore, a special SuccessFactors adapter is provided in SAP HCI to seamlessly integrate with SuccessFactors, in case you decide to develop your own custom integration flows.

- **Integrating with SAP FSN**

  SAP FSN uses SAP HCI as its ESB to facilitate the integration between different corporations and financial institutions.

- **Integrating any cloud-to-cloud scenario**

  If different cloud-based applications need to be integrated and exchange data, then SAP HCI can be used to facilitate the building of custom integration flows.

- **Integrating any other cloud to on-premise applications**

  In addition to working with cloud applications provided by SAP (such as SuccessFactors), you might encounter a situation in which custom applications built on top of SAP HCP need to exchange data with their on-premise counterpart applications. In such a case, SAP HCI can be used to facilitate the building of custom integration flows. In this situation, an integration flow might need to be developed from scratch, because the likelihood of having existing prepackaged integration content for such a scenario will be small.

10.3   Getting Started with the Eclipse IDE

In order to perform development activities for SAP HCI, you will need to use an IDE, such as Eclipse. SAP HCI uses Eclipse to contain the necessary perspectives that support SAP HCI developments.

In order to use Eclipse for SAP HCI development, you need to install some SAP HCI-specific plug-ins and make sure Eclipse is correctly configured. In this section, we'll walk you through these steps.

10.3.1   Installing SAP HANA Cloud Integration Plug-Ins

SAP HCI is currently supported on Eclipse Kepler, a specific version of Eclipse. Other Eclipse platforms currently do not provide support for SAP HCI. Eclipse

Kepler can be downloaded at *https://www.eclipse.org/downloads/packages/release/kepler/sr2*.

After installing Eclipse Kepler, you will need to install the appropriate SAP HCI plug-ins in Eclipse in order to have the necessary artifacts for creating, designing, and monitoring integration flows. Proceed as follows to add the plug-ins:

1. From the main menu, choose HELP • INSTALL NEW SOFTWARE....

2. On the AVAILABLE SOFTWARE page of the install wizard, add the update site URL: *https://tools.HANA.ondemand.com/kepler*.

3. Select from the following three options:

  ▸ SHOW ONLY THE LATEST VERSION OF AVAILABLE SOFTWARE

  ▸ GROUP ITEMS BY CATEGORY

  ▸ CONTACT ALL UPDATE SITES DURING INSTALL TO FIND REQUIRED SOFTWARE

4. Select the SAP HANA CLOUD INTEGRATION TOOLS category.

5. Click on NEXT.

6. Check the features selected for installation and click on NEXT.

7. Accept the terms of the licensing agreement and click on FINISH.

8. Restart the Eclipse IDE.

The Eclipse plug-in contains the following features:

▸ **Designer for SAP HCI**
This feature contains plug-ins to develop and configure integration flows.

▸ **Operations for SAP HCI**
This feature contains plug-ins to perform administrative tasks related to SAP HCI runtime clusters and to monitor integration flows.

▸ **Certificates and security artifacts**
Depending on the type of scenario in mind, designing and deploying integration flows on an SAP HCI tenant requires you to take security aspects into consideration. Different types of security artifacts might need to be included. This could include SSL (certificate authority, private key, and public key) and SSH (private and public keys). Note that many CAs are currently supported (including SAP Passport CA), and more will be added as time goes by.

Because SAP HCI currently supports SOAP, IDoc, SFTP, OData, and SuccessFactors connectivity options, the security artifacts previously listed can be used in most of them.

▶ **Tenant account**
You need a tenant account to be able to deploy your SAP HCI developments. The details of the tenant includes the tenant ID and the operations server. These details are needed to be able to configure your Eclipse environment. For more information about how to apply for a tenant account, please contact your SAP representative. The tenant will facilitate the execution of different integration operations, including the deployment of integration flows and the runtime monitoring of running flows.

10.3.2 Configuring Eclipse

When configuring Eclipse for your SAP HCI environment, you will need to configure two different preference aspects in Eclipse: the operations server and the ESR.

The operations server is required to be able to deploy your SAP HCI integration flows to the server. To set up the operations server, perform the following actions:

1. From your Eclipse IDE, navigate to WINDOWS • PERSPECTIVES • SAP HANA CLOUD INTEGRATION.

2. From there, enter the necessary details to connect to the operations server, based on the tenant details (see Figure 10.4).

3. You can test the connection by using the TEST CONNECTION button. When the test is successful, click on the OK button.

REPOSITORY CONNECTION will normally point to the Enterprise Service Repository (ESR). This configuration will enable the importing of SAP PI/SAP PO objects and artifacts, such as message mappings, operation mappings, and WSDL files. This feature is very useful and facilitates the use of existing SAP PI objects. You will need to input the required details under the REPOSITORY CONNECTION section (see Figure 10.5).

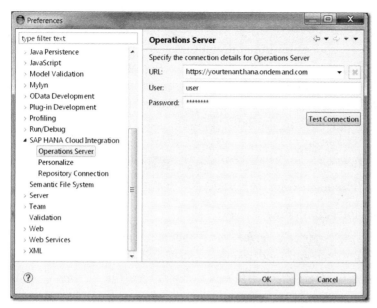

Figure 10.4 Setting Up the Operations Server in Eclipse

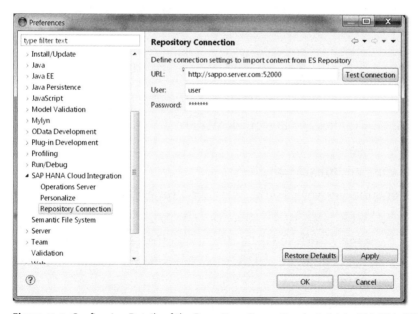

Figure 10.5 Configuring Details of the Repository Connection to Point to SAP PO's ESR

10.4   Implementing a Simple SOAP-to-SOAP Scenario

Back in Section 10.2, we discussed the different use cases for SAP HCI. As you'll recall, one such use case was the ability to integrate a cloud application with an on-premise application. To understand this use case in a little more detail, consider an example where a cloud-based custom application needs to exchange data with an on-premise application, and both applications can be interfaced to and from using the SOAP adapter. In such a case, SAP HCI can be used as the ESB to perform integration using a simple SOAP-to-SOAP integration flow.

The general steps in implementing such a SOAP-to-SOAP scenario are as follows:

1. Create an initial integration flow.

2. Configure the sender system, receiver system (name of the sender and receiver system; this is optional), and sender authorization (this is the public key pair).

3. Import the WSDL file from the SAP PI repository or local file system.

4. Create a parameters file that contains attributes and metadata that can be referenced from the communication channels.

5. Create a mapping between sender and receiver systems, or import existing mapping objects from the SAP PI repository.

6. Create sender and receiver communication channels.

7. Deploy the integration project.

8. Monitor the project to make sure everything is running smoothly.

Each of these steps is discussed in more detail next.

10.4.1   Creating an Integration Flow

To create your initial integration flow, follow the steps below:

1. Switch to the INTEGRATION DESIGNER perspective by going to WINDOW • OPEN PERSPECTIVE. Choose OTHER and then INTEGRATION DESIGNER.

2. Create an integration project by clicking on the PROJECT EXPLORER palette and selecting NEW • OTHER.

3. Then, select INTEGRATION PROJECT from the SAP HANA CLOUD INTEGRATION folder (see Figure 10.6).

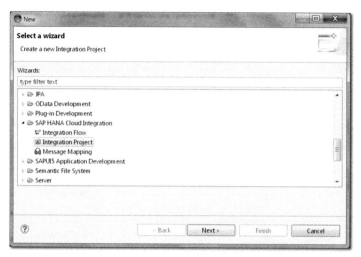

Figure 10.6 Specify Details of the Integration Flow and Its Pattern Template

4. Click on NEXT, and then name your integration flow.

5. Proceed with the wizard, and provide details about the integration flow to be created. In addition to giving it a name, you will also need to specify a pattern to be used to create it. Each of the provided pattern templates contains an explanation of what it can be used for. For the sake of simplicity, choose POINT-TO-POINT CHANNEL (see Figure 10.7).

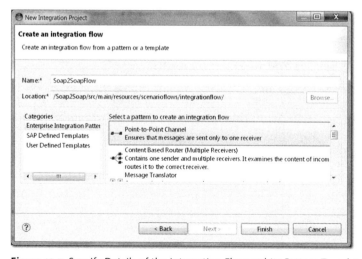

Figure 10.7 Specify Details of the Integration Flow and Its Pattern Template

> **Note**
>
> You can define your own set of integration flow patterns; these are the so-called *user-defined templates*.

6. Click on the FINISH button to complete the initial creation steps.

The resulting integration flow generated from the point-to-point channel template looks like the image shown in Figure 10.8.

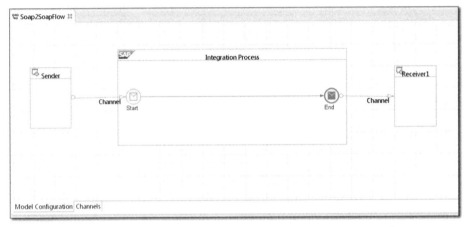

Figure 10.8 Basic Integration Flow from the Point-to-Point Channel Pattern Template

Now it's time to extend this empty integration flow and further configure it.

10.4.2 Configuring Sender and Receiver Systems

To properly configure the sender and receiver systems, follow the steps below:

1. From the integration flow presented in Figure 10.8, click on the sender system (on the left side of the diagram), check the property area, and enter an appropriate name without whitespaces for your sender system.

2. Under SENDER AUTHORIZATION, click on the BROWSE option to import your public SSL key (see Figure 10.9). Adding the SSL key is required for certificate-based authentication.

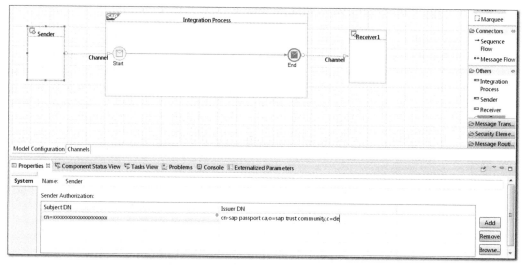

Figure 10.9 Configure the Sender System and Maintain Authorization

3. Repeat the previous steps to configure the receiver system name. Note that there is no need to browse for the public key on the receiver side.

10.4.3 Importing WSDL Files from SAP PI or Your Local File System

For the sake of simplicity, we will assume that you will reuse existing service interfaces for this scenario. You will then need to import them from your ESR. In order to import the service interfaces, proceed as follows:

1. Right-click on the name of the integration project in the PROJECT EXPLORER palette, choose the IMPORT PI CONTENT option, and choose the type of artifact to be imported. You will be asked to choose from among MESSAGE MAPPING, OPERATION MAPPING, and INTERFACE. For this example, choose the INTERFACE option, which will load the list of service interfaces for you to choose from. After selecting the desired service interface, click on the FINISH button.

2. Import the WSDL/service interface for the receiver system as well. These two service interfaces (for the sender and receiver) will be used during mapping. Note that the WSDL file could also be imported from a local file system instead of the ESR.

445

10.4.4 Creating a Parameters File

The parameters file contains the reference parameters to be used in your integration flow. Parameters can be created for a variety of attributes. A typical example includes the location of the WSDL file and the endpoint to be used during the configuration of the communication channels. To create the parameters file, proceed as follows:

1. Right-click on the integration project and choose NEW • OTHER. From the subsequent screen, select GENERAL and then FILE. Enter "parameters.prop" for the file name.

2. Follow the wizard, and make sure that the newly created file is saved in the *src.main.resources* directory.

3. Click on the FINISH button.

4. Populate the newly created file with different parameters and their corresponding values (see Figure 10.10 for an example configuration file).

Figure 10.10 Parameters File

To reference these parameters during the configuration of a communication channel, the values on the left-hand side of the = sign are enclosed in double curly braces—for example, {{SOAP_soapWsdlURL}}.

10.4.5 Mapping between Sender and Receiver Systems

There are two possible ways to implement the mapping between the sender and receiver:

▸ Reuse an existing mapping.

▸ Create a new mapping from within SAP HCI Designer.

If you opt to create a new mapping, then proceed as follows:

1. Right-click on the integration project and select NEW • OTHER. Under SAP HANA CLOUD INTEGRATION, choose MESSAGE MAPPING, and then follow the wizard.

2. Specify the name of the message mapping, and click on FINISH.

3. The OVERVIEW screen of the newly created mapping opens. Choose the DEFINITION tab to select the source and target structures to be used in your mapping.

4. Create a mapping between the source and target structures. The structure needs to be selected from the WSDL file imported earlier (see Figure 10.11).

   Here, the mapping capability is equipped with a number of predefined functions that can be used for defining the mapping logic.

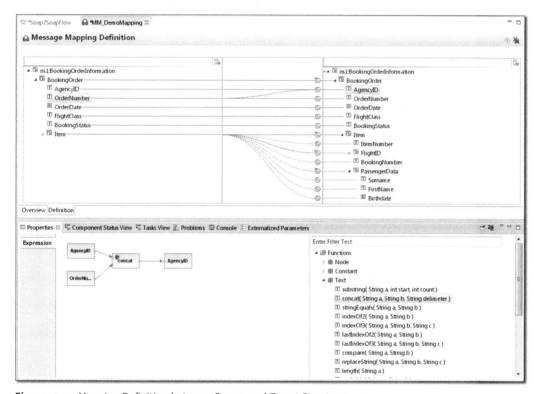

Figure 10.11 Mapping Definition between Source and Target Structures

5. Go back to the integration flow and add a mapping artifact. This can be achieved by using the context menu on the horizontal line between the START

and END icons within the INTEGRATION PROCESS box. Select the ADD MAPPING option. A new mapping artifact will be placed.

6. Use the context menu on the newly added mapping artifact, and select the ASSIGN MAPPING option. On the resulting selection screen, select the previously created message mapping.

10.4.6 Configuring Sender and Receiver Communication Channels

The communication channels need to be configured to the desired adapter type. To configure a communication channel, proceed as follows:

1. Right-click on the channel artifact on the sender side. This is the horizontal line between the sender and the INTEGRATION PROCESS box. Choose the CONFIGURE CHANNEL option.

2. The integration flow jumps into the CHANNELS tab. From there, provide a name for the communication channel and choose the desired adapter type. In this case, choose the SOAP adapter.

3. You will also need to go to the ADAPTER SPECIFIC tab to specify further adapter details. The details to be specified include the endpoint and a link to a WSDL URL. The parameters defined in the parameters.prop file can be used here.

4. You will need to perform the same configuration steps for the receiver communication channel.

The final configuration of the integration flow looks like the one presented in Figure 10.12.

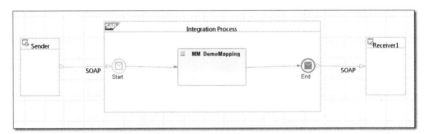

Figure 10.12 Final Simple Integration Flow Configured in SAP HCI

If a red marker appears on the integration project after saving, then that signals that the configuration is not complete. Please check the problem console to see more details about the error.

10.4.7 Deploying the Integration Project

Once all the configurations are done and all the changes saved, it's time to deploy the integration flow to your SAP HCI tenant. To deploy the project to the cloud, right-click on the project and choose the DEPLOY INTEGRATION CONTENT option. A popup will ask for the tenant ID. Once you've provided the ID, the deployment will be performed.

10.4.8 Monitoring

To monitor your flows directly from the Eclipse IDE, switch to the INTEGRATION OPERATION perspective. Figure 10.13 shows the sample messages received by SAP HCI and further detail; different search functionalities can be used from the monitoring tool.

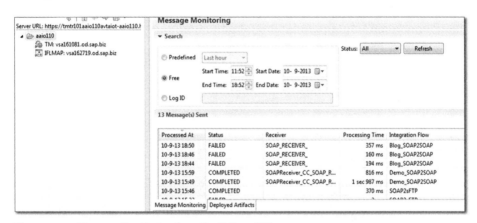

Figure 10.13 Message Monitoring from the Eclipse IDE

In MESSAGE MONITORING, you can search messages based on different filtering criteria. The monitoring screen shows different messages that have been received by the server. You can also see their statuses. Note that this perspective also provides a DEPLOYED ARTIFACTS tab. As its name indicates, this tab lists all the artifacts that have been deployed to the SAP HCI server—including integration flows.

Now that you have a pretty good understanding of what it takes to use Eclipse as the development IDE for SAP HCI, it's time to look at the web UI.

449

10.5   Introduction to the Web UI for SAP HANA Cloud Integration

As an alternative to the Eclipse IDE, you can use the web UI client for SAP HCI. The SAP HCI web UI is a web-based IDE; it's also known as SAP HCI Spaces. It has numerous advantages compared to the Eclipse IDE. One of the most significant ones is that developers don't need to install anything locally; there is no need to worry about the consistency of versions between the local IDE and the server. The developer only needs a browser and Internet connection in order to start development activities. This fact alone reduces the development effort and saves costs.

In this section, we will explore the different tools that make up the web UI development platform. The landing page of the web UI can be accessed via *http:// <operations server url>/itspaces*.

As can be seen on the left side of Figure 10.14, the SAP HCI web UI consists of the following four main sections:

- ▶ DISCOVER
- ▶ DESIGN
- ▶ RUN
- ▶ MONITOR

Figure 10.14 Landing Page of the Web UI

Each of these sections will be explored in more detail next.

10.5.1 The Discover Section (Integration Content Catalog)

With SAP HCI, SAP provides prepackaged integration content that can be found and accessed via a web-based (SAPUI5) application known as the Integration Content Catalog (see Figure 10.15).

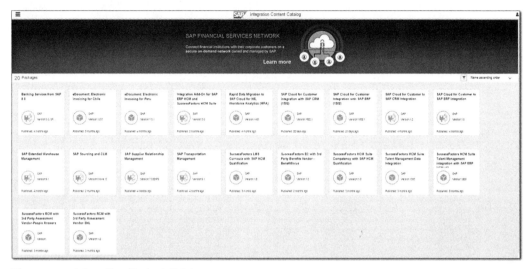

Figure 10.15 Integration Content Catalog

The SAP HCI web UI can be accessed from the DISCOVER section on the left-hand menu, as shown in Figure 10.14. Alternatively, the Integration Content Catalog can be publicly accessed and explored via *https://cloudintegration.HANA.ondemand.com*. You will need to log in with your SCN username and password.

This prepackaged content contains value mappings, mappings, data integration flows, and other integration artifacts. This content can be used directly by partners and customers or can be modified to fit your specific needs.

The content presented in the landing page shown in Figure 10.15 includes a number of content bundles, such as SAP SUPPLIER RELATIONSHIP MANAGEMENT, BANKING SERVICES, SUCCESSFACTORS, and so on. Upon selecting one of these bundles, you are redirected to a page containing more details.

As you can see in Figure 10.16, a name and description of the bundle are presented. You can also find the following:

- ▶ ARTIFACTS

  Includes a list of value mappings, mappings, data integration flows, and other integration artifacts that make up the bundle.

- ▶ DOCUMENTS

  Includes guides and links to provide more documentation and information about the integration content to further assist the user.

- ▶ TAGS

  Provides different tags to help classify the content, including industry, line of businesses, keywords, supported platforms, and so on.

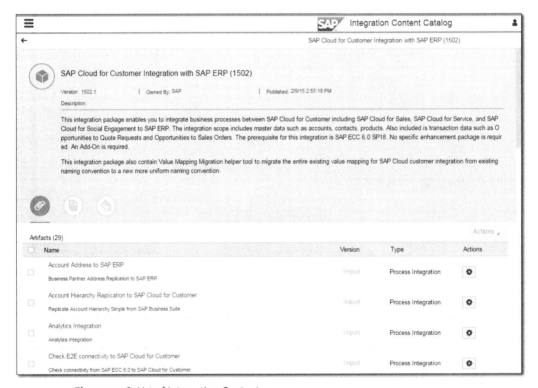

Figure 10.16 List of Integration Content

Click on the items listed under ARTIFACTS to see their graphical representation. In Figure 10.17, you can see an example of an integration flow after it's been clicked on. Any part of the graphical representation of the integration flow can be selected to see more of its details in the bottom part of the screen (as shown in Figure 10.17).

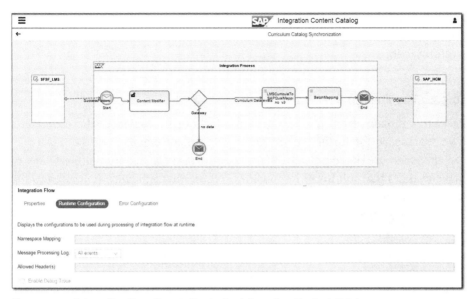

Figure 10.17 Integration Flow Perspective in the Integration Content Catalog

Looking at the graphical representation shown in Figure 10.17, you can see that the integration flow contains a mapping. When you click on this mapping, the name of the mapping is presented in the bottom section of the screen. Click on this name to open a view showing the details of the mapping, as shown in Figure 10.18.

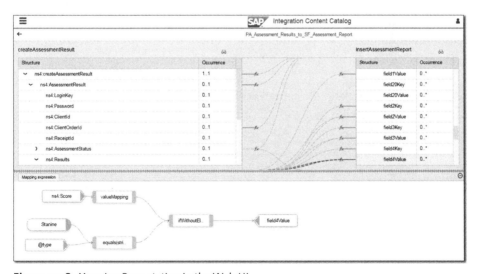

Figure 10.18 Mapping Presentation in the Web UI

The list of integration packages presented in the DISCOVER section can be considered templates. To make changes to these templates, you'll need to explore the DESIGN section.

10.5.2 The Design Section

Package templates from the DISCOVER section can be copied to the customer's own workspace for further modification and enhancements, and the customer can choose to use the template contained in the package as a basis upon which to make changes that suit his or her business requirements. Figure 10.19 shows the button (circled in the figure) that allows you to copy the package template into your own workspace.

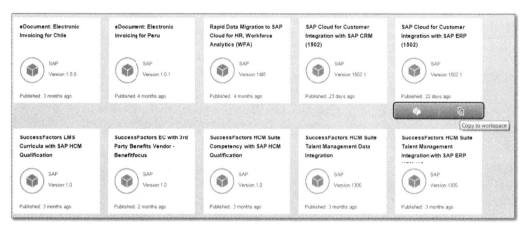

Figure 10.19 Copy Templates to Your Own Workspace

After copying a template, the copied artifact shows up in the DESIGN section and can now be enhanced. Figure 10.20 shows a copied package available in a customer's workspace (see the left side of page).

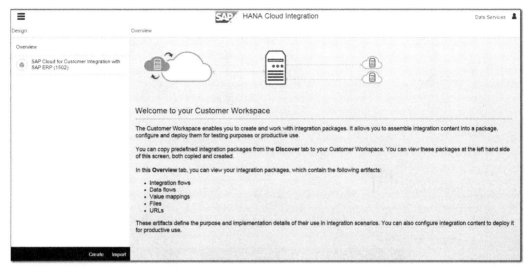

Figure 10.20 Design Component with Copied Templates

The content of the package presented in Figure 10.20 can be modified via the following steps:

1. Click on the package name on the left-hand menu (see Figure 10.18 under OVERVIEW).

2. The menu will be filled with the full list of all artifacts contained in the template package. Note that the artifacts can be made of a mixture of integration flows, data flows, value mappings, files, and URLs (see the left-hand menu in Figure 10.21).

3. Select an integration flow of your choice to have its content graphically displayed, as shown in Figure 10.21.

4. In order to change any aspect of the integration flow, you will need to click on the EDIT option on the bottom-right side (see Figure 10.21) to make the integration flow modifiable. Note that when you're in EDIT mode, the integration package editor locks the object and prevents any other user from changing it.

5. After the desired changes have been made, click on the SAVE button (see bottom-right corner in Figure 10.22). Alternatively, click on the SAVE AS VERSION button to save a new version of the integration flow. You will be asked to provide a comment for the new version. Note that the version number is also automatically incremented.

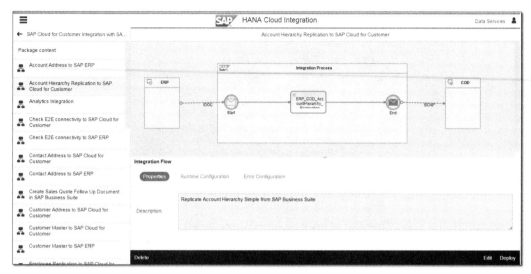

Figure 10.21 Displaying Integration Flow Content

6. After saving your work in the previous step, you can now choose to deploy the integration flow to the server by using the DEPLOY option, as shown in the bottom-right corner of Figure 10.22.

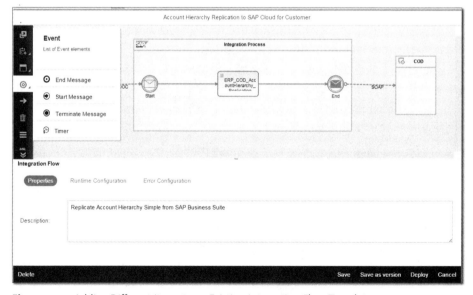

Figure 10.22 Adding Different Items to an Existing Integration Flow Template

7. You will be taken to a new overview of the package, in which you can see that the version of the integration flow has been updated (see the VERSION column in Figure 10.23).

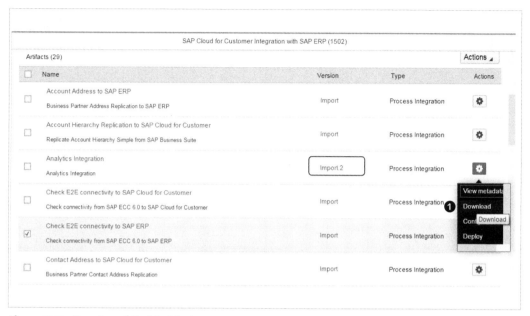

Figure 10.23 Overview of Updated Package

Figure 10.23 also shows that it is possible to download the content of an integration flow. The content is downloaded to your local machine in a form of an archive file (ZIP file) containing the entire integration flow project. This integration flow project ZIP file can then be imported into another package or used in Eclipse.

Note that it is also possible to create your own content package. You will need to use the CREATE button, which is available in the DESIGN section (refer back to Figure 10.20).

10.5.3 The Run Section

The RUN section enables the developer or operator to view a list of all artifacts deployed on the tenant, including integration flows (see Figure 10.24).

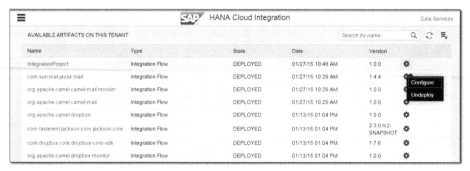

Figure 10.24 View of the Run Section, with a List of Deployed Artifacts

For any of the listed integration flows, the following actions can be performed:

▶ **View details**
Clicking on the name of any presented integration flow will take you to a page in which the details of the integration flow can be seen.

▶ **Configure**
This option provides the functionality to quickly modify some attributes.

▶ **Undeploy**
This option undeploys (or removes) the selected artifact from the SAP HCI server.

10.5.4 The Monitor Section

The MONITOR section enables users or operators to monitor processed messages using the web UI. From this page, you will need to click on the MONITOR link from the menu. You will then land on a page that looks the one presented in Figure 10.25.

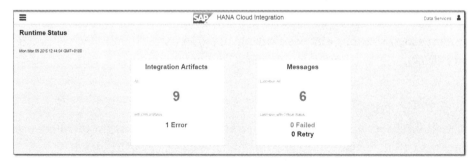

Figure 10.25 Runtime Status from Web UI

This page presents a high-level overview of messages and artifacts with their statuses. You can click on the numbers presented in Figure 10.25 (in the INTEGRATION ARTIFACTS box) to get more details about the objects in question. The details page is shown in Figure 10.26. This new page presents details such as instances, time, and endpoints. The page presents the possibility to filter the entries based on different statuses.

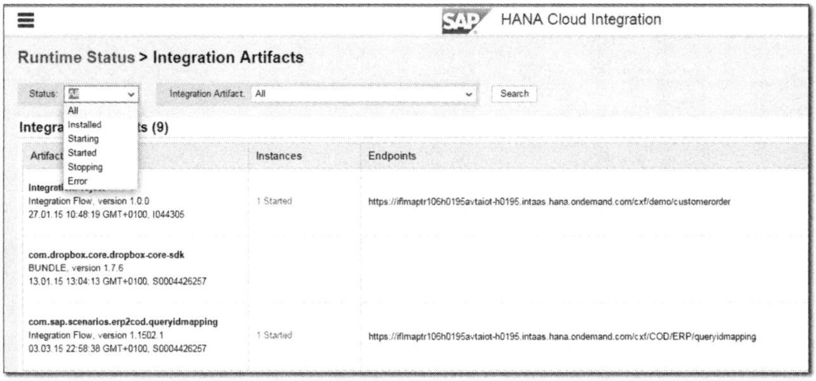

Figure 10.26 Monitoring Details Using the Web UI

It is also possible to see details of messages by clicking on the numbers presented under the MESSAGES box. You will then see more details about the messages that have been processed through your SAP HCI tenant, as shown in Figure 10.27. From this message monitoring page, information such as processing time, statuses, and relevant integration flows can be found.

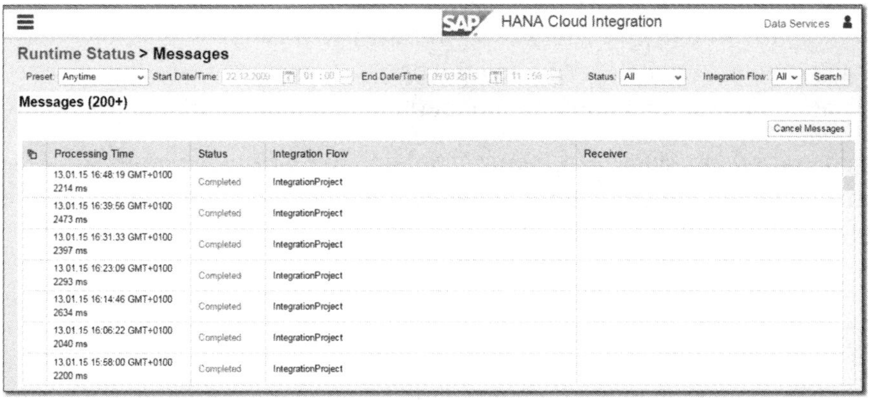

Figure 10.27 Message Monitoring Page

The status of every message line of the table presented on the message monitoring page can be clicked on to get detailed runtime information and processing logs, as shown in Figure 10.28.

Figure 10.28 Message Processing Log

Note that the MESSAGE PROCESSING LOG page also allows you to perform a free text search, as shown in Figure 10.28.

10.6 Summary

This chapter has introduced SAP HCI and provided an overview of the possibilities and features it offers. We also explored SAP HCI's different development tools and provided step-by-step guides to help you build your first integration flow and content in SAP HCI. With much more functionality and features planned in the next releases, we wish you a fun journey in the cloud with SAP HCI!

In the next and last chapter of the printed book, we'll bring together all of the information you've learned so far to demonstrate how SAP HCP can be used to build extension applications for SAP's existing cloud products.

This chapter introduces a number of options to extend existing cloud products from SAP using SAP HCP applications. We'll look at the different integration options, the technology aspects involved, and the underlying infrastructure required for an end-to-end solution.

11 Extension Scenarios with SAP HANA Cloud Platform

In previous chapters, you learned about the core features of SAP HCP and how to create and deploy real applications both on the local development server and on the cloud. In this chapter, we will explore how to put that knowledge to good use to extend some of the SAP Cloud products. We start the discussion of extending applications with SAP HCP by explaining why there is a need to do so in the first place (Section 11.1). After that, we'll dive into the details: the architecture of an extension (Section 11.2) and the specific integration points that you can use (Section 11.3). The chapter concludes with an overview of the process of extending SuccessFactors using SAP HCP (Section 11.4).

There are three key principles that SAP follows for every SAP HCP extension integration project:

▶ One unified experience for SAP partners creating extensions for all SAP Cloud products: the same development process, onboarding, support, and operations

▶ One unified experience for SAP customers leveraging and managing extensions: tightly integrated administration experience, embedded extensions catalog, and optional trial for certified extensions

▶ Zero integration costs for running SAP HCP applications next to an existing SAP Cloud solution

> **Note**
>
> This chapter focuses mostly on the SuccessFactors Employee Central product and the specifics when extending it, but the principles outlined in the chapter are generic

enough to be applied to other SAP Cloud products as well—for example, Ariba, SAP Fieldglass, hybris, Concur, and so on. Thus, when we use the phrase "the extended SAP Cloud solution" in this chapter, we are using it as a generic term to refer to any of these products.

Nevertheless, keep in mind that there are always specifics to consider when working with the APIs of the different solutions.

11.1 The Need for Software-as-a-Solution Extensions

One of the major differences between the Software-as-a-Service (SaaS) world and the on-premise world is that in the on-premise world, IT teams are fully in control to plan process updates and execute on new requirements and ideas. They can directly influence every layer starting from the bare metal hardware, through the network, system setup, and business objects model, and reaching to the UI-level customizations. In such an environment, meeting business commitments is only a matter of good organization, technical ability, and budget. The head of corporate IT has the responsibility to control the ratio between risk and innovation from one side and actively manage the demands from the different business units from another.

On the other hand, SaaS solutions typically strongly emphasize the fact that there is "one code line" and a "continuous flow of innovation" with frequent release cycles. Cloud applications typically provide only the industry best practices, common to the complete customer base. Introducing customer-specific features in the main code line is practically not possible in an economically efficient way. Because the product is provided "as a service" by the vendor, corporate IT teams no longer have influence over any of the underlying layers. They effectively become key users, and their new role is to educate business users and channel feedback to the corresponding vendor. In many cases, corporate IT has to defend and explain why an anticipated business workflow can't be put in production in the same short timeframes that were possible previously with on-premise systems. In the aviation industry, this phenomenon is called *loss of control* (LOC). Some would argue that this is a good thing, because cloud vendors would know better how to run their software at scale in an efficient manner—but, as we've outlined in this paragraph, it does have its drawbacks.

At the same time, transition to the cloud and SaaS is an unstoppable trend. In order to address the loss-of-control issue associated with the transition to cloud solutions, SAP is on a journey to equip corporate IT teams with the necessary tools and practices to keep providing high-quality services to their respective business stakeholders.

Depending on the market and the industry, there are a number of white space areas that SAP will not have the capacity to get into on its own any time soon, making them perfect for cloud extension applications. (Though at a later stage, these might be covered by standard SAP products.) One example is that of country-specific scenarios, which are impacted by the regional regulatory frame. Let's look at some particular cases:

▶ **Company car management**
Germany is known as a car country. More than 85% of the high-end cars purchased there are registered to companies. The tax frame in the country stimulates companies to offer company cars as an employee perk. A potential HR extension application in that space could cover all the processes around choosing, ordering, managing, servicing, and finally returning a company car. The same practice is not at all common in the United States or in Asia, making the scenario a niche one.

▶ **Employee health and safety**
Another example from Germany is the regulatory frame defining how employee health and safety are to be managed by large companies. This includes emergency phone numbers, regular first aid training sessions, and so on. An extension application would ideally cover all the specifics of that process for a large company with multiple office locations in Germany. There are similar (but still different) corporate requirements for companies in other regions, such as Russia, Singapore, China, and so on.

Another dimension on top of the local regulations are industry-specific scenarios:

▶ **Pharmaceutical industry**
Companies in the pharmaceutical industry in Europe are required to maintain a set of certificates for each of their R&D employees, ensuring that they are qualified to work on certain types of drugs and have been trained to work with particular dangerous substances.

▸ **Automotive industry**
Large automotive companies in Europe are obliged to provide mandatory training to employees prior to allowing them to operate certain classes of equipment.

When combining country-specific and industry-specific requirements on a global scale, the result is countless niche scenarios that are perfectly suited to be implemented as extension applications. And this doesn't even take into consideration all the company-specific practices that enable different business to stand out and differentiate from the competition.

In an ideal world, all of these scenarios would be covered by corresponding standard cloud products. However, from a pure effort perspective, doing so is not realistic. The regulatory framework is constantly evolving. Therefore, the only way to scale in this global environment is to enable customers to cover their specific process variations without being dependent on a single vendor.

This situation also opens up a significant business opportunity to application development partners. Despite the push towards software standardization, specific customizations will always be required. The region- and industry-specific requirements, combined with the constant strive of companies to compete, will grow the extension application market in the next years to come.

11.2 The Architecture of an Extension

SAP HCP is positioned as the extension platform for all SAP products going forward. Throughout the book, you've learned that SAP HCP is a secure and scalable application container that can integrate in a secure manner to both cloud and on-premise systems (Figure 11.1). You can develop extension applications on SAP HCP, granting them access to the SAP Cloud solution APIs. In that way, you can create tailored business workflows that fit precisely to your specific business needs. This approach requires no structural changes in the underlying SAP Cloud products, and therefore there is no need to avoid subsequent frequent product updates. At the same time, this approach strongly relies on the availability of stable and robust APIs. In order to achieve this and provide a first-class experience to customers, SAP HCP is being integrated deeply in all SAP Cloud products both from administration and end user perspectives.

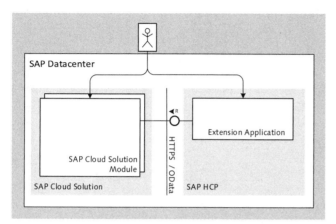

Figure 11.1 SAP HCP Serving as a Secure Application Container for SAP Cloud Solution Extension Applications

The typical SAP HCP-based extension application follows the classical three-tier software architecture, and brings in solution-specific native artifacts to be imported in the extended SAP solution. First of all, it is a normal SAP HCP application. It integrates with the extended SAP solution via (typically OData) APIs. Ideally, it is running on SAP HCP in the same (or a close enough) datacenter together with the extended solution. In any case, both the extended SAP Cloud solutions and SAP HCP are hosted by SAP and enable applications to communicate through a secure, SSL-encrypted connection. In some cases, extension applications also consume data from other backend systems that reside either in the cloud or on-premise. An extension application may also bundle native artifacts specific to the extended SAP Cloud solution, such as custom business objects, generated UI definitions, data view definitions, roles, permissions, and so on (Figure 11.2).

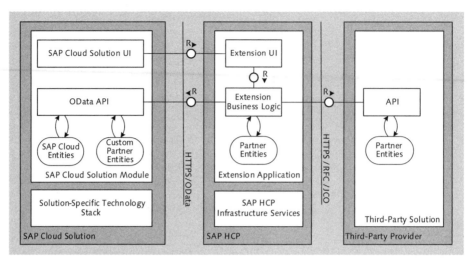

Figure 11.2 SAP HCP Extension Application Interaction Points

On one side are the SAP HCP extension applications, which are specifically implemented to interact with the extended solution via APIs. Underneath is the SAP HCP account, defining the environment for the extension application to run in (Figure 11.3).

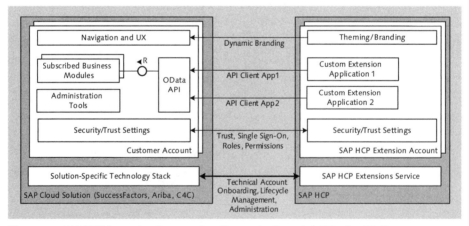

Figure 11.3 SAP HCP Extension Account Coupling to the Extended SAP Cloud Solution

Please note that SAP HCP extension accounts do not function separately from the extended SAP Cloud solution. What makes extension accounts special? Figure 11.3 shows some of the reasons:

► There is a hard 1:1 mapping between SAP Cloud solution accounts or tenants and SAP HCP extension accounts. If you happen to have 10 SuccessFactors tenants, for example, then you'll have 10 SAP HCP extension accounts.

► Centrally configured single sign-on (SSO) is used with the same identity provider as the extended SAP solution. Any application deployed or subscribed to that SAP HCP account will use the same default identity provider to authenticate end users. Typically, all involved trust certificates are generated and exchanged on initial account onboarding.

► Standardized (by naming convention) Connectivity Service destinations perform transparent identity propagation to the underlying extended SAP Cloud solution.

► SAP HANA Cloud Portal is configured to enable all installed portal sites to transparently adopt the branding and color scheme configured in the corresponding extended SAP Cloud solution tenant.

► A custom security role provider allows SAP HCP extension applications to check for role assignments of the currently logged in user in the underlying SAP extended solution. From a development perspective, there is no change in APIs. Java applications still call the standard Java EE `.isUserInRole()` APIs, as described in Section 8.4 of Chapter 8, but the calls will transparently query the extended SAP solution and return the role assignment as configured there.

SAP Cloud Identity Adoption Impact on SAP HCP Extension Accounts

The 1:1 account mapping restriction will loosen up over time with the increasing adoption of the SAP Cloud Identity product. Nonetheless, it's important to understand why that restriction exists in the first place. All applications within the same SAP HCP account automatically receive the same default authentication URL. This means that any unauthenticated request to any of the applications accessible within that account will end up on the same login page—and therein lies the conflict. SuccessFactors tenants typically come with their own identity provider (IdP) tenant, whereas Ariba customers typically use on-premise IdP to authenticate. If we end up mixing extensions for both products in the same SAP HCP account, there is no way to determine the authentication page to redirect end-users to. Should it be the one of the SuccessFactors IdPs or the on-premise Ariba IdP?

Another problem is that, if mixed in the same SAP HCP account, a request that went through SuccessFactors IdP for authentication could end up in an application that attempts to query the Ariba Business network in the backend. What should it do? It might well be the case that this particular user has no permissions whatsoever to work with the Ariba solution. Even worse, this user may have another account in Ariba, but due to the already initialized web session, is not able to log in accordingly.

Due to these special cases and also based on feedback indicating that people working on extension applications for those two solutions are typically not one and the same, SAP decided to establish the 1:1 account restriction rule for the time being.

Extension applications built with SAP HCP run in a managed standardized environment and have three core building blocks. Let's explore these elements in more detail.

11.2.1 Extension Application Frontend Layer

The vast majority of SAP HCP extension applications start "UI first" by creating a "clickable" UI mock. SAP clearly recommends using an SAP HCP HTML5 application for this layer. If you decide to leverage SAPUI5 as the UI technology for your extension, then you could also benefit from the SAP Web IDE. Particularly for SAPUI5, SAP HCP supports additional integration features as well, such as dynamic branding for SAP HANA Cloud Portal sites.

> **What Is Dynamic Branding?**
>
> One of the most commonly configured features in SAP on-premise products is to rebrand the product UIs in corporate colors and to place corporate logos. A few of the most notable publicly known brand color association examples are Coca-Cola™, with everything in the red spectrum, PepsiCo™, with everything predominantly blue, Shell in yellow, and LEGO™ in red. Because one of the requirements for extension applications is to integrate smoothly in the extended SAP solution like just another native module, branding is an essential part of that story. Therefore, by using SAP HANA Cloud Portal sites, an extension application has the opportunity to leverage dynamic branding and get automatically rethemed in the color scheme configured in the extended SAP Cloud solution.
>
> Currently, this feature is only supported for SAPUI5-based applications, but depending on the customer or partner demand, support for dynamic branding may be extended toward other popular open-source UI frameworks.

The most commonly used approach to decouple the UI from the backend is via OData/JSON services. This also allows you to cleanly separate the UI development from the backend service development with a clean contract and reliable testing frame in between. Despite the widespread hype of cross-functional experts, practice shows that having specialized UI designers and skilled backend developers working together pays off in the long term. In such a team, a reasonable question arises: How can you scale out the development process in order for people not to depend on each other all the time? We'd strongly recommend exploring SAPUI5 Mock Server for that purpose.

What Is SAPUI5 Mock Server?

SAPUI5 Mock Server mimics OData backend calls, simulating an OData provider that runs completely in the client (browser). We strongly recommend this for experimenting with different options for backend calls while designing the UI, thus eliminating the overhead to develop throwaway code that might have to be changed multiple times before the user interaction and the UI are finalized.

To instantiate SAPUI5 Mock Server, create an instance of `sap.ui.core.util.Mock-Server` in your JavaScript tier, and then use the `.start()` method to start the server.

Important: Make sure to comment out that functionality once you're ready with the final version of the UI!

Now that we've clarified the basic setup, let's explore the different UI-level artifacts that may be delivered as part of an extension application. To start, frontend artifacts define content, structure, and metadata. All of these are delivered as part of the extension solution.

As you can see in Figure 11.4, UI artifacts are handled in multiple different layers in SAP HCP and in the extended solution. SAP HCP is being integrated deeply in all SAP Cloud solutions in order to enable a seamless experience for both administrators and end users.

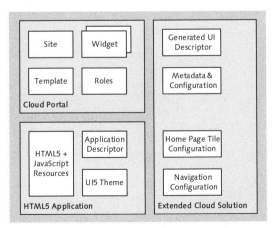

Figure 11.4 Types or UI-Related Artifacts and Where They Are Handled during Installation

You can imagine that this is naturally a constantly evolving architecture, designed to accommodate new cloud acquisitions as they come on board for SAP.

Many of the extension application projects start with the overly simplistic perspective to create "a simple, client-side only" application that leverages existing OData APIs from the extended SAP Cloud solution to better represent data. Although this is a good starting point, projects quickly face the limits of that approach. There are several possible pitfalls:

▶ **Better data representation**
In this scenario, you're recreating an already existing product UI, adding additional details, or presenting the data in a different form. Chances are high that the needed data is already available in some form via OData services and can be used as is. However, chances are rather low that those OData services will return exactly and only the data that your new UI would need. Always keep in mind that those APIs were created for a particular purpose other than yours. In most cases, you can still use $filter and $skip query options to narrow down API call results to improve the situation. At the end, however, you will probably do additional data adaptation on the client side in JavaScript. Try to limit that where possible.

▶ **Data aggregation**
In this scenario, you're creating a brand new UI, which aggregates data from multiple modules in the extended solution. In this case, you'll face several challenges:

  ▷ The OData protocol itself doesn't support joins. Relationships are represented as navigation properties, and the actual joins have to be defined on the server. In this case, they probably will not be in place as needed.

  ▷ You have to deal with the fact that OData backend calls will return more data than you actually need.

  ▷ If you have a read/write scenario, then first you have to ensure that the OData service you're using actually supports modifications of the required entities. In general, SAP Cloud solutions expose read-only data access APIs. Therefore, we strongly recommend that you not underestimate the initial feasibility analysis.

▶ **Combining data from multiple business systems**
In this scenario, you're creating a brand new UI, which uses data from the extended SAP solution, combining it with data from other backend systems (be

they in the cloud or on-premise). Our recommendation is to avoid implementing this scenario in the frontend layer. It's clear that hello-world-grade showcases with weather forecasts and avatar picture REST services will fit in that frame, but when you consider real business scenarios involving access to critical business-level data, there are a number of requirements to consider prior to diving in. We've outlined some of these requirements ahead.

HTML5 vs. Java Application on SAP HCP

With the growing popularity of HTML5/JavaScript frameworks, it becomes more and more tempting to implement scenarios quickly in HTML5 and move forward with it. The main pitfall of that approach is security. You have to always keep in mind that 100% of your HTML5 and JavaScript code executes in a browser, which is by definition untrusted and prone to being compromised. You should only consider implementing business data manipulation in HTML5 in the following cases:

▶ All of the backend systems (including your application) use one user base and have SSO configured to a common identity provider.

▶ All data-manipulation operations are available as backend service APIs, which enforce adequate authorization and authentication checks.

▶ You have to carefully manage role assignments for your HTML5 app; they are doomed to be outdated.

In addition, you have to write your code in such a way to be prepared for failure and crashes at any step for the following reasons:

▶ You have no control over the network stability and reliability, and having a guarantee that you've received all the data from the backend might turn out to be critical for your application (consider a scenario relying on a list of all due invoices, for example).

▶ You have virtually no control over the stability of the browser environment in which your JavaScript code will be running and what browser plug-ins are interfering with your logic (e.g., Google Translate, AdBlock, etc.).

Here's a very simple example: If you have to implement the logic to transfer X amount of EUR from bank account 1 to bank account 2, *never ever* think about implementing such logic in HTML5! Create a Java backend service instead, which will handle authorization, atomicity, and failover of the operation and will guarantee consistency. Then, create the corresponding REST service, which your UI can reliably call. This way, you'll be sure that on the backend side, the operation is either executed consistently or fails consistently, giving your UI a chance to react accordingly.

For any HTML5 app, we strongly recommend describing all backend service API endpoints in the neo-app.json application descriptor, which will result in the endpoints being proxied in SAP HCP. This is required to mitigate the so-called Cross

Origin Resource Sharing (CORS) mechanism in browsers, preventing JavaScript code from loading resources from multiple different domains that the user hasn't explicitly interacted with before in the current browser session.

What Is Cross Origin Resource Sharing (CORS)?

CORS defines a set of HTTP headers that provide guidance to browsers for whether they are allowed to embed content coming from one site into a page hosted in another site. All major browsers support CORS for all types of HTTP requests.

Let's look at the interaction in a nutshell:

1. Your browser is loading a page served from *https://www.siteA.com*.

2. JavaScript code on the page tries to retrieve user details by calling a REST API on *https://www.siteB.com*. In this case, it will send an additional header stating `Origin: https://www.siteA.com`.

3. The Site B web server has the option to respond in several different ways:

   ▸ It can return a response with an `Access-Control-Allow-Origin: http://www.siteA.com` header, indicating which sites are allowed to embed content from Site B.

   ▸ It can return an error page outlining that the CORS request is not allowed.

   ▸ It can return a response with an `Access-Control-Allow-Origin: *` header, indicating that any site is allowed to embed content from Site B. This is typically used for content that is completely public.

In the SAP Cloud solutions extension scenario, having a mutual CORS/ACAO setup will significantly complicate the integration and require the extended solution to know and particularly recognize each and every extension application for each of its tenants. As SAP Cloud solutions content is typically not public, this leaves no viable options for managing the integration. That's why SAP HCP handles all OData backend calls in a uniform way, proxying the calls via the SAP HCP Dispatcher service and implementing the required session handling and identity propagation centrally for all HTML5 apps.

As seen in Figure 11.4, your extension application may also include an SAP HANA Cloud Portal site, complemented by one or more OpenSocial widgets. You learned how to create portal sites and register OpenSocial widgets in Chapter 9, so we won't drill deeper into this topic here.

Last but not least, you may deliver native UI elements that are to be imported in the extended SAP solution during installation. This might include, but is not limited to, home page tiles, navigation entries, UI generation metadata, or other embeddable UI fragments. SAP's midterm goal is that all of the imports are handled by the low-level infrastructure integration between SAP HCP and the corresponding extended SAP Cloud solution.

A typical extension application will have a combination of one or more of the described UI artifacts. If there are none, then you should seriously consider using SAP HANA Cloud Integration (SAP HCI), instead of implementing the data transformation logic yourself.

11.2.2 Extension Application Backend Layer

Similar to the frontend layer, there are a number of artifacts that belong to the backend layer and contribute to the overall solution (Figure 11.5).

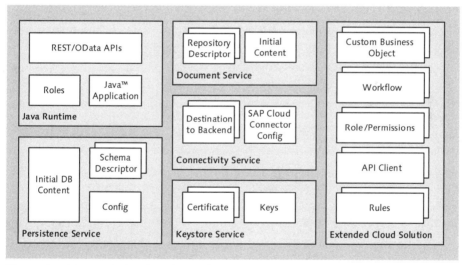

Figure 11.5 Extension Backend Artifacts and Where They Are Handled during Installation

The main part of the business logic is typically implemented in Java or accessed via remote API services in the extended SAP Cloud solution. Depending on the complexity of the application, you're free to choose any of the Java runtimes available. We strongly recommend that you not use Java 6, but select from Java 7 or Java 8. Java 6 is still supported on SAP HCP, but it's mostly there to cover backwards compatibility scenarios, because Java 6 itself is long out of mainstream maintenance in the developer community. While implementing your application, you have to consider which end user roles you'd like to define as part of your extension application and which roles from the extended SAP solution a user requires in order to access the needed data via APIs. Some examples for application-level roles are as follows:

► A car fleet operator would typically be responsible for approving company car orders, reviewing global fuel consumption, and acting on fraud detection alerts. This requires permissions in the corresponding backend systems to access employee profile details, fuel card provider reports, and so on.

► A social benefits administrator would typically be responsible for defining new social benefits and managing social benefit campaigns for employees. This requires permissions in the application to manage those entities, but does not require any additional backend permissions.

► For all the cases in which backend permissions are required, you have the option either to reuse an existing role there or to define a new end user role. There are pros and cons for both. At one extreme, there is a risk of overexposure of data by reusing a role intended for something else. At the other extreme, you might end up with hundreds of custom end user roles and have a hard time managing them in a consistent manner. It's a matter of taste, although we would prefer to have the latter problem rather than the first one.

The API endpoint definitions described in the neo-app.json file in the frontend layer generally cover both backend APIs and APIs exposed by applications running on SAP HCP. Therefore, in order for the API wiring to work, you have to provide the corresponding required destination descriptors as part of the application. The same is true for the Java applications themselves. You also need to specify the corresponding destinations in order to get access to the underlying extended SAP Cloud solution.

SAP has already defined a naming convention for naming some of the different SAP Cloud solution API destinations in order to ensure portability for partner applications across different extension accounts. Some examples of the established naming conventions of destinations include the following:

► `sap_hcmcloud_core_odata`
SuccessFactors OData API using identity propagation. Recommended for interactive extension applications.

▶ `sap_hcmcloud_core_soap`

SuccessFactors SF API using a service user. Recommended for data integration and replication scenarios. Must not be used for interactive extensions.

▶ `sap_jam_odata`

SAP Jam OData API using identity propagation. Recommended for interactive extension applications.

For the majority of extension applications, it will be sufficient to get a single API endpoint to communicate with the extended solution. The same API endpoint will be used for interactive API calls whenever there are actual users working with the extension application. However, there are special cases (such as background scheduled jobs) that don't have an interactive user but have to run at a defined point of time on behalf of a predefined user.

Another major consideration for extension applications is where to store data. We've briefly touched on a number of extension scenarios that generate a fair amount of data; let's dig one level deeper:

▶ In the company car example, you store data for the different car brands, engine sizes, additional equipment, tire change schedule, expiration of insurances, warranty expiration, and so on for employee company cars. You also have to enable the scenario for employees to be able to find each other by searching for a car's license plate.

▶ In the employee health example, you store data for emergency numbers and location data of the different company offices, schedule of planned fire drill events, and so on.

All of that data needs to be stored in an efficient and reliable manner, preferably not bloating the extended solution database with random data.

As you learned in Chapter 6, SAP HCP offers two storage options: relational (Persistence Service) and unstructured storage (Document Service). The Persistence Service offers both SAP HANA and SAP (Sybase) ASE as database options. They naturally come at different price points and provide different capabilities. The Document Service offers unstructured storage based on the open CMIS protocol, facilitating access to a folder-like structure of files and allowing you to define access control lists, object attributes, and so on.

An extension application has the freedom to expand into one or more database schemas and to one or more Document Service repositories. This need is determined during extension application installation and is of course implementation and scenario specific.

Another option facilitated by SAP HCP but not directly provided by it is to store data in the extended SAP Cloud solution. If your extension application has packaged one or more custom business objects, then the object definitions will be imported in the extended SAP Cloud solution during installation. Once imported, instances of those objects can be created and will be accessible via the solution OData API.

Another critical aspect you have to think about is how to persist keys and certificates that your application eventually has to deal with. Keeping them safe is your responsibility both in motion and at rest. For that purpose, SAP HCP offers a *Keystore Service* that is accessible programmatically by looking up an instance of `com.sap.cloud.crypto.keystore.api.KeyStoreService` from JNDI. Inserting keys there can also be done programmatically or via the SAP HCP command-line client.

Further Resources

For more information about this, we would recommend that you consult the SAP HCP keystore service documentation at *http://help.hana.ondemand.com*.

11.2.3 Extension Application Connectivity Layer

Leveraging the fact that SAP HCP is naturally well integrated in all SAP Cloud and on-premise solutions, extension applications typically will access a number of additional backend systems in order to implement their respective business scenarios.

Some examples already emerged from the fictional scenarios we've been growing since the beginning of the chapter:

▶ A typical company car extension would integrate with the following:

▶ A financial system or business network, in order to access ongoing invoices related to services provided for the company cars, which in some cases have to be approved by employees

▶ A payroll system, in order to track monthly taxes on the provided company car benefit

> ▶ An external fuel card system, providing a monthly breakdown of the fuel
> consumption of every managed company car

▶ A typical employee health and safety system would integrate with the following:

> ▶ A global weather forecast service to get severe weather alerts

> ▶ A global country-specific alerts provider, warning employees depending on
> their location

The required backend system connection details must be filled in during the extension application installation. This covers both Internet-accessible systems and on-premise systems, reachable using *SAP Cloud Connector*. This is valid for both HTML5 and Java applications.

It's generally tempting to take a shortcut and implement the queries to, for example, a weather forecast service directly in the frontend layer. Yes, you can do that, and it'll certainly work for simple interactions. However, if the service goes down for some reason, then the first ones to notice will be your end users. SAP HCP has no means to facilitate the process within your frontend tier, neither from alerting nor from a reliability and failover perspective. However, if you model your dependencies in the neo-app.json descriptor and then create the corresponding Connectivity Service destinations, then the least SAP HCP could do is to send you alerts that one of the backend services your application depends on is down. With subsequent releases, there are plans to expand backend connection failovers to improve uptime for SAP HCP applications.

Another aspect you should consider is the storage of connection details to the backend systems your application depends on. In SAP HCP, the persistence of usernames, password, certificates, and access keys is transparently handled by the Connectivity Service. A prerequisite is that you properly utilize connectivity destinations and don't store connection details within your application.

One particularly important aspect of Connectivity Service destinations is *identity propagation*. For extension applications, identity propagation ensures that extended SAP solution APIs are called on behalf of the same user that is logged into the application via SAML. Having the frontend SSO is clearly important. However, what's also critical for extension applications is to access the extended SAP solution APIs on behalf of the same logged in user in order to retrieve user-specific data. If we consider what you learned in Chapter 8, then it should be straightforward to configure, right? However, if we go that way, then every individual user would have to grant access to the extension application. This is clearly not what we want in an enterprise environment.

What Is SAP HCP Identity Propagation and How Does It Work?

As you learned in Chapter 8, Section 8.5, it's fairly easy to configure SSO between an SAP HCP application and another system by using a common identity provider system. Whenever you request any of those systems for the first time, you'll be presented with a login screen. After successful login, you'll be redirected back to the original solution, supplying a signed SAML assertion confirming the successful login. Based on that, a subsequent web session is established.

The OAuth 2.0 SAML bearer assertion flow defines the process to use a SAML assertion to request an OAuth access token for a certain user, which is used to authenticate the user and perform OData API queries. All of that implementation is encapsulated in the SAP HCP Connectivity Service, making the whole process transparent for extension application developers.

From a development perspective, the code looks relatively simple:

```
Context ctx = new InitialContext();
HttpDestination destination =
 (HttpDestination) ctx.lookup("java:comp/env/sap_hcmcloud_core_
odata");
HttpClient client = destination.createHttpClient().execute(…).
```

As a result, the query will always execute on behalf of the currently logged in user without any need for the application to handle it.

11.3 Integration Points for Extending SAP Cloud Solutions

As Figure 11.4 and Figure 11.5 outline, a number of native artifacts are delivered with the extension application in order to find their way into the corresponding extended SAP Cloud solution during installation. Different SAP Cloud solutions currently allow integration of a different subset of the more generic list ahead. This section aims to provide an overview of what's possible today without getting into particular details. By no means does the list pretend to be complete, but it should give you a general perspective on how serious SAP is about extensibility and making sure that corporate IT teams can be as productive with SAP Cloud solutions as they have been for the last 40-plus years with on-premise solutions.

SAP will keep expanding the list as new SAP Cloud solutions integrate with SAP HCP.

As a general rule, SAP HCP is already able to import most of those artifacts into the solutions for which tighter integration is already in place. Enabling full coverage for all SAP Cloud solutions is planned with upcoming releases and is subject to integration API availability.

11.3.1 Custom Business Objects and Views

Most of the SAP Cloud solutions allow developers and administrators to create a limited number of custom business object definitions, which each solution handles differently. Some allow defining formatters or validators for the different fields, and others allow you to put in some metadata description outlining how the object will be visualized and to which screen it'll be attached. With some of the solutions, it's possible to define a simple workflow describing how that custom object is filled with data and what steps the data goes through. What is common among all solutions is that those objects are stored in the SAP Cloud solution database and become part of the solution's object model.

The following are a few examples:

▶ In SuccessFactors, custom objects are managed by the Metadata Framework (MDF) as part of the solution object model. This is a key design principle from the first day MDF was introduced.

▶ In Ariba, it's possible to create Ariba Query Language (AQL) views over the data stored in the solution. This feature is not exposed to customers yet.

▶ In all SAP Business ByDesign-based solutions, you can use the SAP Cloud Application Studio SDK and create new custom entities via business object definition language (BODL).

▶ In SAP Jam, you can register custom business objects in the form of external OData endpoints that are subsequently introspected for the list of available fields.

You typically have the flexibility to define the cardinality of how instances of the custom object relate to other entities in the solution object model. Custom object instances typically get exposed automatically for read and write via REST/OData API, unless explicitly specified otherwise.

11.3.2 Workflows

Every SAP Cloud solution has the internal notion of workflows (one or more), implementing a large variety of industry best practices. At the same time, almost none offer a programmatic way to interact with these workflows, beyond triggering a new cycle. However, there are some exceptions to the rule:

▸ SuccessFactors offers the ability to define MDF object workflows, defining how object data is to be filled. What's coming in late 2015 is programmatic access to the solution workflow engine, allowing developers to interact with the already defined standard workflows.

▸ For SuccessFactors performance management, it's already possible to shift a performance form to the next step via an API.

▸ SAP Business ByDesign-based solutions allow for defining new workflows and triggering existing ones. No modification of the existing predelivered workflow steps in the system is allowed.

11.3.3 Roles and Permissions

Many of the SAP Cloud solutions allow for the creation of custom security roles, and practically all allow administrators to manage the role assignments in groups via administration tools. Most of the solutions offer field-level security with fine-grained operations control (create/read/update/delete). What SAP HCP provides in that space for extension accounts is to enable transparent role assignment propagation to SAP HCP applications from the extended SAP Cloud solution. This allows administrators to keep on working in the original SAP Cloud solution, managing extension application role assignments from there the same way they do for standard product entities. SAP HCP already provides transparent role and permission checks for Java applications when extending SuccessFactors. The same level of integration is in the works for the other SAP Cloud solutions.

11.3.4 API Clients

In order to communicate with SAP Cloud solutions, SAP HCP needs registered API endpoints/client keys. The majority of SAP Cloud solutions support OAuth, some even with OAuth 2.0 SAML bearer assertions. This approach eliminates the need to hardwire service users and use static passwords. It provides flexibility to manage fine-grained access by controlling the issued OAuth access tokens. With identity propagation, SAP HCP is able to transparently call underlying SAP Cloud solution APIs on behalf of the logged in user, providing an end-to-end integrated experience for developers and end users.

In addition to pure data-access APIs, some SAP Cloud solutions also expose theming APIs, allowing you to generate consistent extension application UIs in line with the configured customer corporate branding in the extended SAP solution.

Last but not least, some of the SAP Cloud solutions provide a way for extension applications to register on their event bus and listen for events. This eliminates the need to have heavyweight, constant polling for updates, something that was generating needless load for the last few years.

11.3.5 Rules

Many SAP cloud solutions allow for configuring business logic when filling the fields of custom business object instances. Similarly, SAP Business ByDesign based solutions allow for defining field constraints and dependencies. SAP HCP naturally offers packaging and import of such rules for the solutions for which this is supported.

Using SAP Cloud Application Studio, developers are able to define association valuation rules both during the creation and saving of data.

11.3.6 Configurable UIs

SuccessFactors in particular offers developers and administrators the ability to define configurable UIs so that you can specify which pages the object will be rendered in and in what form.

Another example is SAP Jam, which offers the possibility to provide a manifest that specifies how the different entities in an external OData business object are to be rendered.

11.3.7 Custom Code

Practically the only SAP Cloud business solution that allows full-featured custom code execution on the application stack is SAP Business ByDesign. Development is done using SAP Cloud Application Studio in an SAP-specific scripting language, allowing you to implement custom add-ons.

11.3.8 Home Page Tile Configuration

Most of the SAP Cloud solutions provide some flavor of a welcome page, rendering a number of different widgets. With the transition to SAP Fiori, most of those welcome pages will transition to SAP Fiori Launchpad over time. To check out the always up-to-date version of SAP Fiori, you can explore *www.sap.com/fiori-demo* at any time.

SAP already allows extension application developers to define an embeddable HTML fragment, which can be registered as a custom widget in the corresponding SAP Cloud solution home page. There is one pitfall here, which we've looked at in Section 11.2.1: CORS. The problem lies in the fact that each of the SAP Cloud solutions is served out of its own domain, whereas SAP HCP applications reside on the *hana.ondemand.com* domain. Because most of the SAP Cloud solutions leverage CORS, this leads to the result that the straightforward approach to create a simple iFrame on a home page that embeds content from SAP HCP will be blocked by the majority of modern browsers. How do we proceed, then? We can solve this problem by employing IdP-initiated SAML login, in contrast to the widely used SP-initiated SAML flow.

SP-Initiated vs. IdP-Initiated SAML Login Flow

Figure 8.12 in Chapter 8 illustrates the typical SAML SP-initiated authentication flow. In a nutshell, this means that when a client browser without a valid security session accesses a SAML-protected web resource, it'll be redirected to the configured identity provider for authentication.

There is also a less popular (but very useful) IdP-initiated SAML authentication flow. In this scenario, a client browser accesses the identity provider for authentication directly, passing over a specific mapping key. Once authenticated, IdP automatically forwards the browser along with a signed SAML response to the web resource corresponding to the specified key. The corresponding web application (in the cloud extension scenario, this is handled by SAP HCP) will validate the incoming SAML response and establish a security session as usual.

When the SAP Cloud solution home page is rendered, the IdP URL is already known to the browser, because authentication took place there earlier on. Therefore, referring the extension application via IdP-mapped URLs eliminates the problem of CORS-enabled browsers blocking custom home page tile content.

11.3.9   Navigation Configuration

It's important for extension applications to be reachable for end users from within the extended SAP Cloud solution. In order to achieve that, a number of navigation plugs are available for registration. In SuccessFactors, this includes top-level page navigation, employee profile navigation menu, to-do list, and so on. It's also possible to define a URL exit point from pretty much every configurable UI in the system. From an extension perspective, it's important to automate that flow. Therefore, whenever an extension application is published, it will be plugged into all defined placeholders, thus effectively becoming accessible for end users. For the majority of SAP Cloud solutions, that integration is still ongoing and the configuration will have to be performed manually.

11.4   Extending SuccessFactors with SAP HCP Applications

SuccessFactors is the cloud HCM suite from SAP and is identified as a leader in 18 out of 18 recent analyst reports in its respective HR areas. SuccessFactors allows companies to deploy the different modules at their own pace, because it has multiple possible starting points. With more than 28 million users in over 177 countries, SuccessFactors provides a rich set of customization and configuration capabilities. The core SuccessFactors HCM module, Employee Central, is globalized to support legal compliance in over 71 countries and over 40 languages. SuccessFactors has over 1,000 certified implementation consultants globally.

You can explore SuccessFactors Employee Central in more detail by reading *SuccessFactors Employee Central: The Comprehensive Guide* by Luke Marson, Murali Mazhavanchery, and Rebecca Murray (SAP PRESS, 2016).

Regardless of the feature richness of a solution, there will always be special case scenarios or local market specific niches left open. Therefore, back in November 2013 SAP kicked off the SAP HCP extensibility story at the annual SuccessConnect conference in Las Vegas by announcing the SAP HCP extension package for SuccessFactors. Since then, SAP HCP has gone a long way, integrating much deeper into the SuccessFactors stack and launching similar integration tracks with all other SAP Cloud solutions in parallel.

In this section, we'll explore how SAP HCP complements SuccessFactors, following all the basic principles defined in Section 11.3, including tooling and account configuration. Following the basic principles defined in the beginning of the chapter, there must be zero operational overhead for customers when running a partner extension as part of their SuccessFactors system. We'll leave it up to you to judge that. We'll point you to a practical example from SAP you can explore on your own, and we'll also iterate over the APIs and possible integration points available for your extension application to leverage.

11.4.1 SuccessFactors Administration Layers

The first thing to keep in mind is that SuccessFactors has two separate layers of administration externally visible:

▸ SuccessFactors Provisioning is used for trained SuccessFactors implementation consultants and SuccessFactors professional services consultants.

▸ SuccessFactors OneAdmin is used by company account administrators and key users.

There is a clear difference between these two roles, which we discuss next.

SuccessFactors Provisioning

SuccessFactors Provisioning is the environment used to configure all the licensed features of the SuccessFactors product. This includes enabling the required modules, configuration, mapping the company business processes to workflows, enabling API access, adding new administration users, and so on. Regular recurring replication jobs are also configured and scheduled in Provisioning.

The general trend is to grow the set of features exposed to key users and company administrators, enabling them to handle the company accounts they are responsible for. At the same time, critical operations will still remain in SuccessFactors Provisioning, where company admins have no access. If any configuration changes are required there, then such changes would be performed either by an implementation consultant or by SuccessFactors professional service teams.

The point here is not that SAP does not want to provide access to customers. It's about making sure that only people with the required qualifications, background, and skills will make low-level configuration changes to customer systems. That's one approach to minimize the risk of destabilizing the account and the productive business processes there.

At the end of every implementation project, a detailed handover document is completed, describing the intended business processes and flows. This is used subsequently as the basis for the SuccessFactors support team to determine whether a certain configuration of the account is working as intended or has to be corrected. Any subsequent change in provisioning environment is considered to be a bug fix or an enhancement.

SuccessFactors OneAdmin

Company administrators and key users get access to the so-called OneAdmin tool, which is embedded in the SuccessFactors product experience. They are empowered to further configure all the installed SuccessFactors module specifics, such as onboarding flow, notification templates, 360 degree review campaigns, user permissions and roles, and MDF object definitions. System administrators also have the permissions required to evaluate and install extension applications. On the user experience side, they are responsible for managing the account branding and theme. One of the important roles of key users is to validate and experiment with new features that SuccessFactors publishes regularly, remaining actively aware of how to leverage the new functionality in their company's productive account.

Company administrators also have direct access to the embedded SAP HANA Marketplace view, which enables them to install trial versions of extension applications. Installing a trial application will automatically initialize the required SAP HCP infrastructure underneath.

11.4.2 Account Onboarding

An SAP HCP extension package is implemented and integrates with SuccessFactors like any of the different modules, such as SAP Jam, Learning, or Analytics. It must be enabled via the SuccessFactors Provisioning administration environment. If you are an end customer, you probably don't have access to that environment, but either the SuccessFactors implementation partner you're working with or your SAP Professional Services consultants will be able to assist you.

Once in SUCCESSFACTORS PROVISIONING, select your respective company from the list of COMPANIES. On the next screen, in the EDIT COMPANY SETTINGS section, choose the EXTENSION MANAGEMENT option. If extension management has not yet been enabled for your SuccessFactors company, then you'll see the screen shown in Figure 11.6.

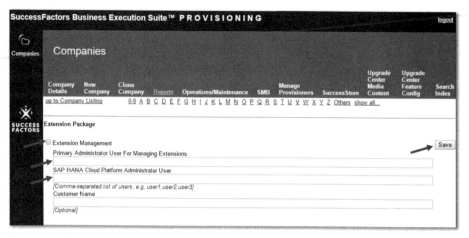

Figure 11.6 SuccessFactors Provisioning Environment Targeted at Professional Services Consultants and Implementation Partners

In this situation, select the EXTENSION MANAGEMENT checkbox. Then, fill in the PRIMARY ADMINISTRATOR USER FOR MANAGING EXTENSIONS field with the name of your SuccessFactors system admin user. This is the first SuccessFactors user who will be granted permissions to customize extension portal sites in SuccessFactors Admin Tools. Later on, he or she can grant permissions to more administrator users. (In future versions of the SuccessFactors Provisioning tool, this field will become obsolete and will be eliminated altogether. Therefore, don't panic if you don't find it in your version at a later stage.)

The second field to be filled in is SAP HANA CLOUD PLATFORM ADMINISTRATOR USER. It defines one (or more; comma separated) SAP Cloud Identity users who will be granted administrator access to the corresponding SAP HCP extension account. Typically, these are the S-users who report issues to SAP and have the permissions to download software from the SAP Service Marketplace.

In case of error, it's always an option to disable the SAP HCP extensions module by deselecting the EXTENSION MANAGEMENT checkbox, fixing the errors, and selecting it again.

With that, your SAP HCP extension account is created (Figure 11.7). The EXTENSION PACKAGE DETAILS section illustrates the current status of the SAP HCP extension account. If onboarding has passed successfully, then you should see EXTENSION PACKAGE STATUS as COMPLETED. This section also includes other details, such as the name of the SAP HCP extension account and a direct link pointing to the SAP HCP Cockpit on the corresponding landscape.

Figure 11.7 Status of SAP HCP Extension Account Onboarding

The EXTENSION PACKAGE RELATED FEATURES STATUS section on the same screen provides some details that come into play when troubleshooting integration issues later on. In Figure 11.8, you can see all the SuccessFactors features that are required for proper functioning of the associated SAP HCP extension account.

Extension Package Related Features Status	
OData API:	ENABLED
Employee Central OData API:	ENABLED
Enable Generic Objects:	ENABLED
Enable the Attachment Manager:	ENABLED
Configure Custom Navigation:	ENABLED
Role-based Permission:	ENABLED
OAuth Client:	ACTIVE
Authorized SP ACS:	CONFIGURED

Figure 11.8 SuccessFactors Features Required for Proper Functioning of the Associated SAP HCP Extension Account

When you click on LINK in the SuccessFactors Provisioning UI (refer back to Figure 11.7), you'll jump to the SAP HCP Cockpit focused on the freshly created SAP HCP extension account for the current SuccessFactors company. Something you'll quickly notice is that the display name of the company allows for quick traceability for what the account is and which particular backend it's configured to extend.

You can examine the account to verify that trust settings are already configured, as shown in Figure 11.9. In upcoming releases of SAP HCP, trust settings and destinations to the extended SAP Cloud solution will become read-only and will be managed automatically by SAP HCP for all extension accounts.

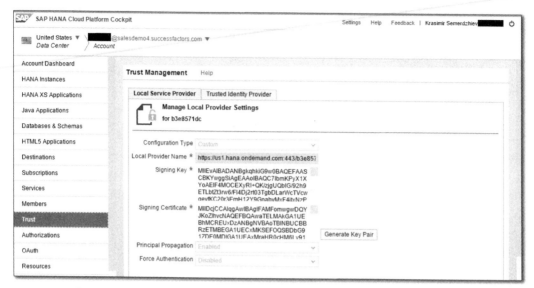

Figure 11.9 SAP HCP Extension Account Trust Settings: Automatically Configured on both the SAP HCP and SuccessFactors Sides

Another aspect worth noting is that SAP HANA Cloud Portal and SAP Web IDE services are automatically enabled for all SAP HCP extension accounts, as shown in Figure 11.10.

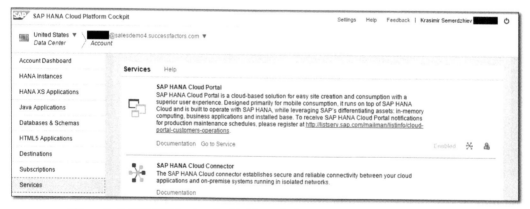

Figure 11.10 SAP HCP Services Enabled by Default in SAP HCP Extension Accounts

Your SAP HCP extension account is now fully configured and is ready to run extension applications.

When deploying additional applications, you'll inevitably reach the configured resource quotas for your account. In order to increase those, you have to either purchase additional SAP HCP resources or (if this was already done) assign additional resources to the newly created extension account out of your central SAP HCP resource pool.

11.4.3 Deploying Your First SuccessFactors Extension

In order to explore what's possible, the best way to move forward is to look at a particular example and try to derive conclusions. For that purpose, SAP has published an official SuccessFactors extension sample application, available under the Apache 2.0 license on GitHub at *http://github.com/SAP/cloud-sfsf-benefits-ext*. The scenario it covers is called *Corporate Benefits*. The purpose of the Corporate Benefits sample application is to offer non-monetary perks to employees while at the same time having a simple process for both employees and the responsible HR managers.

There are two roles in this application: *Employee* and *HR Manager*. The Employee role is practically everyone with a valid user ID in the underlying SuccessFactors system. This means that we're not going to allow non-authenticated users in the application. The HR Manager role is well defined in SuccessFactors and is simply reused by the application, adding additional responsibilities to it.

Employees are granted a monthly budget of an abstract "currency" called *benefit points*. These points are used to indicate the value of a large variety of nonmonetary benefits—for example, soccer game tickets, restaurant/fitness studio vouchers, and so on.

Each selection period is called a *campaign* and has defined start and end dates. Campaigns also have a particular amount of benefit points granted for each employee. As Employee, you can change your benefits selection for each of the active campaigns and view the history of your orders in previous campaigns. In addition, you can browse the benefits catalog and check what the available benefits per campaign are. As HR Manager, you can manage the campaigns: their start date, duration, and so on. You can also manage the benefits of an employee on his or her behalf.

The same application is used as a main exercise in the openSAP course for building SAP product extensions with SAP HCP. The course is available for free for self-study at *http://open.sap.com/courses/hanacloud3*.

In order to deploy the application, you'll have to go through the following steps:

1. Clone the application's Git repository.

2. Import the sources as a Maven project in Eclipse. Make sure that your proxy settings in the Maven settings.xml file are properly configured.

3. Build the project in Eclipse.

4. Deploy the application to SAP HCP.

5. Depending on whether you have a SuccessFactors system to experiment with, you have two different options to continue:

   ▶ Assuming that you already have a SuccessFactors system at hand, then you'll proceed directly with the steps defined in Section 11.4.2.

   ▶ If you don't have access to a commercial SuccessFactors account, then you can follow the application readme and leverage the public read-only Success-Factors API that the SAP HCP team has set live for developers to experiment with.

You can deploy the application using the SAP HCP command-line tool, SAP HCP Tools for Eclipse, or directly from the SAP HCP Cockpit.

11.4.4 SuccessFactors Extension Administration

When you log in to your SuccessFactors account as a system administrator after successful enablement of the SAP HCP extension package, you'll notice some changes.

All SuccessFactors accounts provide out-of-the-box access to an embedded extensions marketplace used to feature extension applications provided by SAP and SAP partners. This marketplace is accessible in Admin Tools under Company Settings and then Extensions, as shown in Figure 11.11.

For SuccessFactors companies for which the SAP HCP extension package is not enabled, the link will open the marketplace directly, as shown in Figure 11.12.

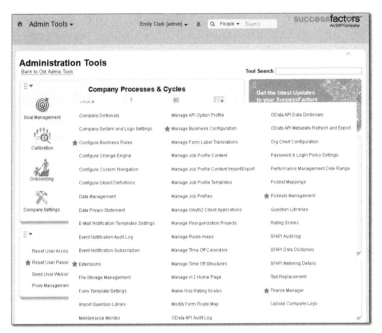

Figure 11.11 Extension Management: Accessible for System Admin Users by Default in Every SuccessFactors Account

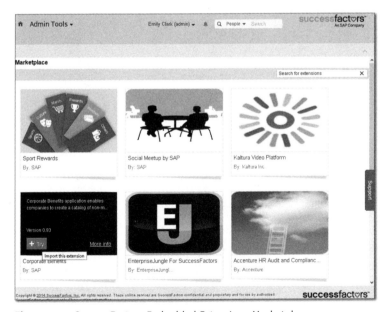

Figure 11.12 SuccessFactors Embedded Extensions Marketplace

Some of the listed solutions will allow free trial installation, thus giving Success-Factors customers an opportunity to evaluate them prior to making purchasing decisions. The follow-up actual contract for a partner extension will typically go through the regular direct sales channels.

Installing a trial extension application will automatically enable the underlying SAP HCP extension package. However, the difference from the approach outlined in Section 11.4.2 is that the SAP HCP account will be completely hidden; no customer users will have access to it. It'll be managed automatically by SAP HCP.

After a short installation cycle (or going through the procedure described in Section 11.4.2), you'll notice a visible difference in the embedded extension administration capabilities. It still contains the embedded extensions marketplace, but it's just one tab in the much more elaborate Extensions Management plug-in, which is now fully functional for this SuccessFactors account.

Figure 11.13 SuccessFactors Extensions Management Plug-In in Admin Tools

The tool has several tabs (as illustrated in Figure 11.13):

▶ EXTENSIONS
Management of extension applications, covering both SAP HCP and MDF artifacts.

▶ MARKETPLACE
The familiar embedded marketplace, filtering extension applications depending on the modules installed in your SuccessFactors account. For example, if you don't have SuccessFactors Learning enabled, then you will not see any extension applications that depend on the Learning module.

▶ CONTENT
Shows a list of reusable OpenSocial widgets that can be combined in different screens to create new mashup pages.

▶ ANALYTICS
Provides an overview of how many clicks were made to each extension application. This view enables company administrators to analyze the penetration and the load for each of the installed or enabled extension applications.

▶ DOCUMENTS
In many cases, it's required to put one document or a larger attachment on a page and perform a rollout. SAP HCP extension accounts come prebundled with a certain amount of unstructured storage, which you can use to store and serve documents.

11.4.5 SuccessFactors APIs

Over the last few years, the SuccessFactors team has put a lot of effort into documenting and releasing OData APIs, in order to OData-enable SuccessFactors by 2016, which will certainly open up a number of opportunities for partners and custom development projects. All released APIs are classified either for extension or integration usage.

You can find all the currently released API definitions in the API INFORMATION section of the SUCCESSFACTORS HCM SUITE page on the SAP Help Portal (at *http:// help.sap.com/cloud4hr*).Here, you will find API documentation for the OData- and SOAP-based SuccessFactors APIs, SuccessFactors Learning API, and SuccessFactors Onboarding API.

The detailed development guide and the OData API for SAP Jam are also on the SAP Help Portal, in the elaborate DEVELOPER INFORMATION section on the SAP JAM page at *http://help.sap.com/sapjam*.

By definition, any available SuccessFactors OData API on the SAP Help Portal can be used to build interactive extensions. In the publicly available SuccessFactors API roadmap, one section is dedicated to API classification, outlining which APIs are intended for interactive end user extensions and which are targeted at integration or replication scenarios. Please take the time to get familiar with that prior to planning your next SuccessFactors extension project.

The next reasonable question is this: How do you create an OAuth API Client in SuccessFactors so that it's consumable from SAP HCP? Simply follow these steps:

1. From SuccessFactors ADMIN TOOLS, choose COMPANY SETTINGS and then MANAGE OAUTH2 CLIENT APPLICATIONS.

2. Click on the REGISTER CLIENT APPLICATION link.

3. In the newly opened view (Figure 11.14), fill in the following fields:

   ▸ TheCOMPANY field is read-only (for a good reason).

   ▸ TheAPPLICATION NAME is the display name for your OAuth 2.0 API Client. It has no functional impact.

   ▸ DESCRIPTION is optional.

   ▸ TheAPPLICATION URL should contain an arbitrary URL; you can use the application login URL.

   ▸ X.509 CERTIFICATE is a critical field! You have to paste in the SAML SP signing certificate, visible in the HCP Cockpit TRUST tab (refer back to Figure 11.9).

   ▸ Once you are ready, click on the REGISTER button.

4. What you'll see is that your newly created OAuth 2.0 API client is visible in the list. Click on the VIEW link next to it.

5. From the next screen, copy the value of the API KEY field.

6. The process continues in the SAP HCP Cockpit, where you will create a destination providing API access to SuccessFactors.

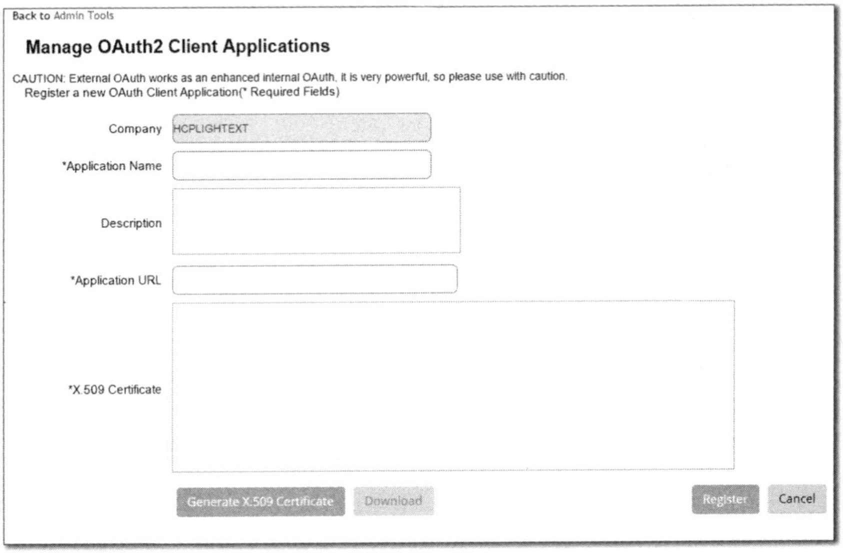

Figure 11.14 Creation of Custom OAuth 2.0 API Client Accessible from SAP HCP Extension Applications

As a prerequisite for the next steps, you have to get your extension application deployed as described in Section 11.4.3.

Once you've done so, continue with the following steps:

1. Log in to the SAP HCP Cockpit in the corresponding landscape hosting your extension account, and click on the Java Applications tab. (Note: If you want to consume this destination from an HTML5 application, then you'll have to create the destination at the global level for the complete account.)

2. Click on the targeted extension application, and then choose the Destinations tab from the left column.

3. In the newly opened screen visible in Figure 11.15, fill in the following fields:

   ▶ For Name, enter "sap_hcmcloud_core_odata".

   ▶ For Type, select HTTP.

   ▶ For URL, you need the API endpoint for your particular SuccessFactors instance. You can find this in the API documentation on the SAP Help Portal.

   ▶ For Proxy Type, select Internet.

► If you'd like to perform OData API calls on behalf of the currently logged in user, then set the AUTHENTICATION field to OAuth2SAMLBearerAssertion. This will open a number of additional fields. Alternatively, you could configure basic authentication here. Keep in mind that basic authentication is acceptable for testing, but is not recommended for production accounts.

► For AUDIENCE, enter "www.successfactors.com".

► Set the CLIENT KEY to the same value you obtained from the SuccessFactors API KEY field in the OAuth 2.0 Client Application view, visible in Figure 11.14.

► Fill the TOKEN SERVICE URL with the corresponding SuccessFactors landscape-specific URL.

► Configure NAMEQUALIFIER to "www.successfactors.com", similarly to the AUDIENCE field.

► For the OAuth flow with SuccessFactors, the COMPANYID field must be filled with the corresponding company ID.

► Last but not least, set the same value you've pasted in to CLIENT KEY for ASSERTIONISSUER.

► Click on SAVE, and you're done.

If you need to create more of the OData destinations, then simply repeat the steps above accordingly, starting with the OAuth client creation in the SuccessFactors OneAdmin tool.

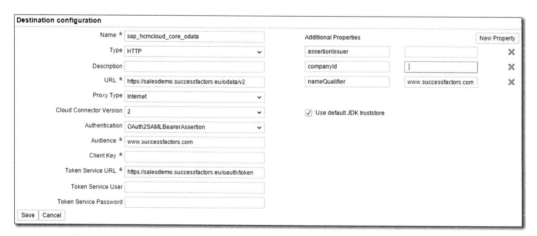

Figure 11.15 Creating a SuccessFactors OData API Destination in the SAP HCP Extension Account

There is one last detail at the end in order to enable successful login from the application through the default SuccessFactors IdP. In addition to X.509 certificates, SuccessFactors utilizes a whitelist of Assertion Consumer Service (ACS) URLs that are allowed to send authentication requests to its IdP. This is implemented to prevent potential denial-of-service attacks on the login screen from multiple URLs.

To configure the authentication whitelist, perform the following steps:

1. Log in to SuccessFactors Provisioning, and select the company you would like to manage.

2. In the SERVICE PROVIDER SETTINGS section, select AUTHORIZED SP ASSERTION CONSUMER SERVICE SETTINGS.

3. You will see a view like the one shown in Figure 11.16.

4. Click on ADD ANOTHER SERVICE PROVIDE ACS, and a new line with empty text boxes will appear.

5. In the ASSERTION CONSUMER SERVICE column, paste the URL of your application (you can obtain it from the SAP HCP Cockpit in the APPLICATION DETAILS view under the APPLICATION URLs section).

6. In the LOGOUT URL and the AUDIENCE URL columns, paste the same values that you can find for the `cloudnwcportal` application (line 5 of Figure 11.16).

7. If you'd like to leverage IdP-initiated login, then you also have to come up with a SP MAPPING KEY value, which can be any string value. We'll need that at a later stage in order to register a new custom tile on the SuccessFactors home page.

8. Don't forget to click on the blue SAVE button!

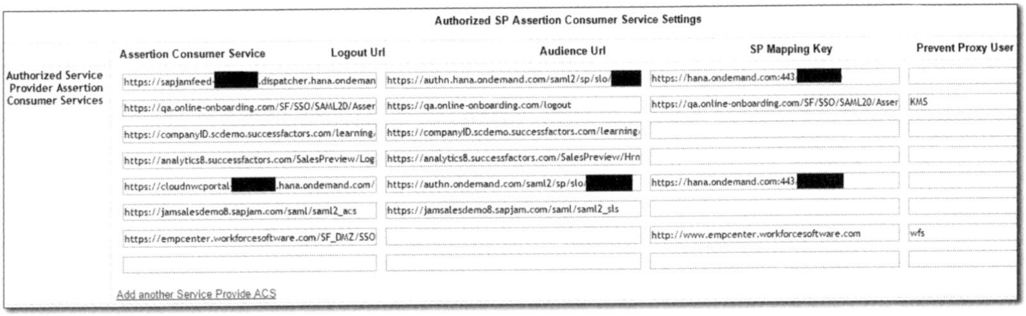

Figure 11.16 SuccessFactors Provisioning ACS Whitelist Configuration

With one of the next releases of SAP HCP, all of the above steps will be incrementally automated for extension accounts and will be triggered during extension application installation. Therefore, you will no longer need to perform any of these steps manually, although it's of course important to be aware of the underlying mechanics, so that you can troubleshoot potential integration issues.

11.4.6 Creating Custom MDF Objects and Consuming Them from SAP HCP

The MDF is an essential part of SuccessFactors' customization and extensibility. Combined with the flexibility of SAP HCP and the low-touch, easy integration, it forms one of the most flexible offerings for customizing and enriching SaaS solutions on the market.

Custom MDF objects always start their existence in a SuccessFactors system. They are modeled using the Object Definitions tool in SuccessFactors OneAdmin. You can access this tool via Admin Tools • Company Settings • Configure Object Definitions. It's critical to set the API visibility flag of newly created objects to Editable or Read-Only. If it's set to Not Visible, then this will mean that the object is not exposed via the OData API and is practically out of reach of SAP HCP applications. All custom MDF objects' names start with cust_ by default. Once you're though with modeling and saving your custom MDF object, don't forget to make it visible to the outside world using the OData API Metadata Refresh and Export tool in Admin Tools. Prior to triggering the refresh, your object won't be present in the OData API data model.

On the SAP HCP application side, you'll work with the custom MDF objects the same way that you work with any other entity in SuccessFactors, by using the sap_hcmcloud_core_odata destination; however, you will query entities starting with cust_ instead.

11.4.7 Creating Custom Home Page Tiles Hosted on SAP HCP

When you log in to a SuccessFactors system, regardless of the modules licensed, you'll be greeted by the SuccessFactors home page (Figure 11.17). The home page enables user-level personalization of the product experience and allows you to collect all the key ingredients in one common screen.

As noted in Section 11.3.8, it's possible to extend the set of visible tiles by registering custom ones. In addition to being a standard feature of the product, tiles are also a great way to incorporate experience and integration with third-party products. SAP HCP extensions make use of that opportunity. Your next question may be: How do I register a tile?

Figure 11.17 SuccessFactors Enterprise Home Page

Once you log in as a company admin, home page tiles configuration is accessible via ADMIN TOOLS • COMPANY SETTINGS • MANAGE v12 HOME PAGE (Figure 11.18).

You will see a comprehensive overview of all tiles delivered as part of the standard product, including some third-party integration tiles. If you want some tiles to be visible to all users in the system, then make sure they are listed in the DEFAULT section. If you want to introduce optional tiles that end users can pull out of a catalog, then have them in the AVAILABLE section. If there are tiles that you want to keep but that are not in use anymore, then move them to the NOT USED section.

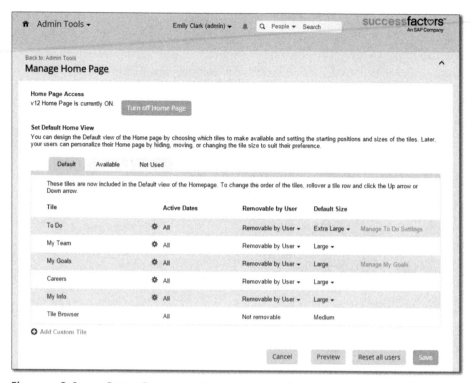

Figure 11.18 SuccessFactors Enterprise v12 Home Page Configuration

For each tile, you can specify whether end users should have the freedom to remove it from the home page and the default size it should be rendered in.

The SuccessFactors home page in version v12 supports three tile sizes:

- Medium: 138 pixels wide
- Large: 296 pixels wide
- Extra-large: 612 pixels wide

All of the tile rules apply both to standard and custom tiles. Having a reasonable strategy for managing the system home page gives you a powerful tool for rolling out new initiatives, campaigns, and tools to the whole employee base.

Looking beyond the standard available tiles, you can register a new one by clicking on ADD CUSTOM TILE (Figure 11.19).

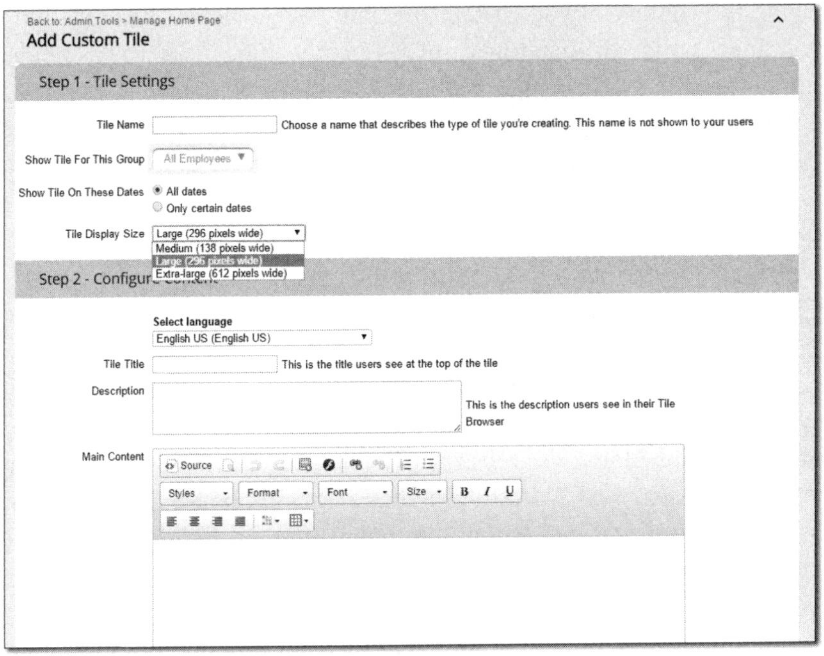

Figure 11.19 Custom Tile Creation Wizard

In addition to the standard properties (e.g., TILE NAME, DISPLAY SIZE, TITLE, and DESCRIPTION), you have the opportunity to specify the target audience and the timeframe you plan to target it in.

The SHOW TILE FOR THIS GROUP field gives you the option to narrow down the group of people who will see the custom tile. We strongly recommend not relying on visibility constraints only, but also performing active group membership checking in the backend services consumed by your tile UI.

Another useful feature defined by the SHOW TILE ON THESE DATES field allows you to specify the effective dating of the custom tile. By default, it's set to ALL DATES. This means that a tile will immediately become visible to the complete targeted population once you click on the SAVE button.

The next aspect of a custom tile to consider is the body it will render. As a rule of thumb, it has to be as informative and as context specific to the current user as possible. Polluting users' home pages with static tiles is generally suboptimal. Users will simply tick that tile away from their home page, or even worse will keep it there and start complaining.

For managing the content of you custom tile, you have a rich wizard, allowing some predefined standard operations, such as embedding flash components, images, links, or pretty much any piece of HTML code. Therefore, you can embed any page that you're serving out of an SAP HCP application in a SuccessFactors custom home page tile. One sample HTML snippet to use is as follows:

```
<iframe border="0" frameborder="0" src="/sf/idp-init/sso/
customWidgetLaunch?parameter1=value&amp;parameter2=value" style=
"width: 100%;height:235px"/>
```

If you look closely at the snippet, you'll notice that there is no pointer to any SAP HCP-specific URL. We could instead have a direct URL to your SAP HCP application, but then you'll see all the CORS issues described in Section 11.3.8. Therefore, we've defined a particular custom SP mapping key, which in turn is used for IdP-initiated SSO, embedding the referenced application content in the defined iFrame. Any parameters you pass to the SuccessFactors IdP URL will be transparently passed along to the target URL. In that way, you can achieve a much more tailored personal experience in your integration.

11.4.8 Managing Custom Navigation Entries

Another key aspect of making your SuccessFactors extension reachable for users is to register it in the different navigation systems inside SuccessFactors, such as the top-level navigation or the personal profile menus. This is done via ADMIN TOOLS • COMPANY SETTINGS • CONFIGURE CUSTOM NAVIGATION (Figure 11.20).

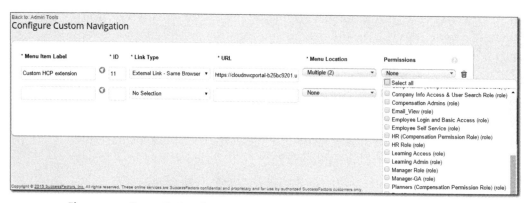

Figure 11.20 SuccessFactors Custom Navigation Management Tool

This management tool allows you to plug any arbitrary link into the navigation menus, specifying certain conditions. One aspect to configure via the LINK TYPE field is how the navigation should behave. Should it open the link in the same window, effectively handing over the control, or should it open the link in a new window, retaining the control in the original one? For SAP HCP extensions using SAP HANA Cloud Portal as the frontend, EXTERNAL LINK—SAME BROWSER should be selected. At first, it looks as if we're navigating away from SuccessFactors. Although technically correct, this is misleading, because the newly opened SAP HANA Cloud Portal site delivers the same header and footer as any other page inside SuccessFactors. Therefore, there should be no visible difference between an extension page and another page inside SuccessFactors.

Another field to consider is the PERMISSIONS field, which lists all existing permissions in the system, thus providing fine-grained access control to navigation. The general philosophy here is that if a user is not allowed to perform some operation, then it should not show up in the menus for that user. Ideally, we should never see an ACCESS DENIED error when simply browsing around.

11.4.9 Troubleshooting SuccessFactors Extension Applications

Once you're done with development and moving toward real business, it's essential to be aware of the different tools offered by the SuccessFactors stack. These tools enable you to develop and troubleshoot applications in the most efficient manner.

We learned about the two different layers of administration in SuccessFactors in Section 11.4.1. We'll leave the SuccessFactors Provisioning environment aside for now, as customers typically don't have access to it. Instead, we'll focus on the tools accessible to customer key users and developers.

As a developer, some burning questions may include the following: Where do I see the results of my API calls? Are they successful? Did they fail? What is the response code returned? For administrators, a reasonable concern might revolve around auditing what data is exposed from the system via APIs and how to keep track of that.

In general, when you're looking for a particular SuccessFactors administration tool, you can always start from the search bar in the OneAdmin view (Figure 11.21).

Figure 11.21 Tool Search Feature in SuccessFactors OneAdmin

If what you're typing doesn't autocomplete, then this means either that there is no such tool or that you don't have the required permissions to access it.

SFAPI Tracing

SuccessFactors SFAPI is practically the oldest public integration API from Success-Factors to be exposed publicly. It is based on SOAP and is primarily used for data replication and synchronization with external systems. It is therefore the basis for many of the prepackaged delivered integrations.

It's worth mentioning that SFAPI has to be explicitly enabled in Provisioning and that the corresponding administrator role permissions need to be granted. Those permissions include the following:

▶ Access to the SFAPI Data Dictionary
▶ Access to the SFAPI Audit Log
▶ Access to the SFAPI Metering Details

When planning to use SFAPI, the first thing to consider is the SFAPI Data Dictionary. It shows you all the available fields and objects you can query on. It also describes the fine-grained permissions for each of the fields. You can find it in ADMIN TOOLS • COMPANY SETTINGS • SFAPI DATA DICTIONARY (Figure 11.22).

There are entities in the object data model that, although accessible through SFAPI, must be explicitly enabled via Provisioning in order to show up in the data dictionary. One example is employee personal information, which is there but not exposed by default.

If you have a scenario where you need to replicate data from a backend system to SuccessFactors or simply keep SuccessFactors in sync with another system, then you'll most probably end up using SFAPI in combination with SAP HCI, Dell Boomi, SAP Process Orchestration, or yet another integration product you might have already. In SAP HCP extension accounts for SuccessFactors, SFAPI would be accessible for applications using the `sap_hcmcloud_core_soap` destination. Keep in mind that due to the service user it's accessible through, it's not suitable for interactive end-user extension applications, but primarily for integration purposes and data synchronization.

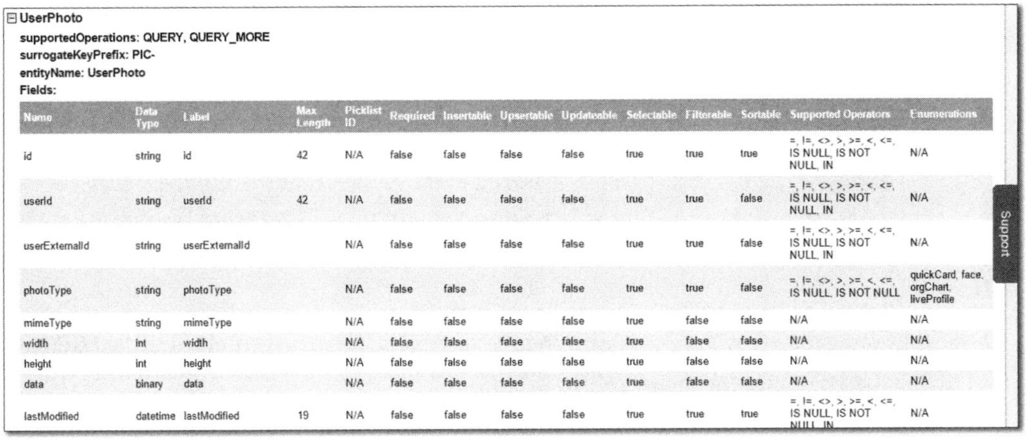

UserPhoto
supportedOperations: QUERY, QUERY_MORE
surrogateKeyPrefix: PIC-
entityName: UserPhoto
Fields:

Name	Data Type	Label	Max Length	Picklist ID	Required	Insertable	Upsertable	Updateable	Selectable	Filterable	Sortable	Supported Operators	Enumerations
id	string	id	42	N/A	false	false	false	false	true	true	true	=, !=, <>, >, >=, <, <=, IS NULL, IS NOT NULL, IN	N/A
userId	string	userId	42	N/A	false	false	false	false	true	true	false	=, !=, <>, >, >=, <, <=, IS NULL, IS NOT NULL, IN	N/A
userExternalId	string	userExternalId		N/A	false	false	false	false	true	true	false	=, !=, <>, >, >=, <, <=, IS NULL, IS NOT NULL, IN	N/A
photoType	string	photoType		N/A	false	false	false	false	true	true	false	=, !=, <>, >, >=, <, <=, IS NULL, IS NOT NULL	quickCard, face, orgChart, liveProfile
mimeType	string	mimeType		N/A	false	false	false	false	true	false	false	N/A	N/A
width	int	width		N/A	false	false	false	false	true	false	false	N/A	N/A
height	int	height		N/A	false	false	false	false	true	false	false	N/A	N/A
data	binary	data		N/A	false	false	false	false	true	false	false	N/A	N/A
lastModified	datetime	lastModified	19	N/A	false	false	false	false	true	true	true	=, !=, <>, >, >=, <, <=, IS NULL, IS NOT NULL, IN	N/A

Figure 11.22 SFAPI Data Dictionary: UserPhoto Object Details

SFAPI also offers a comprehensive audit log, tracing all the calls performed with all the necessary details and allowing further drill down and follow up. It includes HTTP headers, cookies, and calling user details. Another feature you'll find useful is the correlation ID, which allows you to troubleshoot a problem across multiple modules while the other productive requests are running just fine. You'll find the correlation ID attached to all the associated system log records. The SFAPI Audit Log also provides the raw HTTP request, containing all the HTTP headers and the raw SOAP payload. It also does some preprocessing to derive which business object was accessed. Based on all of those properties, there is a powerful filtering mechanism that allows you to get insights over the incoming calls. For example, you can query for a particular timeframe over specific objects in which the query took more than x seconds.

The next tool worth mentioning as part of the SuccessFactors OneAdmin environment is the SFAPI Metering Details, which shows the level of utilization of the API, including number of requests, processing time and throughput, and so on. Historical data is kept for 30 days. Typically, Metering Details would be the tool that administrators monitor for unusual activity. It is one of the first points to start from in the unlikely situation that you observe data inconsistencies between SuccessFactors and other systems that have scheduled synchronization configured.

If you start observing high load volumes, then it might be useful to consider enabling API throttling, which is configurable via Provisioning and defines the number of parallel requests that the system will allow to that particular company account.

OData API Tracing

There are a number of similarities between the features that SuccessFactors OData APIs offer and what you've seen already for SFAPI. From an evolution perspective, OData is the strategic direction in which all SuccessFactors modules are going.

There is a set of permissions that you'd need in order to dig into OData API details:

▶ Access to the OData API Audit Log
▶ Access to the OData API Data Dictionary

The OData API Data Dictionary provides the same overview of all the fields of each of the exposed objects, including all the supported operations, such as `Insertable`, `Upsertable`, `Selectable`, `Sortable`, `Filterable`, and the field `Max Length`.

Similar to SFAPI, the SuccessFactors platform offers a comprehensive audit log for all the performed OData calls. What would you use this tool for? Assume that you have your SAP HCP application, which is calling the SuccessFactors OData API. In SAP HCP extension accounts for SuccessFactors, the OData API is accessible via the `sap_hcmcloud_core_odata` destination.

It's very useful to control both the client and the server at the same time, because you can check the corresponding traces and determine what the potential problem might be. Moreover, you can verify whether your application is really making the API calls you're expecting it to make, using the proper object references. This is increasingly crucial nowadays as development in many areas is moving higher in the abstraction levels and actual API calls are made using code generation.

The OData Audit Log provides the same flexibility to filter the traced requests and get further insights. In the future, both the SFAPI and the OData Audit Logs will leverage the upcoming API management service layer, thus allowing for further improvements and insights into both environments.

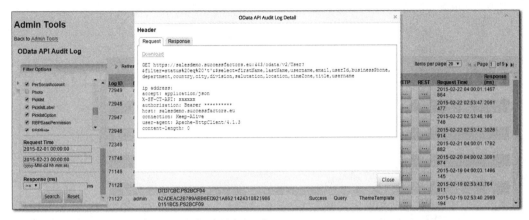

Figure 11.23 SuccessFactors OData API Audit Log Tool

Frequently Asked Questions about SuccessFactors Extensions

One of the most critical aspects to consider when planning your extension scenario is whether it's feasible to implement, given the currently available APIs. By default, you can safely assume that SAP HCP can integrate with any system that is either directly accessible via the Internet or can be accessed on-premise using SAP Cloud Connector. Given the flexible nature of SAP HCP, you can implement pretty much any scenario there, involving an arbitrary set of external services (from SAP and its partners). Therefore, knowing whether certain customizations or extensions can be implemented boils down to answering the following questions:

▶ Is the data required for this scenario available via API for the SAP HCP application to consume or modify?

▶ Is the workflow in which customization is required able to cope programmatically with custom steps and results coming from external systems?

▶ Is the screen in which you'd like to embed a UI allowing UI mashup, or does it have to be rebuilt from scratch on SAP HCP?

Depending on the answers to the preceding questions above, you can judge the feasibility of the scenario in question. Whenever you encounter situations that can't be implemented as of today, don't give up or panic. SuccessFactors has a quarterly release cycle, and new entities are exposed with every release. There is an aggressive roadmap in place to OData-enable all of the SuccessFactors modules by 2016; therefore, chances are high that what's not possible today will be possible in one of the subsequent releases.

Another frequently asked question is whether to use an SAP HCP application to integrate with a third-party system or whether to use Dell Boomi or SAP HCI instead. The answer is that it actually depends. If you're only after headless integration, running on regular intervals and doing predefined attribute mapping, then both Dell Boomi and SAP HCI are good choices. If you're after higher workloads, then SAP HCI should be your default option. However, if you would like to have some user interaction as part of the integration or to have an interactive status presented to end users embedded in the product, then SAP HCP extension applications are the natural choice, building on top and relying on the already configured SAP HCI integrations.

11.5   Summary

The need for extensibility will only grow as more and more companies adopt cloud solutions. Although technically challenging for many SaaS providers to offer as a feature, extensibility definitely will not go away, because businesses are different and will continue to be different 10 years from now. There is also a clear need for standardization and reduced integration costs, which will drive consolidation and support the emergence of a number of extension partner companies specializing in particular product niches in multiple markets and growing side by side with the SAP Cloud solutions. As the default option for building extension applications with zero integration cost for all SAP Cloud solutions, SAP HCP is well set for all of those scenarios, enabling SAP and the vibrant application development partner ecosystem to provide smarter solutions to customers.

A   The Authors

James Wood is the founder and principal consultant of Bowdark Consulting, Inc., a consulting firm specializing in technology and custom development in the SAP landscape. Before starting Bowdark in 2006, James was an SAP NetWeaver consultant for SAP America, Inc. and IBM Corporation, where he was involved in many large-scale SAP implementations. James is also an SAP Mentor and author of several best-selling SAP titles. To learn more about James and this book, please check out his website at *www.bowdark.com*.

John Mutumba Bilay is the cofounder of Rojo Consultancy and contributed Chapter 10 of the book. He currently works as a senior software engineer and enterprise integration consultant. With more than 12 years of international experience in information technology, he has primarily focused on integration technologies for the last eight years. His SAP specialties include SAP integration- and process-related technologies, including SAP Process Orchestration and SAP HANA Cloud Integration. In addition to his daily integration work, he provides integration-related trainings for SAP and for Rojo Consultancy B.V.

Riley Rainey contributed Chapter 12 of the book (available as a download from *www.sap-press.com/3638*). He has been a mobile developer and software architect for the past eight years, during which he has been directly involved in the development and deployment of several major mobile applications for businesses. Riley has been with SAP for the past two years. As part of the Platform Solutions Group, he is actively involved in helping to shape the technology behind SAP Mobile Platform's products and developer tools. Riley has been an SAP Mentor since 2014.

 **Krasimir Semerdzhiev** contributed Chapter 11 of the book. He is a product expert and solution architect in the SAP HANA Cloud Platform team, specializing in enterprise application development, solution integration, and onboarding of new SAP acquisitions. Throughout his 16 years of hands-on experience, he has lead the development of core parts of the SAP NetWeaver Java stack and defined the integration architecture of SAP products such as SAP BusinessObjects BI, Frictionless Commerce, and River. He played a key role in the design and initial inception of SAP HANA Cloud Platform and its integration with a number of other SAP products such as SuccessFactors, Ariba, SAP Jam, and SAP Business ByDesign. He regularly presents at events such as SAP TechEd/d-code, SAP Forum, and SAP User Group gatherings, as well as at industry developer conferences such as JavaOne, Devoxx, Jaxx, and CloudExpo.

Index

K

Interested in reading more?

Please visit our website for all new
book and e-book releases from SAP PRESS.

www.sap-press.com